ROBERT KUTTNER

The Squandering of America

Robert Kuttner is a founder and coeditor of *The American Prospect* magazine, a regular contributor to *The Boston Globe*, a radio and TV commentator, a Demos Senior Fellow, and a contributor to many magazines. He wrote a column for *BusinessWeek* for twenty years. His most recent books are *Everything for Sale* and *The End of Laissez-Faire*.

www.thesquanderingofamerica.com

THE
SQUANDERING OF AMERICA

HOW THE FAILURE OF OUR POLITICS
UNDERMINES OUR PROSPERITY

ROBERT KUTTNER

Vintage Books
A Division of Random House, Inc.
New York

FIRST VINTAGE BOOKS EDITION, NOVEMBER 2008

The Library of Congress has cataloged the Knopf edition as follows:
Kuttner, Robert.
The squandering of America : how the failure of our politics undermines our
prosperity / by Robert Kuttner.
p. cm.
Includes bibliographical references and index.
1. United States—Economic policy—2001– 2. United States—Economic
policy—1993–2001. 3. United States—Politics and government—2001–
4. United States—Commercial policy. 5. Free enterprise—United States.
6. Capitalism—United States. 7. Environmental policy—United States. I. Title.
HC106.83.K88 2007
330.973—dc22
2007022014

Vintage ISBN: 978-1-4000-3363-8

Author photograph © Carolina Manero
Book design by Robert C. Olsson

www.vintagebooks.com

Printed in the United States of America
10 9 8 7 6 5 4 3 2 1

For Joan Fitzgerald

CONTENTS

PREFACE TO THE VINTAGE EDITION

When I finished writing the first edition of *The Squandering of America* in May 2007, the subprime mortgage meltdown was just beginning to be understood as more than a passing blip. The reader will find herein several pages on subprime, but my subject was and is the deeper vulnerability of the U.S. economy, due to three decades of political assault on institutions that once provided broad security, transparency, and shared prosperity.

I wrote fifteen months ago, "I believe that the American economy is in danger, not just of increasing economic and financial inequality. It is at risk of a 1929-scale catastrophe." A financial crisis was not upon us then, but it is now. Some generous reviewers described the book as "prophetic." But it did not require prophesy to detect that our economic path was not sustainable. All it required was a reading of economic history.

The United States now faces its most severe financial crisis since the Great Depression. On the eve of a fateful election, it is not clear whether we will get another Franklin Roosevelt with the political genius to save capitalism from its own self-cannibalizing instincts a second time.

Unlike this decade, the early 1930s were a period of generalized economic collapse. There was broad popular appetite for drastic remedies by the time Roosevelt took office in March 1933. But, as this book suggests, the era since 1973 has been less a general crisis and more a slow erosion of economic security for ordinary people, coupled with escalating risks in liberated financial markets—and little political leadership offering a different path.

Now those financial risks have turned into trillion dollar losses. At this writing, however, the economy is not yet in 1930s-scale free fall—thanks to protections of the New Deal era that were *not* repealed. And though the ideal of self-regulating financial markets has been unmasked as a practical failure, the free-market melody lingers on.

In reviewing the 1920s, I was startled by the near-exact parallels with the abuses of the 1990s and the current decade. The 1920s were rife with convoluted financial scams, but at bottom, all of the abuses boiled down to three. First, in the absence of regulation there was little transparency or disclosure. Investors relied on the prestige and presumed integrity of the investment banks that sold them financial products, many of which turned out to be junk. Second, there were gross conflicts of interest on the part of financial insiders, who could grow very rich even if their customers took a bath. And third, the whole system was sustained by too much speculative borrowing. This is all spelled out in chapter 3 of this book.

One need only review this history against Enron, the bubble in tech stocks, the accounting, stock options, and investment-analyst scandals of the late 1990s, or the subprime mess of this decade, and one appreciates that the game is the same. What is remarkable is not that con artists try these tricks and many investors fall for them. What is remarkable is that these scams were all made illegal by the reforms of the 1930s—and that politicians then were persuaded to repeal most of the protections, on the premise that something new about the new economy meant that financial capitalism was self-regulating after all. We have now learned, painfully, for the second time in less than a century, that markets do not govern themselves.

This book explains how the system set itself up for a second financial meltdown, thanks to the political dominance of economic elites. The chapters that follow, from the hardcover edition, take the story up to roughly June 2007. In the fifteen months since then, the economic unease has gone from one of gradually escalating risks to a full-blown credit crisis.

The crisis began with the collapse of the subprime mortgage sector, which in turn led to severe bank losses and a freezing of many credit markets. But it could have just as well been triggered by the failure of a large hedge fund, or a flight from other derivative securities, or a run on the dollar. These several vulnerabilities are intertwined, because one speculator's debt is another's assets.

As the book recounts, the precarious prosperity of the past fifteen years has been built on cheap money and a series of asset bubbles. Broad-based prosperity has been eroding since the 1970s because of the assault on managed capitalism, but debt has kept the economy on artificial life support. For workers and consumers, increased borrowing partly substituted for declining real wages. People increased their credit card debt and borrowed against their homes. As government withdrew support from public universities, whole families went into debt to send children to college. As the quality of health insurance deteriorated, people incurred more debt for medical expenses.

Between 1989 and 2006, credit card debt grew from $211 billion to $876 billion. College debt has gone from practically nothing a generation ago to an average of $20,000 per graduating student. The ratio of mortgage debt to the value of an average home has gone from under 20 percent in the 1960s to over 50 percent today. All forms of household debt increased from 66 percent of household income in 1973 to about 140 percent today.

In the stock market bubble of the 1990s, inflated stock prices made people feel temporarily richer. Federal Reserve economists have calculated that for every additional dollar of paper financial wealth, people increased their spending by three to five cents. This means that the temporary stock market bubble added between $200 and $400 billion of purchasing power per year in the late 1990s. But when the stock market collapsed, so did this source of consumer spending.

In the current decade, people turned to their one remaining asset— the equity in their homes. Bankers and brokers encouraged consumers to believe that housing prices would keep rising faster than the growth rate of the real economy. They made it ever easier for people to borrow. Between 2000 and 2005, about 5 percent of consumer spending every year was the result of home equity withdrawals. This was another classic asset bubble. It could not continue, because at some point some buyer has to pay the seller's price. If family purchasing power is falling, then housing prices eventually have to fall, too.

The failure of the U.S. economy to modernize its manufacturing industry and to insist on fair play from other trading nations led to another debt crisis. Instead of exporting products, America exported jobs. Instead of using export earnings to pay for imports, America allowed nations like China to accumulate huge trade surpluses—and then borrowed the money back to finance imports. America as a whole went deeper into debt—over a trillion dollars to China alone. As the sinking value of the dollar shows, this strategy has also reached its limits. Creditor nations are diversifying their financial holdings into other currencies and buying up American companies and American real estate rather than American Treasury bonds.

Today, the American worker, the American homeowner, and the American economy are all tapped out. We can no longer borrow prosperity. While the party lasted, Wall Street was happy to prosper by facilitating all of this borrowing and by incurring more debt than any other sector. The financial economy became addicted to ever more exotic products with names like collateralized debt obligations and credit default swaps. Regulators assumed that financial markets knew what they were doing and that the investors were consenting adults.

In fact, these new financial instruments were opaque and untested in crisis, but they had one thing in common—very high ratios of debt to real assets. The financial system was built on the same unholy trinity that wrecked the economy in 1929—little transparency, insider conflicts of interest, and far too much borrowing. When one piece of this exotic financial economy, subprime, got into trouble, investors belatedly began looking more closely at the quality of financial assets in general—and they headed for the exits. Entire categories of financial products became technically worthless because they had no buyers. Subprime was the most dramatic collapse, but the excessive leverage proved to be systemic.

In 2007 to 2008, the Federal Reserve has attempted to cure the crisis with cheap money and selective bailouts, but this strategy has its limits. A cheap dollar only fuels inflation and drives foreign creditors to seek the safety of other currencies. Bailouts reward bad behavior and invite the next round of speculation. It is neither prudent nor practical for government to guarantee the entire financial economy against losses. The alternative is better regulation.

Market fundamentalism, once again, is a proven failure. As a new administration dawns, it will face the simultaneous challenges of reregulating financial markets, devising a very different strategy of engagement with the global economy, generating a domestic recovery with very substantial public outlay and regulation to increase household incomes, and restoring a politics as well as an economics of broad prosperity. All of this will in turn require an ideological reversal as bold as the New Deal and the Reagan revolution. Above all, it will require leadership to mobilize the power of citizens to contest the political power of concentrated wealth.

—Robert Kuttner

The Squandering of America

FAILURES OF POLITICS

Americans have the good fortune to live in a nation that has stood for political liberty and economic opportunity since its founding. Even in the republic's early years, when we cherished our isolation from a troubled world, the American idea was a beacon to other nations. In the twentieth century, a bolder, more outward-looking America came to stand for enlightened leadership globally. At home, a more democratic America became a more balanced society. Public policies promoted broad prosperity and economic security, by harnessing the creative, often chaotic power of capitalism for the general good.

Today, we are seeing the squandering of America, on multiple fronts. The ultimate test of a democracy is whether it is possible for the people to throw out the governing party. In politics, we have come very close to losing our democracy, not just in rigged rules and stolen elections but in the domination of politics by big money, the decline in participation by ordinary people, and the assault on basic constitutional liberties.

America's role as a global leader has been squandered as never before. Our government has been pursuing policies based on fantasies, failing to contain Islamist extremism, failing to promote democratic values and international order. Instead, foreign threats are being used to undermine liberty at home. George W. Bush's bungled war in the Middle East has made a difficult challenge incalculably worse. He has squandered the global goodwill that has long been the necessary complement to America's military might. His policies in general have made America a lightning rod rather than a source of enlightenment.

The squandering of the natural environment is close to reaching a point of no return. As respected experts predict the rising of the world's waters, the extinction of fisheries, the proliferation of tropical diseases, and the intensification of extreme weather, America goes on burning fossil fuels, disdaining development of alternatives, and rejecting international collaboration to reverse the impending calamity.

The potential of our economy to underwrite a society of broad prosperity is being sacrificed to financial speculation. The winnings are going to a narrow elite, jeopardizing not only our broad prosperity but our solvency. In less than a decade, our government budget, gutted by tax cuts, has shifted from endless projected federal surpluses to infinite deficits. Our trade imbalances and financial debt to the rest of the world have grown from a modest concern to levels that could produce a crash.

None of this had to be. All of these disastrous trends reflect a failure of our democratic politics to hold leaders and institutions accountable. With imagination and leadership, much of the damage can still be reversed.

To write about all the ways in which the promise of America is being squandered would require more than one book. This book is about one large dimension: the connection between a precarious economy and a diminished politics.

A Squandered Economy

There is a common thread to the squandering of broad American prosperity and the drastic increase in economic risks to individuals and to the system. What links these trends is the steady dismantling of a balanced and managed form of capitalism, by economic elites. That project, in turn, has required a serious weakening of democratic politics. This book addresses the political dynamics of the reduced living standards for most citizens and the increase in systemic risks to the economy. It concludes by suggesting what it will take to reverse these interrelated trends.

The squandering of America's broad prosperity and solvency has worsened under President Bush, but the roots of the problem go back to the 1970s. For thirty years, the economic condition of most Americans has become ever more precarious, even as the overall output of the economy has doubled. The incomes of two Americans in three have been static or declining. Health insurance and retirement risks and costs are being shifted from private employers and public institutions to individuals and families. Tens of millions of American workers are newly vulnerable to layoffs, outsourcing, and reduced earnings. The role of paid work in the lives of American mothers has undergone a revolutionary change during the same three decades, leaving families more stressed, with no offsetting improvements in social supports. Young Americans find themselves particularly disadvantaged, as their incomes fail to keep up with the cost of housing, tuition loan repayments, and the cost of health insurance. American consumption depends on ever-increasing debt, as people eat into the equity in their homes in order to make ends meet.

The innocent observer would expect that all of this would be the prime subject of political debate. Yet the political system is not taking any of these widely felt economic ills seriously enough.

All of these problems have remedies. Indeed, our political system once addressed similar challenges very effectively, in an era when democracy was more robust. But today the economic frustrations of American families are mostly off the radar screen of public debate. This is a failure of our politics, one that contributes to the weakening of politics.

The hazards are not only a problem for individuals and families; the market economy today faces more systemic risk than at any time since the Great Depression. The real economy of enterprises and workers is hostage to a casino of financial speculation. Our trade policy has squandered American manufacturing, producing a permanent and structural imbalance in which more industries and jobs leave our shores, forcing us to borrow what we no longer finance with exports.

To finance its escalating trade deficit, the United States is ever more deeply in debt to foreign buyers of its bonds, notably Asian central banks. As a consequence of the trade imbalance and foreign debt, sooner or later the U.S. dollar must face a sharp decline in the value of what it can purchase. If that happens in an abrupt collapse, it will lead to more economic damage. Even if the erosion is gradual and we get what is euphemistically termed a "soft landing," it will still mean a further loss of living standards. As a national challenge demanding attention, the issue of foreign debt is mostly beyond political discourse. Both parties, most of Wall Street, and even the Federal Reserve are whistling past the graveyard. This is another failure of politics.

The evisceration of controls on financial speculation not only contributes to a widening of economic inequality, it increases the risk of an economic crash. The stock market collapsed in 2000–01, and remarkably few lessons were learned. No sooner was a very modest reform enacted than banks and corporations found new subterfuges to disguise illicit financial maneuvers, even as they complained about the burdens of honest accounting required by the timid postcrash reforms.

Connecting the Dots

The failure of politics to seriously engage national problems goes hand in hand with the disrepair of democracy itself. For the first time in more than a century, the national government in the Bush era has spent more effort on suppressing voting than on expanding it. Serious people have good reason to believe that one or both of the last two presidential elections were stolen. Political participation is declining, as money crowds out civic engagement.

When politics does not deliver for people, the people give up on politics. Or they see politics as a realm mainly for cultural warfare, for battles over patriotism, or as something for other people. People internalize economic reversals. Pocketbook troubles seem to be private failures rather than the consequence of political choices. The very citizens most exposed to the most severe economic stress have been deserting politics at the most accelerating rate.

This disconnection of the people from their politics, in turn, leaves democracy far less energized. Consequently, when an autocratic administration ignores rights and laws, invents extraconstitutional doctrines such as presidential "signing statements," uses a state of permanent warfare to undermine free debate, or colludes in the suppression of the fundamental right to vote and to have every vote counted, there is far too little popular outcry. This is a recipe for losing both a tolerably just society and our democracy.

This book is an effort to connect those dots—to explore how the instruments of broadly distributed prosperity have been stripped not just from public policy but from public debate; to explain how an economy run by and for elites leaves the society not just less equal and less democratic but more vulnerable to systemic shocks and risks, and less efficient as a matter of economics. The book then goes more deeply into the politics of blockage—and possible remedies.

There is a coherent alternative to what is occurring. It requires a cogent ideology and politics of a managed, rather than laissez-faire, brand of capitalism. It requires political leadership with the courage of its convictions and a stronger set of democratic institutions to offset the power of financial elites. That conception of a mixed economy was once public policy and an animating source of popular politics, during the boom decades after World War II. That model delivered broadly shared prosperity, as well as greater security for both the system and individuals. Contrary to prevailing myths, there is nothing about the structure of the new economy to prevent us from reclaiming an economy of broader prosperity and security. But first we need to reclaim our politics.

Successes of Politics

One citizen's political failure is another's political triumph. The multiple defaults described in this book can be considered political failures—or successes—depending on who you are and what you wish for America. Declining living standards for most Americans should be understood as a political failure. But for the financial elite, this mass quiescence is a great convenience and a splendid political success.

For most Americans, the years since 1973 have been trying times economically, with stagnating real incomes and increased personal financial risks. But they have been terrific times for the top 10 percent, even better for the top 1 percent, and best of all for the superrich. There have been some brief general boom times, as in the late 1990s, but the period as a whole has brought nothing like the economic gains of the previous quarter century to the common American.

Why did this happen? Many observers have blamed changes in the economy; the shift from manufacturing to services; increased global competition; the entry into the workforce of the large baby-boom generation; the economic emancipation of women; the enlarged presence of immigrants; the demand for more highly educated workers. These influences have played a role, but they could just as well have played a different role. People who look purely at technical economic factors to explain why living standards for most Americans stagnated during a period of sharply rising productivity are looking in the wrong place. They should look at the politics.

America as a secure middle-class economy did not jump. It was pushed.

This book argues that the multiple defaults of democratic politics are closely linked. The economic default is substantially bipartisan. Although Democrats have fought skirmishes around issues such as budget balance and tax cutting, too many of them have joined the business class in dismantling a regulated form of capitalism that once produced broader prosperity as well as greater security both for individuals and for the system.

Both parties depend on large donors for the preponderance of their financial support, and election campaigns grow more expensive every year. There are some wealthy liberals, but they tend to be liberal on every issue *but* the core issue of how to housebreak capitalism.

I have attended Democratic fund-raising events in the Park Avenue homes of investment bankers, where there was plenty of enthusiasm for human rights, morning-after pills, and curing climate change but nary a word about financial regulation or social investment. The self-described New Democrats, heavily financed by organized business, counsel the party to shun anything that smacks of class.

Once, progressive party politics was anchored in movements of broad political mobilization, such as the labor movement. Today, organizations that mobilize ordinary people in civic and political roles are weaker than they have been in more than a century. By contrast, an elite version of the America described by Alexis de Tocqueville has never been stronger. Spend a week walking around Washington's hotels, and you will encounter meetings of literally thousands of trade and professional associations, corporations, and business lobbies, beyond anything you might have imagined. This tiny pinnacle of civic plutocracy could hardly be better engaged, networked, and organized.

Elites have not always been heedless of the common good. The American Republic was invented by a planter class that nonetheless believed deeply in democratic values and wanted to improve daily life for the common citizen. Many Americans of financial means were among the leaders of the abolitionist movement. In the Progressive Era, the robber barons who wanted to seize as much as possible for themselves were balanced by patrician reformers who cared about the well-being of the collectivity. Many reforms were the handiwork of the latter. Franklin D. Roosevelt, famously, was a class traitor, as were many of his New Deal colleagues. As recently as the Nixon era, there were influential progressive Republicans who supported universal health insurance, strict environmental regulation, and even a guaranteed annual income. Republicans were the stewards of fiscal responsibility. Today, it is hard to find a patrician who cares more about the republic than his own tax breaks and stock options.

Instead, there are pseudocrises of national concern loudly articulated by the financial elites of both parties, such as the alleged bankruptcy of Social Security and Medicare. A book with my title could have been about the grave menace of entitlement programs, and there are several such volumes. But these elite alarms are really covert ways of trying to get rid of the remnants of social investments that remain. Solving the projected shortfalls in Social Security and Medicare is easy compared to the real risks created by foreign borrowing and the unleashing of an economy based on speculation.

In American history, such political abdications are rare, but not unknown. The leaders of the early republic failed for decades to treat the festering sore of slavery, which was finally resolved by civil war. The assassination of Abraham Lincoln made the aftermath far more contentious than it might have been, and the full redemption of civil rights for blacks was delayed for another century.

Another period of democratic fecklessness, in the late nineteenth century, entailed a broad failure to address the dislocations of industrialization and the chronically depressed farm economy. That period of default, punctuated by episodic depressions, finally ended with the partial reforms of the Progressive Era. Another intense period of disastrous deferral was the decade after World War I, when the United States, as the victorious power, failed to reach accord with its allies on a politically or economically viable postwar international system. All paid the price in a global depression and a second world war. By contrast, in the period after World War II, American leadership effectively addressed the challenge of postwar reconstruction both domestically and globally. But in many ways that period was exceptional.

Markets Rampant

A decade ago, I wrote a book entitled *Everything for Sale: The Virtues and Limits of Markets*. This book can be read as a sequel to that one.

My earlier work was a challenge to the premise that markets invariably yield superior outcomes and an exploration of the encroachments of markets into the realm of citizenship. This work is an expression of alarm at the effects of political domination by financial elites, the failure of politics to contest that hegemony, and the multiple dangers to ordinary people and the economy as a whole. What links the two is a plea that private market forces be domesticated.

My thesis in *Everything for Sale* was simple, though the details were complex. In much of the economy, the free market worked. But in a variety of sectors, ranging from health care to the environment to the regulation of capitalism itself, markets didn't perform so well. Left to their own devices, they led to outcomes that were not only socially intolerable but economically inefficient as well.

Efficiency is the market's ultimate claim to legitimacy. We might not like its outcomes, but if the market is always the most efficient means of allocating resources and thus promoting prosperity, that reality trumps the other complaints. We can always wage a rearguard campaign to redistribute after the fact, playing the weak hand that we are helping those whom the market has adjudged to be losers. The market itself is not to be contradicted.

But as I demonstrated in *Everything for Sale*, the claim that markets optimize outcomes is true in some realms but blatantly false in many others. Markets do not efficiently deliver health care, research, education, pollution control, or the distribution of income and outlay generally. Trading markets, despite the claims of conservative economists, do not accurately price real assets.

And if markets are not always efficient all of the time, we are in an indeterminate world of multiple options, where choices can and must be made about how government should structure and regulate various sectors of the economy, both for the sake of the distribution of income and wealth and on behalf of efficiency itself. These are, inevitably, political choices. To choose a more egalitarian society requires a robust democratic politics. When democratic counterweights are weak, the power of money prevails.

On one level, the book was a plea for an appreciation of complexity. The economy could not be reduced to a neat set of axioms that were true in all cases. Markets in health care, or in electricity, were fundamentally different from the local farmers' market or the market for men's shirts. Leave health care to the market, and some people will die on the street for want of medical attention, the sick will be ejected from health plans, doctors will be turned against patients, and insurance companies and drug magnates will grow very rich. Leave electricity to the market, and both price gouging and system failures will ensue. Leave the financial market itself to its own discipline, and you court massive insider corruption and the risk of collapse.

On another level, the book invited readers to understand the intensified claims on behalf of the perfection of markets as a fundamentalist ideology and a political counterrevolution. On the ruins of the Great Depression, statesmen had constructed what the Nobel Laureate economist Paul Samuelson came to call the mixed economy. Property ownership remained private. But most of the aspects of the market that had gone haywire in the euphoric, laissez-faire 1920s, were subjected to regulation. This revolution was applied most intensely to the heart of capitalism itself: financial markets. Government regulated commercial banks, investment banks, brokerages, stock exchanges, and the accounting profession, as well as closely allied industries deemed to be natural monopolies, such as public utilities. In the 1920s, these industries had worked hand in glove with financial manipulators on Wall Street to bilk the public and undermine the stability and efficiency of the entire system.

Politically and ideologically, the regulatory revolution of the 1930s and 1940s was possible because the usually dominant business elite was enfeebled (temporarily, as it turned out) by the practical failure of laissez-faire. Government enjoyed rare prestige in a normally libertarian country, because the federal government, under Franklin Roosevelt and Harry Truman, put people back to work, rescued capitalism from itself, then mobilized public resources to win a total-commitment war, and also underwrote new benefits, such as Social Security, unemployment compensation, the G.I. Bill of Rights, and Federal Housing Administration (FHA) loans, which allowed the Depression generation to graduate into the postwar middle class. The enterprise of managed capitalism was a practical success. Though few ordinary Americans understood this success as the achievement of a managed form of capitalism, much less knew the term, the idea was firmly implanted in the popular culture as a broadly shared premise about how the economy is supposed to work.

A new generation of economists lent expert witness to the project. Once, the leading economists were celebrants of Adam Smith. Now economists embraced John Maynard Keynes. Not only did key sectors of the market economy need to be regulated, but the larger economy itself could not function efficiently based solely on the discipline of private supply and demand. In managed capitalism, government was necessarily the steward of the total supply of money and credit, as well as the total flow of private and public demand. The Federal Reserve was given new powers to manage the money supply as well as the stability of financial markets, and to serve as lender of last resort. Presidents began using the federal budget not just as a tool to allocate public spending but as an instrument of active fiscal policy, to make up for shortfalls of private demand in recessions and damp it down in periods of overheating. Treasury secretaries worked closely with chairmen of the Federal Reserve.

Very parallel policies were put into place in all of the advanced democracies. In Europe, the sense of a social settlement between business and labor, with a large role for the democratic state, was more explicit and more expansive.

But by the mid-1970s, a counterrevolution was already brewing. Business, strengthened by the same postwar boom, had regained its political influence, most emphatically in the United States. Oil shocks and the ensuing price inflation caused many economists to sour on managed capitalism. Once-marginal economists such as Milton Friedman, a celebrant of the purest form of capitalism, gained stature and influence. Regulation was made the scapegoat for inflation. A new profusion of business-funded think tanks offered a congenial habitat for conservative public intellectuals to embrace, refine, and promote these views. Many Democrats, as well as Republicans, were rewarded for endorsing this counterrevolution, confusing the Democratic Party's natural constituency of ordinary working Americans. By the time Ronald Reagan took office as president, he enjoyed a political tailwind, buoyed by resurgent business, organized conservatism, and weakened liberal self-confidence. And a new generation set about dismantling much of the mixed economy.

None of this was inevitable or even efficient. How to organize capitalism, and for whose benefit, was and remains a political question. Various models of broadly efficient capitalism are possible, with very different distributive outcomes.

My book received respectful reviews. But when it appeared, in 1997, my timing could not have been worse. The newly liberated financial market was at the zenith of its prestige. Money markets had been liberated from regulation, and stock prices were headed skyward. As in the 1920s, ordinary Americans were playing the market and seemingly couldn't lose. As before, a new era of people's capitalism was proclaimed. As managed capitalism continued to be dismantled, "Depression-era" was the preferred adjective of scorn. Who needed a Depression-era system for regulating banks or for providing for financial security in old age? The markets could do it better.

The collapse of communism, moreover, was taken not just as a repudiation of totalitarian dictatorship but as a vindication of simple laissez-faire. In fact, when the people of Eastern Europe had glimpsed the prosperity on the western side of the wall, they saw and approved a social market economy, not a laissez-faire one. But in the capitalist triumphalism, that detail got lost. The declinists, so-called, who had warned of America's "imperial overstretch" or the growing economic challenge of Europe and Japan, had been proven wrong. Japan was mired in recession, Europe in high unemployment. And as communism fell, the America that seemingly had been vindicated was the America of Ronald Reagan, not Franklin Roosevelt.

In the 1990s, technology itself seemed to enhance the renewed case for the pure free market. A giddy group of high-tech prophets saw in the Internet both the exemplar and the instrument of the genius of markets. Monopoly, if it had ever been a problem, no longer needed to be a concern. Computers could connect willing buyers with willing sellers and the Internet would function as a splendid auction market, with enterprises such as eBay proving that markets could regulate themselves. As the Dow Jones Industrial Average soared through the 10,000 level, having quintupled in a decade, two serious economists actually published a book insisting that the Dow's proper current valuation was 36,000, such was the promise of the new economy.

By 2001, however, the vision of a stock market that could perpetually grow at three or four times the rate of the economy was reduced to ashes. The public learned that the bubble was not the consequence of spontaneous euphoria fed by effusive commentators; it had been deliberately engineered for the fraudulent enrichment of financial insiders. This was the most serious disgrace of American capitalism and its stewards since 1929, and it came on the heels of more than a quarter century of escalating enrichment of the few at the expense of the many.

Yet no political counterrevolution ensued, because financial elites remained firmly in control. Deregulation continues to be the dominant ideology. The years since 2000 have produced new Wall Street scandals, new regulatory defaults, and heightened risks. Democratic politics, with a small "d," is if anything, weaker, and more remote from people's lived experience.

As this book will explain, I believe that the American economy is in danger not just of increasing economic and financial inequality. It is at risk of a 1929-scale catastrophe. Another serious depression would doubtless transform politics, but not necessarily for the better. In the mass deprivation of the 1930s, demagogues and dictators abounded. It was a miracle that the Depression delivered Franklin Roosevelt and an energizing of American popular institutions, rather than a home-grown Adolf Hitler.

I am writing this book not in anticipation of a serious collapse again discrediting laissez-faire—it ill becomes liberals if their idea of politics is to wait for the next depression—but in the immodest hope that evidence and argument can change political discourse and head off the worst.

The Enduring Challenge of Housebreaking Capitalism

In all of my writings about politics and economics, I keep coming back to variations on one big theme: What does it take, politically, to render capitalism a reasonably just and secure economic system for most people? As one who was born when Franklin Roosevelt was in the White

House and began college during the presidency of John F. Kennedy, I have always approached this question as a liberal, not a radical. I have great respect for the dynamism of markets. And when I was a young adult studying politics and economics, recent history suggested that capitalism could indeed be domesticated by political democracy for the benefit of the common man and woman. Liberal reform was entirely plausible.

In the 1950s, John Kenneth Galbraith accurately discerned a capitalism of countervailing power centers: trade unions and government and mobilized voters offsetting the immense economic and political power of business, and business itself divided into divergent interests. It was an astute description of that era. In researching this book, the more deeply I delved into the political influence of financial elites, the clearer it became that democracy is not the counterweight to concentrated wealth that it once was. I am still a resolute liberal, not a Marxist trafficking in class struggle, but the latest phase of American capitalism isn't giving me much help.

This book also brings me full circle to my first book, *Revolt of the Haves*, published in 1980 on the eve of Ronald Reagan's election as president. The subject of that book was the great tax revolt, Proposition 13 in California, which was approved by voters in June 1978, raising the curtain on the current era of assault on government. Yet, as I found in researching that book, Proposition 13, which capped property taxes, was not really a backlash against government; it was voters' response to the failure of the political leadership to prevent the shift of tax burdens from businesses to homeowners as an accidental by-product of the inflation in housing values during the 1970s.

California voters actually liked the state's excellent system of schools, universities, libraries, roads, and other public services, which have now deteriorated, after nearly thirty years of revenue caps, to the point where California ranks down with Mississippi in most public services. What voters didn't like was being taxed out of their homes, as property taxes on homeowners tripled in a decade. They correctly blamed the political leaders of both parties, but the hate-government far Right reaped a political windfall.

The parallel with recent history on a national level is exact. "Tax-and-spend" was once not an epithet, it was a formula for tempering a market economy for the benefit of ordinary people, and the voters reciprocated by supporting politicians who used progressive taxation and social outlays to deliver broad economic benefits. Today, the political Right has succeeded in demonizing both taxation and government. It has done this not just by argument but by repeating deliberately what happened in California accidentally. Tax burdens on middle- and working-class citizens have been raised while public services have been diminished. Tax-and-spend no longer looks like a good deal, and even many liberal Democrats are now fainthearted defenders of the necessary role of government. As a consequence, when ordinary working- and middle-class people experience severe pocketbook frustrations, they are less inclined to look to Democrats as their champions and may not look to politics at all. Or, if they do, they are easy prey for either the fundamentalist or the libertarian Right's preaching that we're all on our own anyway.

This book will explore in detail how democratic checks on financial elites weakened in the era after 1980 and how the elite capture of politics keeps the real issues that trouble American citizens beyond the bounds of public debate. It will conclude by exploring the politics and economics of alternatives to our present course.

The book is divided into four broad sections. Chapters one and two will address how the managed economy, which once provided broad prosperity, opportunity, and security, was systematically dismantled by financial elites. Chapters three, four, five, and six will describe the politics of financial deregulation and explain how increased inequality and greater systemic risk have a common political genesis. Chapters seven, eight, and nine will add the international dimension, exploring how globalization makes the project of managed capitalism that much more difficult, as both politics and economics. The final two chapters will then turn in more detail to why American politics fails to articulate the economic interests of the vast majority. I conclude on a hopeful note by suggesting broad political and economic strategies that could restore a brand of managed capitalism, limit risks to the system and to individuals, broaden prosperity, and reclaim democracy.

CHAPTER ONE

A HIDDEN DEPRESSION

SELDOM IN AMERICAN HISTORY has prosperity been more narrowly concentrated. And never has presidential politics been less serious about proposing real remedies to broadly felt economic problems.

In 2006, for the sixth straight year, the U.S. economy grew at a decent rate—on average. Gross domestic product (GDP) growth was up by not quite 3 percent. But that comforting average conceals a widening gulf. For the vast majority of Americans, wages and salaries declined and economic life became less secure. Layoffs accelerated. Health insurance costs were shifted onto employees more and more. Pension coverage deteriorated. Reconciling work and family life became more of a struggle. The notable gains went to the top 10 percent, and most of that to the top 1 percent. Since 2000, median income, adjusted for inflation, has actually fallen by 5.4 percent for all families of working age, despite GDP growth of more than 18 percent. On average, only the 3.4 percent of the workforce with advanced degrees had increased earnings.

It would be no big surprise if this pattern of widening inequality in America had begun with the George W. Bush administration, with its tax cuts for the top and reductions in social spending for the rest. But though the trend accelerated under Bush, it actually started in the 1970s, when the postwar pattern of high growth producing more broadly shared prosperity went into reverse. Between 1947 and 1973, the economy grew at an average annual rate of nearly 4 percent and became more equal in the process. In what the economist Claudia Goldin termed "the Great Compression," the incomes of the lowest fifth increased by 116 percent, while those of the top fifth grew by 85 percent; the middle also gained more than the top. But then, in a fundamental shift, the economy steadily became more unequal.

. . .

This story of widening inequality is not exactly breaking news. It has been the subject of several popular and scholarly books, and economic stagnation is experienced every day by most Americans. My purpose here is not to repeat thrice-told economic tales but to explore a *political* mystery: Why is this fundamental issue off the political radar screen except in symbolic ways that address neither cause nor remedy? Why are people not demanding that the political system respond? Where are the leaders?

The Republican contention is that less government is good for economic growth and that growth ultimately helps "everyone." But the economic history of the past thirty years and the lived experience of most Americans suggest otherwise. Government domestic spending and tax levels have been cut, regulations have been repealed, all according to the conservative recipe—and opportunity, security, and living standards have diminished for the vast majority of Americans.

While there are some Democrats who are populists, the Democrats as a party are too cowed by federal deficits, too in thrall to their donors, too modest in their strategic sense of the economy as a political issue, and too complicit in the general attack on "big government" to offer more than token remedies. Yet there is, in the phrase of the political scientist Walter Dean Burnham, a "politics of excluded alternatives" waiting in the wings that could command broad majority support. It is an economic populism, even a politics of class. But it is not class politics in the sense of poor against rich. The class that needs a political champion isn't just the 12 percent of Americans who are officially certified as poor; it is the broader vulnerable class that comprises all but the economic elite.

This politics, remarkably, is mostly absent. To hear most commentators assess the political reality, the task of Democrats is to move to the political center, a place where fundamental changes in the structure of the economy are unlikely to be found. Yet in the 2006 midterm election, something hopeful and unexpected happened that most press accounts were reluctant to acknowledge. Virtually every Democrat, House or Senate, who took the seat of an incumbent Republican ran as an economic populist.

The economy was not supposed to be a prime issue in the 2006 election. Republicans were expected to lose seats because of voters' disaffection with the Iraq War. A secondary cause was broad public backlash against a series of scandals that bordered on farce. On the eve of the election, the government reported unemployment as being at a four-year low. But the good economic news did not help the Republicans because it did not help most voters.

The press looked at the Democrats who had taken Republican seats and saw an ideological melange. There were Democrats who were against gun control, Democrats who were antiabortion, Democrats who stressed their military credentials and their godliness. Many commentators saw a party moving to the center. But what every one of these socially diverse Democrats had in common was an economic populism. Lori Wallach, director of Public Citizen's Global Trade Watch, reported that every Democratic candidate in the House who picked up a Republican seat, save two, ran as a "fair trader"—a critic of job-killing trade deals such as NAFTA—against a Republican free trader.

Ballot initiatives to raise the minimum wage were placed before voters in six key states and won by huge margins in all six. Organizers from the group Association of Community Organizations for Reform Now (ACORN) and several trade unions had shrewdly targeted swing states in the hope of raising turnout among less affluent voters, who often stayed home. Turnout rose in all six, helping populist House and Senate candidates in close elections or adding to their winning margins.

Probably the emblematic populist candidate was Ohio's Sherrod Brown, who won election to the Senate in that usually Republican state, ousting the incumbent by an unheard-of margin of 12 percentage points. Brown did not shrink from supporting liberal social positions such as gay rights, gun control, or reproductive rights, but he didn't really run as a liberal. He ran as a populist. So did the other five Senate Democrats who picked off Republican seats. In Virginia, James Webb, a military man initially given no chance of defeating the incumbent, George Allen, began by running mainly on his national defense credentials and ended up sounding like a New Dealer.

The new current of economic populism in Congress at least puts the issue of economic insecurity into political debate. But, as we shall see, the populists are up against potent forces that militate against a fundamental change in the structures of the economy that generate the insecurity and the inequality. There is an immense political opportunity here. It remains to be seen whether progressive leaders will seize the opportunity and turn pocketbook frustrations into a winning politics and a shift in national policy.

Most people do not give a lot of thought to an abstraction called inequality or distribution of income. They worry about their own economic situation. Indeed, pollsters have long demonstrated that Americans "identify up." Americans, typically, do not begrudge the millionaire his good fortune; on the contrary, they hope to emulate him. Nonetheless, polls show that most Americans are deeply frustrated with their daily economic struggles. A May 2006 poll by Greenberg Quinlan Rosner Research found that 62 percent of Americans agreed that "The economy is not good for the middle class and working people. Jobs are scarce, incomes stagnant, and benefits being cut back" (and this at a time when the unemployment rate was under 5 percent). About 71 percent think that "we are becoming a society of the haves and the have-nots," as a June 2006 poll by Syracuse University's Maxwell School found. A July 2006 survey by the Pew Research Center reported that a large majority said workers had less job security and faced more job stress than two or three decades ago. The nonpartisan Pew center concluded, "The public thinks that workers were better off a generation ago than they are now on every key dimension of worker life—be it wages, benefits, retirement plans, on-the-job stress, the loyalty they are shown by employers or the need to regularly upgrade work skills."

So if "equality" as an abstract ideal is not a pressing issue except to hard-core ideological liberals, the condition of one's own pocketbook is a clear concern. Beyond self-interest, there is broad support for the ideal of America as a middle-class society. People are all too aware of what a huge percentage of two paychecks it costs to buy and maintain a house; the precariousness of health insurance; the increased risk of layoff; the escalating pressure of personal debt; the time squeeze; the ever-higher cost of college; the uncertainty of secure retirement; and, for many middle-aged and middle-class Americans, the financial and personal stress of simultaneously helping aging parents and young adult children.

Yet the connection between the top getting virtually all of the growth and the rest working longer hours to barely stay even has not yet become a first-rank political issue in national debate. Though politicians like Sherrod Brown talk about it in a serious way, expectations have been so lowered that few Americans look to politics for remedy. Meanwhile, the instruments that government might use to restore a more equal sharing of economic growth have been stripped from the cupboard of thinkable public policies.

How did the income distribution become so skewed? How was politics removed as an avenue of redress? How might politics be reclaimed?

How Most Americans Missed a Boom

In September 2005, Robert Gordon, an eminent and mainstream economist at Northwestern University, and his colleague Ian Dew-Becker presented a scholarly paper at the Brookings Institution entitled "Where Did the Productivity Growth Go?" They found, studying Census Bureau and Bureau of Labor Statistics data, that during the entire period 1966–2001, "Only the top ten percent of the income distribution enjoyed a growth rate of real wage and salary income equal to or above the average rate of economy-wide productivity growth." Just one American in ten captured the lion's share of society's productivity growth—for three decades. And even this understates what actually occurred. It was the *top one tenth of 1 percent* that gained the very most. Those between the 80th and 90th percentiles about held their own. Those between the 95th and 99th percentiles gained 29 percent, those from 99 to 99.9 gained 73 percent, and the top one tenth of 1 percent of the population—one American in a thousand—gained a staggering 291 percent. By 2004, more income went to the top 1 percent than to the entire bottom 50 percent.

Studying a longer time period and using a slightly different methodology, the economists Thomas Piketty and Emmanuel Saez found even more striking results. Their regularly updated papers for the National Bureau of Economic Research have become the gold standard of income distribution research. They use a more comprehensive data set, the government's National Income and Product Accounts, to look at the changing income distribution since 1917. The two scholars calculated that pretax and transfer earnings for the average American in the bottom 90 percent of income distribution—nine Americans out of ten—were almost exactly flat over thirty years: $27,060 in 1970 and $27,035 in 2000 (measured in inflation-adjusted 2000 dollars). Those near the top of that 90 percent did slightly better, those closer to the bottom somewhat worse. But above the 90th percentile, incomes for the top 10 percent, on average, went up by 89 percent. For the *richest one tenth of 1 percent*, inflation-adjusted income soared by 550 percent, from about $3.6 million in 1970 to $24 million in 2000. And at the very top, the richest 400 people had 1.1 percent of all the income in America, more than double their 1992 share.

The Economic Policy Institute reported that in 1979, the top 1 percent had 9.3 percent of all income. By 2000, this share had almost doubled, to 17.8 percent. Were it not for the fact that the average family was working at least 500 more hours a year in 2000 than in 1970, mainly because of women's mass entry into the paid labor force, incomes for the vast middle would have fallen even farther behind. This increase in the work hours required to make ends meet, and the concomitant reduction in leisure and in time for child rearing, is also a real decline in living standards that doesn't show up in the household income statistics.

The experience of the two postwar eras is a story of two entirely different societies. The first era was one of broadly shared gains. Between 1947 and 1973, productivity rose by 103.5 percent and median family income rose by almost exactly the same amount, 103.9 percent. But between 1973 and 2003 productivity rose by 71.3 percent, while median family income rose by just 21.9 percent. Factor out the extra hours worked by wives, and median family income rose scarcely at all.

Between 2000 and 2006, the productivity of American workers increased by 19 percent. But the total increase in the wages paid to all 124 million non-supervisory workers was less than $200 million in six years—a raise of $1.60 per worker—not $1.60 per hour but a grand total of one dollar and sixty cents in higher wages per worker over nearly six years! Labor market researcher Andrew Sum of the Northeastern University Center for Labor Market Studies compares this $200 million for workers to the $38 billion paid in bonuses alone by the top five Wall Street firms during the same period.

One further reflection of increasing economic disparity is far greater concentration of wealth. The wealth gap has widened far more dramatically than the disparity in incomes. In 2001, the top 1 percent had almost 20 percent of the total income but 33.4 percent of total net worth and 39.7 percent of all financial assets. Between 1962 and 1998, the top 20 percent increased their share of national wealth, while all other income classes suffered declining shares. The bottom 30 percent of Americans—100 million people—have an average net worth of $10,000 or less. And more than 50 million Americans have negative net worth—they owe more than they own.

For decades, we have been hearing about the broadening of shareholding. This is the second time that revolution has been heralded. The first was in the 1920s, when boosters talked about "New Era" economics, though even in that decade wealth remained highly concentrated and actually became more concentrated with the stock market boom. In the Reagan era, Congress amended the tax code to allow small savers to put tax-deferred savings into a new form of retirement account, the Individual Retirement Account, or IRA. The hope was that ordinary people would start thinking of themselves less as savers and more as investors. The mutual fund revolution supercharged that hope. But because of all the other policy changes of recent decades that have increased inequality, the hope has been dashed.

More than 150 million Americans are nominally part of the share-holding class. But the reality is that financial wealth is now more narrowly held than at any time in American history other than the late 1920s and the Gilded Age of the 1890s. A majority of us have money invested in the stock market, either directly or through retirement plans such as 401(k)s, but the typical American has only trivial holdings. The bottom 80 percent—four Americans in five—owns just 5.8 percent of the value of all common stocks held outside pension funds. Even when we include pension savings, the bottom 80 percent owns just 10.7 percent of the total. Only 14.6 percent of us have direct holdings valued at $5,000 or more.

The story of widening inequality and income stagnation or decline for roughly the bottom 80 percent is thoroughly documented, whether you measure by wage and salary earnings or by family income. It is only modestly improved by taxes and income transfers. The thirty-year trend has been fairly continuous, despite periods of recession and inflation like the late 1970s and periods of boom like the 1990s. Even with the one bright spot, an increase over time in the real earnings of women, income distribution has been becoming steadily more extreme for families. People tend to marry mates of their own social class. So two-income families have also experienced widening inequality.

Dig deeper, and the story for ordinary Americans is even worse than the gross statistics suggest, in five distinct respects: The prices of things that enable Americans to be middle class have been rising far faster than average prices. Official inflation statistics understate the real cost of living. Young Americans are increasingly reliant on the unequal wealth of their families of origin. The time squeeze on families has increased the stress of raising children in an era with two working parents and no new social supports. And, quite apart from incomes stagnating, new forms of economic insecurity have increased, such as dwindling health care and pension coverage.

The Hidden Hike in Living Costs

The official inflation numbers have been reassuringly low since the early 1990s—less than 3 percent a year. But ordinary people feel seriously pinched by the rising cost of living. People's perceptions are not wrong. The numbers are wrong.

When economists talk about "real" incomes, they refer to wages as adjusted for inflation by the Bureau of Labor Statistics, in its Consumer Price Index (CPI). If your wages go up 3 percent and the CPI goes up 2 percent, you are a point ahead. But what if the official statistics understate the amount of inflation?

The CPI averages all kinds of purchases, gives them relative weights, and announces that the inflation rate last year was, say, 2.5 percent—on average. If you take a closer look, it's evident that some things have been getting cheaper—consumer electronics and clothing, for example—while others are becoming more expensive. For instance, the costs of college education, housing, and medical care have greatly outpaced wages and average prices. It just happens that the prices that have risen most steeply are those of the big items that signal entry into the middle class.

Average college tuition charges at public universities, adjusted for inflation, tripled between 1980 and 2004, according to the College Board. Health insurance costs have been rising at more than triple the rate of inflation generally, and housing costs at about double. According to the economists Jared Bernstein and Sylvia Allegretto of the Economic Policy Institute, who looked in detail at the prices of various goods and services for the years 1991–2002, the nominal incomes (money income not adjusted for inflation) of households in the middle fifth of the economy increased by 41 percent. Inflation during that period, as measured by the government's Consumer Price Index, went up by 33 percent. This implies that real living standards grew by a not very impressive 8 percent during more than a decade of economic boom. But during the same period, the costs of housing, health care, education, and child care went up 46 percent, or 5 points more than incomes.

Even that depressing statistic doesn't tell the whole story. The government also understates how inflation affects actual people in more subtle ways. For instance, the official statistics on the rising cost of health care are scary enough. Medical expenses, according to the Bureau of Labor Statistics, have been increasing at a rate substantially higher than general inflation for more than a decade—about 4 percent per year. This increase is what shows up as one component of the Consumer Price Index. But during the same period, health insurance premiums have been going up at about 10 percent a year, according to the Kaiser Family Foundation. Employers have reduced their own costs by having workers pay more of the premiums, by increasing deductibles and co-pays and by using "managed care" to limit what was covered. So actual health charges to consumers rose far faster than the stated increase in medical inflation. And as out-of-pocket expenses rise, many people forgo needed care; that hidden cost escapes the inflation statistics entirely.

The government's calculation of housing inflation also understates how inflation affects real people, as opposed to statistical ones. Instead of looking at actual changes in housing prices, it computes what econo-mists call the "owner's imputed rent." That statistic infers the economic value of living in your own house, not the market value if you sold it. The theory is that most of the time, most people stay put. True enough. But for those trying to buy in, the index dramatically undercounts the true cost. It particularly understates the toll on young families who are aspiring first-time homeowners.

Since the end of 1982, when the government substituted imputed rent for actual prices, housing costs, accounting for about one fourth of the CPI, have dramatically increased. According to Floyd Norris of *The New York Times*, actual average housing prices doubled between 1996 and 2006, but the imputed rent figure used in the CPI increased by only a third. Norris calculates that if the government had used actual prices instead of this artificial construct, the core inflation rate would have been 4.2 percent during that decade, not the 2.2 percent reported. And with a higher (and more accurate) inflation rate, the aver-age wage, adjusted for inflation, would have declined that much more dramatically.

The government further revises the inflation indexes downward to compensate for supposed improvements in quality. For instance, a 2007 computer is a much more powerful piece of machinery than a 1997 com-puter. So for the purposes of the CPI, its price is adjusted—downward—on the premise that the consumer is buying a far more advanced product for the same money, even though the consumer may never use more fea-tures than word processing, Internet access, and e-mail. Most con-sumers do not use their laptops to design rockets, even though the machines have that capability. The fact that your cell phone is also a camera, plays multiple ring tones as well as songs, and collects your e-mail also results in a downward adjustment of its price as it shows up in the CPI. (The waste of time spent on deleting junk e-mail does not result in an offsetting adjustment.) But these adjustments all serve to lower the supposed overall inflation rate and make the statistics seem more reassuring than the reality. People conclude that the rising cost of living is their own personal problem, since the economy is said to be doing just fine.

In short, the lived experience of economic stress is greater than the statistics on wage growth adjusted for inflation would suggest. If we used a more accurate, higher rate of inflation, we would accurately record that wages have been falling even farther behind. The price of the basket of products that make people middle class (or not) has been rising much faster than earnings. For someone looking to buy a house, acquire good health insurance, or find the money for college tuition, it is relatively small comfort that the cost of plasma TVs or underwear has been declining and that a cell phone is now a hydra-headed appliance.

Reflecting on this trend, I wrote a column in early 2006 titled "The Tchotchke Economy," using a favorite word of my grandmother's (a *tchotchke* is a small trinket). As Americans have trouble affording the big things, many of us comfort ourselves with gadgets. The emblem of the new economy might be a thirty-five-year-old listening to an iPod, with no health insurance, living in a shared apartment much more modest than the house he grew up in, and struggling to pay the rent. It's an economy of ever-cheaper electronic stuff—and ever more costly housing, education, and health care. An iPod is swell, but it doesn't exactly make you middle class.

Napster, the now defunct Internet file-sharing source, used the revealing slogan "Own nothing, have everything." There's a fine sociological insight in that line. It speaks both to the nomadic, antimaterialist ideal of the young—as well as their depressing economic reality. It evokes Jack Kerouac with an MP3 player: you may be flat broke and sharing a roach-infested apartment, but you can have all the world's music. Token luxury consumption is serving as a surrogate for secure membership in the middle class. You can't afford a house or health insurance, but at least you can savor the $3.50 Starbucks latte.

Some critics sidestep the reality of declining real earnings and misstate what has occurred by bemoaning an epidemic of self-indulgent "Affluenza," as the title of one book had it. They counsel the young to forgo the latte and save the money. Damon Darlin, in a Polonius-toned *New York Times* article commending self-denial to the young, calculated that by giving up such small luxuries, a young adult could accumulate more than $80 a month, adding up to $11,500 in ten years. But that sum doesn't even underwrite a down payment on a studio apartment, much less cover the monthly cost of health insurance. The instant gratification promoted by the commercial culture and the fact that the economic deck is so stacked against the young combine to deter the savings habit. For so many young adults, accumulating a down payment is just inconceivable, given soaring rents, tuition debt, and flat wages. The psychology, not without reason, is: Why bother? What the hell, go for the latte.

The Family Welfare State

In this economy, the ability of young Americans to prosper is becoming more a function of the social class of their parents. The sense of having more difficulty "getting ahead" falls with particular force on young adults who lack affluent parents to give them a head start with everything from good primary and secondary schooling to college tuition, down payments on starter homes, and help with the costs of (grand)children. Home ownership rates for young adults aged twenty-five to thirty-four peaked in 1980, at 53 percent. Since then, the rate has declined to 45 percent. About half of all first-time home buyers report getting help with the down payment from their parents. Almost by definition, this has to be people in the more affluent half, since the bottom half of adults has very little net financial wealth; and the further up the income scale, the greater the help. Young adults from nonaffluent families are also disadvantaged in their effort to become well educated and competitive in the labor market. When I attended Oberlin College in the early 1960s, the total four-year cost at a private liberal arts college—tuition, room, board, fees, books—was about $10,000. You could do it on summer jobs and modest help from parents. No longer.

Tamara Draut, in her book on the declining economic fortunes of young adults, *Strapped*, reports that as recently as thirty years ago, in 1976–77, the average cost of attending a private college (in inflation-adjusted current dollars) was $12,837 annually. Today, the cost of attending a *public* college is very nearly that, and four years of private college is fast approaching $200,000. Back in the era of the postwar boom, young people could hang out in coffeehouses *and* have the earnings to subsequently join the middle class without much parental help.

America's welfare state is becoming more of a family affair. The offspring of affluent families benefit from family transfers of income and status literally from birth (and even before birth, given the disparity of prenatal care). A child of affluence is the beneficiary of parental endowments throughout the life course: a decent preschool; residence in a community with better public schools or access to private schools; paid tutoring for college prep; the ability to attend college without regard to cost and without taking on a part-time job or debt; subsidized first-time home ownership—right on to help with (grand)children and, finally, inheritances. Affluence, in this case, begins at about the top 20 percent. At the 80th percentile of family income, annual earnings are about $103,000. Below that level, there is relatively little discretionary income to shower on grown children and not much spare financial wealth. For young adults without family wealth behind them, trying to join the middle class is like running after a departing bus.

For example, economists calculate that helping young adults to get on the home ownership ladder earlier in their lives offers a very substantial economic boost. They begin accumulating equity sooner, they realize tax benefits, and they are spared from having to pay exorbitant and rising shares of their incomes for rent as they have children and need more space. They are likely to acquire better first homes and build wealth earlier in life—and for most Americans, the equity in their homes is their principal form of net worth. As housing prices have outstripped income, delaying first-time home ownership also increases the entry cost.

The financial apple does not fall so close to the tree in other Western nations, where such benefits as prekindergarten, child care, health care, and worker retraining are financed socially. Statistically, American children are more than twice as likely to end up in the same income quartile as their parents compared to grown children in most of continental Europe, where substantial intergenerational income transfers are social, not familial. How Europe does it will be addressed in chapter seven.

America used to be more the land of opportunity for the nonaffluent young, and it is easy to forget how much government helped make that possible. The generation that came of age during the postwar boom went to college at dramatically increasing rates, thanks mainly to public investments such as the G.I. Bill, burgeoning public universities that kept tuitions low, and federal Pell Grants that actually covered most tuition costs. Relatively few parents of the Depression generation had enough spare income and wealth to subsidize the launch of their adult children. And thanks to government-assisted housing and low-interest mortgage loans, few young adults needed the parental subsidy. Home ownership rates rose from 44 percent in 1940 to 62 percent by 1960, and college graduation rates soared from about 5 percent at the end of World War II to more than 20 percent by 1970. Today, the help provided by these opportunity programs has badly lagged behind inflation, due to budget cuts; and one's ability to get ahead is far more a function of family wealth.

The Time Squeeze as an Assault on Living Standards

Between 1979 and 2000, the number of hours worked by married couples increased by several hundred hours a year. Most of this was in the form of hours worked by wives. Among working-class men, it became more common to work two or even three jobs, and average hours worked by men increased slightly, too. Had family members not contributed this increased amount of working time, the decline in real income would have been much worse.

In the 1950s, fewer than one woman in four with small children was in the paid labor force. Since the 1970s, it has become normal for mothers as well as fathers to be in the paid workforce, even parents of young children. Some of this shift was the result of feminism and the long-delayed recognition of women as full economic citizens. But much of it reflected economic necessity. A feminist road not taken could have allowed both parents to share child-rearing responsibilities with part-time careers. One earner's income would still produce a middle-class standard of living, as it did in the postwar era; parents would simply gain new flexibility in how to divide it. But with the real decline in men's wages that began in the late 1970s and early 1980s, coupled with sharp rises in the costs of housing and energy, parents who wanted to retain their living standards were both compelled to join the paid workforce even if one might have preferred to stay home with young children. By 2002, the average wife was working about two thirds the number of hours per year as her husband—1,300 to 1,400 hours for wives, compared to 2,100 to 2,200 hours for husbands. Today, more than 80 percent of mothers of children five and under are in full-time employment.

Absent the social supports that are common in other advanced democracies, such as government-provided child care and paid parental leave, this trend exacts several hidden tolls. The most obvious is economic. For people of moderate income, the cost of having a second parent take a paid job barely exceeds the net income realized from the job. There are expenses for day care, work attire, transportation, meals out, taxes, and the opportunity cost of not performing a range of household tasks, which may incur paid labor costs (housekeepers) or unpaid labor during what would otherwise be leisure and family time.

· · ·

In their best-selling book *The Two-Income Trap*, Harvard Law School Professor Elizabeth Warren and her daughter Amelia Warren Tyagi, a health benefits consultant, compared two families of median income in the early 1970s and the early 2000s. They factored in median wages and median costs of housing and other necessities for the median family of the early 1970s and the early 2000s. In the earlier period, Dad typically worked and Mom raised the children and managed the household. The one-earner family had a total income (in inflation-adjusted dollars) of $38,700. After fixed costs such as mortgage and car payments and taxes, they had disposable income of $17,834 to cover food, clothing, utilities, and optional outlays.

The median dual-income family of the early 2000s earns more, according to the Warrens' analysis of the government's Consumer Expenditure Survey: a combined income of $67,800. But when you factor in the costs of a second car, today's higher housing prices, child care, preschool, other work-related expenses, and being bumped into a higher tax bracket by their higher gross income, their disposable income is actually slightly less than that of the single-earner family of the 1970s.

So is the solution just to revert to an earlier era and have Mom stay home? That won't work, because today's lower real wages and higher housing prices compel her to work, even if a family's true incremental gain in take-home pay is modest. The Warrens make another astute point: Back when mothers typically stayed home, Mom was an "all-purpose safety net" for the family. If a child or an aging grandparent got sick, she was there. If the breadwinner was laid off, became disabled, or died, she could take a job. But families no longer have that extra margin of financial safety because mothers are already in the workforce and the family is already going flat out as a production unit. And if either breadwinner becomes incapacitated or economically displaced, there is no extra margin to fall back on.

Elizabeth Warren, who teaches bankruptcy law, attributes much of the rising epidemic of working-class and middle-class bankruptcies not to people frivolously living beyond their means but to the loss of this extra margin of security in two-income America. Despite their title, the Warrens' book is not a brief for the traditional, paternalist family. The solution is higher wages and better social supports. Then each family with children can decide what blend of domestic work and paid work breadwinners should choose, without having to sacrifice basic living standards.

The cost of the dual-income imperative absent decent wages and social benefits doesn't stop with earnings. The sociologist Arlie Hochschild, studying the effects of women's mass entry into the workforce on the division of labor in the home, referred to household work as "the second shift" and concluded that despite greater opportunity in the workplace, most household and parenting work still fell on women. This, in turn, was a cause of increased stress on marriages.

And there is increasing evidence that while early childhood education is a source of educational enrichment, custodial day care for very young children (under two or even three years of age) is a bad idea. High-quality preschool for three-year-olds can help children become school-ready, and programs such as Head Start can narrow class differences in the capacity to benefit from schooling. But one definitive study of an almost laboratory case looked at children's outcomes before and after the province of Quebec introduced universal, subsidized day care for children under age two. The researchers, who were generally sympathetic to the need for more social outlay on children, found "consistent and robust evidence of *negative* effects of the policy change on child outcomes, parenting, and parent outcomes. Child outcomes are worse for a variety of parent-reported measures, such as hyperactivity, inattention, aggressiveness, motor/social skills, child health status, and illness." Obviously, families that did not need both parents working just to maintain basic living standards could begin child care at a later age and rely on it less intensively.

Ownership and the Shifting of Risks

People are experiencing the stresses of declining living standards in more ways than stagnant salaries and wages. Other mechanisms of economic security have also become far more precarious. During the postwar boom, a good deal of economic risk was socialized. In continental Europe, it was mainly the state that provided health insurance, pensions, and other forms of social income, such as high-quality preschool and child care, that never became universal in the United States. On our side of the Atlantic, many of these protections for the working-age population were provided by paternalistic corporations. In those decades, stable corporations, insulated from Wall Street's pressure to show quick returns, could exercise long-term stewardship for other stakeholders besides executives and shareholders, notably their workers and communities.

It became normal for breadwinners to have jobs that provided decent health insurance and pension benefits. Blue-collar workers, as well as managers and professionals, could look forward to spending their careers with one employer. Occasional layoffs were temporary and substantially covered by unemployment insurance. This whole social model is evaporating, shifting these risks to individuals. The past three decades, with their greater risk of layoff, have also been a period of increased income volatility. According to the Yale political scientist Jacob Hacker, the chance of a family suffering a 20 percent or greater drop in income in a given year has nearly tripled since the late 1970s.

Some argue that the greater technical dynamism of the new economy necessitates more supple firms that have a small core of key employees and a larger force of contingent workers who can expect to change jobs more often. Some even contend that this greater vulnerability is a benefit, because it invites every worker to think like a capitalist, accumulate more wealth, and take greater responsibility for his or her own security. Both premises are debatable. This contingent form of industrial organization is mainly a political choice that moves risks from entrepreneurs to workers. But whether or not this trend is inevitable, efficient, or otherwise desirable, it is definitely making economic life more precarious.

However, instead of public policy working to counterbalance these institutional changes, the risk is being off-loaded from the corporation onto the individual with no offsetting response by government. How often do we hear commentators say that people can expect to change jobs and even careers several times in a lifetime? Wouldn't that signal that health care, pensions, and retraining opportunities should be anchored socially? A more flexible economy implies *more* social bolsters to compensate for the increased individual risk. However, exactly the opposite is occurring: more risk is being transferred back to individuals and families. The two emblematic cases are pensions and health care.

The Republican Right has attempted to disguise this increased individual cost as a benefit. In their view, we should become an entrepreneurial society of risk takers and then reap the financial security of ownership. In his acceptance speech to the 2004 Republican National Convention in New York, President Bush unveiled what he called an Ownership Society. In this vision, various tax-break schemes would help more people own homes, businesses, and savings accounts. The president declared, quite reasonably, "Ownership brings security, and dignity, and independence." Specifically, in the Ownership Society he envisions, "more people will own their health plans and have the confidence of owning a piece of their retirement."

Of course, it's one thing to own your home or your business; it's a far less secure proposition to "own" your own health plan. Individual health insurance policies are notoriously inefficient and expensive. The worst option of all is to be self-insured. An individual, self-financed retirement plan is also a lot riskier than a plan provided through a large pension fund or via government-guaranteed Social Security. Bush was using the appeal of ownership to dismantle the very institutions that help people become more secure owners.

There is a huge difference between knowingly taking a deliberate risk—for example, participating in a hazardous sport, engaging in unprotected sex, or making a speculative investment—and falling victim to a risk entirely beyond your control, such as illness, death of a spouse, loss of employment, or a general economic collapse. Ever since the New Deal, public policy in America has protected ordinary people against unforeseen economic risks precisely so they will have the financial security to take the deliberate and prudent risks of starting businesses, committing themselves to mortgage payments, and becoming owners. What Bush is really proposing is to shift economic risks back onto individuals—at a time when other sources of economic security, such as long-term employment and stable pensions, are dwindling.

In truth, the ideal of an Ownership Society in America is more than two hundred years old, and it has entailed the affirmative use of government mainly to help ordinary people—exactly the opposite of the radical individualism plus tax incentives commended by the Right. America has a high rate of home ownership because Thomas Jefferson was committed to land tenure policies that favored small freeholders; Lincoln gave us the Homestead Acts, which allowed people without financial wealth to become farmer-owners; Roosevelt's administration invented the federally insured self-amortizing mortgage; and Truman's offered even cheaper mortgages via the G.I. Bill of Rights. We are a well-educated nation because we were the first to have free, tax-supported public schools, and government began subsidizing broad-based higher education with land-grant colleges beginning in 1862. We have enjoyed secure retirement because of a blend of Social Security and tax-favored private pensions. In every case, government serves the goal of individual self-reliance and achievement. In no case is the risk piled solely onto the individual. The Right has sought to appropriate this legacy, but its policies would actually reverse it.

There's a wonderful paradox here. Far from promoting dependence, social investment promotes self-reliance. The vision of a society in which everyone has a nice nest egg and thinks like an investor is attractive. But that goal requires substantial government expenditure and regulation of markets, as well as decent incomes. Personal savings rest on an institutional layer of government Social Security and work-related pensions. We will not become a society of secure owners on tax-sheltered savings alone.

The Great Pension Collapse

After World War II, the typical large corporation offered employees what's known as a "defined-benefit" pension plan: the company guaranteed a specified pension for as long as the retired worker lived. A few of these plans antedated the Great Depression, beginning with a plan organized by American Express in 1875, but most were started during or after World War II. One unintended stimulus to this trend was the system of wartime wage and price controls. To damp down inflation, the government strictly limited raises in money wages during the period of wartime labor shortages. With 12 million Americans in uniform and civilian workers suddenly scarce, the government did not want employers bidding up labor costs to attract workers. But the wage-control regulations contained a loophole: they did not prohibit employers from attracting workers with fringe benefits such as pension and health plans.

After the war, a pension plan became one mark of a good employer. Unions bargained for such plans, and companies without unions began offering them as a way of showing that they were just as desirable as unionized ones. Personnel experts commended pension and health plans as a way of rewarding loyal workers and reducing turnover.

The typical pension plan was financed by both employer and employee contributions, and these contributions were tax-deductible. Except in the case of multicompany plans, such as those in the building trades and the trucking industry, which had joint labor and management trustees, pension plans were generally controlled by the sponsoring corporation. Most provided a lifelong guaranteed pension based on a formula that multiplied years of service times a percentage of peak pay or by average pay during the last several years of an employee's service. Many plans were adjusted for inflation. After a spate of bankruptcies deprived workers of pensions, Congress regulated the ground rules for defined benefit plans, under the Employee Retirement Income Security Act of 1974. One rule required plans to prudently diversify their assets.

Beginning in 1956, the IRS permitted employees to shelter lump-sum bonuses from taxation by putting the money into a kind of retirement plan. This option was seldom used, but it was codified in 1978 as Section 401(k) of the Internal Revenue Code. In 1980, a benefits consultant named R. Theodore Benna reasoned that regular wage or salary income might be sheltered from current taxation in the same way. He launched a tax-sheltered savings plan for his own employees. This idea quickly spread. In a 401(k) plan, the employer offered to put in a set percentage of a worker's pay, say 3 percent, subject to the condition that the worker at least match it. The funds would go into an account in the name of the individual worker, partly controlled by the sponsoring company. When the worker retired, he or she could tap the money. In the early 1980s, several large corporations, including Johnson & Johnson, J. C. Penney, PepsiCo, and Honeywell, were among the first to initiate 401(k) plans. Unlike traditional plans, which guaranteed a retiree a set benefit, this approach stipulated only that the company would make a current contribution. When the worker retired, he was on his own.

To a corporation, the enormous benefit of a 401(k) or similar defined-*contribution* plan is that the company is off the hook for everything but its annual payments into the plan. The company owes the worker nothing in retirement. The worker retires with however much money he has managed to accumulate in the 401(k). If he made poor investment choices or has the unfortunate timing to retire during a down market or to outlive his resources, that's just too bad. The plan is not really a pension plan at all; it's just a tax-sheltered savings program. Keeping the plan solvent, or guaranteeing the worker's pension, is no longer the company's problem. A second benefit to the corporation is that employees, such as the hapless Enron workers, could be urged or even required to keep a disproportionate share of their 401(k) holdings in company stock, which pumped up the share price.

Traditional defined-benefit plans are a vanishing species. About 40 percent of private-sector workers have some kind of company-sponsored retirement plan—about the same share as in 1980. But at that time, virtually all were traditional defined-benefit plans. Today, a majority are defined-contribution plans, typically a 401(k) or one of its variations. As the pension experts Alicia Munnell and Annika Sundén have pointed out, the money in these plans is far from adequate. The average American has just $27,600 in IRA, Keogh, and 401(k) savings, according to the Federal Reserve's Survey of Consumer Finances, as tabulated by Munnell. She calculates that for heads of households in their prime earning years—between forty-five and fifty-four—the median balance in IRA accounts and 401(k)s combined is just $37,000. By contrast, the capital accumulated in a traditional pension fund actuarially adequate to cover the anticipated retirement payouts of a median-income worker is several hundred thousand dollars. Even Americans nearing retirement, aged sixty to sixty-four, Munnell and Sundén report, have median IRA and 401(k) savings of only $59,000, enough for perhaps two to three years of decent retirement supplemented by Social Security. Savings held by ordinary Americans have deteriorated, as a consequence of the destruction of the traditional system of pensions and the increase in personal debt, and this financial inadequacy will only become more severe over time. By late 2005, American households were spending a record rate of $531 billion a year more than their earnings, according to a study by Paul Kasriel, chief economist of the Northern Trust Company in Chicago.

The two generations that reached retirement age after 1955 benefited not just from more reliable private pensions. Social Security payouts as a share of lifetime income steadily increased until the early 1980s. Real incomes rose, making it easier to save. And there was a one-time windfall in the rising value of owner-occupied housing. Every one of these supports is going into reverse. A 2006 study by Munnell and Sundén on retirement insecurity calculates the combined effect of all these factors in income adequacy for the elderly. They find that 35 percent of "early boomers," those born between 1946 and 1954, will be at serious risk of not having enough income when they begin retiring late in this decade. For "late boomers," born between 1955 and 1964, the proportion at risk rises to 44 percent. And for "Generation X," born between 1965 and 1972, the number is 49 percent. Of course, it is lower-income people who face the greatest risk, while those who inherit substantial sums from affluent parents, whatever their own lifetime earnings and savings habits, face little risk at all.

In 1985, the takeover artist Ronald Perelman won a bidding war for Revlon, closed down its defined-benefit pension plan, and gained control of its roughly $100 million in assets. Countless others emulated him. After the mid-1980s, virtually no newly created company set up a defined-benefit plan. During the stock market boom, dozens of large corporations raided assets of their traditional pension plans, using outlandish projections of stock market appreciation to make the claim that their plans were "overfunded." Then, when the stock market returned to earth, many companies canceled the plans and gave workers a much-reduced lump-sum payout or annuity, or found other ways to cut benefits. In other cases, companies dumped their pension plans by declaring bankruptcy, reorganizing, and emerging with no traditional pension plan. In still other cases, pension plans, representing deferred workers' wages, were used as the collateral in hostile takeover plays that ended with the company's laying off workers and reducing their current pay.

As a result of these shifts, today's employees will have far less retirement security than the workers of a generation ago. Because traditional pension plans were managed by professionals who aligned the interest of workers (in secure pensions) with the interest of the company (in having a reliable long-term return on their pension plan investments so as to minimize pay-in burdens), traditional pension funds have returned a much better yield than most individual 401(k) plans. Moreover, traditional pension plans, because of their very-long-term time horizon and diversified portfolios, protected individual workers from the risk of unlucky timing or bad investments, risks that are so palpable in their individual 401(k) accounts. A minority of large corporations, such as General Electric and Boeing, have elected to keep traditional pension plans. They still value them as a source of workers' attachment—and as handy pools of spare capital.

It may well be that the traditional defined-benefit plan is doomed. Large, stable, paternalistic corporations are becoming scarce. Most companies are eager to cut costs. Pension plans in America are strictly optional for employers, so it is hard to legislate worker protections for something that is voluntary to begin with.

Of course, with a different politics, workers could regain the security of traditional pension plans, not dependent on the whims of employers. For example, Congress could legislate a second, fully funded tier of the Social Security system. Workers and their employers would contribute equal amounts of payroll deductions. Workers could elect one of several large and prudently managed pension funds with public trustees. These pensions would be totally portable and would guarantee a retirement benefit as long as the worker lived, just like traditional pension plans and traditional Social Security. But unlike Social Security, which is a cash transfer system that uses one generation's payroll taxes to pay the previous generation's retirement benefits, this approach would accumulate a large stock of invested pension capital. The yields on the investment would generate the pension payments. Having a genuinely funded system, in turn, would raise the national savings rate. Such a plan would be beneficial to upward of 80 percent of Americans by increasing their retirement security. It would gradually replace the current system of employer-based pensions, which is unreliable for workers and burdensome for manufacturing corporations that have a high ratio of retirees to current workers. This approach requires a major constructive role for government and a minimal role for Wall Street. Not surprisingly, it is entirely off the radar—another failure of politics.

Savings, Housing, and Debt

If the ideal is to produce a society of people who think like investors, the present set of policies is utterly counterproductive, despite the proliferation of tax-deferred savings vehicles. Not surprisingly, a low ability to save is directly correlated with low or declining real incomes. The decline in the personal savings rate, from about 8 to 9 percent in the 1980s to 1 percent by 2001, and a negative rate in 2005 and 2006, parallels the erosion of earnings. Only 36 percent of Americans under age thirty-five have any retirement savings at all, despite ever more liberal tax shelter incentives for IRAs, Keoghs, and 401(k)s. Of Americans with savings, their median nest egg is just $6,600. Even counting home equity, the most prevalent form of savings for the nonwealthy, fully 30 percent of Americans have less than $10,000 in all net assets. That number has remained stuck during three decades of nearly doubled GDP.

Net savings is what remains after subtracting debt. Although there has been a good deal of clucking about the profligacy of Americans who go into debt to live beyond their means, most credit card, mortgage, and home equity debt is in fact incurred to support basic living standards at a time of dwindling real incomes and increasing income volatility. In 1973, all forms of consumer debt as a share of consumer assets totaled 12.6 percent. By 2003, that had risen to 18.3 percent. The rise in debt measured against incomes was even more alarming: it nearly doubled, from less than 70 percent in the 1970s to more than 130 percent today.

The cost of the interest on that debt has not increased nearly as fast as the debt, because the past several years have been a period of unusually low inflation and moderate interest rates. In fact, despite the piling on of consumer debt, debt service costs relative to income barely increased between 1989 and 2005. But this temporary reprieve disguised the vulnerability. Beginning in 2005, the Federal Reserve started raising interest rates again, in part because of the weak dollar. As many consumers have discovered as interest rates have begun to come back up, their debt is a time bomb. The foreclosure rate has already nearly tripled since the early 1980s.

In the case of housing, an earlier generation of consumers could reap a double bonanza: They could buy homes and watch their net worth increase thanks to steady appreciation of housing values. Then, as interest rates came down in the 1990s, they could refinance and reduce their monthly payments; they could even "take out equity" and still make only modest monthly payments. The ability of consumption to rise faster than income throughout the 1990s was based in part on this happy maneuver. Even if the amount of mortgage debt on a given home remained constant or rising, home owners (and their bankers) could reasonably wager that the net equity in the property would increase because its market value was increasing faster than the debt.

But this defiance of financial gravity could go on for only so long. Housing values could not outstrip incomes indefinitely, because somebody has to buy the house. A recent report by the Brookings Institution showed an alarming deterioration in the number of neighborhoods in American metropolitan areas in which the median-priced house is affordable to a family of median income. With interest rates rising and housing prices flat, young home owners, especially those who took advantage of variable-rate mortgages, are now facing a double squeeze. As real incomes have stagnated, recent home buyers can no longer count on windfall appreciation to increase their equity; instead, they have to earn equity the old-fashioned way, by paying down the loan.

With the air going out of the housing bubble, the assumption that rising housing prices would compensate for rising mortgage debt is no longer viable. Today, mortgage debt as a percent of housing values is at a postwar high. At this writing, Americans' equity in their homes has fallen to about 52 percent, compared to a peak of 85 percent in the mid-1950s. Since January 1999, according to a Federal Reserve paper, some $2.62 trillion in home equity has been taken out by home owners in mortgage refinancings and home equity loans. Home equity withdrawals accounted for 9 percent of total household disposable income by late 2005. In the first six months of 2006, home owners withdrew a record $511 billion in home equity from mortgage refinancings, more than the entire total of 2005.

Meanwhile, a rising fraction of new mortgages are adjustable-rate or interest-only loans, a disaster waiting to happen in a period of rising interest rates, falling housing values, and stagnant incomes. The last time interest rates underwent a long-term climb, in the late 1970s, adjustable-rate mortgages were unknown. *The New York Times* reported a 59 percent increase in adjustable-rate mortgages between March 2004 and May 2006. Interest-only mortgages accounted for more than half of all the mortgages taken out in 2004 and 2005, which means that the home owners are relying entirely on appreciation rather than debt pay-down to accumulate equity.

Comparative studies of national savings rates have noted that the apparently anomalous low rate of U.S. household savings is a reflection of our unusually high rate of home ownership. Middle-class couples have long viewed the equity in their homes as part of their retirement nest egg. When the youngest child has left, you can sell the family home, move to more modest accommodations, and put the difference in the bank. Or stay put and enjoy life with a paid-off mortgage. Two British economists, John C. Carrington and George T. Edwards, concluded that if you factor in what they call "housing savings," U.S. household savings rates historically are not so different from Europe's. To the extent that housing savings have always been the principal form of savings for the American middle class, the tapping of equity to finance consumption further disguises the reduced rate of household savings for all but the rich.

The steady increase in the percentage of Americans who own their own homes has now stalled. America was always a nation of home own-ers, thanks in large part to the egalitarian policies of past centuries. As early as 1900, when we were still mostly a nation of farmers, 46.5 per-cent of Americans were already home owners, the legacy of Jefferson's freeholder land policies and Lincoln's Homestead Act. In some western states that had been heavily populated with homesteaders, home owner-ship rates exceeded 70 percent, according to the Census Bureau. This impressive percentage fell only slightly in the Great Depression because the Roosevelt administration deliberately countermanded market forces that would otherwise have led to mass foreclosures. The government sponsored the Home Owners' Loan Corporation and created the government-insured, low-down-payment thirty-year mortgage. Banks were virtually ordered to forbear foreclosing, pending refinancings. Home ownership bottomed out at about 40 percent in the late 1930s, before beginning its dramatic postwar rise.

The most extreme indicator of the household financial squeeze is the rise in personal bankruptcies, which have quintupled in less than two decades. Between 1981 and 2001, according to the Consumer Bank-ruptcy Project, the number of women filing for bankruptcy increased nearly sevenfold. The Warrens demolish the contention that this greater vulnerability is due to the middle class trying to live like the rich.

Despite a spate of magazine cover stories decrying "McMansions," over-sized homes reflect mainly the warped income distribution, not the profligacy of the middle class. The size of the median owner-occupied home grew only modestly, from 5.7 rooms in 1975 to 6.1 rooms in the late 1990s. What grew dramatically was the price of a typical home. Yes, one can make a case that some teenagers spend too much on Air Jordan basketball shoes, computer games, and junk food. But median families actually spend less of their income per year on clothing and all forms of food than they did a generation ago. And a lot of fast-food consumption reflects the fact that the two-income family has less time to cook. The Warrens point out that middle-class families are strapping themselves to buy homes in districts with decent public schools—places where housing prices have been bid up far faster than incomes. Refuting what they call "The Myth of the Immoral Debtor," the Warrens document that fully 87 percent of families went bankrupt because of one of three causes: unsustainable medical bills, divorce, or because a breadwinner lost a job or became incapacitated. A 2005 Harvard Medical School study found that more than half of all bankruptcies were the result of medical debt and that 80 percent of the medically bankrupt had some form of medical insurance—which had failed to cover needed care.

Health Hazards

The slow collapse of employer-provided health coverage is another case of shifted risks and a hidden decline in living standards for the broad middle class. Like pension coverage, employer-provided health care was a purely accidental side effect of World War II. With lifetime employment becoming far less the norm, it would make sense both for corporations and employees to break this link. Employers have been following this path spontaneously by degrading their workers' coverage, without any social alternatives to take its place. The Bush administration has been promoting a gimmick called health savings accounts, which break up broad insurance pools, allow insurance companies to sell healthy people very lucrative (and inefficient) individual policies at cheap, tax-subsidized rates, and shift the cost of treating sick people onto the rest of the system.

During the past two decades, as insurance premiums have continued to outpace inflation, employers have raised the cost to workers and their families in a variety of ways. Inferior, more intensely managed forms of coverage are being substituted for health plans that give employees and their families a freer choice of doctors, hospitals, and treatment options. Employees are being charged higher co-pays and deductibles. Between 1992 and 2005, the share of insurance premiums paid by workers rose from 14 percent to 22 percent of total premium costs, at a time when those costs were rising. All of this is a disguised cut in wages and salaries.

Here again, the usual statistics understate what is occurring. The number of Americans who are uninsured has continued to creep up, to 45 million at the end of 2006. But in any given year, according to studies by Families USA and the Commonwealth Fund, 85 million Americans—one working family in three—face periods of being uninsured. Many of the supposedly insured are seriously underinsured. When illness strikes, they must reach deep into their own pockets or do without. Many preventable illnesses hit moderate-income Americans disproportionately, either because they lack insurance or because they can afford only inferior insurance that fails to cover medically recommended screenings such as mammograms and colonoscopies.

An ever-increasing percentage of employers either fail to provide coverage at all or offer it on onerous terms that require workers to bear most of the premium cost. The percentage of workers with any employer-provided insurance has declined from 61.5 percent in 1989 to 55.9 percent in 2005. Wal-Mart boasts that it offers health insurance, but since it pays low wages and sticks workers with a large fraction of the costs, only about 25 percent of its employees take the coverage, mainly because they can't afford the premiums. For workers whose employers do not provide health insurance, purchase of a decent plan is often prohibitive. A plan for a family of four costs $6,000 to $8,000 a year, and more if any family member has a "preexisting condition."

Ironically, much of the increase in costs and resulting reduction in coverage is the consequence of the insurance system itself. With private health insurance, approximately 30 percent of total costs go to administering the system and to profits. These sums reflect the expenses of marketing, risk selecting (trying to insure younger, healthier consumers rather than older, sicker ones), profit maximizing, and the expenses of having a fragmented system of duplicative private bureaucracies. Enthusiasts of the free market contend that competition and other market disciplines harness the profit motive to introduce efficiencies and cut costs. But many of the privatized parts of the health care system maximize their profits by maximizing costs. Some of this opportunism is enabled by deliberate public policy.

The public got a vivid sense of just how privatization raises costs when the Bush administration used the broad public support for Medicare coverage of prescription drugs as the pretext for privatizing part of Medicare. The bill was written mainly by and for the drug and insurance industries and required the new drug coverage to be offered only by private insurers even though the rest of Medicare is a government program. Although greater volume ordinarily reduces costs, the prices of the top twenty drugs prescribed to elderly Americans actually increased faster than the rate of inflation in the year after the program was introduced. The prices charged by the private insurers for these drugs was 46 percent higher than the discounted prices for the identical drugs paid by the Veterans Administration, according to a survey by Families USA.

The Bush legislation explicitly prohibited the government from negotiating bulk discounts with drug manufacturers. As a favor to the private insurance industry, the Bush legislation also prohibited public Medicare from offering pharmaceutical coverage directly. Rather than offering head-to-head price competition (which might have reduced costs), insurers maximized their profits by offering a bewildering array of plans that defied transparent comparative shopping. So inefficient was this system that Congress had to build in the infamous "doughnut hole"—the disappearance of coverage after the subscriber incurs about $2,250 of cost every year. Coverage does not resume until the consumer has paid annual out-of-pocket costs totaling $5,100. But insurers save money because many elderly patients cannot afford anything like that sum and never claim benefits to which they are nominally entitled. The economist Dean Baker has calculated that if public Medicare were put in charge, without the profiteering motive of private insurers and with the same power to negotiate bulk drug discounts that the Veterans Administration has, the cost savings would be sufficient to close the doughnut hole and offer comprehensive drug coverage without gaps.

That proposal, uncharacteristically, is actually being debated. A majority of Democrats in the House have offered a watered-down version of it, allowing public Medicare to compete with private vendors of pharmaceutical insurance, but not getting private insurers out of Medicare and restoring its comprehensive status as a public program. What is not being debated, however, is universal, national health insurance, even though polls continue to show that an overwhelming majority of Americans would prefer it. By 2006 America was spending 15.3 percent of GDP on health care and with less coverage than other wealthy nations, which spend an average of about 9 percent, according to the Organization for Economic Cooperation and Development (OECD). For the current total outlay, we could have comprehensive, high-quality coverage for all—if we got rid of the middlemen and instituted a system of national health insurance. The existing fragmented and costly system, run by and for the drug and insurance industries, virtually guarantees that good insurance coverage will gradually be priced beyond the means of more and more Americans. It is another, entirely preventable decline in living standards—the result of elites' domination of political choices.

CHAPTER TWO

The Assault on the Good Society

The widening of inequality has different dynamics at the top, the middle, and the bottom—but the same fundamental cause: the turning away from a managed form of capitalism. At the top, economic deregulation and the unleashing of a pre-1929 speculative form of capitalism has allowed the rich to become superrich. The same deregulation has allowed those who own and control capital to treat wage and salary workers as expendable units of production, making employment and incomes more precarious for the middle and the bottom.

While the income loss has been more severe at the very bottom, the result is that the working middle class has more in common today with the working poor than with the rich. The captains of finance have been pulling away from even the professional class. Skilled salaried professionals are often subjected to the same insecurities as wage workers.

One of the dominant myths about our era is the idea that something has fundamentally changed about the nature of the economy—either its technology or its global character—that moots the role of government. Countless commentators have declared the nation-state an anachronism in an age of global markets. But if anything, the greater speculative instability and the increased risks to individuals call for an increased role for government.

A Counterrevolution of Depressed Expectations

As government has largely ceased to offset the instability of markets, ordinary voters have given up on government making much of a difference in their lives. The ideology of deregulation has become dominant in both political parties. Republicans have been so successful at two rounds of tax cutting and deficit deepening (in the eras of Reagan and Bush I, and then again under Bush II) that many Democrats now see their main task as balancing the budget rather than restoring economic opportunity. This has the handy side effect of neutering the Democrats politically. Budget balancing is not exactly a clarion call to economically frustrated citizens, so the potential alliance between Democrats and alienated voters is never consummated. In addition, since Jimmy Carter's presidency, many Democrats have colluded in the Republican project of government bashing. Even when they don't openly disparage government, most Democrats are unfriendly to economic regulation.

Traumatized as they are by deficits and in league with their own business elites, Democrats offer mainly small, token programs that mock their bold initiatives of the past, such as Social Security, the G.I. Bill, Medicare, the Wagner Act, and serious regulation of financial excesses, all of which really did serve the broad middle class and created a generation of economic opportunity and security.

With the exception of Democrats who run as populists, the Democratic message fails to rouse voters harmed by the new economic realities. "New Democrats" treat the necessary instruments of greater equality as policy anachronisms no longer needed in the new era of a self-regulating economy. Progressive Republicans have simply vanished.

The result is a cumulative depoliticization of economic ills. This revolution of declining expectations is one of the most widely validated findings of public opinion research. Damon Silvers, who directs corporate issues for the AFL-CIO, tells of an open-ended focus group of voters at roughly median earnings—about $55,000. The pollsters first spent more than an hour asking the voters to discuss their lives. They heard stories of couples working extra jobs trying to make ends meet, the frustrations of trying to juggle work and family obligations, rising health care and housing costs—all realms amenable to public policy. Then the pollsters asked how the voters thought different government policies might make a difference for the better. The response was blank stares.

Theda Skocpol, a respected social scientist at Harvard, recounts in her book *The Missing Middle* a similar story of her conversation with a woman named Annmarie. The woman lacked health insurance and was struggling to pay off hospital bills. This was during the national debate about the Clinton health plan. Trying to offer some political hope, Skocpol suggested that Congress might soon enact a universal health insurance program.

Annmarie listened politely and responded in a kindly tone, yet unmistakably looked at me as if I had just arrived from the moon. "Nothing they do there"—meaning Washington, D.C.—"ever makes any difference for people like me."

The health plan, of course, was never enacted. Recalling the conversation more than a decade later, during the Bush years, Skocpol added, "She will be lucky if nothing that government does has any impact on her life." Indeed, in the intervening decade, government policies have made the lot of people like Annmarie worse.

So there is a vicious circle here. Expectations have been so lowered by the politics of the past three decades and the domination of both parties by economic elites that the low repute of government on the part of ordinary working Americans is hardly surprising. People who have low expectations of government are reluctant to support higher taxes, even taxes on the wealthy (whom they hope to emulate someday). Because political leaders fail to frankly address the fact of stalled or declining living standards and because government delivers too little, ordinary people personalize these frustrations and conclude that economic stress is entirely their own fault or at best their own challenge. People give up on politics as a way of restoring opportunity and equity—the way politics once served to expand broad opportunities during the great postwar boom. The Right has played on this cynicism to market an ethic of every man for himself, which promotes politics such as privatization of Social Security.

To review this history is to appreciate just how far politics has shifted to the right in three decades. Instead of a genuine concern for the common good, we have a fable of economics being reduced to personal virtue and everyone a capitalist. But these are constraints of a particular political era, not eternal verities. Chapter ten will examine the politics of diminished expectations and possible remedies in greater detail.

Recalling the Politics of Equality

President Kennedy famously declared that a rising tide lifts all boats. Economists have long argued that we have a better chance of building an egalitarian society when the economy as a whole is booming. The classic scholarly exposition of this issue, by the economist and economic historian Simon Kuznets, held that initial phases of economic development often lead to increased inequality because of displacements; but that as societies become richer, they tend to become more equal. Education and basic public services become universal, the rule of law constrains aristocratic privilege, and opportunities widen. In a boom, moreover, voters are often more willing to be generous with tax revenues aimed at expanding opportunities for have-nots. There is the sense of more money "left over" for the needy. In a tight labor market, workers enjoy more bargaining power. An economic boom, with a shortage of workers, breaks down social barriers.

The association of growth with broadened equality, however, is at best a gross generalization. Good economists always add the caveat "Other things being equal." Recent history dramatically demonstrates that not all booms are created equal—and not all booms create equality. The great postwar boom of 1948 to 1973 did produce a more equal economy. The boom that began in 1983, and that has now lasted nearly as long as its postwar predecessor, produced dramatically rising inequality. Diametrically different policies, undergirded by very different politics, made the difference in the two booms.

The greater equality that our economy experienced in the 1940s, '50s, and '60s was not the automatic result of high growth rates and relatively tight labor markets, although the latter were helpful. Rather, the economy benefited from a variety of deliberate *equalizing institutions* that moderated the tendency of a laissez-faire economy to produce an income distribution of extremes.

Why does an unregulated market economy produce extremes? For one thing, its most successful winners can abuse their power. The usual story is that big winners "must have" made enormous contributions to the economy and therefore have earned their rewards. But in reality, many big winnings are the result of insiders taking advantage of privileged positions to reap excessive gains. Today's CEOs earn astronomical pay packages not because they suddenly became ten times more productive but because crony boards of directors enable them to cash in. Today's investment bankers and hedge fund operators make so much money because the rules have been changed to encourage more purely financial engineering and manipulation of paper. Many other big winnings are the result of abuses of monopoly positions. The drug companies and their executives would not be cashing in so exorbitantly at public expense if their lobbyists and allies in Congress hadn't rewritten the patent laws to discourage the use of cheaper generic drugs.

None of this pulling away at the top and widened inequality is the result of "the market," as if markets were spontaneous creations of nature. All functioning markets are creatures of laws, beginning with laws defining and protecting basic property rights, laws creating and privileging corporations as legal "persons," and laws defining the rights of shareholders and duties of corporate boards. Laws can lead to a narrower or broader diffusion of an economy's benefits. In the past three decades, because of the capture of the political process by economic elites, the movement in the evolution of laws governing capitalism has been entirely in one direction—toward a legal conception of markets that narrows rather than broadens concentrations of wealth.

The market's allocation of wealth also tends to undervalue social goods. Social investments can contribute to economic growth even as they distribute it more broadly. Public education allows ordinary people to make contributions to the national well-being. It allows prospective scientists, engineers, doctors, teachers, and nurses, as well as other good citizens, to realize their economic potential. Public outlays on health and research make the society more prosperous as well as more equal. Unless we tax those who win big in the market lottery, we will not have the resources to invest in public schools, public health programs, research universities, training programs, social insurance, and the other elements of a society that is both efficient and just.

Moreover, a pure market system lacks social mechanisms to protect against unanticipated risk. Many economic losses that hit individuals are the result of plain bad luck or bad timing—working in an industry suddenly overwhelmed by outsourcing, a breadwinner's succumbing to an incapacitating illness, reaching economic adulthood just as the economy goes into recession. The more a market turns everything into a commodity, the fewer are the protections against dislocations produced by market forces or random ones. Finally, a totally unregulated market is vulnerable to financial panics (often the result of overreaching by the same insiders) and episodes of boom and bust. While occasionally a billionaire loses everything, little people with limited financial resources are generally more vulnerable to the consequences of economic shifts and shocks. So on all counts, the more laissez-faire an economy, the more unequal it tends to be. All of economic history demonstrates this.

An Exceptional Moment

In our own national experience, several things about the 1930s and 1940s America were politically unique. Most important, a laissez-faire economy was disgraced by the Great Depression as a practical failure.

Not only did this lead to a whole decade of legislation regulating the instability and the opportunism of pure capitalism, as well as expanding security and opportunity for ordinary citizens; but as a political by-product, it put in the White House an exceptionally popular, progressive president committed to the activist use of government and willing to use his political capital to educate public opinion about the evils of "economic royalists." All of this in turn weakened the usual political influence of organized business. The major business groups and their political allies issued the usual dire warnings about economic ruin as the New Deal rolled on, but for once they lacked the public sympathy and the votes to block at least some regulatory remedies. Market excesses had wrecked capitalism, so you couldn't intimidate liberals and Democrats by warning that their policies were bad for the business climate. This political shift was reinforced via a much-strengthened labor movement that was a close ally of the Roosevelt administration.

Then, coincidentally, the prestige of the national government as reliable problem solver (in a country with a history of distrusting government) was further enhanced by the successful prosecution of World War II. The war also contributed to feelings of cross-class empathy, trust, and solidarity. The sacrifices of the Depression and then the war led a generation of Americans to feel that they had paid in advance and had earned a new era of broad prosperity; and that government had a major role to play in helping to make it happen. The war was not just a success of battlefield valor; it was a triumph of public planning. It was World War II, even more than the New Deal, that allowed Roosevelt to proclaim in 1944, in his Four Freedoms speech, that freedom from want was a public responsibility. It was the war that allowed the public to support a massive expansion of public support for higher education and home ownership under the banner of the G.I. Bill of Rights.

Even with this unusual tailwind, however, many of the New Deal–Great Society policies were not as robust as they first seemed. Much economic regulation was industry self-regulation. After World War II, planning fell into ideological disrepute (though it lived on in tacit form, thanks to the Cold War and the Pentagon's need for advanced technologies). The tapestry of social protections was far from complete. The largest social programs—Social Security and later Medicare—were mainly for the elderly, not the working-age population. Unions were far less well tolerated by business than they appeared to be; and as soon as organized business regained political power, it reverted to strident antiunionism.

Nonetheless, the rough political consensus on behalf of a social, managed form of capitalism had enough momentum to continue into the immediate postwar period, with bipartisan programs of broad opportunity such as the G.I. Bill and the expansion of Social Security, and on into the Eisenhower era, when government dramatically expanded support for community colleges and public universities, subsidized housing, and built the Interstate Highway System. To win Republicans' support, legislation promoting social objectives often had to be disguised with an ostensible Cold War rationale, such as the National Defense Education Act, which increased college aid the better to combat the Soviets, or the National Interstate and Defense Highways Act, which built roads for motorists on the premise that they might be needed for tanks.

Whatever the stated rationale, unlike today's token initiatives, these programs made a real difference in people's lives. Voters noticed, and they supported politicians who offered such programs. Meanwhile the regime of tight limits on financial speculation remained snugly in place, and the real economy thrived. It was not until the 1970s that business recovered its latent political influence and began its successful campaign against progressive taxation, regulation, unionism, and social outlay.

To review this history is not to express nostalgia for the good old days but to make three arguments about the American future: First, a society of broader opportunity and security was rooted in a very different politics, and it could be again. Second, though the particulars would be somewhat different in a twenty-first-century egalitarian society, progressive taxation, social investment, worker representation, and economic regulation remain key. And third, despite a massive propaganda blitz to the contrary, a managed form of capitalism is more efficient as well as more socially just. With that prologue, here is a brief tour of the mixed economy's golden age—and its undoing.

The Politics of Tax, Spend, and Regulate

The greater equality of the postwar boom was built on several pillars. One was greater progressivity in the tax system. Although government outlay was roughly the same share of GDP as it is today, working and middle-class people paid far less of their income in taxes than they do today, and wealthy individuals and corporations paid a greater share. But even without the impact of taxes, the economy had several equalizing institutions. They included wage regulation and stronger unions, economic regulation that created greater institutional stability of enterprises, tight controls on speculative capital, and a trading system that limited low-wage competition. All of these factors—some deliberately aimed at promoting security and equality, some achieving that result secondarily—counteracted the market's tendency to produce extremes of wealth and poverty.

The postwar economy relied on progressive taxation and the use of revenue proceeds to increase opportunities for the nonwealthy. Before the 1970s, the top marginal rate on incomes was as high as 91 percent, and taxation on the wage and salary income of ordinary workers was relatively low. A median-income worker typically paid a total tax rate of less than 10 percent. This is not because government spent less—the composition of government outlay has varied, but its overall spending relative to GDP has not changed much in fifty years—but because the tax system was so much more effectively progressive.

Most of the federal tax load was carried by individual and corporate income taxes, both progressive forms of taxation. As recently as the Johnson administration, the corporate income tax equaled about 4 percent of GDP, or over 20 percent of federal revenues. Today, it is down to just over 1 percent of GDP. Meanwhile, the regressive Social Security payroll tax, paid on an income currently capped at $97,500, has accounted for an ever increasing share of federal revenue. As late as 1970, the maximum annual Social Security tax was $327. By 2007, it was $5,785. And with husband and wife both working, you can double that. Today, three working Americans in four pay more in regressive Social Security taxes than they do in progressive personal income taxes, while the rich man's Social Security tax is capped. A worker at minimum wage pays 6.2 percent of earnings in Social Security taxes. An executive earning $2 million pays about one third of 1 percent.

Worse still, the well-meaning people who designed the political compromise that shored up Social Security's finances in 1982–83 made one huge political blunder: they enacted a multitrillion-dollar tax increase on America's wage workers, with no current benefits to match it.

The slower-than-anticipated wage growth of the 1970s (and with it reduced tax receipts), coupled with the projected retirement of the large baby-boom generation after 2010, had left Social Security with a projected shortfall. A bipartisan compromise negotiated by the then-Democratic Congress and the Republican Reagan administration raised the retirement age by two years and increased payroll taxes. The idea was that higher taxes, collected decades in advance of the system's projected payouts, would allow the Social Security trust funds to bank a huge surplus, reserves that would cover the shortfall of current revenues well into the twenty-first century.

Social Security taxes are the most regressive taxes we have. But instead of supplementing payroll taxes with more progressive general revenues, as Roosevelt's architects of Social Security had recommended in 1935, the bipartisan compromise relied entirely on far higher payroll taxes. As a consequence, America's working and middle classes were hit with a tax hike that totaled more than $2.3 trillion between 1984 and 2007, and this will only compound in coming decades. Worst of all, this was exactly the money that underwrote George W. Bush's several rounds of tax cuts for the richest. The "surplus" that Bush raided to finance his tax breaks was mainly the Social Security reserves.

Virtually all of the press coverage of the tax-cut debate noted that the lion's share of the Bush tax breaks went to the wealthiest but that working Americans got a little something, too. This is entirely misleading, since it excludes that multitrillion-dollar tax increase inflicted on wage and salary earners, in advance, over more than twenty years. That tax hike dwarfed the middle-income tax cuts. This immense tax increase might have paid for, say, universal health insurance, universal child care, subsidized starter homes, universal reduced college tuitions, or labor market programs to help displaced workers back into good jobs—any of which might have left voters believing that the higher taxes had produced some valuable return. Instead, more than $2 trillion in higher taxes paid for nothing at all other than a long-run accounting entry on the books of Social Security and financed tax breaks for the rich in the short run, during a period when public services were being cut. No wonder the working middle class concluded that government was a bad bargain.

As a result of the several tax cuts sponsored by Ronald Reagan and George W. Bush, the tax code is now only very marginally redistributive. The overall federal tax burden is now about 15 percent of national income. According to tabulations by *New York Times* reporter David Cay Johnson, since the enactment of the third round of Bush tax cuts in 2003 the very wealthiest are paying a net tax rate of about 17.5 percent, or just barely above the average overall rate. With the additional tax breaks enacted in 2005–06, the wealthiest are paying an effective rate lower than that paid by a majority of working people. Because of the rising hostility to taxation, Republicans were also able to ram through Congress a "taxpayer bill of rights" that crippled the ability of the IRS to audit tax shelters and other cases of high-income tax evasion. At least

$300 billion a year of easily collected taxes are owed but unpaid every year, enough money to eliminate the deficit or underwrite national health insurance.

The same tax cuts have starved the public sector for revenues with which to underwrite public programs of economic opportunity and security. By contrast, the postwar era saw very substantial increases in social investments. These contributed to a more egalitarian society, both directly and indirectly. Social insurance protected ordinary people from economic setbacks beyond their personal control. Public-sector jobs tended to command decent wages, benefits, and employment security. Public services allowed moderate-income citizens access to amenities (and necessities) that they might not be able to afford if they had to purchase them at market prices. This includes everything from free public parks to public health inoculations to subsidized mass transit, plus "positive externalities" such as clean drinking water. As these services are reduced or privatized, and as tax-supported free services become more reliant on fees, access becomes a matter of what people at a given income level can afford.

Given the widening disparity in pretax income as the economy has become privatized, deregulated, and globalized, it would take serious increases in progressive taxation and compensatory social outlay to offset the greater pretax inequality of income and wealth. However, far from using the public sector to lean against the wind, the Right's program of tax cuts to the upper brackets, coupled with a cynical strategy of permanent structural deficits, has caused social outlay to be reduced while reinforcing the extremes of pretax incomes. Domestic spending relative to GDP is now back to the level of the 1950s, and most of what remains is Social Security and Medicare. This shift in burdens and benefits reinforces conservative politics.

Economic Regulation and Trade Unions

During the postwar boom, wage and labor regulation, such as minimum-wage and prevailing-wage laws, unemployment compensation, and legal recognition of trade unions not only raised wages directly, they served to increase the bargaining power of both individual workers and organized labor on behalf of the whole umbrella of social protections. The new commitment by the state to maintaining full employment created a relatively tight labor market in which employers had to pay decently to hire qualified workers.

For a time, employers concluded that labor unions were a permanent fixture of the modern industrial landscape that had to be lived with. They bargained hard over shares of company earnings but did not try to put unions out of business. This entente changed radically in the 1970s, when business, especially in the United States, faced with declining profits, new international competition, and new pressures from financial markets, took off the gloves. Today the unionized percentage is below 8 percent of private-sector workers, down from about 30 percent in the early 1950s.

The deregulation of labor standards has gone hand in hand with the weakening of unions. As of January 2007, the federal minimum wage, adjusted for inflation, was at a fifty-year low of less than 30 percent of the average wage. Unemployment compensation now covers relatively fewer workers and replaces a lower percentage of wages than at any time since FDR. The average weekly benefit of this mostly state-administered program was just $262.50 a week in 2006, about 10 percent less than the poverty line for a family of three.

It is hard to overstate the constructive role of unions in both the economics and the politics of maintaining a broadly egalitarian economy. Unions, by their very nature, serve to equalize wages and to increase labor's share of the total pie, as well as increasing workers' "voice." During the postwar era, this union wage premium affected the wages and benefits not just of unionized workers but of employees in competing firms that hoped to remain union-free.

Unions, moreover, were the core political constituency for the rest of the liberal agenda. Union lobbyists, backed by millions of members, worked to pass not only labor legislation in the narrow sense but comprehensive social legislation such as Medicare, Social Security, federal aid to education, financial regulation, and the great civil rights acts. In the effort to win enactment of these landmark laws during the 1960s, Lyndon Johnson gave great credit to the legislative efforts of the unions. Public opinion polls demonstrate that union membership tends to offset the social conservatism of many white working-class voters, especially white men. In recent years, as Democrats have lost many "Reagan Democrats" on such issues as guns and religious fundamentalism, a postelection poll conducted by Peter Hart found that not only did unionists vote for John Kerry by a margin of 68–32 in battleground states, but Kerry carried a majority of union members who were gun owners and who were evangelical Christians. Even in the weakened union climate of 2004, Hart calculated, without the characteristic differences in the voting tendencies of working-class voters who were union members, John Kerry would have lost seven additional states and won only 175 electoral votes rather than the 252 that he actually did win.

Despite a legacy of corruption in a small minority of unions and a history of racial exclusion in craft unions before the civil rights era, the labor movement today is the most racially and ethnically integrated large institution in America. Unions are the only such economic institutions organized along democratic rather than hierarchical or financial lines. Membership in a union enables workers to gain a clearer sense of their economic interests. It also helps bridge racial and ethnic divides. In this respect, a monumental difference between the era of greater equality and the present one is the relative decline of unions as a political force.

Today's dwindling share of union representation is not the result of workers deciding that unions are not for them. It is the consequence of a no-holds-barred attack by corporations on unions, with the complicity of government. A recent Hart poll shows that 53 percent of America's nonunion workers would like to be represented by a union. But in 2004 just 80,000 workers succeeded in organizing one—because management so efficiently and costlessly fires workers who sign union cards, in flagrant violation of the Wagner Act.

Even in an era of all-out war on unions, the economic advantages of being a union member are impressive. According to the Bureau of Labor Statistics, the average union wage premium is 28 percent. By coincidence, union members also have 28 percent more paid vacation days than nonunion workers. Fully 73 percent of union members have defined-benefit pensions, compared to 16 percent of nonunion workers. And 92 percent of workers in unionized companies receive employer-provided health insurance compared to 68 percent of nonunion workers (whose policies are also often inferior). Lest the reader conclude that all these workers are in declining, old-economy companies whose generous compensation policies are rendering them uncompetitive, the same differences hold up if we compare the average hourly pay of workers in the low-wage service economy, the one sector where unionization is growing:

HOURLY WAGES ($)	UNION	NONUNION
Cashiers	11.22	8.63
Child care workers	11.19	8.83

HOURLY WAGES ($)	UNION	NONUNION
Cooks	11.64	9.05
Janitors	13.71	10.43
Maids	11.67	9.19
Receptionists	14.02	11.47
Telephone operators	19.85	11.86

Source: U.S. Bureau of Labor Statistics.

In the postwar era, several other forms of economic regulation served to insulate workers from pressures to cut wages. An old labor slogan (and strategy) sensibly declares: Take wages out of competition. If companies in the same industry all have labor contracts that require roughly comparable wages for comparable work, they must compete on the basis of customer service, innovative technology, brand loyalty, and other factors that make for more efficient production. A laggard company cannot compensate for management's inefficiency by demanding wage or benefit cuts. Conversely, if companies can compete with lower prices by pressuring their workers to lower wages, the result is a never-ending race to the bottom. This strategy of industry-wide wage standards was employed in the heyday of industrial unionism and has been successfully used more recently by service sector unions that seek to negotiate citywide agreements with hotels and janitorial-service companies.

Before the late 1970s, industries with tens of millions of workers were subject to economic regulation of their prices, terms of service, and market entry and exit. This type of regulation was legislated to prevent monopolies from abusing their market power, but it had the powerful secondary effect of protecting wages. For example, since the 1930s, industries such as airlines, broadcasting, telecommunications, gas and electric utilities, trucking, railroads, and hospitals, as well as banks, insurance companies, and brokerages, had all been subject to diverse forms of price regulation. In the case of airlines, railroads, telephones, and public utilities, the premise was that these industries had elements of "natural monopoly." It was not economically efficient to string two parallel sets of electric wires; one provider was more cost-effective than two or three. But if you left a sole-source public utility or telephone company unregulated, incipient monopolists would use their market power to gobble up competitors, dominate the provision of an essential service, and then gouge the consumer.

In these industries, a combination of state and federal regulation granted a particular company, such as AT&T, Con Edison, or American Airlines, a monopoly franchise for a particular service, customer base, or route. In turn, government subjected the company to a regulated rate of return and price structure that protected both the company and its consumers. In other industries, such as broadcasting, where a private firm was understood to be using a public resource (the airwaves), the terms of competition were closely regulated and the public interest was a criterion to be balanced against the goal of private profit. As part of the New Deal system of regulation, various subterfuges such as holding companies, which had been used to circumvent utility regulation, were also reined in.

Though this system violated textbook free-market economics, it created a climate of institutional stability and predictability, in which entrepreneurs maximized their profits via technological innovation and market deepening, not wage cutting or union bashing. In the case of airlines, better planes led to expansion of markets, reductions in consumer prices, more widespread flying, and more company profits. (Since airline deregulation, most airlines have run at a loss, and customers complain about deteriorating service, aging planes, and a crazy quilt of fares.) In the case of electric power and telephones, where the rate of return was regulated, companies could increase their earnings by expanding their customer base. They grew by devising better technologies that lowered costs and made electricity or phone service more affordable to more people. As the utilities invested more capital, having a larger capital base also increased their earnings because depreciation was part of the formula that determined the permissible rates of return. Real prices declined, service proliferated as more and more people became customers, and industry enjoyed a stable and steady income.

Perhaps the most underappreciated side effect of this whole system of regulated industries was protection of wages. If a monopoly provider's prices were regulated, its wage costs were part of the overall expenses on which its rate of return was calculated. There was nothing to be gained by pressing labor to accept wage cuts. On the contrary, it made more sense to pursue a strategy of retaining well-trained, loyal workers and labor peace. Not by coincidence, these regulated industries tended to have strong unions and decent (though not exorbitant) wages. The unions, in turn, were a force not just for good wages but for a more egalitarian pay structure.

Unions, as a matter of core values, seek to raise the wages of the lowest-paid workers. The main blue-collar union in the airlines, for example, is the International Association of Machinists and Aerospace Workers. A skilled airline mechanic requires several years of training and commands excellent pay. In the heyday of airline regulation, the machinists' union also represented baggage handlers, a relatively unskilled job. However the union succeeded in raising the pay of the baggage handlers to a level well above the minimum necessary to recruit a worker. Other unions worked to narrow wage gaps among occupations in other industries. Public utility regulation also served to moderate executives' compensation, because the management's paychecks were also subject to public scrutiny.

When deregulation came to these industries, all of these egalitarian pressures evaporated. Once public utilities were free to milk whatever profits they could get away with and to outsource work and cut workers' pay, wages were suddenly back in competition with a vengeance. New, low-cost airlines could pay far lower wages, putting pressure on established competitors to follow suit. New telecom companies resisted unionization by outsourcing call centers. Even unions at unionized companies had to work with management to cut costs and often did so by acquiescing in the outsourcing of job categories deemed peripheral. This process undercut the unions' influence on equalizing wages.

In principle, this greater freedom for companies (that still enjoyed a degree of monopoly power) liberated them to innovate and to pass the fruits of innovation along to customers. But it didn't quite work out that way. The actual experience of the 1980s and 1990s shows that companies in these industries took advantage of market power and, on balance, abused customers as well as workers. Electricity deregulation is a failure. Adjusted for the price of fuel, the retail cost of electricity has increased at a faster rate after deregulation than before. Deregulation has invited merger and market power, not competition. Costs would be rising even faster if most states had not opted to retain some caps on retail charges. Telephone deregulation opened the doors to an orgy of mergers, acquisitions, and stock market frauds, which ended up wasting nearly $2 trillion of capital, invested in projects that were written off as losses.

Leave aside for a moment whether a "high road" of stable employment and good pay is ultimately more or less efficient for the economy as a whole than a "low road" of deregulation, contingent work, job insecurity, and declining wages. This book will demonstrate that the high road is at least as efficient for the economy generally, and much better for workers and their families. But for now, it ought to be crystal clear that economic regulation contributed mightily to broadly distributed prosperity.

Markets Unbound

As I argued in *Everything for Sale,* many realms of economic and civic life that were relatively less marketized have become more intensely commercial. In a decade, this trend has only intensified. It is not healthy for a democracy when market values crowd out civic values.

Take, for example, college tuition. As higher education costs have risen, universities have increasingly thought of themselves as creatures of the marketplace. Universities make deals with industry partners. These arrangements render a great deal of their research proprietary, rather than part of the pool of common knowledge. University admissions offices market their schools as commercial products, to raise their standing in the annual *U.S. News & World Report* rankings. The College Board reported that by 2006, less than half the aid granted by public institutions was based on financial need and the trend was to give more aid based on "merit," in order to attract high-scoring students, usually from affluent families. A 2006 research study by the Education Trust found that universities were actually giving more financial aid to upper-class students than to poor ones in their quest for students with higher College Board scores.

As public support for higher education has dwindled, university presidents and deans spend an ever-increasing percentage of their time cultivating wealthy benefactors, rather than presiding over a community of higher learning. All of this undercuts the university's core mission. Rather than requiring college presidents to pay court to the caprices of billionaires (which leads to an often weird allocation of endowed chairs and named institutes), it would be far more efficient, as well as more equitable, to raise taxes on those billionaires and use some of the proceeds to give universities and their students and faculty more adequate core support.

Egalitarian norms have given way to a system that disproportionately rewards supposed superstars and downplays the economic contribution of the rest of the team. In some cases, this is just the market working, as people with unique talents bid up their market price. In other cases, it is pure insider opportunism. Would American industry wither if CEOs reverted to a system in which the chief executive earned "only" sixty times the pay of the ordinary worker in the 1960s? Hardly.

The Windfall Economy

There are two ways to think about what is happening to the income distribution in America. The first holds that the narrowing of prosperity is necessary for economic efficiency. The second holds that the concentration of wealth and income reflects changes in American institutions and political power, and that an equally dynamic but far fairer America is available, given different political and economic rules.

The defenders of the present system contend that in the new, high-tech, high-skill, global economy, the innovators deserve their astronomical gains—that they are smarter, or more inventive, or better trained than ordinary Americans. There is germ of truth to this contention, especially when it involves technology. Cornell economist Robert Frank describes a "winner-take-all" economy in which financial and entertainment superstars now have the whole world as their stage, and unique talents or technical breakthroughs can legitimately produce astronomical gains. Arguably, Pierre Omidyar, inventor of eBay, earned his multi-billion-dollar fortune. Likewise Sergey Brin, who created Google, and of course Bill Gates. Even in their cases, however, the public may be overpaying, and Gates may well be collecting monopoly profits at public expense. The collapse of antitrust enforcement under the Republicans has allowed Microsoft to abuse its monopoly Windows operating system to crush purveyors of often superior applications software (for instance, WordPerfect versus Word or Mosaic versus Outlook) by making sure that the non-Microsoft product is harder to use with Windows. Google, likewise, is now getting sued for lifting other people's copyrighted content, in video and printed books.

However, if anyone deserves large returns as the fruits of their innovation, these high-tech entrepreneurs do. They have actually created something of broad value. If we want to prevent them from becoming an American plutocracy, the remedy is tougher antitrust laws and progressive income and estate taxes. Plenty of innovation will still occur. Back in the era of a more equal America, entrepreneurs innovated even though their financial returns were only in the tens of millions rather than the billions. And some, like Jonas Salk, or Tim Berners-Lee, who created the World Wide Web, did it for the sheer joy of making a better world and settled for a decent professional income. Indeed, the whole culture of windfall gain is at risk of crowding out the necessary public-mindedness of scientists, doctors, and educators, most of whom would happily take a congenial work environment and a good professional salary, but whose peer culture is signaling them that they are suckers unless they go for astronomical incomes. This trend is corrupting the values of fields like scientific research.

But if some technical entrepreneurs arguably deserve large earnings, the Wall Street billionaires are a whole other story. There is a very good case that their windfall profits are actually making the economy worse off. The gains to hedge fund operators and merger-and-acquisition specialists in the newly deregulated environment are often not a case of inventing something new and valuable, but rather taking advantage of an insider position to capitalize on information that will move markets before it becomes widely known, or manipulating those markets for personal gain, or rearranging assets for the value that can be extracted from the transaction. While some Wall Street insiders do add value, spillover costs of the windfall economy frequently exceed the benefits.

The costs are both to economic efficiency as a whole, and to the distribution of prosperity. When self-dealing on Wall Street produces a spectacular collapse, such as Enron, there are huge losses. When a merger deal mainly rearranges assets, the financial engineers take out profits at the expense of the operating company. And when a merger or a breakup is promoted mainly for the transaction profits that can be gained, there also is a shift in who gets the benefits of the company's profits. The new owners inevitably squeeze the employees. Reduced wages, increased layoffs, outsourcing, and the looting of pension funds often result. This is less a case of improved efficiency than a narrowing of who receives the fruits of production. The examples are legion.

To take one recent case, the real estate mogul Sam Zell in April 2007 made a winning offer for Chicago's Tribune Company. The Tribune and its subsidiary, the Los Angeles Times, previously had poor employee relations because the management was trying to compensate for losses by resorting to many hundreds of newsroom layoffs. Zell was able to get control of the Tribune by putting up just 3.4 percent of his own money in the $8.2 billion leveraged buyout. The rest of the money was borrowed, by using the tax benefits of a newly created employee stock ownership plan (ESOP) to reduce tax liabilities. This sounds like the employees will become partners. In fact, the employees get no governing power. Zell is in a position to rake off profits and capital gains should the venture succeed, but stick the employee-shareholders with most of the loss if the venture goes bad. Zell borrowed over $8 billion in order to consummate the deal, on top of the company's existing debt of nearly $5 billion. As a result, the interest costs to the operating company will increase dramatically, causing bond-rating agencies to downgrade its debt, thus further raising costs. All of this created the expectation of even deeper layoffs. This was less a case of improving efficiencies than extracting cash flow.

Deals like this, which are profitable because of the tax laws, specifically the tax treatment of interest payments, enable financial engineering that worsens the income mal-distribution. They enrich a small number of insiders, whose gains are ultimately financed by extracting pay cuts on ordinary wage and salaried workers. The resulting narrowing of prosperity has nothing to do with technology or genuine entrepreneurship. It reflects shifts in political power both inside the corporation and in the halls of Congress.

One other hallmark of the postwar boom, of which more is discussed in chapters six, seven, eight, and nine, was that the United States was relatively insulated from global competitive pressures—to deregulate markets or to reduce wages. For the three decades after World War II, tariffs were gradually reduced from a high level. But there remained a variety of nontariff barriers that protected the mixed economy, such as a monetary system with fixed exchange rates and financial regulations that discouraged speculative money movements. Governments were also free to pursue industrial and technology policies and to favor domestic producers in their procurement policies, without being hauled before the World Trade Organization (then called the General Agreement on Tariffs and Trade) to be accused of discrimination. Until the 1960s, only about 5 percent of the value of the U.S. economy was traded.

This was also an era of controlled immigration. Until Lyndon Johnson signed the Immigration Act of 1967, immigration was tightly capped. There was not much illegal entry because there was far less interpenetration of the U.S. economy with other economies. South of the Rio Grande, economic conditions for ordinary Mexicans were relatively better than they are today, and there was far less of a desperate push to find work in the north. The 1967 law liberalized annual limits, getting rid of the discriminatory national origin quotas that were the basis of the highly restrictive 1924 legislation. In its place, the new law substituted such principles as reuniting families and taking in refugees and needed specialty workers. The national identity of most immigrants rapidly shifted from Western European to that of a broad tapestry of nations. Illegal immigration increasingly became a problem, as more people swam across the Rio Grande or overstayed student or tourist visas to work illegally. Taken together, the earlier limits on trade and on immigration had protected American workers from pressures to cut wages for either foreign or immigrant workers willing to perform the same work for less.

The effect of immigrants on wages is disputed by economists. Clearly, a large influx of relatively uneducated workers adds to the labor supply and puts downward pressure on wages among those with low skills. But how much? This is the subject of intense debate. Professor George Borjas of Harvard, the best known of the academic immigration hawks, has written studies suggesting that wages among the unskilled fall as much as 3 to 4 percent for each 10 percent increase in immigration. The net loss is lower than the gross loss because immigrants become consumers of goods and services and their purchases also create jobs.

Other economists calculate the downward wage pressure from immigrants to be far less severe. But two points are clear. First, higher unionization rates and higher minimum wage laws would offset most of the wage drag produced by more liberal immigration. The highly successful organizing drive to unionize every major hotel in Las Vegas has turned poverty-level jobs into middle-class jobs, even though most members of the Las Vegas local are immigrants. Second, at the top of the income distribution, the capture of so much of the national income by the richest 1 percent has nothing whatever to do with immigration.

The Great Reversal

In the 1970s, the entire egalitarian system that was built after World War II unraveled. Imagine if the sponsors of this economic reversal had practiced truth in advertising and simply declared that the proposed policy changes would be terrific for the richest 10 percent of the population and make everyone else relatively worse off, and more than half the people absolutely worse off; that overall economic growth rates after 1973 would be roughly a third lower than during the postwar boom; and that risks to the system and to individuals would be dramatically heightened. Of course, this is not what was advertised.

Regulation was blamed for several ills of the 1970s. And a newly resurgent business elite and their economist allies took advantage of a bout of inflation to make a fresh effort to deregulate the economy. Economic regulation was widely faulted for causing price pressures, most of which actually originated in the OPEC oil shock and in Lyndon Johnson's overheating of the economy in the late 1960s to avoid choosing between "guns and butter." Competition was advertised as the cure for America's economic torpor.

Say what you will about the violations of free-market economics, a system that produced nearly three decades of egalitarian economic growth with an average annual growth rate of 3.8 percent cannot be all bad. There were perhaps some excesses and inefficiencies in the postwar economic system, but with a different politics we could have a very different set of remedies and still preserve the system's equalizing institutions.

Increasing income inequality was already apparent by the late 1970s and was addressed by commentators as an economic puzzle, presumably a temporary one. At the time, most economists attributed the rising inequality to everything but political power. One leading suspect was the shift from manufacturing to services, since service sector pay tends to be concentrated at the bottom. Another was the entry of large numbers of new workers with lower-than-average skills into the labor market, especially younger workers and women. Other things being equal, a wider dispersion of skills should widen income inequality. Still another prime candidate was the slower growth and "stagflation" of the 1970s. High unemployment always produces low bargaining power for wage workers. The industrial restructuring of that era also killed off lots of well-paid factory jobs.

In a 1983 article for *The Atlantic Monthly* titled "The Declining Middle," I questioned the view that these income shifts were merely temporary results of technical changes. My argument was that the shifts in the rules reflected shifts in political power. Time has confirmed that view. It's true that a shift away from manufacturing employment, other things being equal, will widen income inequality, because manufacturing wages tend to be relatively equal and cluster somewhat above the median. But this greater income equality is largely the result of the earlier successes of trade unions; it is not inherent in manufacturing, as any Mexican or Chinese sweatshop worker can testify. By contrast, the service sector is made up of brain surgeons at one end and fast-food workers at the other. Shift to a service economy, and you will get a more unequal distribution of income.

As things turned out, the rising inequality of the 1970s was no technical or temporary phenomenon. When the economy resumed growing at close to normal postwar rates in the 1980s and then soared in the 1990s, women and baby boomers were fully absorbed into the workforce, and productivity growth regained high levels, the inequality just kept widening. The bottom made relative gains only for a couple of years, at the peak of the late-1990s boom, when labor markets were briefly so tight that even the lowest paid could get modest raises. Even so, the top kept pulling away from everybody else. The widening inequality, it turned out, reflected not a temporary recession or temporary demographic factors but deep structural changes in the organization of the economy. These, in turn, reflected a massive shift in political power.

Several other key factors are vividly evident now that were only embryonic in 1983. Despite its high and rising productivity, manufacturing is no longer a wage leader. The gap between average manufacturing and service pay has narrowed to about 20 percent. The industrial sector is particularly vulnerable to low-wage global competition, and real wages in industries such as autos and steel, once the heart of the blue-collar middle class, have been falling as automation as well as trade continue to replace manufacturing jobs. Productivity in manufacturing has soared, but the fruits are not shared with the workers, whose real pay is steadily declining. That disjuncture reflects disparities of power. Today, more service sector jobs are more amenable to unionization, because many of them can't move offshore.

Quite apart from the shifting composition of the labor market, inequality continues to widen for more fundamental reasons. The most powerful of these forces, which now loom far larger than they did in 1983, are the globalization of commerce under laissez-faire auspices and the deregulation of much of the economy, most importantly of the financial sector. These two trends, taken together, have undermined most of the equalizing institutions of the postwar boom (except for taxes and income transfers) and make them difficult to resurrect.

In the standard analysis of why inequality has increased since the 1970s, deregulation and the rules of trade receive far too little attention. Deregulation is held simply to improve economic efficiency; its benefits receive nearly all the attention, and its costs are widely ignored. Anyone who questions the rules of the current trade regime and whose interests it serves is dismissed as a flat-earth protectionist. Instead, a great many economists, journalists, and politicians of both parties emphasize education as both the source of rising inequality, and its cure.

Education: The Wrong Explanation

The education story has two parts. First, with the globalization of commerce, decently educated Indians and Chinese are happy to do the work of comparably educated Americans for something like one tenth to one fifth the wage. Therefore, in this account, if we want to remain a high-wage economy and keep the high-end jobs, we had better become the best-educated workforce on the planet.

The second part of the story has to do with purported shifts in the demand for workers. Supposedly, with the new, advanced economy, industry now demands much higher skill levels. Not surprisingly, merely ordinary skills do not command the good wages that they once did. This trend, known in the economics literature as "skill-biased technology shifts," is said to account for much of the widening of wage and salary inequality. Princeton economist Alan Blinder, in an article warning that the moving of jobs offshore was a much bigger problem than many of his colleagues thought, pinned most of the blame on the shift in demand for skills: "The labor market has turned ferociously against the low-skilled and the uneducated." But Blinder explicitly warns that more education, by itself, is not the cure. The economist Benjamin Friedman, in a discussion of growth and equality, likewise writes that "the increasing inequality in the United States and in many western European countries reflects just such a widening of pay differentials, as the shift from industrial production to information-based services accelerated while many workers initially lacked the new computer skills rewarded in the labor market."

There are several flaws in both parts of the analysis. First, trade with workers in lower-wage economies does not just put low-skilled American workers at risk. Indian engineers, not just Indian textile workers and call center operators, can perform American jobs at far lower wages. Thomas Friedman, among the most euphoric of the cheerleaders for the great opportunities in the new, globalized economy, acknowledges what he calls "a dirty little secret." In *The World Is Flat*, he writes, "A lot of the jobs that are starting to go abroad today are very high-end research jobs, because not only is the talent abroad cheaper, but a lot of it is as educated as American workers—or even more so."

Even Friedman does not think that we can compete by lowering our salaries to Indian or Chinese levels, and he has seen too much in his travels and interviews to believe that the Indians and Chinese will be satisfied with the routine jobs such as factory operative and call center worker so that Americans can hold on to the high end. China already turns out more engineers a year than we do.

Elsewhere in his book, Friedman imagines a conversation with his daughters. "Girls," he advises them, "when I was growing up, my parents used to say to me, 'Tom, finish your dinner—people in China and

India are starving.' My advice to you is, Girls: finish your homework—people in China and India are starving for your jobs." It's a clever one-liner, but Friedman can't be serious. He's just told us that well-educated people in Bangalore will work for a fifth of the wages of their American counterparts, and he surely doesn't want that for his daughters. Yes, we need a very well-educated society, but the cure for declining American incomes and widening inequality largely lies elsewhere.

As for the claim that wider inequality reflects a shift in demand for the workers' current skill levels, careful economic analysis shows that this just isn't true. Ian Dew-Becker and Robert Gordon, in their paper "Where Did the Productivity Growth Go?," write that the skill-mismatch hypothesis is just not plausible for three distinct reasons. First, it "fails to explain the absence of an increase in income inequality in Europe despite the free flow of technology across borders." Second, inequality increased fastest during 1977–92, "when growth and presumably technical change was slowest." And third, if a changing demand for skills associated with computerization were a major factor in rising inequality, it should have been reflected in rewards to skilled workers. "Yet in the 1989–97 period, total real compensation to CEOs increased by 100 percent, while those in occupations related to math and computer science increased only 4.8 percent, and engineers decreased 1.4 percent."

In a recent exhaustive summary of the skills debate, the sociologist Michael J. Handel observes, "Any skills mismatch explanation of U.S. inequality growth and poor economic performance in the 1980s has to account for the turnaround in the 1990s that seems largely independent of trends in the stock of skills." Handel adds, "One of the more unexpected findings that casts doubt on the more extreme skills mismatch argument is the remarkable employment rate of the large number of former welfare recipients who have left the program since the mid-1990s and the generally favorable evaluation of their skills and performance by employers." More important than shifts in skills in explaining rising inequality, Handel suggests, is the shift in relative bargaining power of workers and employers.

There is in fact substantial divergence between skills and earnings. Doctors, for example, are among the most highly trained and skilled of all the professions. Yet doctors in most specialties lately have been asked to work longer hours for less pay, reflecting an increase in the power of the insurance industry relative to that of the medical profession. Today's auto and steel workers typically have college degrees and are asked to master technologies unknown to the rank-and-file members of Walter Reuther's United Automobile Workers (UAW), many of whom had not graduated from high school. Yet autoworkers' real earnings have fallen by a third in two decades. The technician who comes to install or fix your cable TV has a degree of computer literacy that his predecessor a decade ago would not have recognized. Yet as nonunion telecom companies have gone head-to-head with unionized outfits, a technician for nonunion Comcast is making six or seven dollars an hour less than his unionized Verizon counterpart doing the identical job.

It is certainly true that a high school education is no longer enough to command a middle-class standard of living. But while more years of education are necessary to earn a higher income, they are by no means sufficient. Indeed, during the postwar boom, when half of Americans had not completed high school, there were wider education gaps between the top and the bottom but a far more equal allocation of income and opportunity. Tens of millions of American college graduates today are working in jobs that do not require a college degree.

The weakening of all the equalizing institutions mentioned herein contribute far more to the new inequality than changes in demand for skills. Yet emphasizing skills and education neatly allows politicians, economists, and commentators to avoid discussing the other, more politically loaded factors. Moreover, focusing on education conveniently blames government's administration of public schools, promotes privatization via vouchers, and makes rising inequality largely the individual worker's fault rather than a function of how the system is organized and for whose benefit.

At the other end of the income spectrum, twenty-six-year-olds manipulating bond markets in the 1980s and 1990s became multimillionaires. They knew next to nothing about the underlying industries whose fates they were dictating. They were adroit at a very narrow set of number-crunching skills and found themselves in the right place at the right time. Somehow, this does not comport with Tom Friedman's picture of a competitive economy based on rare "skills." At the very top, the ability of corporate chief executives and Wall Street moguls to command earnings that routinely exceed $50 million a year has less to do with skills in the usual sense of the word and more to do with skill at rearranging paper assets and the system's rules.

For every genuine entrepreneur who invents something truly new and who arguably "deserves" annual income in the tens or hundreds of millions, there are countless routine corporate CEOs tending mature companies who have increased their typical earnings tenfold since the 1980s without adding anything like that multiple to the corporation's wealth creation. They are simply taking a free ride on the shifting norms of what CEOs are paid, norms that are largely the fruits of the winner-take-all psychology promoted by deregulation. Every year, the financial press reports on innumerable CEOs whose pay rose while the company's earnings fell.

The Liberation of Capital

Financial deregulation was a serial offender in worsening the income distribution. In the regulatory regime that prevailed between the 1940s and 1970s, the financial part of capitalism was constrained to playing its appropriate role: providing capital to the "real" part of the economy that produced goods and services. The ability of Wall Street to make money for insiders purely by rearranging assets was restricted by both norms and laws. Several things that are now commonplace simply were not done. Mergers occasionally occurred, but not hostile takeovers arranged with borrowed money. Investment bankers underwrote stock issues to take new companies public and arranged bond financing for clients but did not promote an orgy of mergers and acquisitions mainly for the value of the fees they generated. Corporate chief executives commanded generous salaries (at a far lower multiple of workers' salaries), and stock options and bonus compensation related to the share price were virtually unknown.

Beginning in the 1970s, a whole new style of capitalism was set in motion. Soon, nearly every corporation was at risk of being on the auction block all the time. The game became: Acquire or Be Acquired. A company with a rising share price had more value to borrow against in order to put annoying competitors out of business. Size per se became prized because higher executive pay generally went hand in hand with higher corporate worth, quite apart from earnings.

This new brand of capitalism affected the incomes of both the top and the bottom. The pay of corporate executives rose dramatically, as did the fees earned by middleman investment bankers. Almost overnight, investment bankers were ubiquitously pitching possible mergers that made little economic sense except as sources of fees. In the middle and at the bottom, workers who had made careers in stable corporations were suddenly vulnerable to layoffs and pay cuts.

The new rules fundamentally changed the nature of the corporation, and not for the better. Back when the financial markets were servants of corporations, rather than their masters, corporations enjoyed a degree of stability over time. Executives generally came up through company ranks and had a sense of loyalty to the communities where they lived, as well as to their workers and suppliers. Some even made an effort to get along with unions. This is not to sentimentalize the 1950s. Plenty of corporate leaders were soulless money-grubbers. But at least the institutional structure made possible, in blue-chip corporations, an ethos in which corporations could make investments for the long term, both in technologies and in people.

We will explore the multiple consequences of financial deregulation in greater detail in later chapters. For now, it is enough to appreciate how these changes widened the income distribution—at the top, the middle, and the bottom—by subjecting the real economy to increased pressures from the trading economy.

Like deregulation, globalization of commerce and finance undermines equality in far-flung, mutually reinforcing, underappreciated ways. The increasing subjection of American workers to direct wage competition from people willing to work for a fraction of the U.S. wage is only the most overt aspect. Globalization undermines the politics of remedy, because it weakens the ability of national governments to levy taxes and to regulate capital and labor, and it strengthens domestic constituencies for laissez-faire.

The regulation of commerce can best be understood as a political struggle spanning more than a century of popular government, intended to broaden economic prosperity and to temper the profit motive with a modicum of social accountability. Since political democracy necessarily operates through the nation-state, globalization of commerce allows organized business to make an end run, to a realm in which there is no democratic sovereign. I am a citizen of the United States, not a citizen of the WTO or of NAFTA. Regulation of labor, health, the environment, taxation, and provision of social goods are all necessarily done mainly by national governments. The embryonic European Union is making an effort to accomplish some of this on a continental scale, so that it can carry on the project of balancing commercial goals with social ones. By contrast, NAFTA, which has no civic component, is a pure triumph of commerce over democratic citizenship.

Few American politicians are serious about addressing the question of how a nation that values decent wages and social balance ought to engage with the global economy. The current dogma of globalization, defined as global deregulation in the interest of the business elite, is intellectually and politically hegemonic. It simply can't be challenged in respectable company. It is assumed that those with a different view are irrational or self-serving nativists, rather than people seeking to preserve the demonstrated benefits of a managed form of capitalism. You literally cannot find an editorial writer on a mainstream daily newspaper sympathetic to this view. And you have to go well to the left within the Democratic Party to find anyone who will defend principles for organizing an economy that were once standard American practice and that once served the bottom 80 percent far better than the current organization of capitalism does. This is another failure of politics.

Globalization and financial deregulation work hand in glove. The ascendancy of the Wall Street view of what is good for the American economy goes a long way toward explaining why a different politics and different principles for organizing the U.S. and global economy are only at the margins of political discourse. It is to this logic that we now turn.

CHAPTER THREE

WALL STREET RULES

SEVEN YEARS after the fact, the general understanding of the Wall Street scandals of the 1990s and the stock market crash of 2000–01 is that the system averted wider catastrophe and largely fixed what was broken. Congress responded with a potent reform, the 2002 Sarbanes-Oxley Act, which required honest corporate accounting and prohibited the kinds of conflicts of interest that led to cooked books and manipulated share prices. The SEC may have been too cozy with Wall Street, but Eliot Spitzer, then the New York State attorney general, stepped into the breach with masterful investigations. The big banks and brokerage houses signed an unprecedented consent agreement that prohibited a range of dangerous practices and required a collective fine and disgorgement of nearly $1.4 billion. The worst scoundrels were convicted of felonies, and several went to prison. Even Martha Stewart, found guilty of selling a small number of shares based on an insider stock tip, served five months. Shareholders were in a new mood of activism, and the corporation was at last being rendered more accountable. CEOs and their accountants, bankers, and stockbrokers have been put on notice to play it straight or face the consequences.

This chapter and the two that follow will argue that almost none of the above is true. Nearly all the conflicts of interest that set into motion first the stock bubble and then the crash, the fleecing of investors, and the waste of trillions of dollars of investment capital are alive and continuing to do damage. The Sarbanes-Oxley Act, now under broad assault by business as excessive, addresses only a tiny fraction of what's wrong, and the Securities and Exchange Commission (SEC) remains largely passive. New conflicts of interest and financial plays that enrich insiders at the expense of small investors are being invented with new ingenuity and ferocity, concentrating income and wealth and putting the entire financial system at risk. Meanwhile, the temporary cure for the economic downdraft caused by the 2000–01 crash—a cheap dollar, large public deficits, and ever-greater international borrowing—is doing hidden damage and deferring a more dangerous day of reckoning. Wall Street's lock on economic policy removes from public debate the instruments of broader prosperity and security that characterized the economy of the mid–twentieth century.

All of this is a monumental failure of democratic politics—and a great success for wealthy insiders at the general expense. Worse, it is not as if one political party were demanding remedy and the other resisting. As in the case of the stagnation of living standards, the real remedies are not to be found in mainstream political debate. Only a few scattered politicians are willing to take on even the flagrant and easy-to-grasp abuses, such as manipulation of stock options. Hardly any are interested in the deeper regulatory questions that directly affect both income distribution and systemic risk, such as the governance of corporations, the regulation of hedge funds, private equity, and mutual funds, and the multiple conflicts of interest still built into the entire system. The issues of deepening risk and grotesque inequalities of reward are directly interrelated. Each reflects a failure of politics—either elite politics or mass politics—to take regulation of capitalism seriously.

Alan Greenspan famously referred to the stock market bubble as "irrational exuberance." That was in December 1996, when the market still had another several thousand points of growth to go before it collapsed, in part because of Greenspan's own regulatory indulgence. One can point to the dot-com euphoria of the late 1990s as a classic case of speculative wishful thinking, of a piece with tulip bulb mania and the South Sea Bubble. But the exuberance, however irrational, was not a spontaneous madness of crowds. It was force-fed.

A System Built on Conflicts of Interest

In their essence, the Wall Street scandals of the 1990s were about conflicts of interest—invited by deregulation and abused by insiders to their own financial advantage. In almost every case, the speculations involved borrowed money, often deliberately concealed and thus exponentially increasing the risk of loss in the event of a sudden downturn, miscalculation, or exposure of fraud. Far from enhancing economic efficiency—always the rationale for giving financial markets and their speculators more license—deregulation promoted insiders' enrichment at the expense of small investors, ordinary employees, and pensioners and jeopardized the efficiency and solvency of the system as a whole.

Every category of gatekeeper who had a fiduciary relationship with small shareholders was corrupted. Social scientists call this a failure of "agency"—a corruption of intermediaries charged with acting as agents of individual investors and of the public in general. The supposed representatives of shareholders simply became confederates of insiders, suborned by the prospect of their own enrichment.

In the idealized financial system of textbook economics, small investors are the instruments of an efficient market. They discipline the companies whose shares they own by buying and selling securities at a price that reflects accurate information. Technically, the market price is the present discounted value of an expected future earnings stream. Different investors, of course, will place different bets because of their different guesses about the future—that's why trading markets exist. But in an efficient market, these expectations are based on honest bookkeeping and arm's-length trading. Small investors depend on the integrity of "agents": accountants, lawyers, stockbrokers, underwriters, and corporate boards of directors.

Curiously, it took substantial regulation to compel actual financial markets to resemble the efficiency of textbook ones. To facilitate accurate information, honest fiduciaries, and well-informed investors, the scheme of financial regulation created during the New Deal requires corporations to make a variety of disclosures. Independent audits are mandated by law. Stock manipulation, self-dealing, insider trading, and other conflicts of interest are supposedly proscribed. Fiduciary norms of self-restraint are backed up by regulators and the risk of civil and criminal penalties as well as private lawsuits. After the great crash of 1929, it became clear that the risk of being penalized after the fact is often too weak a disincentive. Entire categories of temptation had to be ruled out by structural barriers, such as those prohibiting commercial banks from floating stock issues. Although these regulations were far from complete or foolproof, they created a transparency that made U.S. capital markets the envy of the world.

In the 1980s and 1990s, however, every element of agency failed. Deregulation and lax enforcement of the regulations that remained eroded professional norms that had constrained rank opportunism. Supposedly independent auditors colluded with management to dress up corporate books. Ostensibly fair-minded securities analysts serving investors turned out to be stock touts looking to bring their firm underwriting business based on their success in running up a client company's share price. Boards of directors that allegedly represented shareholders helped crony CEOs reap astronomical compensation packages largely disconnected from actual company performance. Corporate boards promoted stock options that gave executives incentives not to optimize true performance but to inflate the share price in the short run. Mutual funds, rather than serving as the agents of investors, took huge transaction fees and invariably voted their shares with management. Brokers and investment bankers helped themselves and their favorite clients to new stock issues (IPOs) at preferential prices not available to the public. Institutions of self-regulation, such as the National Association of Securities Dealers, the American Institute of Certified Public Accountants, and the New York Stock Exchange, went after minor infractions but not the deeper corruption.

What all of these insiders had in common was a self-interest in manipulating share prices. A rising market draws in more investors, further inflating stocks. In an era of exploding mergers and acquisitions collateralized by company stock, a corporation with swollen share prices had more money with which to buy competitors, reduce competition, and reward insiders. A bigger merged company naturally (or unnaturally) led to bigger executive pay packages. Mergers and acquisitions inflated the fees of investment bankers. With executive compensation itself increasingly based on stock options, the ability to cash in big also depended on high-flying stock.

The supposed premise was that a bonus paid in the form of stock options would "align incentives" between the executive and ordinary shareholders, who presumably had a common interest in a rising share price. But the way options were structured, the executive had no interest in the long-term performance of the company or even of the stock. The idea was to create a quick spike in the share price so that the executive could cash in—and often quickly cash out. This perverse incentive supercharged the incentive to manipulate balance sheets and stock prices. Options were often backdated, so that executives could realize gains whether or not the company had actually performed well. So much for alignment of incentives.

The relentless increase in CEOs' pay, largely unrelated to actual corporate performance, had already been a public issue for more than a decade. The game was well described in former compensation consultant Graef Crystal's 1991 book, *In Search of Excess*. Between 1970 and 1990, CEOs' pay increased about fourfold, while workers' median earnings stagnated. Subsequently, during the 1990s, the reported pay of senior corporate executives increased almost fivefold. If workers' median pay had grown at the same rate as CEOs' pay, it would today be over $200,000 a year. CEOs and their boards worked hand in glove to trade favors. Even in 2002, after two years of corporate meltdown, the median pay of the *Fortune* 100 CEOs rose by another 14 percent, to $13.2 million.

Students of economic history learn that "interlocking directorates" were prohibited in 1914 by the Clayton Antitrust Act. But that turns out to mean only interlocks between direct competitors. Executives in a position to do one another favors at the expense of investors—vendors, bankers, traders, customers—routinely serve on one another's boards. At the time Crystal wrote his indignant book, the average chief executive's pay was roughly 150 times that of the typical worker. Fifteen years later, it is about 400 to 500 times, mocking the premise that the risk of hostile takeovers and a "market for corporate control" would somehow render CEOs more accountable.

So much money was there to be made that even the system's most cautious and prudent players, certified public accountants, were corrupted. Fees were relatively modest for the accountants' bread-and-butter business, annual audits of financial statements. So the firms set up a lucrative sideline of offering consulting services. At bottom, the main "service" was advising the corporate client how to game its own books and still pass muster in an audit. Accountants were literally reaping fees for advising clients how to deceive accountants. Their own professional association, the American Institute of Certified Public Accountants, empowered by the SEC to be the system's watchdog, became a lobby for the loosest possible regulation.

These scandals required the convergence of several different pieces of deregulation. Enron, for example, was nominally an energy company, but at heart it was a Ponzi scheme built on extensive borrowing and gambling in derivatives markets. It covered its losses by using off-the-books entities to book sham transactions and borrow increasing sums of money. Big banks, enriched by Enron's fees, willingly lent the company and its executives money, collateralized by Enron stock. Enron and its insiders used much of the money to buy more stock. The whole scheme depended on excess borrowing and bankers' complicity. As long as it had favorable notices and a high-flying share price, the money kept flowing. Once the company burned through its borrowed assets and the spiral went into reverse, the money evaporated because the stock price was never backed by real earnings.

None of this would have been possible without multiple forms of deregulation. Just before she left office in early 1993, Wendy Gramm, George H. W. Bush's chair of the Commodity Futures Trading Commission, issued a midnight order sought by Enron allowing it to make over-the-counter trades in exotic derivatives of its own creation, exempt from CFTC supervision. Her husband, Senator Phil Gramm, was subsequently rewarded with a seat on Enron's board. This regulatory lapse, among many others, allowed Enron to set itself up as a derivatives trading company and largely evade detection of market rigging. But it also fed on other regulatory defaults. Electric power deregulation broke up integrated utilities and created opportunities for Enron and other intermediaries to manipulate energy supplies, causing prices to spike and creating huge trading profits. The lax supervision of accountants and the delegation of many regulatory standards to their own trade association invited the basic conflicts of interest that led auditors not just to bless so much phony bookkeeping but to earn fees helping to devise it. And, perhaps most important, the weakening of supervision of the banks virtually invited banks to provide credit to grossly overleveraged and undermonitored outfits such as Enron and WorldCom.

Several of the meltdowns of the 1990s involved the telecom sector. Prior to 1996, the telephone industry had been governed by traditional regulation by the Federal Communications Commission (FCC) and state public utility commissions. This was modified by the 1979 antitrust consent agreement that had broken up the old AT&T monopoly, bringing competition to long-distance service while local companies remained regulated monopolies. In 1996 Congress agreed that one company could provide both kinds of service, as long as there was adequate local competition. The "Baby Bells" could enter long-distance service if they offered access to their grid to local competitors. Congress hoped the result would be more head-to-head price competition (rates did fall for a time but then began climbing in the late 1990s). But there were two unforeseen results. First, a new wave of consolidation helped big companies like Verizon maintain high prices. Second, new players using borrowed money could expand overnight into multibillion-dollar enterprises. With the expansion of the Internet, investors were told that the demand for broadband service was almost infinite.

Fully $1.8 trillion was poured into the broadband craze, and 92 percent of that market value was ultimately lost. Global Crossing, from a standing start in 1997, burned through more than $12 billion during its brief lifetime before going bust in early 2002. Its executives were already

dumping stock during 2000 and 2001, even as they and their confederates, such as the stock analyst Jack Grubman at Salomon Smith Barney,
were talking up the stock to the public. Telecoms with excess capacity
puffed up their balance sheets by swapping broadband leases with one
another for identical amounts of cash. The transactions thus existed
solely on paper. No money changed hands, but each company fraudulently booked the money as income. Amazingly, the accounting firm
Arthur Andersen not only signed off on these deals; in its capacity as
consultant, it helped orchestrate them. This brand of fraud is a criminal
violation of the securities laws. But Global Crossing CEO Gary Win-
nick, who personally pocketed more than $735 million, was never even
charged with criminal wrongdoing. A few months later, in July 2002,
WorldCom filed for a much larger bankruptcy, $66 billion in the red.

When the scandal finally erupted, two relatively minor sets of players
took the fall: the accountants and the stock analysts. The new law and
regulations required the separation of accounting and consulting; and it
also added a new (easily breached) "wall" between the role of stock analyst and that of stock underwriter. But the deeper systemic corruption
went largely untouched, and more fundamental walls came down.

Even as the abuses became widely known, Congress continued to
loosen several regulatory strictures against conflicts of interest, culminating in repeal of the 1933 Glass-Steagall Act, which had prohibited
commercial banks from underwriting or marketing securities. Congress
also weakened the remedies of the common law. In 1995, a bipartisan
majority passed legislation over President Clinton's veto, the Private
Securities Litigation Reform Act, making it much more difficult for
shareholders to win lawsuits against corporations or underwriters that
deliberately falsified information. The law was amended in 1998 to
require all such class action suits for securities fraud to be brought in
federal court, making it more difficult to prove breach of fiduciary duty.
Dozens of Democratic legislators joined Republicans on these bills,
including the current chairman of the Senate Banking, Housing, and
Urban Affairs Committee, Christopher Dodd. Litigation is the last
resort when public regulation fails and the last deterrent in an era of
weak government supervision. These moves were also the result of
extensive lobbying by industry promoters looking to evade liability for
dishonest claims made to investors.

Fittingly, one of the leading architects of the fraud-inviting 1995 law,
former California Congressman Christopher Cox, was named chairman
of the Securities and Exchange Commission by President George W.

Bush. In the 1990s, the SEC was chaired by the relatively public-minded Arthur Levitt. But whenever Chairman Levitt tried to enact tough new regulations to deal with newly invented abuses, he was reined in by a bipartisan consensus in Congress that threatened his appropriations. Many of Levitt's aborted proposals would have made it much more difficult for the Enrons and WorldComs to reach the extremes that they did.

The consequence was that markets were gulled by engineered euphoria and investors were induced to overprice financial assets by trillions of dollars. When reality finally intruded, a crash was inevitable. Conservative economists and their corporate allies obsessively calculate the supposed costs of inefficient regulation to air travelers, utility ratepayers, consumers of trucking services, and so on. But how much regulatory inefficiency would it take to burn $7 trillion, the amount of investment capital misallocated by the stock bubble and ensuing crash? The financial economists who promoted deregulation are oddly uninterested in that question.

A relatively small number of the most spectacular cases, such as Enron, WorldCom, and Global Crossing, got most of the headlines. While a few corporate CEOs actually went to prison, their partners on Wall Street got off very lightly. Blue-chip commercial and investment banks were enablers of these abuses (they still are, even more so with the repeal of Glass-Steagall). Hungry for fees and for underwriting business, they kept lending to fraudulent companies such as Enron and its executives long after they knew that the balance sheets were fishy. They tossed good money after bad in the hope that investors would be reassured and greater fools would somehow keep the game going. A list of the banks and investment banks that paid fines to settle Spitzer's litigation includes ten of the ten largest, including Goldman Sachs, Morgan Stanley, Citigroup, Merrill Lynch, and JPMorgan Chase.

Despite the handful of spectacular cases, no major player on Wall Street admitted criminal wrongdoing, much less went to jail. The bar had been so lowered, and the concern about spooking financial markets in the aftermath of a crash so raised, that criminal charges, let alone convictions of blue-chip banks or their executives, were considered out of the question. Eliot Spitzer got a very respectful press for having the courage to use even the possibility of criminal charges in bargaining for a settlement.

The Spitzer settlement required the financial houses to undertake three modest reforms. Management was required to compensate stock analysts without considering what they had contributed to the firm's investment banking business. The firms paid a total of $450 million to fund new, ostensibly independent research services for investors, for a period of five years. Finally, the firms committed to cease giving early access to hot new stock offerings as disguised bribes to favored clients. But the practice continued, only with greater discretion. Stock analysts who were actually investment bankers simply changed their titles, and the game continued. Nomi Prins, a former managing director of Goldman Sachs, observed, "Despite the settlement requirement, little has changed in the way of fee-linked bonuses." In her 2004 book, *Other People's Money*, she quotes a senior executive at one of the firms that signed the settlement as saying, "It's not like junior analysts in training are being told they'll get penalized for bringing in deals."

Two of the most notorious analysts-cum-stock-touts, Henry Blodget of Merrill Lynch and Jack Grubman, got off with individual fines equal to a small fraction of their gains. Blodget, whose cumulative earnings totaled at least $40 million, was made to pay $4 million. Grubman, whose severance payment alone from Salomon Smith Barney was $32 million and whose annual salary and bonus were in the $20 million range, paid $15 million to settle all charges. Neither man admitted criminal wrongdoing.

Their bosses, who were in charge of the larger game, paid nothing. The price tag for Spitzer's "global settlement" was $1.388 billion. That seems a huge sum of money. But to the banks and investment houses that signed the settlement, it was chump change—a minuscule fraction of what they had made via the wrongful activity. Nomi Prins calculates that the investment banking earnings alone of the ten top banks from 1998 to 2002 totaled $62 billion and that their total earnings during this period came to more than $1 trillion. As Prins further notes, the collective fines in the Spitzer settlement were modest compared to the fines paid by offending firms in the mid-1990s, before the extent of the systemic damage was fully known. Prudential Securities alone paid $1.5 billion in fines for its part in securities scams. Merrill Lynch paid $470 million. Salomon Brothers, then a principal dealer in government securities, paid $250 million for defrauding, of all customers, the U.S. Treasury.

The government's settlement of the $11 billion WorldCom accounting fraud, which cost investors upward of $180 billion in evaporated market value, was a travesty. No criminal charges were lodged. The company was permitted to stay in business, change its name back to MCI, the untainted name of one of the companies it had acquired, and roll merrily along. By going into bankruptcy, WorldCom got rid of $41 billion in debt. The only regulatory penalty was a fine of $500 million levied by the SEC, which the judge in the bankruptcy reorganization, Jed S. Rakoff, indignantly raised to $750 million. The message: Hire more clever lawyers and let the game continue. At this writing, the company has a sole-source U.S. government contract to rebuild Iraq's mobile phone system.

Interestingly, a much larger sum was paid by WorldCom's investment bankers, thanks to a class action lawsuit filed by then New York state controller Alan Hevesi on behalf of pension funds. Hevesi's suit charged that underwriters of the deals had been party to the cooked books and had fraudulently promoted WorldCom stock in violation of the securities laws. More than a dozen banks ended up paying a record settlement of $6 billion to state pension funds in 2005. It's a good illustration of why litigation is a necessary fallback against the weaknesses of a feeble SEC and why corporations want so eagerly to restrict private legal remedies with what they call "tort reform."

A hilariously revealing counterpoint to the blue-chip stock-hyping scandals involved a fourteen-year-old named Jonathan Lebed, the youngest person ever to be prosecuted for running what in the 1920s was called a stock pool. From his bedroom in suburban New Jersey, Jonathan had done essentially what major investment banking houses, their stock touts, and retail sales forces do routinely, only he did it rather more crudely. Jonathan bought small stakes in selected stocks, having cashed in some savings bonds. Then he peppered financial sites on the Internet with favorable comments, posing as an insider. He'd learned the game from watching the pros do it on CNBC and CNNfn. The stocks he picked were small, thinly capitalized companies, so just a few buy orders could spike their prices. Gullible investors who read Lebed's postings bid up the prices of stocks in eleven companies that he favored. Jonathan then cashed in. Starting with a stake of just a few thousand dollars, in six months his trading profits totaled not quite $800,000. This was stock manipulation, pure and simple.

When word of these exploits reached the authorities, a very embarrassed SEC shut Jonathan down. A deal negotiated with the family's lawyer in late 2000 required Jonathan to give up $285,000 of his improper gains, leaving the young stock manipulator with more than half a million dollars. The story was all over the financial press and networks that winter. In a retrospective article on the Lebed affair, the business writer and former bond trader Michael Lewis, author of *Liar's*

Poker, chased down senior SEC officials and discovered why the commission had gone so easy on Lebed: to throw the book at him, the SEC would have had to throw the book at all of Wall Street. "That's the trouble with fourteen-year-old boys—from the point of view of the social order," Lewis wrote. "They haven't learned the more sophisticated forms of dishonesty."

The Compulsion to Repeat 1929

Despite the self-serving propaganda of the free marketeers, nothing about the market system has changed in eight decades to make capitalism more self-regulating. On the contrary, three important things have changed for the worse: Technology and globalization have created even more opportunities for speculative abuse and a greater capacity for financial operators to outrun nation-bound regulators. Politics has dramatically shifted away from forces that favor regulated capitalism and social balance. And the Federal Reserve has gotten better at bailouts—so far—which only makes the Fed more complicit in risky behavior.

This expanded rescue role for the Fed is highly ironic, for the central bank is part of the government—in an era when markets supposedly don't need governments. Free-market fundamentalists rarely comment on the Fed's enlarged role but are quietly grateful that it's there. Since the early 1980s, the Federal Reserve and the U.S. Treasury have countermanded damaging market verdicts with one bailout after another. If they hadn't done so, the epidemic of speculation would have crashed the economy.

The Fed's much-expanded systemic responsibility creates what economists call "moral hazard." Players take ever more risks. Only the most grotesque abusers are ever punished. The "too big to fail" doctrine once applied only to large, federally insured and supervised banks. It has been tacitly extended to institutions not covered by federal supervision, such as large hedge funds, whose license to speculate is based on the premise that the only money at risk is that of their investors. As various international bailouts beginning in the early 1980s demonstrate, too-big-to-fail has been extended to entire countries.

A comparison with the Depression era suggests uncanny parallels in financial abuses—and a total divergence when it comes to remedies. After the 1929 crash, a less empowered and less sophisticated Federal Reserve System failed to prevent a monetary implosion from turning into a Great Depression, and in the 1930s Congress remade the financial system. After the collapse of 2000–01, however, the Fed adroitly contained the damage (for now). No depression resulted, and no impeachment of the broader system. Congress saw no reason to reregulate except in the most modest way, and Wall Street continued to reign.

In the 1990s, as in the 1920s, speculative schemes, largely unregulated and increasingly reliant on dishonest books and borrowed money, drove up the price of stocks even as the insiders who organized the schemes pulled out their own money and gulled small investors. The nearly exact parallels have received far too little attention.

In the 1920s, one favorite device was "stock pools." Their organizers, often floor traders at either brokerage houses or allied investment bankers, bought securities at cheap prices and then devised calculated campaigns to drive up the prices of stocks, luring outsiders to buy into a sure thing. The insiders then cashed out, leaving the suckers holding the bag. These were not just penny stocks in obscure companies but corporations such as RCA and Anaconda Copper. The organizers of the pools were not shabby operators of "boiler rooms" but blue-chip outfits such as the House of Morgan and National City Bank of New York. Often, bank executives used money borrowed from the bank to buy shares on credit before dumping them. The architects of the New Deal thought they were outlawing stock pools, but precisely the same brand of insider larceny occurred in the 1990s. This time the corporations had names like Enron and Global Crossing. The banks had many of the same names, including Morgan and Citibank. This time, it was stock "analysts" who colluded with their investment banker colleagues to run up stock prices with borrowed money and promote them to pension funds and small investors, even as the promoters knew that the shares were junk. Executives who gave lucrative business to the investment banks were added to the pool of insiders who were rewarded with new stock issues at below-market prices. And since the 2000 crash, it has been hedge funds manipulating the markets. The game is the same.

In the 1920s, another much-abused insider device was the holding company. The Morgan interests, and others, had organized holding companies for railroads and other industries, allowing them to control vast industrial empires with a relatively small amount of their own equity. Most of the money was borrowed—from depositors in Morgan banks—or absorbed from shareholders who had no meaningful control over the enterprise. Perhaps the single most notorious speculative abuse of the 1920s was the use of public utility holding companies to loot the assets of operating utility companies, their ratepayers, and shareholders.

The Insull family, the most brazen of the holding company operators, ran pyramids with as many as seven layers. At each layer, the Insulls acquired voting control of the subsidiaries for a tiny amount of cash; the rest of the deal was backed by an exchange of watered-down securities. At their peak, the Insull companies had assets of over $2.5 billion, but their actual equity was around $100 million—leverage of twenty-five to one.

These pyramids were deliberately impenetrable to state public utility commissions responsible for regulating rates. Ferdinand Pecora, chief counsel to the Senate Banking Committee, investigating the causes of the crash, later wrote, "It is said that only twelve men were qualified to understand the Einstein theory of relativity; but the Insull structure was so complex that no one could fully grasp it, not even, probably, Mr. Insull himself." The pattern of utility holding companies made no technical sense in terms of actual power grids or service delivery networks. Their purpose was purely financial—to allow the Insulls to water down stock, divert operating income "upstream" to the parent companies, deceive regulators, and have ratepayers make up the difference. Subsequent investigations revealed that sales of services by operating companies declined by only 16 percent after the stock market crash, but the unwinding of all that leverage once the share prices started falling left the companies financially worthless. When the pyramids collapsed in the general crash, investors lost hundreds of millions of dollars, and ratepayers' money that should have been invested in maintenance and upgrading of facilities was either diverted to the Insull fortune or lost in the crash—and had to be paid all over again.

Note the exact parallels to Enron: the regulatory indulgence, the financial manipulation, the multiple conflicts of interest by insiders; the absurd and opaque level of pyramiding and borrowed money; the enabler role of investment bankers; and the cost to employees, ratepayers, and the public. Here again, the New Dealers thought they were making the holding company abuses of the 1920s impossible. But in the 1980s and 1990s, deregulation of public utilities allowed not just the return of holding companies that acquired and then pillaged underlying utility companies that actually delivered the services. Deregulation invited outright frauds like Enron. Where the Insull empire had used opaque holding companies, Enron used off-the-books "special entities" whose sole purpose was to camouflage the degree of borrowing that had been used to pump up the stock.

A third core abuse involved the three-way conflict of interest on the part of investment bankers, who could simultaneously underwrite securities, make commercial loans to themselves and other insiders, and peddle the securities to the public. Morgan and other giant banks put up money for dubious securities issues, everything from the aforementioned holding companies to loans to sovereign countries. Their offering literature made gross misrepresentations of the securities' safety as investments. They then used their retail network to palm them off on an unsuspecting public. Banking executives secretly dealt in their company's stocks, trading on insider information, often to the detriment of shareholders. In 1929, one of the most notorious pool operators, Albert Wiggin, the president of Chase National Bank, sold short his own company's shares, pocketing $4 million. Charles E. Mitchell, chairman of the archrival National City Bank, just before the crash was trying to orchestrate a merger with the Corn Exchange Bank. Since the deal was collateralized with stock in City Bank, he needed to maintain a share price of at least $450 if the deal was to close. Mitchell got a $12 million personal loan from well-interlocked allies at Morgan to buy shares and pump up the stock.

When unearthed a few years later by congressional investigations, this sort of insider scheme was widely deplored as scandalous behavior, to be prohibited by the new SEC's proscription on insider trading. But the exact same behavior would be repeated, on a much larger scale, in the 1990s. Bankers of virtually every elite house, including Citicorp, Morgan, Chase, and Goldman Sachs, lent small fortunes to the executives of their best corporate customers. The loans were collateralized by the same company stock. Their proceeds were used to buy more of the stock, in the hope of bidding up the price. An alert eighth-grader, not to mention a regulator, might have noticed that this was all a speculative bubble—the collateral, the shares, and the loans would be worthless when the game unwound. Insiders at investment banking houses similarly bought newly issued stock for their own accounts, and doled them out to favored corporate clients at low prices not available to the general investing public, often financing the purchase with loans.

This story of bidding up stocks on credit may remind the reader of a quaint word from a bygone era: margin. One of the best-documented causes of the crash of 1929 was the buying of securities with borrowed money, conveniently lent by the same broker who was promoting the sale of the stock. The investor could put up as little as ten cents on the dollar. As Fred Schwed described the practice in his droll 1940 retrospective on the crash, *Where Are the Customers' Yachts?*, "We assume that it is a wise and profitable venture to buy 100 shares of United Fido at ten, paying $1,000 for it. Ergo, wouldn't it be even better to buy 200 shares paying the same $1,000? And even better to make it three or four hundred if we can find a sufficiently kindly broker to do us the favor?"

The crash proved otherwise. The miracle of margin worked only on the way up. On the way down, the value of the collateral quickly sank below the value of the loan, the broker demanded his money back—via the dreaded "margin calls"—and the overleveraged investor was wiped out. These wipeouts compounded the market's volatility by creating downdrafts in which there were no buyers, only sellers. Once again, Congress thought it had solved the problem of margin abuse by empowering the Federal Reserve Board of Governors to regulate margin requirements—in a rule named Regulation T. Writing from the vantage point of 1940, Schwed confidently declared, "Margin requirements are now fixed." He added in a slightly scandalized tone, "but formerly many customers used to shop around in different houses to see where they could buy the most stock for the least pledge of money."

But once the speculative impulse revived (as it always does in rising markets) it turned out that Congress had managed to regulate margin only for unsophisticated small fry. In recent years, high rollers have gotten around Regulation T by using derivatives such as options and other instruments of futures markets, where the ability to speculate with borrowed money is limited only by the investor's taste for risk. Hedge funds have astronomical leverage ratios. As in the 1920s, the risks to the system remain. And in the many scandals in which banks had both personal and commercial relationships with corporate customers, they lent money to executives knowing it would be used to purchase stocks, without even bothering with the subterfuge of derivatives. Despite the obvious violation of Regulation T, the regulators did nothing.

Even a cursory review of this financial history makes clear that these insider abuses are hardy perennials. The new contrivances are variations on the same basic story. They can be prevented only by alert regulation that keeps adapting itself to new inventions aimed at circumventing conflicts of interest. But regulation is only as good as the politics that undergirds it. Having served as chief investigator of the Senate Banking Committee in the 1970s, when the impulse to speculate and deregulate was just gaining fresh momentum, I didn't find it shocking that insiders were seeking the restoration of privileges that had been damped down by the New Deal. More appalling was the collusion of their expert accomplices. Financial economists, who insisted that something about the new economy made it self-regulating after all, seemed to know little or nothing of this institutional history of how markets have been corrupted by insiders in practice. Their equations simply "proved" that markets worked in theory.

Resisting Regulation: A Forgotten Story

When the stock market crashed in October 1929, the initial impact was on Wall Street financial houses and large investors. Just over 1 percent of Americans—about 1.5 million investors out of a population of 120 million—owned shares. Despite the imagery of "New Era" economics that capitalism was being democratized and stories of shoeshine boys passing along stock tips, shareholding, as measured by the value of investments (as opposed to the number of small shareholders), was even more highly concentrated. Unlike in the 1990s, there were relatively few pension funds, and no IRAs, Keoghs, or 401(k) plans, to spread holdings (and losses) to small players. But because banks were on the hook for a badly overleveraged market, the crash soon turned into a financial panic. Then, as loans were called, banks declared insolvent, viable businesses shut down, and workers laid off, it cascaded into a general depression.

The largely privatized Federal Reserve of the early 1930s had neither the wit nor the authority to flood the system with liquidity, as Paul Volcker would do in the crisis of 1987 and Alan Greenspan would repeat for three years after the crash of 2000–01. John Maynard Keynes had not yet written his masterwork on shortfalls of aggregate demand, and President Herbert Hoover's notions of public spending were far too feeble to jump-start the stalled economy.

After Roosevelt's election in November 1932, a newly Democratic Congress belatedly got serious about sorting out the origins of the crash and reforming the financial system. We have grown up learning that the New Deal was a revolutionary transformation that saved capitalism from its own worst excesses. This is substantially true, yet even in the depths of depression a justifiably discredited business elite retained the political power to neutralize much of the regulatory structure that the Roosevelt administration proposed and to preserve special privileges for insiders. Whole libraries of books have been written on what Roosevelt wrought. In many respects, the more instructive story is what the New Deal was politically unable to achieve.

The New Deal attempted to restart the faltering economy in multiple ways: by putting money back in workers' pockets, by underwriting public works, by restoring confidence in the badly damaged banking system, and by making sure that the speculative excesses typical of the 1920s would never again bring the system down. It is sobering to compare what the Roosevelt administration originally sought with what it was able to get through Congress after Wall Street lobbyists got finished. The Securities Act of 1933, according to Professor Joel Seligman's definitive history of the SEC and corporate finance, "was more remarkable, considering the sentiments of the day, for the powers it did not grant than for the limited powers it did."

The 1933 act required that issues of securities be registered with the Federal Trade Commission; that certain financial disclosures be made; and that a corporation's officers, directors, accountants, and investment bankers could be held liable for material untruths or omissions. This last provision was the law's only real teeth, and Wall Street successfully fought to water down its application. A disappointed William O. Douglas, then a young law professor, later chairman of the SEC, and ultimately a Supreme Court justice, wrote, "[T]here is nothing in the Act which controls the power of the self-perpetuating management group. . . . There is nothing in the Act which purports to deal with the protection of the rights of minorities [meaning minority shareholders]. There is nothing in the Act which concerns the problem of capital structure, its soundness or unsoundness."

Even before Roosevelt signed the 1933 act, Wall Street went on a massive lobbying blitz to weaken the liability section and head off other regulation. The business lobbies contended that the bad publicity and clamor for heightened regulation were depressing the ability of money markets to raise capital and prolonging the Depression. This was a preposterous assertion; the Depression itself had massively undercut the demand for new enterprises. If investors were staying away from Wall Street, it was for lack of funds. Nonetheless, the financial lobby won over several in the administration who were eager to restore "business confidence," including top officials of the Treasury and Commerce Departments, who urged FDR to weaken the act. Roosevelt's intimate Felix Frankfurter, in contrast, wrote that the financial lobby was engaged in a "bankers' strike," and warned the president that Wall Street was out to "chloroform" the act.

Roosevelt initially sided with the reformers. New legislation was introduced in 1934, to complete the work of the 1933 act. The original draft, written in large part by James Landis and Benjamin Cohen and supported by Roosevelt and New Dealers in Congress, reads almost as if its sponsors had a crystal ball and foresaw the multiple abuses of the 1990s. Among other protections, the bill proposed prohibition or very strict regulation of self-dealing, insider trading, stock pool operations, margin loans, and short selling. It required all stock exchanges to register with the FTC, which was to be given very wide authority to set standards and to regulate over-the-counter markets as well. The bill proposed to separate brokers from dealers, so that the same firms making markets in securities would not be selling them to the public. Floor traders were to be abolished and "specialists" drastically constrained, so that brokers could not make money at customers' expense by trading for their own accounts. As Seligman observed, "If enacted, it would have ended all private transactions on the Exchange floor, transforming the Exchange into a clerical agency for execution of off-floor orders." The legislation also encouraged the FTC to drastically democratize corporation governance by requiring the election of corporate boards and officers under new proxy rules.

At the time, there was not exactly overwhelming public sympathy for Wall Street. Unemployment was running at 25 percent. In July 1934, while the New York Stock Exchange was indignantly pressing to retain its prerogative of self-regulation, a 1920s-style pool operation was found to have manipulated the share price of the American Commercial Alcohol Company. Ferdinand Pecora requested the New York Stock Exchange to investigate, but the Exchange uncovered no wrongdoing. Pecora quickly discovered that during a period when American Commercial's share price had abruptly tripled, some 75 percent of the trades had been executed by the pool operators. Even after all that had been learned, Wall Street seemed incapable of policing itself. Indeed, the insider abuses of the 1920s suggested that a passive "clerical agency" taking reasonable fees to connect investors with productive users of capital, uncompromised by middleman conflicts of interest, was just what the economy needed.

Yet by playing on fears of a prolonged financial depression and using small regional stock exchanges to cultivate sympathy with congressmen unsympathetic to Wall Street, the financial industry succeeded in weakening every key provision of the bill. By the time the eventual Securities Exchange Act of 1934 was adopted, it left the broker-dealer and floor specialist system unchanged, dropped the provisions on insider trading, gave margin regulation to the Federal Reserve, and empowered stock exchanges to pursue self-regulation under loose supervision by federal regulators. For good measure, Congress removed the Roosevelt-oriented FTC from the business of securities regulation and created a new agency called the Securities and Exchange Commission, which was expected to be friendlier to Wall Street.

Conservatives in Congress and their financial allies were not disappointed. Roosevelt knew when he was licked and extended a remarkably generous olive branch to the financiers. To chair the new commission, he appointed a Wall Street man to whom he owed a political favor. Joseph P. Kennedy, the father of the future president, was the rare Wall Streeter who had supported Roosevelt in 1932. Kennedy had himself been a notorious stock pool operator and was friendly to the idea of self-regulation. Later, in 1938, even after the chairman of the New York Stock Exchange, Richard Whitney, had been led away in handcuffs for looting several funds, the Roosevelt administration, on the defensive because of a deep recession and a stock market nosedive, approved legislation explicitly making stock exchanges responsible for policing most regulation of listed companies, with the SEC acting only at one remove.

A second strand of New Deal financial regulation dealt with banks. One systemic problem was that commercial banks, despite the Federal Reserve, were subject to "runs" during severe financial panics. This could, and did, cascade into an epidemic of bank failures, producing massive losses to individuals and businesses and a general economic contraction. To prevent a repetition, Congress approved federal deposit insurance and increased the supervisory powers of the Federal Reserve and other federal bank regulatory agencies.

A separate banking problem was the inherent conflict of interest that occurs when a bank both underwrites securities as an investment bank and takes in deposits and makes loans as a commercial bank. The landmark 1933 Glass-Steagall Act created deposit insurance and prohibited the same institution from engaging in commercial banking and investment banking so that there would be no speculation with insured money. In both the 1920s and the 1990s, commercial banks relaxed their supervisory and fiduciary role by conflating three functions: lending money; reaping fee income from underwriting stocks and bonds; and making more money from marketing securities to the public. The triple role was rife with conflicts of interest. The more money that insiders could make from fees, underwriting, and selling securities, the less eager the banks were to be vigilant about the true quality of assets. The temptation was to unload the junk on the public and keep the choicest bits. A rising market led them to further relax their stewardship; mistakes would wash out in rising share prices. Risks could always be packaged as securities and sold off to unwary investors. Although some revisionist historians have contended that the Glass-Steagall Act was a misplaced act of retribution against the House of Morgan, there is no doubt that the conflicts of interest that pumped up share prices were one major cause of the crash of 1929. As Glass-Steagall was gradually gutted and then officially buried, its demise served to enable exactly parallel behavior in the 1990s and beyond.

An even more contentious issue was control of the money supply itself. As all students of economics know, banks "create" money when they make loans. Modern central banks govern that process by controlling loan-to-deposit ratios and raising or lowering short-term interest rates, mainly by buying or selling government bonds in the open market. In 1935, over substantial opposition from bankers and their conservative allies in Congress, the Roosevelt administration only partly succeeded in remaking the hybrid Federal Reserve System into a true central bank.

The Fed was less than three decades old. It had been conceived to create an elastic monetary system and prevent the periodic credit crunches characteristic of the nineteenth century. In the 1913 legislation creating the Reserve, the banking industry had appropriated a populist idea and placed it in safe hands. Most of the power was deliberately vested in the regional Federal Reserve Banks, which were dominated by their private industry board members and reflected their interests. In the crash of 1929, it was the powerful New York Federal Reserve Bank that played the role (dismally) of crisis manager, while the publicly appointed board of governors in Washington had little power. Marriner Eccles, the rare populist banker whom Roosevelt later appointed to chair the board, proposed legislation to at last shift the real power to control the money supply to the presidentially appointed Board. The 1933 banking legislation had already given the Board the authority to regulate the ratio of bank reserves to deposits.

What remained was the single most important lever—open-market operations, namely the buying and selling of Treasury securities to affect the money supply and interest rates. That authority was vested by the original legislation creating the Fed in a committee of private bankers from the boards of the regional Reserve Banks. Eccles felt passionately that the existing Federal Open Market Committee had been singularly unhelpful in supporting the administration's policy of low interest rates, and that the money supply was public business that should be regulated by a government body. The banking lobby fiercely opposed Eccles's plan to give open market authority to the publicly appointed Board of Governors. The bankers were backed by Senator Carter Glass, the principal author of the 1913 act and, at seventy-seven, still the doyen of banking legislation. The stated concern was that "political" (which is to say democratically accountable) control of monetary policy would court inflation. Private creditors were defenders of "sound money," even in the teeth of a Great Depression whose main problem was deflation. FDR's treasury secretary, Henry Morgenthau, was also ambivalent.

In the end, even at the height of the New Deal and the depths of depression, the best the Roosevelt administration could manage was a compromise, changing the membership of the Open Market Committee to a blend of public and private appointees. It remains the case that the trial by fire of every new Fed chairman is to gain effective control of the Open Market Committee. On more than one occasion, even chairmen as powerful as Volcker and Greenspan have had to get contingent authority to vary rates as necessary and even threaten to resign, and on occasion they still have been outvoted. Such is the residual power of the banking industry.

A fourth set of New Deal laws and regulations was intended to prohibit other kinds of speculation and conflicts of interest on the part of insiders. The most egregious abuse was the aforementioned public utility holding company. Various congressional and regulatory agency committees had been investigating utility holding companies since 1928. A leading expert, Judge Robert E. Healy, wrote that the holding company system was "a parasite and excrescence on the actual operating companies." The Insulls were ultimately acquitted of federal and state charges of mail fraud and embezzlement. Existing law was simply too weak to prohibit their scheme. The larger problem was systemic.

Legislation introduced by the Roosevelt administration in 1935 authorized the Federal Trade Commission to break up holding companies and reorganize the operating companies on the basis of regional and technical efficiencies, with the federal government sharing rate regulation with state public utility commissions. Once again, the New Deal had to settle for half a loaf. Despite the overwhelming majority of Democrats and progressive Republicans in Congress, broad popular indignation, and the widely publicized disgrace of the Insulls and the other holding companies, industry lobbyists descended on Washington. Prefiguring the blitz tactics of the drug and insurance and banking industries decades later, the holding companies literally had more lobbyists on the case than there were members of Congress. The entire corporate establishment opposed the administration's bill. A leading industry opponent was Wendell L. Willkie of Indiana, then representing the Commonwealth & Southern and later the Republican presidential nominee in 1940, hailed as a moderate internationalist (and ridiculed as "the barefoot boy from Wall Street"). Industry advocates, who had made dire prophecies of a bankrupt utility system, succeeded in watering down the bill in the Senate and in conference committee. Rather than abolishing holding companies outright, the Public Utility Holding Company Act of 1935 bucked the question to the regulatory commissions and the courts, where the utilities and their allies knew they could fight another day.

Not until the national emergency of World War II produced unusual government leverage was the SEC able to compel most public utility holding companies to either sell off most of their assets or reorganize their empires into geographically contiguous service units that made engineering sense. This process was completed only in the early 1950s. Studies showed that the government's ultimately successful efforts to improve utilities' operating efficiencies through simplification of their tortuous capital structure and regional integration of their networks saved consumers billions of dollars. Shareholders, meanwhile, got a safe rate of return slightly above the stock market average. By finally getting rid of holding companies, federal regulators enabled state public utility commissions to do their jobs. Money paid by consumers, based on utilities' costs of operations, improvements, and a reasonable profit, could not be diverted to speculative ventures.

But this regulatory regime lasted barely three decades. Beginning in the 1980s, electricity was gradually deregulated, culminating in the repeal of the holding company act itself in 2005. Instead of retaining integrated and regulated utilities, the industry was broken up into producers of power, traders of power, and local retail suppliers. Deregulation ushered in a new era of consolidation, speculation, corruption, and wild spikes in consumer prices. According to an authoritative review by the Tellus Institute, in the period from December 2005 through October 2006, average electricity rates in the states that had deregulated were 55 percent higher than in the states that had retained regulation and that gap has widened over time. In some states, such as Montana, cheap hydropower plants were sold off to multinational corporations, which promptly jacked up rates. Despite visions of more competition and cheaper, more reliable power, deregulation raised consumer prices and was mainly a boon to traders and investors. When a cascading blackout hit the Northeast and Midwest in 2003, investigators found that the breakup and deregulation of the industry had left nobody with clear responsibility for investing the money to maintain the grid. (In the days of regulation, this prudent expense could be charged to the rate base.) Deregulation had emphasized the superior efficiencies of trading markets. Few people remembered the importance of network engineering efficiencies or the value of cheap, reliable power. Even fewer seemed to have any appreciation of why Congress and the SEC had had to shut down holding companies in the first place.

There was, of course, a great deal more to the New Deal, but these were the key elements of its partial reform of financial markets. These moderate reforms, which produced a stable and equitable form of managed capitalism, required an alignment unique in the history of American politics: the worst depression in the nation's history, an overwhelming Democratic majority in both houses of Congress, a popular and populist chief executive, and the utter political disgrace of the banking and business elite.

Even so, the Roosevelt administration often had to settle for far less than it wanted and frequently accepted the delegation of crucial authority to private-industry bodies. The SEC was compelled to delegate much of its regulatory authority to stock exchanges, and industry-dominated bodies such as the American Institute of Certified Public Accountants, the National Association of Securities Dealers, and the Financial Accounting Standards Board. All this suggests how overwhelming is the power of organized business in a political democracy that is also a capitalist economy and how hard it is for reform and genuine public-private balance to endure. For the past three decades, even the partial counterweights to organized financial interests have been steadily weakened.

Liberating Speculative Finance

The reforms that were blocked in the New Deal era and afterward literally anticipated every form of corruption and inefficiency that began recurring in the 1980s. For example, there were periodic attempts to reform corporate governance by requiring large corporations to obtain federal charters rather than letting them shop for the state (usually Delaware, New Jersey, or Nevada) that would give the management the greatest insulation from accountability to shareholders and creditors. This sensible reform was originally proposed early in the nineteenth century by President James Madison and later embraced by the populists of the 1890s. It was again raised by Pecora and Roosevelt himself in the 1930s, and once again in the 1960s by President Kennedy's first SEC chairman, William Cary. Each time, it was buried by industry lobbying.

Every proposed expansion of direct SEC authority, and every proposed restraint on insider trading, was defeated with the usual fearmongering that it would be bad for business. The Cary SEC documented continuing abuses by floor traders and specialists trading for their own accounts, but its efforts at serious reform were beaten back. A similar investigation after the 2000–01 meltdown also came to nothing. The basic privileges of the larger financial system and its insiders remained politically untouchable.

Democrats might expand Social Security, raise the minimum wage, and launch a "War on Poverty," but even during the Great Society era, with its Roosevelt-scale majority in Congress, the power of Wall Street was too great to allow serious reforming of the very heart of financial capitalism. The Democrats' failure to constrain the power of Wall Street insiders not only rendered the economy less equitable and efficient; it also set in motion a wider reversal that would soon undercut the other instruments of broadly shared prosperity.

The Roosevelt reforms, however partial, did constrain the grosser forms of insider opportunism for about three decades. They created a platform for unprecedented economic growth on egalitarian terms. The United States of that era was operated as an economy in which real enterprises and their employees were not just tails on the kites of financial speculators.

This all worked because the speculative impulse and the related self-dealing were substantially contained. During the three decades from 1951 through 1980, commercial banks charged off bad loans totaling $28 billion. In 1985–87 alone, they charged off $45 billion. In the years before 1980, savings and loans almost never went broke, and both the Federal Deposit Insurance Corporation (FDIC) and its counterpart for savings institutions, the Federal Savings and Loan Insurance Corporation (FSLIC), returned an annual surplus to the Treasury. In the years after 1980, the S&L bust cost taxpayers over $200 billion.

Did this more prudent financial regime starve industry for capital? An economy that grows at 3.8 percent annually for three decades is not hurting for capital. Personal savings rates were far higher than today, and the economy did not have to borrow from abroad. Between the 1940s and the 1960s, neither political party was inclined to tamper with the basic financial regulatory structure bequeathed by the New Deal. Indeed, as late as the early 1970s new forms of regulation to protect consumers kept being added, including laws such as the Truth in Lending Act of 1968, which required banks and thrifts to quote interest charges in a clear and consistent annual percentage rate, and the Fair Credit Reporting Act of 1970, which legislated standards for the private credit bureau industry and allowed consumers to correct errors in their credit reports, as well as the Community Reinvestment Act of 1977. But while liberal legislators were adding some nice extras, the entire edifice of managed capitalism was about to be sundered.

The oil shock of 1973 and higher inflation created an opening for financial deregulation in several ways. The fixed exchange rates that had anchored the global trading system failed to hold. With U.S. inflation rising and foreigners clamoring to exchange dollars for gold, President Richard Nixon abruptly delinked the dollar from gold and shifted to a regime of floating exchange rates. Floating rates, whose values were set daily by trading markets, quickly offered a whole new set of opportunities to speculate in currencies, often destabilizing entire economies. Inflation also played havoc with the regulation of the interest that federally insured banks and thrift institutions could pay on savings and checking accounts. The regulatory premise was that if banks got into the game of bidding for deposits, as they had done in the 1920s, they would then need to earn higher rates of return and might take unacceptable risks with depositors' money (which in fact they did, both then and now).

As long as the rate of inflation was low and stable, the New Deal set of financial rules could work. Banks were more like public utilities, taking in deposits, making commercial and family loans, playing their designated role as servants of the real economy. Rising inflation, however, meant that depositors were losing money on savings accounts that paid fixed interest rates. When Merrill Lynch in 1972 persuaded the SEC to allow it to offer small investors shares in a "money market mutual fund," which behaved very much like a bank account but offered higher yields, and state regulators permitted banks under their jurisdiction to pay interest on checking accounts, so-called Negotiable Order of Withdrawal (NOW) accounts, federally regulated and insured banks found themselves squeezed on both sides of their balance sheets. Depositors were abandoning banks for institutions that offered higher returns. Merrill Lynch was quickly followed by Fidelity Investments. Money market mutual funds went from holding just $1.7 billion as late as 1974 to $233 billion by 1982. Congress was induced to repeal the whole set of New Deal regulations limiting the interest that banks and thrifts could pay depositors. This set in train a broad movement for further financial deregulation.

At the same time that banks faced new competition for depositors' money, the banks' best loan customers, blue-chip corporations, were bypassing the banks and borrowing money directly in financial markets by simply issuing IOUs, so-called commercial paper. The outstanding volume of commercial paper increased from just $4.5 billion in 1960 to $90 billion by 1979 and more than $200 billion by 1985. Nonbanks, such as credit card companies and the financing divisions of automakers, were also invading banks' traditionally lucrative consumer credit lines of business.

Meanwhile, with memories of 1929 fading, outsiders were crashing the clubby corporate world and devising new ways to make quick money by manipulating assets. Until the 1970s, mergers, acquisitions, or changes in ownership were consummated by mutual consent or because an investor simply purchased controlling interest in a corporation. An investment banker would not have dreamt of imposing a takeover on a target company whose board did not wish it to be bought. The canary in the coal mine was an upstart named Saul Steinberg. Not yet thirty years old, Steinberg, operating from a small computer leasing company called Leasco, decided that he wanted to run a diversified financial conglomerate. The word "conglomerate" had entered the financial vocabulary only in 1964. Big conglomerates, such as Textron, Gulf + Western, Ling-Temco-Vought, and Litton Industries, were the hot new thing. Rather than growing organically, they were the result of mergers.

A whole new financial literature promoted the benefits of "synergies." Accountants could creatively value the merged entity as greater than the sum of its parts, leading investors to bid up the stock. Investment bankers could make fortunes underwriting mergers; then, when the advertised benefits failed to materialize, they could make more money underwriting the breakup. As John Brooks, the author of one of the best histories of finance in the 1960s, wrote, "The conglomerate needed neither toil nor spin—only keep buying companies and writing up earnings. It was magic, until the pyramid became top-heavy, and fell."

Within three years, Steinberg managed to buy up several other leasing companies, increasing Leasco's worth from just $750,000 when it went public in 1965, to $74 million by 1968. But then he invented something wholly new: a minnow swallowing a whale, using the whale's own assets as collateral. Steinberg targeted a company with a net worth ten times that of Leasco, an old-line fire-and-casualty company called Reliance Insurance. He coveted Reliance in part because it had about $100 million in excess reserves. Steinberg began by quietly accumulating 3 percent of Reliance's outstanding stock. After pitching a merger to Reliance executives in May 1968 and predictably being turned down, he made a "tender offer" to Reliance shareholders. They could tender (swap) their Reliance stock for Leasco convertible debentures and warrants, for a substantially higher cash value. Steinberg was happy to pay a premium over what the market was valuing Reliance. His bet was that he could use that spare $100 million to make more earnings than the staid incumbent managers were achieving and to further expand his empire. By September, management capitulated, and Steinberg had control of Reliance.

Tender offers quickly proliferated. During the merger boom of the 1980s, some ten thousand deals took place, valued at more than a trillion dollars, culminating with the takeover of RJR Nabisco by Kohlberg Kravis Roberts, for a cool $30 billion. Some of these mergers were legitimate and made business sense, and only a minority were hostile takeovers financed with borrowed money. But a sizable number of the deals mainly enriched their promoters. The leveraged buyout (LBO) craze left corporations saddled with debt, and by the late 1980s, many of the progeny of the LBO boom had crashed and burned.

Though regulators could have prevented hostile takeovers if they had so chosen, Congress and the SEC opted for only the mildest requirements of disclosure and required opportunities for other suitors to put forth competing bids. This buyout trend was less a shift in regulations than a change in norms—a move away from the prudent if sometimes clubby habits of an earlier era.

The boom in private equity, in the current decade, relies on many of the same practices as the LBO fad of the late 1980s, notably the use of tax-deductible borrowed money to take over a target company using its own assets as collateral. But whereas the earlier LBO craze was self-limiting once several such acquisitions proved to be economic failures, with relatively little damage to the larger economy, the current role of private equity is much larger and likely to produce much more systemic damage during the next bout of higher interest rates or economic downturn. Private equity already has many of the characteristics of a bubble, and a collapse of the value of many of these over-leveraged companies is likely to occur before Congress gets around to reforms. If reforms such as repeal of the use of tax-deductible debt in leveraged buyouts had been enacted at the time of the LBO bust two decades ago, the economy would not be so vulnerable today.

A Fake Populism

The hostile-takeover movement ostensibly united three sets of interests: investors, investment bankers, and the ideological cheerleaders for laissez-faire. In the 1970s, investors were restless. The stock market was in the midst of a decadelong slump. As late as the mid-1970s, the Dow was no higher than it had been in the mid-1960s. To some extent, the culprit was inflation, which is always bad for stock prices. But with the economy faltering and major industries facing the first wave of import competition, corporate chief executives were said to be lazy and unimaginative, sheltered from competition by regulation and oligopoly and protected by chummy boards. The hostile-takeover movement was seen as a novel way to achieve an accountability to markets and to shareholders that the conventional assumption of corporate governance—shareholders electing boards, boards appointing executives—was plainly failing to achieve. If a new, more aggressive owner, however bizarre his means of acquiring control, could achieve higher returns for shareholders, he was doing the Lord's work.

Conservative economists blessed the first boom in mergers and hostile takeovers as "maximizing shareholder value," relying on the splendid efficiencies of a hitherto unknown market, "the market for corporate control." The question of which executives and entrepreneurs were given operating control of a corporation's assets should be considered unsentimentally as an issue to be resolved by a bidding market just like any other spot market. Incumbent managers had no special claim on keeping their jobs, nor should corporations or their workers presume any institutional loyalties.

In this story, indolent corporate executives were in league with overpaid, redundant workers. A virtuous corporate raider, playing the role of market discipline made flesh, could use borrowed money collateralized by the target corporation's own assets, or later by junk bonds, and set off a bidding war for control of the corporation. This pleased shareholders, at least in the short run, because it raised the trading price of the company's shares. Eventually, someone got operating control, reaping windfall profits on the transaction but leaving the corporation saddled with new debt. Even this inflated debt, however, was held to be salutary because the burden of paying it forced the new managers to realize ruthless cost savings—often hiving off divisions, laying off workers, and cutting wages.

A new current of academic literature cheered on this new brand of financial engineering, and despite periodic setbacks like the stock market crashes of 1987 and 2000, they continue the cheerleading. In the 1970s, it was hard to pick up a business or financial-economics journal without seeing an article extolling efficient markets, the maximization of shareholder value, and the market for corporate control. The "efficient market hypothesis" held that markets, by definition, optimized outcomes. So if a market invented something new that fetched buyers, by definition it was efficient. No distinction was made between arm's-length "markets" and insiders opportunistically taking advantage of unequal power and information. The fact that the market itself was the creature of laws defining property rights, differentiating legal activity from illegal fraud, was deemed not to be especially interesting. Given that markets were held to be efficient by definition, economists of this school disparaged all forms of regulation as equally suspect distortions of market forces.

Ordinary Americans, commentators in the financial press, and many moderate and liberal members of Congress were confused by the pretend populism. The advocates of Wild West fights for corporate control using borrowed money cast chief executives and pliant boards as villains and small shareholders and consumers as victims. There was more than a germ of truth to the tale of unaccountable executives. Any student of the corporation and financial markets was acquainted with the critique by A. A. Berle and Gardiner Means, whose 1932 book, *The Modern Corporation and Private Property*, famously lamented the separation of ownership from control. In the 1920s (and again in recent decades) executives and their cronies on corporate boards chronically failed to act in the interest of the owners—shareholders—much less other stakeholders such as employees. New Dealers, having read their Berle and Means, sought to make corporations more accountable via greater disclosure and by prohibition of corrupt insider behavior.

Shareholder democracy, however, never took hold. Proxy fights seldom materialized, in large part because the weak SEC regulation demanded by corporate elites prevented minority factions from effectively communicating with shareholders. Insider groups allied with management invariably prevailed. By the late twentieth century, a majority of shares were held by large institutions: pension funds, insurance companies, and mutual funds. Under the cozy Wall Street system, these institutions, with a tiny few exceptions, were traditionally passive owners. By convention, they cast their proxy votes with management; if they didn't like management's performance, they just sold the shares. This custom even had a revealing name. It was called the Wall Street Rule.

A corporation perennially at risk of being taken over was one way of keeping management on its toes, but it was hardly the only remedy, much less the best one. Mostly, the "market-for-corporate-control" story was self-serving. The exercise was mainly about quick enrichment of traders and takeover artists, and the cure was often worse than the disease. Synergies that supposedly made sense in the first wave of conglomerate mergers often turned out to be illusory a few short years later. Corporate executives sometimes used their privileged knowledge to take temporarily undervalued companies private. At other times, companies with spare cash engaged in buybacks, purchasing their own shares in order to boost the value of their stock, suggesting that they were not especially astute at making investments, nor solicitous of the interests of the broader shareholding public.

The investment banking fraternity found ways to make money from every one of these maneuvers, coming and going. Investment bankers could be found with elaborate hypothetical deal "books," promoting any conceivable merger or hostile takeover that might net fees. Well-run corporations, as well as lazy ones, were compelled to make economically destructive "poison pill" maneuvers to defend themselves against takeovers. Often it was workers who paid the price when takeover artists who "leveraged up" had to engage in excessive cost cutting that did not make the enterprise more efficient. After three decades of corporate raiding, many studies have concluded that a "market for corporate control" and the constant fear of a hostile takeover is in fact a highly inefficient form of corporate accountability. Often, the acquiring firm overpays for the target, and the newly merged entity, saddled with debt, operates far less efficiently than the two predecessor firms. The merger occurred not because "markets" demanded it but because middlemen saw money to be made and appealed to the vanity (and purses) of the executives of the acquiring company.

Morgan's Revenge

The emblematic case of bogus populism was the gradual evisceration of the Glass-Steagall Act. In the go-go years of the 1960s and 1970s, it was investment banks that thrived and commercial banks that suffered. The more new forms of mergers and acquisitions became prevalent, the better investment bankers did. Old-line houses such as Goldman Sachs once prided themselves on never competing with their customers. But by the 1980s, any sense of old-fashioned honor was long gone. Investment houses happily advanced the money to help corporate raiders take over targets. They also dominated new exotic plays such as junk (high-yield) bonds, and the conversion of once-staid assets such as mortgages into tradable securities, in addition to their traditionally lucrative business of underwriting new securities issues and promoting conventional mergers.

In the changed regulatory climate, commercial banks bitterly complained that the division of roles ordered by the Glass-Steagall Act left them with the crumbs. The lifting of the cap on interest rates for large certificates of deposit and the final elimination, in 1980, of Regulation Q, which had capped the interest rates that banks could pay small savers, finally allowed them to compete with money market mutual funds, which were acting more and more like banks. But then the banks had to earn the higher returns to pay the higher interest rates. They were increasingly forced into risky plays, such as petrodollar recycling and Third World loans, because deregulation was also letting new players compete with their loan operations, drying up their traditional safe lines of lending. It was a "fence with a one-way hole." Bank stocks, in the 1970s, badly lagged the stock market as a whole, and the stock market was generally flat. The investment bankers were making huge profits. Why not let more competition into their private preserve? Surely it would lower the excess profits and benefit the banking public.

This argument was yet another with a pseudopopulist flavor. I vividly remember, from my days at the Senate Banking Committee, how the then chairman, Senator William Proxmire, one of the most principled and progressive legislators ever to lead the committee, came to feel substantial sympathy for the commercial bankers' position. This was at the very dawn of the period of financial deregulation. My mentor, the committee's staff director, Ken McLean, who had written landmark consumer protection legislation, largely bought the commercial bankers' argument that more competition could only benefit the public. I was literally the only member of Proxmire's senior staff who thought that weakening or repealing Glass-Steagall was a dubious idea.

In private meetings, Proxmire informed Fed officials that he would not object if the Fed allowed banks to underwrite some categories of securities. Proxmire and McLean expected that if commercial bankers could break some of the investment banking monopoly, salutary price competition would ensue, to the benefit of consumers. They did not imagine that financial conglomerates combining both functions would quickly reemerge, repeating the same conflicts of interest that had crashed the markets in the 1920s, whose recurrence Glass-Steagall had been intended to prevent.

I did not have much company in my views in those days, but quality made up for quantity. A fellow skeptic was Federal Reserve Chairman Paul Volcker. In February 1987, Volcker called a rare hearing at the Federal Reserve to allow commercial bankers to make their case. Representing the bankers were senior executives of Citicorp, Bankers Trust, and J. P. Morgan. The bankers requested dispensation to underwrite some categories of securities that were generally the province of investment banks—not stocks but municipal bonds, commercial paper, and securities backed by mortgages, as well as credit card receipts. Volcker, according to a tape of the hearing later obtained by *The Wall Street Journal*, rejected their pleas. Volcker read from a 1934 letter from the belatedly contrite chairman of the National City Bank of New York, Citicorp's predecessor, to the bank's shareholders: "I personally believe the bank should be free from any connections, either directly or in any way, which might be taken by the public to indicate a relation with any investment banking house."

"The world has changed a hell of a lot," one of the bankers declared. "But the law hasn't," replied Volcker. Banks enjoyed federal deposit insurance, as well as access to membership in the Federal Reserve System; speculation was not their business, he pointed out. Volcker, however, had been named by Jimmy Carter and reappointed once by Ronald Reagan. The Board was now dominated by Reagan appointees. Three months later, Volcker was on the losing side of a 3–2 vote by the governors of the Federal Reserve, allowing commercial banks to sell some kinds of securities.

That fall, Volcker, sensing that he'd be on the short end of minority votes, resigned. His fourteen-year term had almost six more years to run, and he had not yet turned fifty-nine. His successor, Alan Greenspan, formerly on the board of J. P. Morgan, was far friendlier to the idea of breaching Glass-Steagall. In January 1989, the Fed under Greenspan permitted commercial banks to underwrite corporate bonds, and by October, J. P. Morgan had issued a bond for the Savannah Electric and Power Company, the first such commercial bank transaction since the early 1930s.

That same month, Willard Butcher, chairman of Chase Manhattan, complained about what had befallen the banks' traditional, safe lines of business. "When I started in the bank 42 years ago," Butcher said, "90 percent of our business came from loans to U.S. corporations. Today, they account for less than 4 percent of income." With commercial bankers desperate to pursue new lines of business, a small breach quickly became an open floodgate. Commercial banks became principal creditors of public utility and energy companies. They became enablers of Enron. Regulators, with the acquiescence of most in Congress and the Clinton administration (represented by Robert Rubin), viewed Glass-Steagall as a defunct formality. Greenspan was a strong believer in the idea that American banks should divide not into commercial and investment bankers but into either very large national players who could compete with foreign international giants or small, locally based retail banks. He actively promoted the squeezing out and absorption of midsized institutions, as well as nationwide branching. By 1997, commercial bankers were given explicit permission to acquire investment houses.

In New York, the financier par excellence Sanford Weill adroitly maneuvered himself to run the biggest of the newly permitted, pre-Depression–style superbanks, what would eventually be Citigroup. In 1985, Weill had taken control of Commercial Credit Company and then of Primerica Corporation. From this banking base, Weill acquired Travelers Corporation in 1993. Insurance companies were regulated by the states, and mergers with banks or brokerages were generally resisted by regulators. But this one was permitted. Then, in 1997, Weill took over Salomon Inc. and began discussions with then Citicorp chairman John Reed of a supermerger. This explicitly defied the essence of Glass-Steagall. Yet by October 1998, Travelers and Citicorp merged. The lawyers found a loophole in the 1956 Bank Holding Company Act that allows a two-year period for the Federal Reserve to review large mergers. The Fed, of course, could have disallowed the combination outright as a violation of Glass-Steagall. As recently as the late 1980s, such a merger would have been unthinkable. But now, repeal was welcomed by Greenspan, Rubin, and the key players in Congress, all of whom saw the Citicorp-Travelers merger not as a brazen violation of law but as the final push that would render Glass-Steagall moot. It took Congress just another year to make repeal official.

The Financial Services Modernization Act, signed by President Bill

Clinton in November 1999, was snidely termed in some quarters the "Citigroup Authorization Act." By no small coincidence, Robert Rubin, who as Treasury secretary had relentlessly promoted Glass-Steagall repeal within the Clinton administration, resigned that fall to return to the private sector. His new position was chairman of the executive committee of the newly created Citigroup. Call it a success of politics.

The next two chapters describe the multiple abuses and systemic risks made possible by this cumulative regulatory laxity. As this book was going to press, financial markets were starting to balk at hundreds of billions of dollars worth of pending private-equity deals, with investors fearing that stock prices had peaked and credit terms tightening. A serious economic contraction could be triggered by any of several factors, which would then feed on each other—a softer dollar, higher inflation triggered by oil and food prices, a stock sell-off, a weakened housing market, rising interest rates, anxious credit markets, and tapped out consumers, most of whom have less real income and more debt today than in 2000.

One cannot predict the precise sequence of events, or how steep the decline. But from the perspective of August 2007, it is painfully clear that all the elements of a severe downturn are in place, and that their common genesis is financial deregulation and speculation. The gross inequality of our era only compounds the risk, by removing one of the automatic stabilizers of that characterized the postwar era—broadly distributed mass purchasing power. And the unregulated global market makes it more difficult for nation-states to contain the damage.

CHAPTER FOUR

FINANCIAL ENGINEERING AND SYSTEMIC RISKS

THE EXCESSIVE SPECULATION that dominates the real economy widens inequality, reduces economic efficiency, and increases systemic risk. There is no shortage of dire warnings about risks to the U.S. economy. The problem is that most of the Cassandras are raising alarms about the wrong set of ills. Or, more precisely, these warnings serve the interest of the very class of people whose control of economic policy has been putting the economy in such jeopardy for everyone else.

One favorite nemesis is the federal deficit and the related national debt. Another is the projected ruinous cost of "entitlements" such as Social Security and Medicare. In each case, the preferred remedy seems to be deeper cuts in federal regulation and in public outlay. We will return to these trumped-up risks in chapter six.

There really are, however, some alarming systemic threats to the economy. Most are the consequences of the increasingly speculative financial markets permitted by cumulative deregulation and supercharged by globalization. The top two sources of risk are the exponential proliferation of hedge funds and private equity and the increased dependence of the entire economy on borrowing from abroad.

Hedge Funds: Betting the Farm

The name "hedge fund" implies an investment fund with a particular sort of hedging strategy. In fact, hedge funds are merely creatures of a loophole in the Investment Company Act of 1940. The act, which regulates mutual funds, allowed private funds for very wealthy investors to avoid the entire New Deal regulatory structure. They could put their money wherever they wanted to, with no registration or disclosure requirements for these private funds and no limits on their borrowing. The theory was that this was high-stakes gambling for sophisticated, consenting adults. The popular name, "hedge fund," derives from one such fund founded in the 1940s, which adopted a strategy of hedging its risks by going long in some investments and short in others. For nearly half a century, hedge funds remained niches for the very wealthy, almost like private investment clubs. They were no threat to the system.

Then, in the 1990s, more and more people got in on the game. Hedge fund operators realized that this loophole could be used as a blanket exemption from nearly all forms of financial regulation other than willful fraud. Two decades ago, a relative handful of hedge fund operators produced above-market returns for their wealthy sponsors and investors. Much of their activity involved currency speculation and other creative uses of derivatives. George Soros, for one, had a golden touch. In those days, there was unexploited knowledge about the blend of political and economic factors in various countries that hinted at the likely future value of their currencies. There were highly technical strategies for taking advantage of temporary anomalies in markets. No conflict of interest or manipulation of share prices was required, though some traders were accused of manipulating currency markets. An analyst with an astute feel for markets and a taste for huge risk could make a fortune for himself and his investors.

Lately, thousands of analysts have started hedge funds. This has created a Lake Wobegon problem: everyone wants above-average returns. Otherwise there is no point in paying the huge fees commanded by hedge fund operators. In the days when hedge funds were small niche players, exceptional returns were possible for very astute strategists. But, alas, everyone can't be above average.

As hedge funds have proliferated, often the most expedient way to get above-average returns is to cheat. Increasingly, their operators have relied less on genuinely unique investment strategies and more on the same kinds of insider trading, market manipulation, and conflicts of interest that characterized the scandals of the 1920s and the 1990s. But with hedge funds, the stakes are far higher because of the immense borrowing that the funds do and the fact that they are a regulatory black box. Even hedge funds that don't resort to cheating pose a systemic problem because they tend to exaggerate the market's herd instincts and intensify market volatility. As Keynes famously wrote, "Speculators may do no harm as bubbles on a steady stream of enterprise, but when enterprise becomes the bubble on a whirlpool of speculation, the job of capitalism is likely to be ill-done." That was during the Great Depression. We are destined to learn this lesson over and over again.

As long as hedge funds controlled only a tiny fraction of all financial transactions and kept their own borrowing within prudent bounds, there was no systemic risk. Today the potential risk is huge, because of the almost infinite leveraging and the lack of transparency. Regulators literally do not know what hedge funds are up to until one gets into serious trouble.

The first sign that something ominous could be at stake occurred in 1998, with the collapse of Long-Term Capital Management. LTCM was something special, a hedge fund advised by Nobel laureates with arcane formulas that simply couldn't lose.

LTCM was the brainchild of John Meriwether, formerly a successful risk arbitrageur at Salomon Brothers. The heart of Meriwether's trading model was the premise that if yields on basically similar bonds diverged over time, they were very likely to converge. By cranking into a computer the history of such movements, you could build a model predicting likely future behavior. The model could guide your bets, using various derivative instruments, which also had the benefit of allowing an astronomical ratio of borrowed money to actual capital. The more confident you were of the model, the more you could finance these bets with other people's money.

Meriwether brought in two distinguished academic economists who would later win the Nobel Prize for their models of financial market pricing behavior, Robert Merton and Myron Scholes. Merton and Scholes were on display, both to refine the models and to add cachet. Meriwether began borrowing immense sums of money. In the mid-1990s, he was the envy of Wall Street. For four years running, LTCM produced seemingly riskless annual yields averaging about 40 percent. Though scarcely known beyond the rarified circle of financial elites, LTCM soon had more capital entrusted to its care than Fidelity's famous Magellan Fund. Meriwether required investors to have a net worth of at least $10 million and to tie up their investment for three years, and he had no shortage of takers.

It is one thing for a commercial bank to lend sums at several multiples of its own capital, as long as it avoids concentrations of highly speculative investments like Third World loans. Most of its ordinary assets are loans to businesses and consumers, each one carefully vetted and unlikely to default all at once. Even so, regulators require banks not to be leveraged beyond roughly fourteen to one, and bank assets (loans) are subject to government supervision. If the loan is nonperforming, the bank may be required to put up more capital. But a hedge fund like LTCM is far more thinly capitalized than a bank, its investments are far more speculative, regulators know nothing about the quality of its assets, and if its core assumption about market behavior turns out to be mistaken, the whole thing can blow up. In its heyday, LTCM was betting its entire capital on a single trade. Just before its collapse, the ratio of borrowed money to its own capital was more than 100 to 1.

In 1998, the behavior of markets unaccountably defied the LTCM model. Spreads that logically should have narrowed kept widening, and LTCM was on the wrong side of astronomical bets made with borrowed money. By this point, Meriwether and his partners had bought out most of the fund's investors; they wanted the returns for themselves. LTCM now had equity capital of well over $4 billion and thousands of trading contracts using mostly borrowed money, adding up to a net debt of more than $100 billion with every major Wall Street bank. Given that most of its investments were in derivatives that added another layer or two of leverage, the total value of its contracts (and the exposure of the financial system) was more than a trillion dollars.

In the normal course of events, LTCM would have unwound these positions, paid off the debts as its strategy indicated, made money on the spreads, and replaced old bets with new ones. But when spreads between similar securities widened rather than narrowed, violating the hedge fund's core strategic premise, the very highly leveraged LTCM was suddenly at risk of total default literally overnight. And a default of this scale could crash the whole system.

On September 23, 1998, New York Fed president William McDonough, working closely with Alan Greenspan, summoned the heads of every major New York bank and explained the stakes: the Fed had no authority over hedge funds whatsoever, but the whole financial system had been put at risk by its most arcane speculators.

As Roger Lowenstein recounts the story of the collapse in his definitive book on LTCM, *When Genius Failed*, there was little love lost between the other banks and LTCM, whose "secretive, close knit mathematicians treated everyone else on Wall Street with utter disdain." But McDonough soon got the assembled money cartel to appreciate their common prisoners' dilemma. If each acted in his own self-interest and began dumping LTCM's securities, there could be an old-fashioned nineteenth-century-style financial panic. McDonough asked for, and got the banking executives in the room to put up, just under $4 billion, so that trading positions could be liquidated in orderly fashion. The banks briefly owned LTCM and collectively lost a bundle when it finally went under. But the system held. This was a problem—created by the arrogance of pure speculators—that market forces simply could not solve.

Alan Greenspan had been a champion of derivatives. He had bought the premise that they were agents of greater market efficiency. After the crisis passed, analysts asked themselves just what LTCM had contributed to economic prosperity or market efficiency by exploiting tiny discrepancies in the pricing of bonds and stocks. Despite the claim that its actions had rendered markets more liquid, LTCM had added nothing to the real economy, except (while its luck held) to the net worth of its organizers and their wealthy investors—and to the risk of the entire system.

An All-Purpose Loophole

Today, LTCM is gone, but unregulated hedge funds have become the fastest-growing entities on Wall Street, each one a time bomb of risk. Every effort to regulate them seriously has been beaten back. In the early and mid-1990s, even before LTCM blew up, frauds and losses involving derivatives already extended into the billions. In 1998, the very year that LTCM collapsed, Brooksley Born, then President Clinton's chair of the Commodity Futures Trading Commission, solicited comments on whether certain swaps and other derivatives traded directly between buyer and seller (over the counter), currently exempt from regulation, should be subjected to greater scrutiny. In a very rare joint statement, Fed Chairman Alan Greenspan, Treasury Secretary Robert Rubin, and SEC Chairman Arthur Levitt denounced Born for even raising the subject and browbeat her into withdrawing the solicitation for comment, much less mandating closer supervision. Rubin subsequently endeavored to reduce CFTC's jurisdiction. Even after the LTCM collapse, Greenspan continued to favor less regulation of derivatives.

The nonregulation of derivatives is closely linked to the failure to regulate the hedge funds that make heavy use of them. Beginning in the early 1990s, congressional committees, then still in the hands of Democrats, took a close look at derivatives and became very alarmed. There was a nascent effort to tighten regulation, but it came to naught. With the Republican takeover of Congress in January 1995, the issue essentially vanished from political debate. After Long-Term Capital Management, the issue briefly surfaced again. The Basel-based Bank for International Settlements, a kind of central bankers' clearing bank but without real political or regulatory power, convened an expert panel and issued a report. The experts essentially concluded that because funds could so easily borrow and be hidden offshore, serious regulation of hedge funds was not in the cards.

In 1998, hedge funds held about $250 billion in assets. Today, they hold an estimated $1.3 trillion, and nobody really knows the number for certain. There are no fewer than eight thousand separate hedge funds. Once the premise was that hedge funds were for large and sophisticated investors who could afford big risks and occasionally big losses. Today, more than a thousand so-called funds of funds—mutual funds that invest in hedge funds—allow investors to play the hedge fund game with as little as $5,000.

With hedge funds, the investor bears all of the downside risk but is expected to share a large fraction of upside gains with the fund's management. Hedge funds typically charge fees of 2 percent of the funds they manage and 20 percent of the profits. Managers' annual compensation can run into the hundreds of millions of dollars in a good year, and most of the compensation is treated as capital gains for tax purposes. In 2006, the top hedge fund manager took in $1.7 billion. Pension funds, representing the deferred savings of workers, are investing heavily in hedge funds. Corporations control the investment decisions of their pension funds; the more money the pension fund makes, the smaller the annual contribution that must come out of company profits. At this writing, some unions are challenging pension investments in hedge funds as violating the fiduciary duty of prudent investment. University endowments have also moved heavily into hedge funds.

As hedge funds have proliferated, their average rate of return has steadily dropped. Whereas returns in excess of 20 percent were once common (supercharged by the hot stock market of the 1990s), today the average hedge fund often fails to beat the S&P 500. The Hennessee Group, which tracks hedge fund returns, calculates that the average hedge fund produced returns of 14.9 percent annually from 1987 through 2004, compared to 11.9 percent for the S&P 500. But in 2005, the average hedge fund returned only 8.3 percent, which was actually 2.6 percentage points below the S&P average.

Several critics have observed that even these statistics overstate how well hedge funds actually do. In any given year, hundreds, even thousands, of new hedge funds are launched, and hundreds go bust. For instance in 2005, there were 2,073 hedge funds newly started, and 848 closed down, according to the firm Hedge Fund Research. But the conventional statistics track only the returns of the firms that stay in business, producing a systematic bias that overstates the earnings of the industry as a whole.

Since hedge funds charge exorbitant commissions and often require their investors to lock in funds for an extended period, the pressure to increase returns has intensified the tendency to engage in risky and often extralegal practices. Once, hedge funds used mainly abstruse formulas of their own invention. Today, they do many of the same things that investment bankers do. They account for nearly half the trading volume on the New York Stock Exchange and more than half the volume in derivatives transactions. They buy and sell entire companies, then make complex market plays in a variety of commodities. Indeed, some hedge funds are owned by investment banking conglomerates. And with the immense pressure for high returns to justify their high fees and commissions, they are systematically repeating the abuses that characterized the scandals of the 1990s—only with much greater systemic risks because of the very high leveraging and absence of regulatory scrutiny.

Today hedge funds orchestrate takeover fights, often for the sole purpose of manipulating the share price. Since hedge funds rely so heavily on borrowing and make such risky bets, their risk is transmitted to the institutions that lend them money. These are Wall Street's most blue-chip institutions—the same ones almost taken down nearly a decade ago in the collapse of Long-Term Capital Management.

Like the hedge funds that pay them premium rates, banks and brokerages are looking for new ways to make market-beating returns. According to *Fortune* magazine, "prime brokerage," the lending of money to hedge funds by investment bankers, is one of the fastest-growing lines of business on Wall Street. Not only do the big Wall Street houses make money on the loans; they derive additional fees by executing trades for their hedge fund clients. *Fortune* estimates that Goldman Sachs makes at least 10 percent of its earnings from hedge fund business, including $1.3 billion in 2005.

In an era of derivatives, margin regulation has become a joke, something that restricts only the small and the unsophisticated. Banks collude in the circumvention of margin limits, and regulators collude in the banks' behavior. Hedge funds borrow their money from the largest money center banks, often at preferential rates because they are such large borrowers. The transactions are presumably safe, because many trades in derivatives are settled daily, although some hedge funds have bargained for, and received, long-term lines of credit. In ordinary transactions, banks are owed the money to settle a hedge fund market play. But in another major hedge fund collapse, there would be no market for these derivatives, the hedge fund would quickly run out of money to pay off the banks, and liquidity would dry up. Moreover, with the merger and consolidation of major lending institutions into a handful of trillion-dollar behemoths, a great many hedge funds are making essentially the same bets, financed by the same banks.

The increased risk of this whole brand of financial capitalism cannot possibly be justified by the supposed gains to economic efficiency. The game of banks financing hedge funds to invest in derivatives operates at three removes from the normal banking or venture capital business of supplying capital to actual enterprises, which requires careful monitoring of what the enterprises actually do rather than the manipulation of formulas. The former activity adds value; the latter kind of pyramiding mainly extracts fees and adds risk. At each layer of remove from the real economy, middlemen take a handsome cut. They are parasitic on the real economy. In this respect, the hedge fund game is reminiscent of the watered-down stock pools of the 1920s, the S&L speculation with brokered money of the 1980s, and the scandals of the 1990s.

In the case of LTCM, the hedge fund spread its borrowing business around to dozens of banks. Each bank knew only its own exposure; it had no idea of the vulnerability of the banking system as a whole. The total risk became apparent only when LTCM ran out of money and the Fed had to organize an emergency rescue. Today, that systemic exposure has been multiplied at least a hundredfold, and the plays that each hedge fund pursues have become even more opaque. When LTCM blew up, McDonough sent two of his deputies on an urgent mission to its Greenwich, Connecticut, headquarters to determine the extent of its total exposure and the identities of the banks at risk. Because of the greater complexity of trades and the proliferation of funds, "I could not do that today," McDonough told me.

In the late 1990s, "stock analysts" such as Jack Grubman turned out to be stock touts. They were rewarded for talking up bad investments in which their investment banker allies had a stake. The postcrash reforms supposedly put an end to this kind of conflict of interest and market manipulation. But today, many hedge funds orchestrate an inversion of the analysts' ploys of the 1990s. They aggressively take short positions in stocks, betting that the price will fall. They then talk down the value of the stock, hoping to create a self-fulfilling prophecy.

In a fine irony, one of the remedies intended to cure the conflicts of interest endemic in the scandals of the 1990s has turned into a tool of hedge fund stock manipulators. The Sarbanes-Oxley Act tried to strengthen the wall between supposed securities analysts in the employ of investment banks and investment banking activity. The Spitzer "global settlement" required the Wall Street banking houses to contribute funds to bankroll new, wholly independent analysis and research firms whose sole purpose would be to serve investors. But somebody has to pay the freight for this research. It turns out that many of the investors retaining the services of independent analysis firms are hedge funds—which expect the analysts to help them engage in the same sort of stock manipulation that marked the earlier scandals.

With hedge funds sometimes in the role of creditor as well as borrower, new opportunities for conflicts of interest arise. When a company borrows money, it has to provide the lender with confidential information. If the company is considering a merger, sale, or acquisition, the lender becomes privy to that information. In several cases being investigated by the SEC, hedge funds that were lenders to corporations may have used privileged information to trade in the corporation's stock.

Because hedge funds control so much capital, they are a prime source of business for investment banking houses. Investment bankers seeking to curry favor with hedge funds have been known to tip off fund managers to pending stock offerings. French securities authorities are investigating a London-based hedge fund, Marshall Wace, for allegedly ordering a huge sale of Alcatel shares, just before the French telecom giant unveiled a stock offering that was likely to water down the value of existing shares. A manager at the hedge fund, according to *The Wall Street Journal*, had been tipped off by a friendly investment banker. Marshall Wace, which at this writing manages some $7 billion in three hedge funds, paid around $250 million in commissions in 2004 and again in 2005, and accounts for 2 to 3 percent of all trades on major European stock exchanges. Investment banking houses want this business. Britain's Financial Services Authority, the equivalent of our SEC, believes such insider trades based on privileged information are widespread.

As noted, there is no such thing as a hedge fund in the sense of a fund that pursues a unique investing strategy. The only difference between so-called hedge funds and the regulated mutual funds to which ordinary investors entrust their money is that hedge funds enjoy a special exemption from ordinary disclosures mandated by the SEC. But as hedge funds have proliferated, both the legislators and the regulators have forgotten the other great lesson of the Great Depression: that financial regulation is also needed to reduce risks to the system. Back when private, unregulated millionaires' investment funds were small players, they didn't pose a systemic risk. Today they pose a huge one. And the more they play on a global stage beyond the reach of national regulators, the greater the risk that they could take down the whole system.

The SEC has proposed only the most minimal regulation of hedge funds. In 2004 the commission required funds to register with the SEC, but its requirements even for a modest set of disclosures were thrown out by the courts, on the grounds that the commission had exceeded its statutory authority. Congress would have to tighten hedge fund regulation, and Congress has no such plans. Despite the risks, there are no limits placed on hedge fund borrowing, or on the lock-in terms they require of their investors. In late 2006, the SEC announced plans to increase the minimum investment required, on the premise that the risk was to the individual investor. But the SEC had no plans to address the risks to the system.

Who Needs Hedge Funds?

To get rid of the hedge fund menace, Congress would have to repeal the special exemption and require all funds selling shares to the public to register and provide the same kind of disclosures. Congress would also need to limit the permissible leverage allowed investment funds to a more prudent level. Congress would also have to amend the banking regulations, so that banks did not collude with hedge funds to use ever more esoteric derivatives to get around the newly enforced margin limits.

But wouldn't hedge funds just move offshore and borrow in unregulated banking and tax havens? Many such funds are already incorporated in the Cayman Islands, as LTCM was. This problem could also be addressed by greater coordination of financial regulation among the leading money center nations.

My interviews suggest that all of this deeply worries some of the best-informed senior people on Wall Street and in the central banking system. These interviews with some of the best-known people in American finance are on background, because they are as reluctant to be identified as skunks at a picnic. One surprising exception to the happy talk from Wall Street is William Rhodes, CEO of Citibank—the commercial bank part of the giant financial conglomerate Citigroup. Rhodes went public with a surprising op-ed piece in the *Financial Times* in late March, warning of a very major stock market correction in late 2007. Rhodes cited excess liquidity fueling too many dubious deals and the "possibly destabilizing effect" of hedge funds, private equity, and derivatives as liquidity recedes. His piece ended with a warning against "any temptation to relax standards." Rhodes had been a major player in the debt workouts of South American countries in the 1980s and 1990s, after banks had been overly lax with their lending standards. The piece was a remarkably public dissent by a senior Wall Street banker, especially given that other subsidiaries of Citi are in the business of promoting hedge fund, private equity, and derivative activity, and Citi is also part of the chorus calling for loosening of the Sarbanes-Oxley Act. None of these remedies are anywhere in mainstream political debate. But that is not a consequence of globalization or financial technology or New Era economics in which financial markets are self-regulating. It is another failure of politics.

You don't need a crystal ball to know that when the next major financial meltdown occurs—and it will—those who clean up the mess will hold hearings, just as they did in the 1930s. And just as then, it will quickly be clear that one of the prime causes was far too much speculation with borrowed money. One of the first things Congress will do will be to put hedge funds out of business. And commentators will ask why nobody acted before the crash came.

The answer, again, is that too many people are making too much money; too many Wall Street elders supposedly concerned about systemic risk are more concerned about their good relationships with their financial peers; and too many supposed liberals are drunk on the same Kool-Aid of deregulation, washed down by a lot of campaign funding.

One interesting footnote to the hedge fund story: *The Wall Street Journal*, the ideological organ of free markets, has been a great defender of hedge funds (in its editorial pages—its news stories have done a fine job of exposing the risks). But the same editorial page is on a relentless tear to attack the Federal National Mortgage Association (Fannie Mae) and the Federal Home Loan Mortgage Corporation (Freddie Mac), two large private, once public, financial companies created by Congress to inject liquidity into mortgage markets. Fannie and Freddie buy mortgages, bundle them as securities, and infuse banks, thrift institutions, and mortgage companies with access to additional funds with which to originate new mortgage loans.

The *Journal* doesn't like Fannie and Freddie for two main reasons. First, these are quasi-governmental entities that tap capital markets for huge sums (Fannie is the second largest borrower after the U.S. Treasury). Because Fannie and Freddie have a public purpose and were government agencies until being privatized in 1968, markets assume that the government would bail them out in a crisis, so they can borrow at rates lower than their purely private competitors. Second, Fannie also has something of a Democratic flavor. During the Clinton era, despite its ostensibly public purpose, Fannie's top executives, Democratic ex-politicians, managed to award themselves outsized pay packets; and Fannie, like many other corporations during the 1990s, played games with its balance sheet in order to inflate its stock price and the value of its executives' stock compensation.

In one of the rare cases of regulatory zeal under the Republicans, the small agency that supervises Fannie Mae, the Office of Federal Housing Enterprise Oversight, or OFHEO, has kicked up its heels and become an aggressive regulator. An OFHEO report issued in May 2006 faulted "illusions deliberately and systematically" manipulated by top executives in an $11 billion accounting scandal intended to inflate Fannie's stock price, and by extension, the compensation paid to CEO Frank Raines, a former Clinton administration budget director. Raines's pay rose steadily from about $8 million a year in 1999 to almost $25 million in 2003, just before he was forced to resign when accounting irregularities came to light. The OFHEO report noted that of the $90 million in compensation that Raines was paid over six years, $52 million was directly tied to meeting earnings-per-share targets that Fannie's executives rigged. At this writing OFHEO has ordered Fannie to limit its total portfolio to $727 billion and to pay a fine of $400 million to settle OFHEO and SEC charges of bogus accounting, and Raines is expected to have to repay some of his windfall. Leading Republicans in Congress, including Senator Richard Shelby, who chaired the Banking Committee, have pressed for even tighter regulation.

An oft-stated concern of the *Journal*, Senator Shelby, and other critics of Fannie and Freddie is that these two large financial institutions are very highly leveraged; that they make exotic market plays using complex and arcane derivative instruments; and that because so much money is involved, if ever they make a fundamental miscalculation in their investment strategy, the financial consequences could be disastrous. The parallel to hedge funds is hard to miss, and the double standard is telling. Indeed, Fannie and Freddie are closely regulated, and their balance sheets and business operations are subject to normal disclosure requirements by the SEC and additional ones by OFHEO. No such scrutiny is applied to hedge funds. Fannie and Freddie, moreover, are just two entities. Every one of these well-placed concerns applies in spades to hedge funds, now numbering in the thousands, which are more opaque, more arcane, more highly leveraged, and collectively more of a financial risk. On this issue, *The Wall Street Journal* and the Republican congressional elders are silent.

Private Enrichments

Once, private-equity funds, like hedge funds, occupied a fairly small niche. In recent years, private-equity firms have become very major players. In the first ten months of 2006, there were 2,163 private buy-outs valued at a total of $538.67 billion, according to the tracking firm Dealogic. This was about double the value of similar deals a year earlier. Worldwide, by the end of 2006, private-equity buyouts had risen to a rate of $1.4 trillion a year, from under $400 billion in 2004, according to Thomson Financial, and by May 2007 the annual rate was on track to reach $2 trillion. In Britain, an estimated one employee in five works for a company owned by private equity.

Superficially, these firms resemble investment banks and venture capitalists. But unlike investment banks, they share with hedge funds a broad exemption from most regulatory requirements, since they neither take in deposits like banks nor sell securities to the investing public like regulated brokerages. When a private-equity firm buys a corporation, that company is suddenly exempt from the usual disclosures required of public companies by the SEC. This loophole makes it far easier for manager/owners to mulct the assets of the company for their own private enrichment. Disclosures required of public companies by the SEC are narrowly intended to protect investors, but more broadly they require information and accounting standards and protections against conflicts of interest needed to keep the whole system honest. And unlike venture capitalists, who raise capital mainly to finance new enterprises, the new wave of private-equity firms are mostly doing deals for quick returns.

A characteristic form of conflict of interest, which became increasingly fashionable in the years after the crash of 2000–01 and the supposed reforms, is the management buyout. Once upon a time, a successful entrepreneur would work with venture capitalists or investment bankers to take a new company public. An initial public offering would allow the innovator to reap a nice cash reward for a new company judged promising by the investing public. Some of the proceeds would go to the entrepreneur. Most would be invested in the expansion of the enterprise. This is just how financial markets are supposed to work—connecting investors with innovators. The entrepreneur, compensated with stock, would retain an interest in pleasing the markets.

Lately, this process has gone into reverse. Managers, who typically inherited a large, publicly traded company, contrive to buy it for themselves. Often working with private-equity firms, the managers put together the capital to "take the company private." In 2005 and 2006, there were about a hundred management buyouts, valued at a total of about a trillion dollars. The largest was the $31.6 billion buyback by the Frist family and private-equity partners of HCA, the scandal-ridden hospital conglomerate first founded by Tom Frist, the brother of former Senate Majority Leader Bill Frist, in the 1970s.

The apologists for this practice contend that it is good for everyone. Shareholders typically realize a premium over the prevailing market price. Managers are freed from the relentless pressure to meet analysts' expectations of quarterly returns. They are also, conveniently, freed from the reporting and disclosure requirements of public companies.

What enthusiasts don't tout, however, is the massive conflict of interest. Managers supposedly operate the company as agents of shareholders. Indeed, in the earlier wave of leveraged buyouts, the hostile-takeover artists contended that existing management was performing poorly, so outsiders had to wrest control from them in order to serve shareholders better. But what happens when managers wrest control from shareholders to enrich themselves?

Studies show that in the months preceding a management buyout, the managers often seek to depress the stock price so they can buy the company cheaply. Nominally, it is the board of directors that negotiates the sale and sets the price, but as we've seen, the directors are typically cronies of the managers, appointed by them and loyal to them. One study of management buyouts in 2004 and 2005 found that when management purchases the company, it typically pays shareholders about 30 percent less than it pays outside buyers in mergers and acquisitions.

Researchers have found that managers preparing to take a company private also sometimes manipulate balance sheets to make earnings look as low as possible, to depress the share price. Sharon Katz, of the Harvard Business School, calculated that in the two years preceding a management buyout, corporations underreported accounts receivable. This reduced nominal earnings. Another study found that managers planning buyouts were likely to speed up the booking of expenses and slow down the booking of revenue. So the management buyout is often less a case of managers improving actual performance after taking a company private than cooking the books in advance of the deal.

And in sharp contrast to the fable about managers having an incentive to run the enterprise more efficiently, what managers and their private-equity partners want most is to make a quick killing. Often a company is taken private, only to be taken public again, with the managers and their private-equity partners making a short-term windfall. Or sometimes the managers sell off some divisions and keep the rest.

In principle, these gains render the market more efficient. In practice, they frequently put well-run companies at the mercy of short-term trading profits. The increase in private-equity activity has only intensified this pattern. The sale of the Knight Ridder chain to the McClatchy Company in June 2006, forced by a private-equity firm, was followed by the sell-off of twelve of Knight Ridder's papers. The spin-offs yielded $2.1 billion, which McClatchy needed to reduce the debt it had taken on to finance the merger.

Knight Ridder was a relatively benign corporate owner. Over the years, its papers had won a total of eighty-five Pulitzer Prizes. But in recent years, newspaper stocks have lagged the broader stock market, because of fears that Internet advertising is gradually crowding out newspapers' ad revenue. Knight Ridder stock declined from a high of $80 a share in 2004 to a low of $52.42 in 2005. This, in turn, led to pressure from its largest shareholder, Private Capital Management, which held 19 percent, for management to take drastic action. This meant, first, severe cost-cutting measures, and the private-equity firm eventually forced the sale to McClatchy for $4.5 billion, or $67.25 a share. Cost cutting is continuing under the new owners.

Burger King was taken private in 2002. In February 2006, it was taken public again. The private owners, a consortium of the Texas Pacific Group and Bain Capital, more than tripled their stake in less than four years. Burger King is roughly as profitable today as it was in 2002, though its market share has continued to fall. Is it really possible to triple the efficiency of a commodity business such as selling fast food? Or were these private-equity firms cooking the books along with the burgers? Barring a lawsuit charging outright fraud (which is far more difficult today, thanks to the legislation passed by the Republican Congress in 1996), we'll never know, since once a company is taken private it enters a regulatory black hole.

Private-equity funds promote these deals not just for the opportunity to make a quick killing on the acquisition and resale. There are also lucrative fees to be had. For instance, in the Burger King buyout from a British-owned chain, the two private investment firms collected an initial $22.4 million in unspecified fees. Burger King then began paying its new owners quarterly management fees for monitoring its business and serving on its board. In 2006, these fees added up to $29 million. And just before the new public offering, the owners voted themselves a handsome $367 million dividend. Finally, the two private investment firms collected a $30 million "termination fee" from the company for selling it off.

One of the owners who flipped Burger King for a quick profit, Bain Capital, is a well-established private investment firm cofounded by former Massachusetts governor Mitt Romney. In 2005, it tried to buy the entire National Hockey League. The other owner, Texas Pacific Group, works closely with Goldman Sachs. With private-equity firms proliferating, the big, established Wall Street houses are not about to let independent operators make off with this lucrative business. Goldman has so many fingers in so many pies that it can make money on fees, commissions, underwriting, lending, and in this case as an owner/speculator. When Burger King started selling shares to the public again, Goldman reaped another $6.3 million in underwriting fees. The two private-equity firms ended up tripling their original investment, yet, after selling some shares to the public, still retained a 76 percent stake. What, exactly, did the new owners contribute?

It is one thing for traditional investment bankers to extract fees for advising companies on buyout deals and for finding the capital to finance them. But the new private-equity firms also take fees for "advisory" work on their own deals, in addition to making windfall profits on the purchase and sale of the assets. The Blackstone Group, which took the Celanese Corporation private and became its owner in 2004, then billed itself $45 million in fees for executing its own deal.

Like the earlier boom in leveraged buyouts of the 1980s, the private-equity boom relies heavily on borrowed money, both to finance the purchases and even to pay out the dividends and fees. According to *The Wall Street Journal*, loans to pay out dividends to private-equity owners rose from less than a billion dollars in 2001 to more than $20 billion in 2005 and were on track to hit $40 billion in 2006. All these loans are burdens on the actual operating company. Unlike the earlier leveraged-buyout boom, which involved mostly one public company acquiring another, private-equity deals are far less transparent. Details emerge only in lawsuits or when the firms attempt a round-trip and cash out by taking the private company public.

In one such case, retirees of Intelsat sued the company for walking away from its pension obligations. The owners maintain that the newly privatized company is a wholly different corporate entity with none of the former obligations to pensioners. You can be sure that Intelsat respects its obligations to the private-equity firms that bought it, but why do they have more contractual rights than the pensioners? The 2001 buyout was financed with $515 million in private equity and $3 billion in borrowed money. By 2006, the owners had taken out management fees and dividends totaling $576 million, equal to more than their original investment. As a result of the heavily leveraged buyout, Intelsat's net worth fell from a positive $2.3 billion to a negative $290 million. It is inconceivable to imagine a public company with negative net worth voting its shareholders a large dividend. Basically, a good piece of management's fees came directly out of the pockets of its retirees.

It would be one thing if private equity were mainly in the business of taking over stagnant companies. But the ideal private-equity target is a well-run business that sets aside plenty of money to invest in workers, R&D, and its future. A classic example is the German manufacturer of high quality plumbing fixtures, Friedrich Grohe AG. In 1999, a majority stake in the firm was sold by the Grohe family to a British private-equity fund, BC Partners, which financed its purchase mostly with borrowed money. BC Partners, in turn, sold Grohe again to two other private-equity firms, Texas Pacific Group and Credit Suisse First Boston. As a result of these two debt-financed sales, Moody's has reduced Grohe's once-outstanding credit rating, and an increasing portion of the company's cash flow goes for interest payments. The new owners planned to move a large fraction of Grohe's craft jobs to China. But thanks to Germany's system of co-determination and worker representation on the company board, this kind of mass layoff and outsourcing cannot be done quite as abruptly as in the United States. The employees made a strong case that Grohe, as a premium brand, could not just hollow itself out without destroying the company's reputation for quality. At this writing, Grohe's private-equity owners and its workers are still negotiating about the number of job relocations, which will be smaller than originally planned. The private-equity firms may end up with slightly less of a windfall, as Grohe's other stakeholders compel management to take a longer term view. This was not a problem when the firm was locally owned.

The proliferation of private buyout deals offers new, secondary opportunities for previously unimagined insider gains, based on the leaking of confidential information. Among the new popular derivative instruments are financial contracts called "credit default swaps." These are private contracts against the risk of a company going bankrupt. Their legitimate use is as a kind of inexpensive insurance policy taken out by creditors. There is also a huge trading market in these derivatives, which are popular with hedge funds.

When a company is about to be bought in a highly leveraged buyout, it takes on more debt, and its existing debt becomes a little riskier, because of the increased possibility of default. The greater the risk of default, the more costly the credit default swaps. According to *The Wall Street Journal*, in the five days before the HCA deal was disclosed on July 19, 2006, the price of HCA credit default swaps rose by 11 percent, suggesting that at least some insiders had knowledge of the pending deal and were trading ahead of it. Word of the deal could have simply leaked. More likely, insiders used their knowledge of the pending deal to make some additional profits on the side or to tip hedge fund chums as part of what novelist Tom Wolfe termed "the great favor bank," doing a favor to be called in later.

The newest wrinkle is the emergence of hybrid firms that are part hedge fund, part private-equity firm, part corporate conglomerate—and, if they get their way, part commercial bank. One such fund, Cerberus Capital Management, well named for the mythical three-headed dog that guarded the gates of Hell, now controls companies worth $30 billion, according to *BusinessWeek*. Its holdings currently include car rental franchises, fast-food restaurants, and Kmart. In mid-2007, Cerberus bought the Chrysler division of Daimler-Benz.

Megafunds like Cerberus may soon be able to own federally insured commercial banks as well. Thanks to a loophole in federal banking law, Utah, the home of former Senate Banking Committee chairman Jake Garn, was permitted to allow a unique hybrid known as an industrial bank. These small financial institutions, a throwback to Utah's era of frontier economic development, were allowed to own ordinary businesses as well as to operate banks. This practice breaches the most fundamental doctrine of U.S. banking law, the wall between commercial banking and ordinary commerce. If banks, with their deep access to federally insured depositor money, are allowed to compete with other businesses, it invites both excessive risks and unfair competition. When limited to small-town banks, this loophole was no big deal. But in an era of nationwide banking, any enterprise can set up shop in Utah. Wal-Mart tried to use the industrial bank loophole to get into the banking business but was beaten back by the commercial banking lobby. At this writing, hedge funds like Cerberus still hope to use the Utah loophole to set up megabanks.

As private equity got bigger and bigger, private-equity firms, like their hedge-fund cousins, also fell victim to the law of large numbers. It is simply not possible for everyone to make above-average returns. Unsavory temptations increased—to profit from illegal insider information, to strip sound companies of assets, to shift from long-term holdings to quick trades, and to unload overpriced assets on greater fools. By mid-2007, the boom in private equity looked like nothing so much as a bubble that would soon be popped.

One leading indicator was that the Blackstone Group, whose owners had grown very rich by promoting the virtues of private equity, decided to go public. Or rather, Blackstone offered to sell ordinary investors a slice of its operations, while leaving the power in the hands of the general partners. In a column titled "Making a Play for the Dumb Money," *Washington Post* financial columnist Steven Pearlstein acidly observed, "Don't fall for all those explanations about how Blackstone needs to raise capital or find a way for its visionary founders to cash out. Blackstone has a proven record of being able to raise all the private capital it needs. . . . No, the reason Blackstone is considering going public is simple: It's at the market tops like this that the dumb money will overpay. The smart money is getting out while it can."

As evidence, Pearlstein got hold of a memo from another private-equity pioneer, Bill Conway, a founder of the Carlyle Group. Conway warned: "Frankly, there is so much liquidity in the world that lenders (even 'our' lenders) are making very risky credit decisions. . . . I know the longer it lasts the more money our investors (and we) will make. . . . And I know that the longer it lasts, the worse it will be when it ends." Pearlstein and other commentators pointed to the huge potential for conflicts of interest between the general and limited partners of Blackstone and their public shareholders. "[W]hen the market finally turns and deals blow up," Pearlstein warned, "you can be pretty sure that fund managers will do everything they can to protect themselves and the interests of their limited partners and let the saps who are public shareholders take it on the chin."

Unfortunately the "dumb money" that could end up as big-time losers when the private-equity bubble pops is not just the gullible individual investor. University and foundation endowments and pension funds have all been flocking to what are euphemistically called "alternative investments"—mainly hedge funds and private equity. The more money they put up, the more deals private-equity firms can do. The financial managers of university endowments are compensated according to how well the endowment performs. Foundations love high rates of return; they can keep funding favored grantees without dipping into principal. And pension funds need high returns to meet obligations in the face of longer-lived retirees. *The Chronicle of Philanthropy* examined large institutions such as foundations, universities, charities, research institutes, and museums. Traditionally, these endowments were heavily invested in blue-chip stocks, safe bonds, other fixed-income securities, and a reserve of cash. By 2006, the *Chronicle* reported that the median endowment worth more than a billion dollars had fully 34 percent of its money in speculative alternative investments, spurred on by financial advisers. America's nonprofit civic institutions will be among the victims of the hedge fund and private-equity bubble when the party ends.

Note the difference between these supposed apostles of market efficiency and a true Wall Street hero, Warren Buffett. Superinvestor Buffett consistently beats the market averages by deeply researching the fundamentals of the stocks and companies that his holding company, Berkshire Hathaway, acquires. Unlike hedge funds and many private-equity funds, Berkshire Hathaway typically holds on to its acquisitions as a long-term investor. And though Buffett could have chosen to operate Berkshire as a private equity fund, his company is publicly traded and makes all the usual SEC disclosures.

The larger point here is that the proliferation of exotic instruments and deals simply overwhelms regulators and enriches insiders at the expense of the broad investing public and the efficiency of the system, which depends on honest and transparent information. Since the crash of 2000–01, all of this has only worsened.

The cycle of ignoring lessons of history is speeding up. It took more than four decades for American capitalism to forget the lessons of the great crash of 1929 and begin repeating the same abuses. It took less than four years to forget the lessons of the crash of 2000.

What's the Matter with Markets?

If the claims made by today's private-equity firms sound familiar, exactly the same claims were made by apologists for this brand of financial engineering two decades ago, just before innumerable hostile takeovers and mergers orchestrated with borrowed money collapsed. These deals supposedly "maximized shareholder value." By "leveraging up"—borrowing lots of money—the LBOs' sponsors put pressure on managers to perform and to find new efficiencies. By going private, companies could be insulated from Wall Street's relentless demands to meet or exceed quarterly profit targets and could tend to the business of managing the company. All this was said to serve ordinary investors by raising share prices.

These claims turned out to be mostly self-serving. Those who got rich were the middlemen. Stock prices often rose on the eve of a deal, but the stock of a company suddenly burdened with new debt often sank just as fast. By the late 1980s, Wall Street was littered with the remains of LBO deals that had gone bad. The "efficiencies" demanded by managers often turned out to be cuts in wages, benefits, and pensions. This was less a case of running the company more efficiently than an income transfer from ordinary employees to executives and financial engineers. Moreover, the contention that taking a company private insulates it from the quarterly pressure to perform is also backward. As financial engineering becomes more dominant, short-term performance drives the whole system.

The latest wave of asset rearrangement is fueled by four realities. First, in the aftermath of the stock market bust of 2000, investors are hungry for the supernormal yields they briefly enjoyed in the bubble of the 1990s. Money from quasi-public institutions such as university endowments and pension funds, as well as individual investors, has been pouring into hedge funds and private-equity funds. Second, a climate of low interest rates makes these deals irresistible, especially since the interest is tax-deductible. Regulatory laxity is a third factor, and the use of hedge funds or private-equity firms evades even the minimal regulation required of normal mergers and acquisitions. Finally, these deals are relentlessly promoted by other middlemen—commercial banks and investment bankers, which make money off the fees.

This trend invites several big questions. How could financial markets be so inefficient that insiders could find literally billions of spare dollars to exploit in a single deal, by cashing in the difference between the price that the stock market places on a company and their own valuation of the underlying assets? This practice, known as risk arbitrage, has been around for decades—Robert Rubin made his money as a "risk arb"—but it has never been so central to financial markets.

And is the stock market really so undervalued? In the 1970s and

1980s, when the movement to deregulate financial markets gathered force, we heard a lot about a core postulate of conservative Chicago School economics: the Efficient Market Hypothesis. Supposedly, markets were efficient by definition. Whatever the market deemed to be the price of a stock was its true value. Therefore, regulators should leave markets alone. Today, the same Chicago School economists, who once touted the efficiency of stock market pricing, are apologists for private-equity deals that supposedly take advantage of the same stock market's *inefficiency*—its apparent failure to price shares accurately. But both claims can't be true. Either way, the markets are not as efficient as they're cracked up to be.

And what about the stock market itself? In principle, stock markets exist to connect entrepreneurs with investors. There is a legitimate middleman function in underwriting new securities: taking the risk of evaluating an entrepreneur, floating a new issue of stock, pricing it, and selling it to the investing public. Investment bankers can make fortunes performing that role. But what is so seriously the matter with the stock market that a whole new layer of essentially parasitic middlemen is necessary to carry out the ordinary functions of capital markets?

It would make more sense to expose the stock market to greater public scrutiny and increase its efficiency directly—and to get rid of the incentives that allow windfall gains to the new middlemen. Some private-equity firms do add value, especially when they supply equity capital and when they hold stock and improve the management of a firm for the medium or long term. But public policy needs to change the current incentives that reward the short-term acquisition of sound corporations and allow middlemen to strip them of assets. Specifically, the interest on the borrowed money that underwrites leveraged buyouts should not be tax-deductible. Deal makers who take entire companies private only to take them public again in a short period of time should be subject to a windfall profits tax. New owners of a firm acquired mostly with borrowed money should be prohibited from voting themselves extraordinary dividends. There should be limits on the transactions fees paid to middlemen. And, in the case of a company with assets over a set amount, say $50 million, exactly the same public disclosures should be required, whether the owners are the general shareholding public or private-equity firms and hedge funds.

You can bet that this proposal, like the reining in of hedge funds, is nowhere on the public regulatory agenda. But that is just a mark of the degree to which regulatory policy has been captured by Wall Street.

Wouldn't such a proposal gum up the efficiency of markets? On the contrary, it would take a lot of the profit out of deals aimed mainly at the enrichment of middlemen. It would put pressure on companies to improve their performance organically. It is bizarre to use the highly leveraged sale and resale of entire companies as the preferred way of holding their managers accountable. Taking some of the profit out of these superheated buyouts would also redirect more investment capital and entrepreneurial zeal to the creation of real wealth rather than the manipulation and rearrangement of paper.

Defenders of private equity make three arguments. First, they contend, there are many badly managed companies. By grasping the potential for changes in how an enterprise is run, private-equity owners can pay above-market prices, unlock hidden value, reap just rewards, and improve the efficiency of the economy. Back when private equity was a small niche, this picture described at least some private-equity owners; and there are still some private-equity firms that buy and hold for the long term. But today the norm is becoming a strategy of stripping assets for quick return. The new wave of private-equity funds do not get involved in the details of running firms. They are the antithesis of careful management.

A second oft-heard argument is that private-equity purchasers of companies "must have" some special proprietary knowledge or skill; otherwise, they would not pay above-market prices. And to compel additional disclosures would destroy their ability to bring new economic efficiencies to the company, and by extension to the economy. But today's private-equity players increasingly are using a generic cookbook: borrow a lot of money, take the company private, pull out windfall dividends, and sell off the remaining assets. There are few genuine management secrets worth protecting.

This brings us to the trump card in the defense. Obviously, say apologists for private equity, the whole process would not work if private-equity owners could not find buyers. And if buyers are willing to pay more than the private-equity owners' own previous purchase price, then by definition private equity "must have" added value. But take a closer look. If the whole deal is financed with tax-deductible borrowed money, and private-equity owners make windfall gains by paying themselves exorbitant special dividends, then a private-equity firm can actually sell the company, or its pieces, for less than its own acquisition price and still come out way ahead.

In a rising stock market, with low interest rates, private-equity owners can make exorbitant short-term gains by putting up a small amount of equity and borrowing the rest. Their windfall is the difference between the return on total capital, which need only be normal, and the return on equity—even if they bring no additional management expertise. But in a down market, or a period of rising interest costs, the magic of leverage goes into reverse. So private-equity fever brings risks both to sound enterprises and to the economy as a whole.

There have been times in American history when regulators have stepped in precisely to throw a little "sand in the gears" of financial speculation, as the Nobel laureate in economics James Tobin famously put it. Tobin was no wild-eyed radical. He was a member of the Council of Economic Advisers under President Kennedy. Tobin made his sand-in-the-gears comment in the course of proposing a special tax on short-term financial transactions, aimed at discouraging so much speculative activity. The Tobin Tax was never enacted, but it won the support of other mainstream economists such as Lawrence Summers, the former Treasury secretary and before that the chief economist of the International Monetary Fund. The whole series of post-1929 reforms was aimed at making either illegal or unprofitable entire categories of speculative financial transactions. All of these, from stock pools to evasions of margin requirements to insider trading, have been reborn in the financial engineering of the current era.

The addition of a new layer of middlemen and the dysfunctional operation of corporate governance and capital markets are two sides of the same coin. If corporate executives were more effectively accountable to boards of directors and directors more accountable to shareholders, the system would not need private-equity firms and hedge funds to claim that they were rendering managers more responsible and markets more efficient by buying and selling entire companies with tax-deductible borrowed money.

Unfortunately, serious reforms of financial markets are nowhere on the horizon. Instead, in the deregulated climate, new abuses and risks continue to proliferate.

CHAPTER FIVE

The Casino Continues

Less than seven years after the crash of 2000–01 and just five years after Congress in a fit of self-congratulation enacted the Sarbanes-Oxley Act, new forms of insider self-dealing, speculative excess, and gambles with the entire system are continuing to proliferate. Trading ahead of customers, known as "front running," continues to be epidemic. The practice of "spinning," or favored allocation of hot initial public offerings to insiders and preferred business clients, has simply gone further underground. New stock options abuses seem to be reported almost daily.

These exploits filled the financial pages in 2005 and 2006, as if the system had learned nothing from the abuses of the 1990s. And it hadn't. For the most part, the SEC and the other regulatory authorities have remained remarkably complacent. Treasury Secretary Henry Paulson has been the cheerleader for a privately funded task force, the Committee on Capital Markets Regulation, which promotes multiple forms of financial deregulation. The committee's principal underwriter was Hank Greenberg, who was forced to step down as CEO of the insurance giant AIG after a $2.7 billion accounting scandal and other run-ins with regulators. In its first report, in late November 2006, the committee recommended watering down several provisions of the Sarbanes-Oxley Act, further weakening shareholders' right to sue, restricting lawsuits by state attorneys general such as New York's Eliot Spitzer, and limiting the SEC's enforcement powers. The committee's co-chair was R. Glenn Hubbard, a former chairman of President George W. Bush's Council of Economic Advisers. It continues to work closely with major business lobbies to push the deregulatory agenda. The committee has been a cornucopia of funding for friendly academics. As the business lobbies geared up for their massive lobbying campaign to weaken Sarbanes-

Oxley, almost every ill afflicting U.S. capital markets was attributed to the rather mild anti-corruption requirements of the act. Former Democratic Treasury Secretary Robert Rubin, now a senior executive at Citigroup, joined Republicans in pressing for a weakening of the act, at a March 2007 conference sponsored by the U.S. Treasury. Treasury Secretary Henry Paulson was the administration's quarterback of the effort.

Some of the financial industry executives and their academic allies associated with the Committee on Capital Markets Regulation tried to promote a deal in which the key section of the Sarbanes-Oxley Act—Section 404 requiring genuinely independent audits—would be seriously weakened in exchange for auditors being given immunity from investor lawsuits. But the accounting profession, having been badly burned by the Enron scandal, wanted no part of the deal and neither did the SEC.

Sarbanes-Oxley is still sorely needed. An exhaustive compilation by the independent research firm Glass, Lewis & Co. in early 2007 found that in the first year of more stringent audits required under Sarbanes-Oxley, 16 percent of all publicly traded companies were compelled by auditors to report "material weaknesses" in their internal standards for assuring accurate books. By 2006, 1,118 U.S. companies—11 percent—had to make such disclosures, suggesting that inaccurate books are still widespread. Companies reporting sloppy controls underperformed the broad stock market in 2006 by 18 percentage points. The authors of the report commented: "At a time when regulators are proposing less testing of internal controls—and thus less disclosure of weaknesses—we think you'd be left with the same question we have: What are they *thinking*?" (italics in original).

The one legitimate problem with the enforcement of Sarbanes-Oxley has been an overly rigid application of a checklist approach to the auditing of small- and medium-sized companies. At this writing, the Public Company Accounting Oversight Board, which was created by the Sarbanes-Oxley Act, is in the process of working with industry to allow more flexible auditing criteria for small corporations but without gutting the key investor protection provision of the act. Four former chairmen at the SEC, speaking at a Council on Foreign Relations forum in New York in February 2007, warned against exempting any companies from the internal controls provisions of Sarbanes-Oxley. Yet the pressure to water down investor protections continues, and the financial industry plays on fears that New York could lose market share as a financial center to offshore locations. In May 2007, New York Governor Eliot Spitzer, formerly the crusading attorney general who brought to light many of the abuses, appointed a state commission to "Modernize the Regulation of Financial Services." Members include Lloyd Blankfein, chief executive of Goldman Sachs; Charles Prince, chief executive of Citigroup, as well as Stephen Cutler, former director of enforcement of the SEC, and Spitzer's longtime lieutenant, Eric Dinallo, now the state insurance commissioner. No serious observer expects this commission to call for tougher regulation of Wall Street's continuing abuses.

One widely repeated contention was that the requirements of the Sarbanes-Oxley Act were driving deals offshore and weakening New York as the world's preeminent financial center. In this decade, an increasing number of initial public offerings and stock listings have in fact been done in London and in Hong Kong. As part of the lobbying campaign to weaken the act, one of the innumerable articles published on the editorial page of *The Wall Street Journal*, "What Sarbox Wrought," by Jonathan Macey, deputy dean of the Yale Law School, lamented "the relative decline of U.S. capital markets since Sarbox," blaming "the dreaded one-two punch of the U.S. plaintiff's bar and the SEC's regulatory juggernaut." But in fact, this is the most docile SEC in decades, and the commission is already taking steps to exempt small and midsized corporations from many of the Sarbanes-Oxley requirements. And thanks to the very legislation sponsored by then Congressman Christopher Cox, now chair of the SEC, plaintiffs who allege fraud in securities offerings have a much higher bar before they can collect damages. Some juggernaut.

Ironically, the most compelling rebuttal to this set of claims came from Goldman Sachs, the firm formerly headed by the same Henry Paulson. A lengthy report by Goldman's London office debunked the claims that Sarbanes-Oxley was responsible for New York's relative decline, and pointed out that "natural advantages such as time zone, geographic adjacency and language suggest that other strong markets will enjoy strong growth ahead. . . . It seems likely that capital markets outside the U.S. will develop more quickly. In this regard, both London and Hong Kong have natural advantages that New York lacks." The reality is that the U.S. share of all IPOs began a steady decline in the 1990s, from about 60 percent in 1996 to just 8 percent in 2001, before Sarbanes-Oxley was enacted. The domestic share actually increased after Sarbanes-Oxley, to 15 percent by 2005, according to Charles Niemeier, a member of the Public Company Accounting Oversight Board.

In reality, as the United States becomes more and more of a debtor nation and capital markets become deeper and more mature in Europe and Asia, it is only normal that New York should cease to dominate financial transactions. And, indeed, as American investment banking firms have globalized, they have simply followed the business abroad. Morgan Stanley continues to be the world's leading issuer of new stock offerings, even as their location becomes more diversified.

Historically, U.S. financial markets were the gold standard for investors because good financial regulation assured transparency. Corruption is hardly a calling card we should be proud of. One of the worst distortions in the valuation of corporate securities was the series of manipulations caused by the backdating of stock options for senior executives. This abuse came to light only because the maligned Sarbanes-Oxley Act required full disclosure of changes in executive compensation within two days of any change. Previous law had allowed protracted reporting delays, which allowed companies to hide backdating of stock options so effectively that not even the SEC noticed. With the enactment of Sarbanes-Oxley, fraudulent use of stock options came to a halt. Thanks to Sarbanes-Oxley, investors get more accurate information, and markets are more transparent and hence the economy is more efficient because capital is not invested based on misrepresentation and misinformation. In 2006, the requirement for honest bookkeeping led to no fewer than 1,420 U.S. publicly traded companies to file restatements of past financial reports with the SEC. That equaled one public corporation in ten. And despite all the fear-mongering, New York continues to set records for financial transactions. A Thomson Financial survey of Wall Street IPO activity reported that 189 IPOs in 2006 raised a total of nearly $43 billion—another banner year. Despite Sarbanes-Oxley, or maybe thanks to the reassurance that it provided investors, Wall Street executives took home record bonuses in 2006. If executives hate the Sarbanes-Oxley Act, it has far more to do with the act's insistence on honest books than with excess paperwork.

The Subprime Scandal

As 2007 dawned, the new year brought a new financial scandal, and a new risk of systemic contagion. The so-called subprime mortgage lending sector began incurring large losses, bringing heightened risks to the much larger $6.5 trillion mortgage securities market. "Subprime" is the broad term for credit extended to people who would not ordinarily qualify for loans, either because their income is too low to meet the anticipated payments or because of a poor credit history. In the early 2000s, mortgage lenders introduced ever more complex variants on the traditional home mortgage. These included not just variable-rate mortgages, but mortgage loans with no down payment, mortgages with low "teaser" rates that rose after a brief period even if the prevailing interest rate did not; and mortgages, amazingly, that required no credit check. An estimated 60 percent of subprime loans required either no income verification or only the most cursory check.

Mortgage companies were able to make these loans because they did not bear most of the risk. Typically, these mortgages were sold off as soon as the loan closed, and packaged as securities known as collateralized debt obligations (CDOs). The securities carried rates of return supposedly aligned closely to the risk. According to *The Wall Street Journal*, subprime loans increased more than twelvefold, from about $50 billion in 2001 to over $600 billion in 2005. From 2005 to 2006, the value of high-risk mortgage securities more than doubled.

One might have expected trouble to begin when prevailing interest rates went up, but ominously enough, when the subprime sector got into serious difficulty in early 2007, interest rates were flat or falling. One can only imagine how much more dire the losses—to home owners, lenders, investors, and the larger economy—will be in the next round of interest-rate hikes. One industry study projects that about 32 percent of loans with teaser rates of 4 percent or less will be in foreclosure by 2010.

Rather than higher prevailing rates causing increased defaults, two predictable things happened in early 2007. First, thanks to the lax standards, an increasing number of borrowers had undertaken larger obligations than they could financially bear. Any unexpected slight financial reversal could cause them to default on their loans and lose their homes. For many, the end of the teaser period meant they could no longer afford their payments. Second, subprime lenders looking for quick profits had gone ever farther downward into the pool of risky borrowers, increasing the risk of defaults. By March 2007, about 15 percent of subprime loans were in default.

As in the case of so many other financial bubbles of the past decade, this one was driven by the search for abnormally high returns. Wall Street seemed to have forgotten the most elementary of lessons: higher yield is associated with higher risk. And the subprime mortgage brokers were not some set of shady characters one degree above Mafia lenders— they were bankrolled by the most blue-chip names on Wall Street. But these companies did not bear the full risk—they were middlemen, since most of the securities were sold off to investors such as pension funds.

When one of the biggest of the subprime lenders, New Century Financial Corporation, went bankrupt in April 2007, it was revealed that its own biggest creditor was Morgan Stanley. New Century and other subprime mortgage originators were also heavily financed by hedge funds. And the subprime loan debacle had familiar insider conflicts of interest. New Century originated $60 billion worth of mortgages in 2006, second only to London-based HSBC in its volume of subprime loans. The three founders of New Century, perhaps sensing what was to come, cashed out about $103 million of their own stock in the company over four years at an average price of $42.46 per share, much of it in 2006, even as they continued touting it to investors and analysts. As of April 2007, they were under investigation by the SEC for possible insider trading violations. And even in its bankruptcy, New Century generated profits for investment bankers and Wall Street lawyers on both sides of the case—more sheer economic waste.

The lessons are also familiar from other cases of financial excess over the past decade. Both public and private regulation failed. As the early warnings of this saga were unfolding in the financial pages in 2005 and 2006, the regulatory agencies did nothing. Mortgage companies, as opposed to banks and savings and loan associations, are not directly regulated by the federal government. New Century was given a cursory examination in 2006 by California's regulators, who have a staff of just twenty-five to police 4,100 mortgage origination companies, and was given a clean bill of health. As lightly regulated mortgage brokers have taken increasing market share from traditional thrift and banking institutions, only 23 percent of subprime loans in 2005 were originated by federally regulated lenders. This makes perfect sense, since regulated lenders at least worry about government scrutiny. But in this scandal, little was forthcoming. The Federal Reserve had residual authority to investigate abuses that could disturb financial markets, but as the subprime sector got into ever riskier territory, the Fed undertook no investigation and issued exactly one cease-and-desist order against a subprime lender affiliated with a bank.

In principle, the secondary mortgage market, dominated by Fannie Mae and Freddie Mac, polices the standards. Bad loans, supposedly, are not certified by Fannie and Freddie for resale or securitization. But, as we have seen, Fannie Mae was having its own major scandals. And remarkably enough, the agency that monitors Fannie Mae, the Office of Federal Housing Enterprise Oversight, had little interest in the subprime problems. Freddie Mac only tightened its standards in February 2007, after much damage was done. In the meantime, subprime lenders had found ways to package their loans as high-yield securities without Fannie's or Freddie's seal of approval, so the subprime scandal reflected a dual failure. Private markets did not accurately price CDOs and failed to prevent behavior that had serious risks not just for consenting individual investors but for the financial system. And public regulatory agencies, in the hands of close allies on Wall Street who oppose regulation, failed to act.

Only in the spring of 2007 did Congress belatedly begin investigating. And when Congress scheduled hearings, the Mortgage Bankers Association (MBA) defended its most reckless members, using the low-income home buyer as its poster child. Regulating this sector, the association contended, would only deprive some borrowers of credit. When Freddie Mac belatedly tightened standards, MBA chairman John M. Robbins warned that the move "will limit the product options and the access to credit for those individuals most in need, many of whom are first time, underserved or minority homebuyers. The mortgage products that these new standards target are important financial instruments, crucial to helping borrowers get into homes and repair their credit. Regulation that further limits consumer choice is unwarranted."

It was the same argument used to justify the savings and loan excesses of the 1980s. In both cases, the real intent was to make middlemen rich; if some people of modest means got help purchasing homes, that was purely incidental. The mortgage brokers seemed unconcerned that a large fraction of these Americans would lose their homes, as long as the formulas worked and there was good money to be made on average.

If public policy makers wish to help more low-income Americans become home owners, there is a far better approach than relying on sleazy mortgage brokers peddling bait-and-switch products that leave a trail of foreclosure and heartbreak. At other times in our history, the government has offered subsidized mortgages to first-time home buyers, through the VA and FHA. The 3 percent down payment loans offered through FHA have a far lower default rate than those of subprime lenders. Government-backed nonprofits such as Neighborhood Housing Services of America are not in the mortgage business for a quick buck but to counsel low-income home buyers and to work with them for the long haul. Neighborhood Housing Service's foreclosure rate is close to zero.

At times, the government has also stepped in to prevent foreclosures. The Home Owners' Loan Corporation of the mid-1930s worked with homeowners and lenders to encourage forbearance by lenders and renegotiate mortgage terms that allowed hard-pressed home owners to keep their homes in difficult times. Some states, such as North Dakota, created state banks and legislated temporary moratoria on foreclosures. Had the fate of home owners been left to private markets, there would have been a cascade of foreclosures and an even deeper collapse of local housing markets. Today, there is no national Great Depression, but there is a severe depression in some local housing markets requiring more than the tender mercies of private creditors. In early 2007, Ohio, with the nation's highest foreclosure rate, passed a $100 million bond issue to refinance mortgages.

In housing policy, the road not taken includes sound underwriting standards coupled with subsidized mortgages and starter homes, as well as credit counseling, to help new home buyers. Decent housing for moderate-income people requires social subsidy, not just market gymnastics and the quest for the quick buck. Government aid also moderates housing prices, since it adds to the housing supply. But even as markets brace for the wider fallout of this latest financial excess, and regulators belatedly tighten standards, these fundamental lessons seem not to have been learned.

Legal Scandal: The Mutual Fund Industry

One very large player figured only marginally in the scandals of the 1990s, the $7 trillion mutual fund industry. There has been relatively little exposure of wrongdoing and even less reform when it comes to mutual funds—because, in the immortal words of former *New Republic* editor Michael Kinsley, the scandal is what's legal.

The more than six thousand mutual funds hold the assets of over 100 million small investors and pensioners. The legal scandal comes in two parts. The first is the exorbitant amount of money that flows to mutual fund managers at investors' expense. The Investment Company Act of 1940, which governs mutual funds, explicitly requires them to be operated in the interests of their shareholders "rather than in the interests of their managers and distributors." Yet the amount of money taken from investors by mutual fund company managers is outsized and little appreciated.

John Bogle, the retired founder of the Vanguard Group, has become a crusader for reform of his industry. Bogle calculates that between 1950 and 2004, the assets held in mutual funds increased more than a thousandfold, from about $2 billion to more than $8 trillion. One might have expected that as the amount of funds under management grew, economies of scale would reduce the expense ratio paid by investors to fund managers. In fact, the expense ratio more than doubled. Because of the miracle of compounding, mutual fund transaction costs and other fees consume a far higher percentage of returns than most investors realize. According to Bogle, "Equity fund investors paid costs estimated at $72 billion in 2004 alone, and as much as $300 billion in the past five years."

The net return of the average mutual fund was substantially lower than the average return of the stock market, not because the funds' very expensive advisers were bad stock pickers—their gross returns just about matched that of the broad market—but because of the huge transaction costs and profits to managers. Between 1985 and 2004, Bogle calculates, the average mutual fund annual return, not adjusted for inflation, was 10.4 percent. That sounds good until you realize that the comparable return from the stock market itself was 13.2 percent. The difference was the mutual fund fees. The ordinary investor would have been better off using a dartboard to select a random basket of stocks or investing in a broad-based, low-fee index fund.

Bogle reports that $10,000 invested randomly in the stock market in 1984 would have returned an average profit of $109,800 by 2004. The same money placed in the average mutual fund would have returned a far smaller profit of $62,900. He observes, "[T]he investor put up 100 percent of the capital and assumed 100 percent of the risk, but collected only 57 percent of the profit. The mutual fund management and distribution system put up zero capital and assumed zero percent of the risk, but collected 43 percent of the return." Timing can make that split even worse. During the boom and bust of 1997–2002, mutual fund managers collected $250 billion, while millions of investors suffered a net loss.

The second part of the legal scandal helps explain the excesses of the first. Although mutual fund managers are perfectly positioned to be agents of small investors, they fail utterly to serve investors' interests in a more transparent system. When I served on the staff of the Senate Banking Committee, you could count on the mutual fund lobby, the Investment Company Institute, to be on the wrong side of every consumer and regulatory issue. Nothing has changed. Bogle reports that not a single mutual fund has ever sponsored a proxy resolution opposed by management, supported efforts to reform option compensation, or testified in favor of the Sarbanes-Oxley Act.

When the SEC in 2003 put out for comment a proposal requiring mutual funds to disclose to their owners how they had cast their proxy votes, the industry united in opposition to the idea. The regulation was adopted in 2004 over the industry's objection, and it has actually led to a modest increase in shareholder activism directed against excessive CEO compensation.

Current law requires a majority of mutual fund directors to be independent of the fund's managers. But the independent directors are among the best compensated and most docile on Wall Street and invariably do what management wants. One study reported that the average compensation to mutual fund directors, for attending a few meetings a year, was $386,000. The superinvestor Warren Buffett once criticized the activity of independent mutual fund directors as "a zombie-like process that makes a mockery of stewardship." Buffett added, "A monkey will type-out Shakespeare before an 'independent' board will vote to replace management."

After the Enron scandals, a reformer, William Donaldson, briefly served as SEC chairman. In 2003, the Donaldson SEC, by a 3–2 vote, issued a proposed regulation that would have required that 75 percent of mutual fund directors, including the chairman, be independent of the management company that organizes, markets, and profits from the fund and that the independent directors meet separately at least quarterly. This was opposed by the mutual fund industry and the U.S. Chamber of Commerce, which represents large corporations and successfully sued to block the regulation.

Mutual funds themselves have not been immune to corruption. In 2003, Eliot Spitzer brought civil charges against four major mutual management fund companies for "market timing" and other forms of late trading: executing trades after U.S. markets had closed, based on breaking news events that influenced foreign markets that were still open, which accurately predicted the direction of the next day's market in New York. These illegal trades were primarily for the benefit of managers. Putnam Investments, one of the industry's largest fund sponsors, paid a fine of $193 million. Bank of America paid $600 million. All told, 24 mutual fund management companies paid a total of $2.5 billion in fines by mid-2004. One academic study estimated that market timing abuses cost ordinary investors on the order of $4 billion and that the practice had been common for at least two decades before regulators were pushed to intervene. Fund managers have also taken bribes to promote favored funds to their retail customers.

Financial conglomerates that own mutual funds also frequently promote their own funds to retail customers, giving sales incentives to brokers. Morgan Stanley paid $70 million in fines for such practices, and Merrill Lynch and Citigroup are targets of class action suits.

The abuses of the mutual fund industry nicely illustrate how self-regulation and the premise of "agency" break down on Wall Street. In theory, mutual funds could solve the problem of the atomized shareholders failing to hold corporate management accountable. In practice, mutual fund managers are doing very nicely and don't want to rock the boat.

Mutual funds are a sleeping giant. If their own outside directors were to push them to become more active on behalf of corporate governance, it could shake up corporate America. The reformers' longtime dream of having boards truly hold top managers accountable might come closer to reality. One awaits a set of "Bogle Principles," modeled on the Sullivan Principles of the late 1970s and the 1980s, in which activists and shareholders pressed American corporations to use their leverage to bring racial reform to South Africa. Under the Bogle Principles, investors would put their money only into mutual funds that had genuinely independent directors and that used their political influence to lobby for, rather than against, systemic reforms.

Into the Stratosphere

Despite the contrition and reformism that briefly pervaded Wall Street after the collapse of 2000–01, the abuses of executive compensation only intensified. Exorbitant pay for chief executives continued to soar, unrelated to corporate performance. Stock options, always a somewhat questionable way to supposedly align the interests of shareholders and executives, frequently turned out to be rigged so that the executive would get the bonus whether or not the company met performance targets.

By the end of 2006, the SEC and the Justice Department were investigating more than 150 major corporations for backdating options awards given to chief executives. Backdating ensures that a bonus payout is guaranteed. A variation on this abuse was called "reloading." If the stock did not perform in a way that produced the expected benefit, the board would simply rescind the old options and structure new ones to ensure the desired benefits.

Since the whole premise of options compensation is to reward executives for company performance, it would be hard to imagine a more cynical money grab or default on the part of the corporate board. A study by the finance professors Randall A. Heron and Erik Lie found that 14 percent of options grants to senior executives between 1996 and 2005 were backdated or manipulated. And even options grants that were not backdated often gave windfall bonuses unrelated to actual performance.

In one high-profile case, William McGuire, the chief executive officer of UnitedHealth Group, was forced out in October 2006 after a seven-month investigation by an outside law firm ordered by his board under SEC and Justice Department pressure. The investigation revealed that "most of the 29 stock grants" accounting for gains running into the hundreds of millions of dollars over a twelve-year period had been deliberately backdated, with each being timed to be granted just before a spike in the company stock. That way, McGuire was guaranteed a payout after the fact. An analysis by *The Wall Street Journal* calculated the odds of the dating occurring randomly at 200 million to one. McGuire's total take was about $1.1 billion, the highest windfall ever captured by a corporate chief executive.

The outside report by the law firm Wilmer Cutler Pickering Hale and Dorr also found that the director responsible for signing off on options negotiations, William G. Spears, had close financial connections to McGuire. Spears served as the personal investment manager for McGuire and his family, and in 2006 his firm managed about $55 million of McGuire's fortune. He also served as trustee for two trusts set up for McGuire's children. Spears was also forced to resign. Spears and McGuire told investigators that the board had been aware of this conflict of interest. But no written record of that disclosure existed, and other board members disclaimed knowledge of it.

When the board of UnitedHealth Group forced McGuire to step down, it named McGuire's protégé Stephen J. Hemsley, a man apparently untainted by the backdating fraud, as the new CEO. The board was subsequently embarrassed when the financial press pointed to an item buried deep in the lawyers' report. When Hemsley joined the company in June 1997, he was awarded 400,000 stock options. But they were dated five months earlier, mooting the premise that there was an incentive to produce and netting Hemsley an instant windfall of about $3 million. There's nothing wrong with a signing bonus, but this one was deliberately concealed from shareholders.

The latest options abuses underscore the continuing corporate efforts to deceive shareholders and the public. It is legal for a corporate board to grant options that allow executives to reap exorbitant gains from options or stocks. The timing of the options need not be backdated in order for that windfall to occur. For example, if a stock is trading at $50 a share, a board could vote the CEO options to buy shares at $10 a share, or it could just vote the CEO bonus compensation by giving additional stock shares.

Why then did so many CEOs, with the collusion of their boards, opt for backdating? The answer is found in pesky accounting and disclosure regulations. If you give a CEO $20 million worth of stock, or options guaranteed to produce a $20 million gain, that gift has to be disclosed and charged against current earnings. That might raise eyebrows and might even reduce the current value of the stock. But if you backdate existing options, you can hide the gift.

CEOs' options compensation now equals about nine times their compensation in salaries, benefits, and bonuses. The continued upward spiral in CEOs' pay, which paused only briefly after the millennial stock market tumble, has been mainly in the form of options. No wonder CEOs wanted to conceal them from public scrutiny.

The newest wave of options scandals, some predating the stock market bubble and supposed reforms but continuing into the new decade, shows how feeble the reforms actually are. Among other goals, the Sarbanes-Oxley reforms supposedly strengthened the accountability to corporate boards, which are ostensibly the representatives of shareholders. But the upward-spiraling executive pay and the crony infestation of boards show how little has really changed. CEOs got these gains with the full complicity of boards.

The Flawed Accountability of Trading Markets

A core question is whether the liberation of speculative finance truly makes American capitalism more efficient. In the usual story, America is uniquely dynamic because it rewards entrepreneurs and has deep and innovative capital markets. However, none of these legitimate rewards depends on the corrupt enrichment of insiders. On the contrary, they divert investment capital from truly productive uses and skew rewards.

The function of capital markets is to connect investors with entrepreneurs. Investment bankers take a legitimate cut when they evaluate, price, and market shares of enterprises to the investing public. But none of these activities requires the conflicts of interest that have proliferated in recent years; their main function is to give insiders a quick killing, often at the expense of arm's-length investors and at the efficient pricing of financial assets. In the case of a company such as Intelsat, the theft of pension fund assets (and there have been hundreds of such cases) has nothing to do with economic efficiency. It is simply about transferring wealth that legitimately belongs to retirees to quick-buck temporary owners.

If the real concern was the accountability of corporate executives to shareholders (and other stakeholders), there was a path not taken—a path hardly even considered. This other path would subject corporate managers to much greater institutional accountability, but without the breakup and recombination of entire companies as paper assets, heedless of their role as collectivities of real people in real communities.

In the economist Albert Hirschman's famous formulation, there are two forms of accountability, Exit and Voice. In our economy, a shareholder unhappy with management's performance nearly always expresses that preference by exiting—selling the stock—because stockholders have no effective voice. Exit is indeed one option throughout society. Immigrants who move to a new country, parents who remove a child from a failing school, workers frustrated by a hostile boss, a spouse walking out of a contentious marriage, all are voting with their feet. But, as Hirschman notes, the alternative to Exit is Voice. This is especially important in a democratic polity, which presumes a continuing existence. Citizens express voice through their elected representatives. Members of a local school board and parents who appear before it are expressing preferences via voice. Trade unionism is a form of voice.

In our capitalist democracy, the great exception to democratic voice is the business corporation. The economist David Ellerman has written of how the history of democracy, from the eighteenth century onward, democratized the polity but not the business enterprise. The corporation is an explicit autocracy. Its workers have no rights as stakeholders unless they have a union. Property ownership trumps the "sweat equity" contributed by workers, who can be terminated at will.

Ironically, the sponsors of greater worker power via ownership ended up empowering financial engineers instead, in a reflection of where the real political power lay. In the late 1950s, an economic visionary, Louis Kelso, proposed tax-favored employee stock ownership plans (ESOPs), through which workers would eventually control a large portion of shareholding wealth. Workers would thus gain influence over corporations, not in their role as employees but as owners. In 1974, Kelso sold the idea to the then chairman of the Senate Finance Committee, Russell Long, son of the populist demagogue Huey Long. Changes in the law were duly enacted to allow tax favoritism to ESOPs and other forms of stock transfer that relied on borrowed money. But as things worked out, it was Kohlberg Kravis Roberts (KKR), one of the original private-equity firms, that figured out how to maximize the use of this tax loophole to buy and sell entire corporations for private gain, while ESOPs benefiting workers languished as a minor appendage.

Elsewhere, inventions in corporate governance, such as German-style works councils and codetermination provisions, mandate employee representation on corporate boards. The idea is to empower other stakeholders besides shareholders. In the United States, we largely fail to empower even shareholders. With rare exceptions, atomized shareholders have too little coordinated capacity to influence management by collective voice. Proxy fights are unusual because the rules have been written to favor incumbent management.

Another option is what some scholars have termed the "blockholding" (as opposed to shareholding) model of corporate governance. In some countries, huge blocks of shares are held by banks or by interlocking corporations that are part of the same industrial group and do not freely trade on stock exchanges. In Germany and Japan, for instance, banks are a much more potent force in corporate ownership and governance than in the United States. In recent decades, the percentage of stocks owned by institutions, such as pension funds, mutual funds, and hedge funds, has grown dramatically in the United States. By 2001, they held more than 60 percent of all outstanding shares. But with the exception of a minority of activist public pension funds like California's CalPERS, most institutional investors in the United States do not behave like owners. They act more as traders, seeking short-term gain.

There are both advantages and disadvantages to the blockholding system. An advantage is that the executives can be held accountable without the constant churning and breakup of entire companies. A disadvantage is that there is typically less of a role for new risk-bearing capital. Yet despite the greater institutional stability, or perhaps because of it, plenty of innovation occurs where it matters in Germany and Japan—in innovative technologies and production processes. Germany and Japan continue gaining market share on the United States in industry after industry. Big banks, at least in Germany, think of themselves more as stewards. Ironically, a German market-liberalization reform passed in the 1990s intended to reduce the banks' role in order to attract more equity capital has opened highly efficient German industrial corporations to asset-stripping raids by hedge funds. And as the Japanese recession of the 1990s suggests, a bank-dominated system can generate its own dysfunctional behavior and its own corruption. No society has yet devised an ideal form of internal corporate self-governance, and government regulation of the entire market system is a necessary check on corporate excess.

It surprises many Americans to realize that the legal regime that governs the modern corporation is not much more than a century old and is not the only possible one. As late as the 1890s, many states demanded that corporations serve public purposes and strictly regulated their internal governance in exchange for the limited liability granted to general corporations in their charters. It was after the Supreme Court, in 1886, held that corporations enjoyed the same rights as "persons" under the Fourteenth Amendment that states began a true race to the bottom. In the 1870s and 1880s, John D. Rockefeller and other magnates devised holding companies, known as trusts, to get around the limitations of state corporation law, which limited corporate activity to a single state. By the 1880s, these trusts were being used to allow Rockefeller's oil trusts, and his imitators in the steel, sugar, beef, rail, and tobacco industries, both to operate nationally and to buy out or crush competitors.

A backlash against the abuses of holding companies led to the federal Sherman Antitrust Act of 1890. But as the act was moving through Congress, the state of New Jersey helpfully amended its chartering law to allow friendly treatment of corporations that wanted to continue to use interstate holding companies. Most of the trusts soon became New Jersey corporations. When a reform governor, Woodrow Wilson, acted to close some of the loopholes, Delaware adopted the original New Jersey law and added a few new wrinkles sheltering management from government, creditor, and shareholder scrutiny. Delaware quickly became the corporate domicile of choice and has continued to lead the race to the bottom in corporate chartering standards. From there it was a quick journey to the insider corporation run on behalf of its managers and banker allies, described so well by Berle and Means less than half a century later.

But the cure is not to turn corporations and their employees and communities into fungible assets, on the auction block all the time. As William Greider has observed, the corporation is not the marketplace. Rather, it is a kind of "shelter from the storms of the marketplace . . . a long-running collaboration, not a daily auction." Yet the preeminence of finance over enterprise is wrecking the corporation as a community of collaborators with long-term stakes.

The spectacular failure of some of the biggest merger deals, and the gap between CEOs' pay and performance, are testament to the feeble role of corporate boards. A study that reviewed the 302 mergers consummated between July 1995 and August 2001 found that the average return was a negative 4.3 percent and that 61 percent of the acquiring companies underperformed peer corporations by an average of 25 percent. This poor performance was not the result of the stock market bust. Other studies showed similar results during the boom years. Acquiring companies often overpay, a problem known as the winner's curse. The motivation is often to enhance the compensation and power of the CEO rather than to serve shareholders.

Even if there were very substantial accountability to shareholders, that would solve only a small part of the challenge of prudent and equitable regulation of capitalism. John Bogle's 2005 book, *The Battle for the Soul of Capitalism*, proposes several regulatory reforms. He would drastically limit stock option compensation, give more power to nonmanagement directors, impose tighter regulation on mutual fund governance, and prohibit a broad range of conflicts of interest. He favors far stronger federal or state regulation of corporations and even has a kind word for the Glass-Steagall Act. Bogle's call to action—literally—is "Owners of the World, Unite."

But reflect further on that bold credo, and you'll realize that it isn't enough. Ownership of shares is astonishingly concentrated. As recently as 1981, "only" 35.8 percent of capital income went to the wealthiest 1 percent of Americans. By 2003, that concentration had increased to 57.5 percent, according to the Congressional Budget Office. Corporate "democracy" by and for the top 1 percent would just be a slightly broader plutocracy.

A balanced and equitable society requires more than a revolution in shareholder power. Just as there was much more to the excesses of the 1920s than a failure of accountability to small investors, the corruption of the 1980s and 1990s went far deeper than the disempowerment of the shareholder. Indeed, many of the worst abuses were perpetrated in the name of "maximizing shareholder value." The deeper problem was a political failure to hold financial markets and corporations accountable to society as a whole, not just to investors.

The remedies launched in the Roosevelt era likewise went far beyond the SEC schema of greater transparency. The New Deal promoted not just disclosure but a far broader strategy to limit the political power of concentrated wealth, to rein in financial conflicts of interest, to use social outlay to complement and constrain private capital, and to assist the fledgling labor movement. The need was to create multiple political and economic counterweights to the abuses of laissez-faire and concentrated financial power, not just to liberate shareholders.

In our own era, there has been a broad political failure to connect these several dots. The deregulation of financial markets, which in turn invited the Wall Street scandals, is of a piece with the weakening of the public sector, the labor movement, and democratic citizenship. At bottom, the problem is the political hegemony of finance. "The market needs a place," wrote the moderately liberal economist Arthur Okun, "and the market needs to be kept in its place." That is not the same as calling for shareholder democracy, which is, in the end, a call for more perfect financial markets.

Weak Politics, Weak Remedies

Every time another crisis hits Wall Street, commentators cry out for systemic reform: more accountability of managers to boards; of boards to shareholders; of corporations to social standards. Some recent proposals would require that a majority of corporate board members be nonmanagement directors, that the job of chief executive officer and board chairman be separated, and that rival directors or slates of directors be easier for shareholders to elect. The point of these and similar reforms is to minimize the conflicts of interest—failures of "agency"—that currently invite managers to serve their own well-being rather than that of shareholders and other clients.

In the current political climate, these proposals invariably fail to win enactment. The stock exchanges are too reliant on the goodwill of the same CEOs. The SEC either is dominated by corporate interests or lacks the nerve. And when it does muster the nerve, it is often overruled by Congress or the courts.

There is also immense resistance to such reforms within the corporate culture. Greater self-policing by the corporation is wildly improbable in today's political climate. New York University Business School professors Roy Smith and Ingo Warner, authors of a recent scholarly book on corporate governance, write:

> Most analyses of director independence fail to recognize the social dynamics of corporate boards, which often serve to persuade their members that the real purpose of outside directors is to support man-

agement and the company as good team players. Board members usually have little contact with each other outside the boardroom, but each has a carefully cultivated relationship with the CEO, who has usually recruited some of the board members—often selecting those who have reason to appreciate the appointment. . . . Any board member who may prove to be difficult can be isolated, given less information than others, or not nominated for reelection.

Genuine reform of corporate governance would require a political transformation. The fact that deeper reform did not occur even in the wake of the scandals of the 1990s suggests something of the obstacles.

To the extent that a nascent movement exists in the United States for greater management accountability and corporate social responsibility and reform of corporate governance, it is mostly a minor distraction. The movement is made up of diverse factions with somewhat different goals. As weak as they are, they often fail to talk even to one another, and they are overwhelmed by the power of the usual suspects.

For instance, the "socially responsible" mutual funds that invest only in corporations with good environmental or labor records play no organized role in the other reform movement that works to render corporations more accountable to their shareholders. An admirable group of CEOs called Business for Social Responsibility emphasizes decent treatment of workers and sensitivity to the environment but does not get involved in SEC issues of corporate governance.

If you look at the participants in a typical SEC or congressional hearing exploring whether to tighten, say, proxy rules to encourage more contested elections for board members or the governance structure of mutual funds, or whether to increase the regulation of hedge funds, you will find an astonishing asymmetry of participants that unfortunately reflects the political reality. On one side you will typically find every major investment bank and commercial bank; every major mutual fund and hedge fund; the U.S. Chamber of Commerce, representing nonfinancial business corporations; and the Business Roundtable, representing the CEOs of America's largest corporations. Even the trade association of accountants, the AICPA, typically weighs in against democratization of corporate governance, because it wants to get along with its clients.

On the other side of the debate, hopelessly outgunned, is the occasional liberal member of the SEC or, even more infrequently, the occasional Republican conservative steward of a transparent system; a tiny trade association called the Council of Institutional Investors, representing public employee pension funds; some of those funds themselves, such as CalPERS; a few assertive state treasurers or controllers, such as New York's former controller Alan Hevesi, some attorneys general, such as Connecticut's Richard Blumenthal; and the AFL-CIO and its larger member unions, some of which have partial control over union pension funds under the Landrum-Griffin Act of 1959. But union and public employee pension funds together hold less than 5 percent of the total funds invested on Wall Street.

It is emblematic that the only large financial players who reliably support greater accountability of corporations are the two that come from the extramarket parts of the system—the parts that exist as explicit counterweights to private profit: the pension funds representing the public sector and those representing unions. Everyone else is a member of the same club.

What about countervailing power within the financial community? Why do regulated mutual funds that are losing business to hedge funds generally defend the right of far more reckless hedge funds to be unregulated? Why do mutual funds, representing millions of small shareholders, resist regulations that might lead to more accountable corporate boards, better financial standards, and a safer and more accountable investing environment? Why are accountants, of all people, not a lobby for greater transparency? Why are the stock exchanges not crusaders for reform of the governance of the companies whose shares they list? You might call it a class solidarity of insiders. The less the whole affair is subject to regulation, sunlight, and accountability, the more money insiders can make.

The stunning weakness of the movement to rein in the power of financial capital is reflected in the docile Democratic Party. The most assertive and best-informed Democrat on issues of financial regulation, Senator Paul Sarbanes of Maryland, the longtime chair of the Senate Banking Committee, retired in 2006. It was only Sarbanes's tenacity that produced the 2002 Sarbanes-Oxley bill. Representative Michael Oxley and the Republicans, who had strenuously opposed further regulation, clambered on board only after the WorldCom collapse, when they had no political alternative. Sarbanes's successor, Christopher Dodd of Connecticut, is a relative liberal on other issues but a close ally of Wall Street. Dodd was one of the Democrats who voted to overturn Bill Clinton's veto in 1995 of the legislation that made it much more difficult for defrauded shareholders to sue. Dodd is one of the leading recipients of financial industry campaign contributions in the Senate. The ranking Democrat on the crucial Subcommittee on Securities is Chuck Schumer of New York, another liberal on social issues and one of Wall Street's best friends in Congress. He is extremely close to the major New York banks and investment houses, especially to the New York Stock Exchange. Schumer has never promoted tough financial regulation opposed by major banks and investment houses.

When Clinton's SEC chairman Arthur Levitt proved to be a somewhat tougher regulator than either Clinton or Wall Street had bargained for, having tried to restrict some (though hardly all) of the conflicts of interest that caused the stock bubble and ensuing crash, Schumer was among those who threatened to cut Levitt's appropriations. And in case the occasional fellow Democrat is tempted to stray, Schumer happens to be chair of the Democratic Senatorial Campaign Committee, which doles out campaign contributions and makes introductions to individual wealthy donors. Deeper structural reform has almost no chance, via conventional politics, of making it onto the legislative agenda or even the Democratic platform.

Even after the scandal-ridden 1990s, during a brief reform era at the SEC when Chairman William Donaldson attempted some modest reforms, Democratic legislators joined Republicans in trying to block them. When the Financial Accounting Standards Board, another of the weak self-regulatory institutions, issued a standard in December 2004 requiring that stock options be expensed (treated as current outlays), the House of Representatives voted to block this move, 312–111. Even Nancy Pelosi, the generally liberal Democratic House leader, criticized the regulation. Pelosi is from San Francisco, and options are especially popular in Silicon Valley. But the Senate did not act, the SEC backed the FASB, and the ruling took effect. However, this step is only the bare beginning of reform and thus far has had little effect on the appetite for stock options of CEOs and their tame corporate boards.

In 2003, during Donaldson's brief tenure as SEC chairman, the commission invited comment on a proposal to allow shareholders to nominate opposition candidates to corporate boards. Current law provides that shareholders, in casting proxies, may withhold their votes on management candidates in annual elections to corporate boards, but may not sponsor or vote for competing candidates. State and local pension funds were major supporters of this reform, but the commission never acted. Consequently, the management slate nearly always wins. The only way to replace incumbent management is by an all-out proxy war for control or the ever-popular hostile takeover.

Donaldson had been appointed in the wake of the stock scandals after Bush's first SEC chairman, the former accounting industry lobbyist Harvey Pitt, had repeatedly embarrassed himself by downplaying the seriousness of the wrongdoing. After Donaldson spent a year promoting modestly tougher regulation, he abruptly resigned under pressure from the Bush White House, after extensive lobbying by the U.S. Chamber of Commerce.

At the epicenter of the Democrats' weakness on financial regulation is their leading voice on economic policy, the same Robert Rubin who headed Goldman Sachs before becoming a Clinton cabinet official and who is currently a top executive of Citigroup. Rubin is held in personal high regard because of the economic performance of the Clinton administration, which is mistakenly attributed to Rubin's policy of putting balancing the budget ahead of all other goals (more on that in chapter six).

Rubin is personally underwriting the Brookings Institution's signature initiative on the U.S. economy, the Hamilton Project, which stresses budget balance, free trade, and reining in Social Security and Medicare. Leading Democratic candidates seek his advice. Rubin, however, is simultaneously offering ideas for the Democrats' next presidential campaign and administration while using his bipartisan Washington access to look out for Citigroup's corporate interests. He is not paid $30 million a year by Citigroup to advance tougher regulation.

In the Bush era, there is said to be a wide gulf between the two political parties. But Goldman Sachs also contributed two top Bush economic officials, Stephen Friedman, director of Bush's National Economic Council, and Henry Paulson, now the Treasury secretary. When Bush named Paulson, the appointment drew rave reviews. After going through two somewhat ineffectual ex-industrialists to head the Treasury, Bush had finally found a serious Wall Street man, press accounts wrote. Never mind that Goldman Sachs had been implicated in the scandals along with the others, paying fines and penalties totaling $110 million. Its blue-chip reputation evidently remained intact.

Nothing quite so perfectly personifies the hegemony of Wall Street as the utterly bipartisan role of Goldman Sachs. Many in the financial industry wondered why Paulson took the job. In late 2006, part of the answer emerged: Paulson was serving as the administration's point man for an industry coalition seeking to undermine the already far too weak structure of financial regulation.

The Complicity of the Federal Reserve

For the past two decades, the story has been one of regulators bailing out speculators with easy money and regulatory indulgence, increasing systemic costs and risks. Our economy has dodged several bullets thanks to a degree of government intervention totally at odds with the prevailing ideology. The ideology says: Leave markets alone. But organized business doesn't really want that result. Business hates regulation of risky practices but depends on bailouts after the fact. Despite the disparagement of government regulation by financial elites and their political and intellectual allies, it is government that permits their current strategy of self-enrichment by ever-riskier behavior to persist without producing a 1929-scale depression. As noted, the key player is the Federal Reserve.

In 2005, an unlikely fan of interventionist government, the late Milton Friedman, at age ninety-three, published a paper in the *Journal of Economic Perspectives* congratulating the Federal Reserve, under Alan Greenspan, for using aggressive monetary intervention to keep the 2000–01 financial panic from cascading into a general depression, as the Fed of 1929 had so clearly failed to do. It was almost as if the libertarian Friedman had forgotten that the Fed is part of the government.

Friedman's paper, his last piece of original research in a remarkable career, explored a natural experiment. He closely compared central bank performance in the United States in the financial crises of 1929 and of 2001 and that of Japan's central bank in the 1990s. According to Friedman, Japan's bank and the 1929 Fed flunked; they let their economies slip into self-deepening deflation. It was Friedman whose authoritative *Monetary History of the United States* had blamed much of the Great Depression on the Fed's failure to act.

Evidently, the government had learned something in seven decades. "Monetary policy," his 2005 paper concluded, "deserves much credit for the mildness of the recession that followed the collapse of the U.S. boom in late 2000." Friedman, as is his penchant, emphasized the Fed's success in combating inflation. But inflation was hardly the problem in 2001—in fact, the economy was on the verge of dangerous deflation. The Federal Reserve of the Greenspan era did far more than keep prices stable; when crises hit, it flooded the system with liquidity, and it made a series of hands-on interventions to rescue specific banks and investment houses and the system itself. It was the most interventionist Fed ever. Friedman, in spite of himself, acknowledged in this paper that capitalism requires massive government intervention at its financial core.

By mopping up the mistakes of Wall Street geniuses who lost huge gambles with other people's money, the modern Federal Reserve has overruled markets in a number of ways, most of them going well beyond the Fed's ostensible charter. In the stock market crashes of 1987 and 2000–01, the Fed flooded money markets with liquidity, persuaded bankers to keep lending, and effectively commandeered private financial institutions to keep credit flowing. In fact, the Federal Reserve System since the early 1980s, under Volcker and Greenspan, aggressively intervened in the economy more than a dozen times to countermand catastrophic market-driven disasters that could have caused repeats of the Great Depression.

The Volcker Federal Reserve bent the regulatory rules in the early 1980s, after speculative Third World loan losses left every major money center bank technically insolvent. Had the Federal Reserve and the other bank regulatory agencies followed the normal practice and marked down nonpaying loans to their true market value, the banks would have been far below their required reserve ratios. They would have had to call in loans, creating a credit crunch, or raise new equity at a time when few people wanted to buy bank stocks.

The banks, having ignored history, convinced themselves that a sovereign state could not go broke. They had overmarketed loans to Latin American and other Third World borrowers. Reversing the usual pattern of borrowers going to creditors hat in hand, bankers practically begged finance ministers of obscure countries to take on more debt. This was the aftermath of the oil shocks of the 1970s and the game of what was termed "petrodollar recycling." With Washington's encouragement, the big New York banks accepted deposits from the swollen treasuries of oil-producing nations. These were then lent out, and a lot of the money went to Third World countries struggling to pay higher oil bills. This system was a very good deal for the banks and sustainable as long as interest rates stayed manageable. But then inflation spiked, largely the result of the same increase in oil prices. And the Third World debt overhang abruptly collided with Volcker's sudden shift, in 1979, to very high interest rates.

In this new climate, Mexico and other nations were unable to roll over debts that were coming due. In August 1982, the Mexican finance minister, Jesús Silva Herzog, contacted both the Fed and the Treasury to advise that Mexico was almost out of reserves and could not pay its foreign debt, $80 billion all told. If a default of this scale occurred, investors would pull out of other Latin American nations, and money center banks would collapse. Despite the Reagan administration's general enthusiasm for market discipline, this was not seen as a good outcome. The Fed, working with the Treasury and the International Monetary Fund (IMF), arranged a huge bailout. To receive new loans with which to repay old ones, Mexico had to agree to a devastating austerity program. It was the lenders and bondholders who benefited from the rescue, not Mexico.

By the end of 1983, fourteen other nations faced the same formula: domestic belt-tightening in order to finance a new round of loans at higher interest rates by foreign banks, an austerity program leading to what Latin Americans would call the "lost decade" of development. Although many loans were ultimately settled at around seventy cents on the dollar or less, the Fed and other U.S. bank regulatory agencies refrained during the crisis from requiring the money center banks to mark down their loan portfolios to their actual, diminished value, which would have inconveniently signaled insolvency.

The crisis was the child of deregulation. It could occur only because the Fed and the other regulators, in the 1970s, had encouraged petrodollar recycling, permitting money center banks to profit from risky Third World loans and other forms of speculative lending. It was exacerbated by Volcker's decision to fight inflation with a sudden shock of very tight money, which greatly increased interest burdens. High interest rates were the only medicine available in the absence of more selective regulatory policies that might have addressed inflation sector by sector.

The Fed was even more interventionist in the stock market crash of 1987. In percentage terms, the market collapse of October 19, 1987, was far worse than the crash of October 29, 1929, the market losing 22.6 percent of its value in a single day. The one-day crash in 1929 lost only 11.7 percent. And more equity was wiped out, relative to GDP, in the bust of 2000–01 than in the extended great crash of 1929–30. In each of these cases, Greenspan persuaded his colleagues to intervene very actively, stretching the limits of the law, to keep the markets from destroying themselves.

When the stock market tanked, just weeks into Greenspan's tenure, the new chairman, working closely with Gerald Corrigan, president of the Federal Reserve Bank of New York, importuned commercial banks to keep lending to brokerages that were technically underwater. The entire credit system was on the verge of seizing up, as panicky brokers resisted paying short-term debts to other brokers. The Fed, with its knowledge of history, basically guaranteed payment.

In a single day, almost a trillion dollars of paper wealth had been wiped out. Early the next morning, Greenspan issued a very carefully worded one-sentence statement: "The Federal Reserve, consistent with its responsibilities as the nation's central bank, affirmed today its readiness to serve as a source of liquidity to support the economic and financial system." Behind the scenes, Corrigan phoned the heads of banks and brokerage houses. The payments system was at risk. Brokerages settle their accounts every day, and on this day brokerages owed one another many billions of dollars. Some were delaying payment, uncertain as to whether they would be paid and who would be in business after the crash. The stock market had momentarily seized up. Sell orders, even for blue-chip stocks, could not fetch buyers at any price, and the vaunted system of "specialists" did not have the capital to maintain a normal market artificially. Trading in nearly two hundred stocks came to a temporary halt. The markets barely stayed open. But the Fed rose to the rescue, convincing banks to keep lending, backed by cheap credit from the nation's central bank. The Fed could not order payments to be made—indeed, Corrigan was exceeding his authority by making the calls at all—but Corrigan could strongly hint that the Fed would flood the system with liquidity and that panicky brokers had better not create a self-fulfilling prophecy of mutual collapse. Once again, this was a crisis that market forces could not handle.

Again in 1990, an examination by the FDIC found that Wall Street's largest bank, Citibank, was effectively insolvent. Citi was still reeling from its losses on Third World loans and had gotten itself deeper in trouble with a series of bad real estate loans and costly acquisitions. The bank needed close to $5 billion in new capital in order to cover its bad loans and avoid insolvency. But how do you float new stock at a time when investors are aware that your bank is underwater?

Gerald Corrigan, still president of the New York Federal Reserve Bank, held a highly confidential meeting with Citibank CEO John Reed. Corrigan calculated the infusion needed, and secretly went to Saudi Arabia to meet with one of Citi's largest shareholders, Prince Alwaleed bin Talal. The prince agreed to put up another $1.2 billion and to abide by a secret agreement to play the role of a purely passive investor, since an Arab takeover of New York's largest bank, despite protestations of letting the markets reign, was politically unthinkable. Citi, in turn, had to agree to detailed supervision by the Fed, the FDIC, and the Office of the Comptroller of the Currency while the bank raised more capital and worked off its bad loans.

The crisis repeated itself, in slightly different forms, at several points in the 1980s and 1990s, as well as in the current decade. In each case, the pattern was the same: regulatory indulgence, speculative lending and financial engineering, collapse, and then government rescue, with debtors, taxpayers, or shareholders paying nearly all the price and speculators surviving to play again.

The savings and loan collapse followed much the same script, eventually costing taxpayers about $200 billion. S&Ls had been among the safest financial institutions, a paint-by-numbers kind of business. They were heavily regulated on both sides of the balance sheet. Their job was limited to taking in deposits, making mortgage loans, and being replenished by Fannie Mae and advances from the Federal Home Loan Banks. S&Ls were a model of how the financial system works when it is the servant of the real economy rather than the overlord. It was the last part of the system that needed to be turned over to speculative forces.

If normal, prudent underwriting of a borrower's qualifications was exercised, home mortgages seldom defaulted and were protected by reliable collateral. It was an easy formula. So safe were S&Ls that in its first forty-seven years, from 1934 to 1981, the FSLIC had had to pay claims of just $630 million. In the next seven years, thanks to deregulation, it would pay more than three hundred times that.

The Logic of Speculation and Bailout

The intensified rescue role of the Federal Reserve and the Treasury in the speculative 1980s and 1990s was the flip side of deregulation—an ideology that ostensibly disdained the need for government. Highly interventionist behavior by the Federal Reserve and the Treasury was unknown in the more regulated 1950s and 1960s. It was never required, because it was precluded by the system's structure. Characterizing the scandals of the 1990s, the free-market political Right has tried to paint a picture of isolated lawbreaking. But to imagine an outbreak of reckless criminality is to misunderstand what occurred. The kinds of speculative activities that got the banks into such trouble after the mid-1970s were not only prohibited in earlier postwar decades, for the most part they were not even possible.

For instance, there was no such thing as currency speculation in an era of fixed exchange rates and capital controls. There was no such thing as S&L speculation in junk bonds, given that S&Ls were explicitly chartered to make only mortgage loans and only in a local area. Even if the odd bank or S&L ventured into forbidden speculative territory that violated loan-to-deposit ratios or the terms of its charter, it would have soon come to the attention of bank examiners.

Later, it was not isolated laws but the whole legal and regulatory system that was deliberately broken. As the pattern of speculation, systemic risk, and costly bailouts kept repeating itself in the late twentieth and early twenty-first centuries, one might think that regulators and legislators had just never learned. In fact, so much money was at stake, some of it channeled into campaign contributions, that the political elite either cheered the affair on or looked the other way.

The populist politics of accountability had been so weakened that neither the Democratic Party nor those few genuine stewards on Wall Street who cared about the stability of the larger system could muster the support to reregulate financial markets. Quite the contrary, the cure for all of these glitches was said to be more deregulation. Because the Fed and the Treasury had gotten so proficient at bailouts, Congress and the regulators became very blasé about speculation and systemic risks. Another day, another bullet dodged.

After the stock market collapse of 2000–01, Alan Greenspan led the Fed to gradually reduce short-term interest rates to as low as 1 percent, in 2004. Greenspan opened the monetary floodgates even as President Bush was pursuing a very expansionary fiscal policy with immense tax cuts (which were also blessed by Greenspan). This was the same Alan Greenspan who had insisted to the incoming Clinton administration in 1993 that the only way to get interest rates down was to drastically *cut* the federal deficit. But circumstances evidently alter cases, especially when a conservative Republican is in the White House.

Moreover, in 2001 the economy was on the verge of a serious recession, and Greenspan was concerned about containing the wider effects of the stock market collapse. Suddenly deficits didn't matter. So it took a very-loose-money policy by the Fed *and* a very stimulative budget based on large deficits (coupled with the convenient willingness of foreign central banks to keep lending America money) to prevent the postcrash economy from sinking into deflation and depression. The need for cheap money was not just macroeconomic; it was required to recapitalize banks still recovering from earlier bouts of speculative excess.

We can properly take issue with the form of Bush's several tax cuts. They were far too heavily tilted to the wealthiest 5 percent of Americans. The same deficit spending, built on public outlays and tax breaks for working people, would have delivered far more stimulus, dollar for dollar. But as a matter of macroeconomics and balance sheet rebuilding, the economy needed this scale of stimulus, such was the damage of the 2000–01 crash. The improbable combination of very low interest rates, large deficits, and ever-increasing foreign borrowing kept the economy growing at tolerable rates in the years after the crash, but in a fashion that disguised underlying weaknesses and that is clearly unsustainable in the long term. This was another cost of reckless financial deregulation whose ultimate price we don't yet know.

Alan Greenspan's Bubble Machine

During and after World War II, the Federal Reserve, needing to fund a large national debt, also kept interest rates low. But unlike in the recent era, the Fed of that period was part of a regulatory system that had strict structural limitations on financial speculation. The easy money financed investment in real homes, factories, and farms. Today's relatively low interest rates, by contrast, are part of a deregulated financial economy in which anything goes.

Much of the speculative boom in hedge fund activity with derivatives and the rise of private-equity firms, described earlier, depended on borrowed money and was fueled by very low interest rates—the same cheap money made necessary by the Fed's previous laxity. Having disdained financial regulation, the Fed retains only the blunt instrument of monetary policy. It can continue to let the good times roll and let speculative excess reach new heights. Or it can turn risk-averse, raise rates, and slow the whole economy. This is a needless Hobson's choice, made necessary only by the embrace of financial deregulation.

In an era of fallen icons, the Federal Reserve is one of the few public institutions that has retained its prestige. Alan Greenspan, during his long tenure as chairman, received an almost universally respectful press. He was very adroit at management of the money supply and at crisis intervention, but he was also a crisis enabler. Even though Greenspan knew better, he did not oppose Bush's tax cuts. And his indulgence of various forms of deregulation helped create the crises he quashed, rather like the arsonist who is also a volunteer fireman. Even after the Long-Term Capital Management fiasco, Greenspan defended hedge funds as instruments of the efficiency of capital markets.

The Fed was famously described by Chairman William McChesney Martin as the fellow who takes away the punch bowl just when the party is getting going. Greenspan had a reputation as a steely inflation fighter.

But a closer look at his interest rate policies suggests that he made the punch bowl liberally available when Wall Street needed it. In the late 1990s, as Greenspan himself had warned, the stock bubble was feeding on cheap money. Yet, as the bubble continued to expand, he neither tightened money nor increased margin requirements.

A key year was 1998. Two members of the open market committee, Jerry Jordan, president of the Federal Reserve Bank of Cleveland, and William Poole, president of the Federal Reserve Bank of Saint Louis, wanted to raise interest rates. Greenspan had expressed the view in delphic testimony to Congress that both the stock market and the economy might be expanding too rapidly.

But at the time Greenspan had two crises on his hands, both born of speculative excess: the Long-Term Capital Management mess and the East Asian currency meltdown. On August 31, 1998, the Dow Jones Industrial Average fell by 513 points. It was no time to raise rates. On September 29, at Greenspan's prodding, the Federal Open Market Committee met and cut the federal funds rate, from 5.50 to 5.25 percent. As the journalist Bob Woodward reports, "The cut had little to do with inflation or even with the U.S. economy in general." Woodward quotes Fed vice chair Alice Rivlin as concluding that "the Fed was in a sense acting as the central banker of the world." Two weeks later, on October 15, after getting his colleagues' consent in a telephone conference call, Greenspan announced another quarter-point cut. The Dow soared 330 points, and the bubble kept expanding. Greenspan did tighten rates slightly in 1999, but that only brought them back to 5.5 percent, where they had been at the beginning of the huge market run-up that had begun in mid-1995.

John Cassidy, *The New Yorker*'s financial writer and author of the definitive book on the Internet bust, *Dot.con*, wrote, "Low interest rates were not Greenspan's only contribution to the stock market boom. His frequent references to the benefits of new technology, and his refusal to criticize excessive speculation, also played an important role." As a free-market man, Greenspan repeatedly made it clear that it was not his job to second-guess the judgments of millions of investors. But, Cassidy added, "Most commentators accepted Greenspan's judgment, but it wasn't supported by history. The very reason the Fed was founded in 1913 was to prevent a repeat of the speculative busts that had been increasingly common in the previous century."

Greenspan was properly worried that stock market mania was feeding on itself. A properly valued stock will increase based on two real-world factors: falling interest rates and rising corporate earnings. In the 1990s, both things were occurring. But one technical study calculated that these two factors explained only 70 to 80 percent of the run-up of the S&P 500 as of early 1998. The rest was pure bubble—expectations driving expectations in a climate when serious people believed that the Dow should be at 36,000.

In early 2000, when Greenspan finally acted to tighten money, his stated concern was that "demand" in the economy was outstripping supply, thus courting inflation. But one of the prime sources of overheated consumer demand, he explained in a high-profile address to the Economic Club of New York on January 13, 2000, was the wealth effects of the stock bubble. As Fed researchers documented, people felt so rich from the stock market run-up that they were spending more than 100 percent of their incomes. Greenspan spoke in his usual oblique and euphemistic language. Asset prices (meaning stock prices), he solemnly declared, should rise "no more than income." Belatedly, Greenspan had found a rather convoluted way to justify intervening to pop the bubble, while preserving his ability to disingenuously deny that he was second-guessing investors. Only the week before, Clinton had appointed Greenspan to a fourth term; now the chairman's job would not be impaired if he were blamed for bringing a crashing end to the party.

The markets correctly read the signal that Greenspan would at last use monetary policy to take away the punch bowl, and the market duly collapsed. If Greenspan had not had to keep rates lower than he really wanted in order to bail out the results of the same speculative excesses that had been encouraged by the Fed, he might have acted sooner and the damage of the crash would have been far lighter.

Despite Greenspan's golden reputation—Bob Woodward's authorized biography was titled *Maestro* in admiration, not in irony—the Fed chairman spent his final eight years using interest rate policy more to mop up the results of earlier speculative excesses than to control inflation and manage a balanced economy. When Greenspan retired in early 2006, more than one commentator observed that he had gotten out while the getting was good. His successor has far less running room.

Fed chairman Ben Bernanke could well face a repeat of the "stagflation" of the 1970s, in even less propitious circumstances. In that period, the United States was still a creditor nation. Even so, the combination of inflation set off by rising oil prices and high unemployment caused by the oil price shock left the Fed with unpalatable choices: low interest rates would feed inflation; high ones would strangle the economy. For several years, the economy suffered from both afflictions. Many bank customers, socked with very high interest rates, defaulted on their loans, weakening the banks' balance sheets and setting off a bout of bank speculation in the vain hope of recouping the losses. This was all before the United States became a net debtor. The Greenspan Fed shares responsibility for a weakened system, having been so complicit in allowing the excesses. If commentators conclude from Bernanke's responses to his impossible choices that they miss his predecessor, that would be far too kind to Greenspan.

In this decade, new speculative abuses have been driven by very cheap money. The world is said to be "awash in liquidity." Bernanke is one of those who accepts the idea of a "global savings glut." Supposedly, the recent expansion of the global capitalist economy to include three billion new souls in India, China, and East Asia, areas with high savings rates, gives the West plenty of access to cheap capital. But there is a lot more to the story. For one thing, the money supply has ramified. The increased use of derivatives and other exotic financial instruments creates forms of quasi-money, leaving central bankers less in control of a well-defined money supply made up of currency and regulated bank credit. Second, the particular imbalance between the trade accounts of China and the United States floods Western capital markets with dollars; and because China's mercantilist strategy supports America's huge trade imbalance, there is little pressure to raise dollar interest rates. Yet ultimately, the central banks led by the Federal Reserve either indulge this cheap money environment or rein it in. The Fed may have blunter instruments than in the past, but it still has the power to bring the party to a halt.

As noted, the period of very low interest rates that prevailed during the two decades after World War II combined cheap money with tight regulation of the speculative impulse, both nationally and globally—so that the low interest rates of the postwar era promoted growth of the real economy. Today's very low capital costs, by contrast, operate in a climate of speculative excess, so they stimulate more financial engineering at the expense of the real economy. If legislators and regulators acted to tighten controls on pure speculation, we would not need to choose between heightened financial risk or tighter money; and the benefit to the real economy would be immense. But there is one common feature to both: low interest rates last only as long as central bankers allow them.

Just as the era of cheap money ended abruptly with the systemic shocks of the late 1960s and 1970s, first as a result of the Vietnam War, then as a consequence of the oil shock, and finally with Paul Volcker's cold bath cure for inflation, we should not regard today's low interest rates as permanent. Increased productivity and global competition do bias the system to low inflation, other things being equal. However, any number of external shocks could lead to higher interest rates, among them loss of confidence in the dollar, or a deepening of the climate-change crisis and a sharp spike in the cost of energy. When such a shock occurs, and interest rates rise, the speculative economy will likely face a very nasty unwinding.

Even as more and more observers express alarm about a speculative crash, the politics of re-regulating the financial industry and holding the Federal Reserve more accountable are extremely difficult. Not only are the issues highly technical and opaque to ordinary citizens, elected officials, even those not dependent on campaign contributions, are extremely reluctant to say anything that might spook markets, and far too many are recipients of Wall Street campaign money. There was a time, three decades ago, when progressive Democrats such as Senator William Proxmire and Congressman Wright Patman chaired the Senate and House Banking Committees respectively, and were willing to promote tough regulation and go head-to-head with Fed chairmen. As recently as 2006, Paul Sarbanes headed the Senate Banking Committee, and used the Enron and WorldCom scandals to push through the legislation that bears his name. Since the election of 2006, the effective liberal Barney Frank has been chair of the counterpart House Committee on Financial Services. But it is unlikely that Frank would have the votes for a latter day set of Pecora hearings. In this era, the conventional wisdom among Democrats as well as Republicans so embraces financial deregulation that even progressives in Congress have a hard time promoting more than modest changes in the regulatory system absent a serious financial crisis.

The Fed's role has never been more interventionist, but the deregulated global economy is rapidly outrunning even the Fed's capacity to bail out calamities. Despite these perils, there has never been a time since the 1930s when politicians of both parties have been less supportive of preventive regulation by government and more willing to indulge deeper damage. There is simply too much money to be made. Until our political leaders put the safety of the economy ahead of narrow financial interests, we will remain at severe systemic risk.

CHAPTER SIX

BUDGET ANXIETY AND RUBINOMICS

FOR DECADES, government budget deficits have received double-standard treatment, depending on whether they are caused by too much peacetime public outlay (hardly ever) or by the gutting of the tax system (almost always). Yet the widespread premise has been that deficits reflect excess government spending. In reality, the sole occasion since World War II when domestic spending was partly responsible for modestly increased deficits was late in the Vietnam War era, when Lyndon Johnson escalated the war but refused to sacrifice his domestic program, and the economy overheated. However, discretionary federal outlay for social purposes has been steadily declining relative to GDP since the Carter administration. And since 1980, deficits have been above the postwar trend for two reasons: permanent cuts in the structure of federal taxation and periodic spikes in military spending.

The United States came out of World War II with a large national debt relative to its GDP—about 120 percent of one year's total production. For the next three decades, the economy grew faster than the debt did, so the ratio of debt to GDP fell steadily until it reached a postwar low of well under 30 percent in the Carter administration. Then came the Reagan deficits, which used tax cuts to create a wholly unnecessary fiscal crisis, to be "solved" by cuts in social spending. The same recipe was repeated by the second President Bush. And on both occasions hikes in military outlay compounded the problem.

The Deficit Wars

The issue of deficit reduction, as currently framed, muddles the choices we need to make as a nation. Instead of debating how we want to finance the public sector, at what levels, and for what purposes, commentators have turned deficit reduction into an all-purpose proxy for political virtue, to the exclusion of far more pressing public questions. The size of the deficit and the size of the government are entirely separate variables. We can have a modest deficit with public spending at 25 percent of GDP or a serious one with public spending at 15 percent. Responsible fiscal policy is a matter of roughly balancing outlays with revenues. By putting the deficit itself at center stage, public discourse conceals the true public issues.

The deficit literally dominated the election of 1992. H. Ross Perot, the late-entering independent who built his entire presidential campaign around the deficit and opposition to the North American Free Trade Agreement (NAFTA), at one point was running in the polls ahead of both the challenger, Bill Clinton, and the incumbent, George H. W. Bush. An elite bipartisan group, the Concord Coalition, was acclaimed in the press for raising the visibility of the deficit as a public issue. An ever-escalating national debt clock was regularly featured on the nightly news. Supposedly, according to many political scientists, you can't get voters to pay attention to an abstract issue like the deficit because specific interest groups benefit from deficit-financed public spending, while nobody benefits from cutting the deficit. But suddenly the deficit became a symbol of bad public management, and voters were demanding that politicians do something about it.

Bill Clinton did. Elected as something of an economic populist ("People who work hard and play by the rules should never be poor"), he governed as the supreme fiscal conservative. Clinton pledged to cut the deficit in half over four years, and he staked his presidency on a 1993 budget plan enacted by a single vote in the House with Vice President Gore casting the tie-breaking vote in the Senate. Clinton's budget dramatically reduced the deficit, partly through reductions in spending and partly through tax hikes on the wealthiest 2 percent of taxpayers. He sacrificed programs of social investment in which he deeply believed to the gods of deficit reduction. Then, as the budget headed into the black, he and his allies made budget surplus the ultimate test of economic stewardship.

Clinton was persuaded by Alan Greenspan that deficit reduction offered a fiscally orthodox path to economic recovery, the opposite of the Keynesian path. At a lengthy private meeting in the Arkansas governor's mansion in December 1992, Greenspan contended that high deficits were leading to high interest rates, even in a recession, because public borrowing "crowds out" business investment and consumer borrowing and bids up the cost of capital. Greenspan indicated that if the deficit was reduced, the money markets would likely approve; the Fed chairman could then reinforce their approval with a somewhat looser money policy. Lower interest rates, in turn, would reduce costs to businesses and consumers, investment would increase, and so would economic growth. Money would move out of lower-yielding bonds and into stocks. This view is now enshrined as national mythology, but almost none of what actually happened in the 1990s followed this logic.

The Greenspan view was strongly seconded by Robert Rubin, then head of Clinton's National Economic Council and later Treasury secretary. In a key strategy meeting, Clinton famously exploded that his whole economic vision and political future were being held hostage by "a bunch of fucking bond traders." At another planning session, dominated by fiscally conservative advisers, Clinton declared with disgust, "Where are all the Democrats? We're all Eisenhower Republicans. . . . We stand for lower deficits and free trade and the bond market. Isn't that great?"

The skeptical Clinton of early 1993 had it right. It's true that very high deficits, of the kind that Ronald Reagan and the elder Bush ran year after year, will cause the accumulated public debt to increase at a faster rate than the gross domestic product. At some point, this will put upward pressure on long-term interest rates, as money markets fear inflation. Clinton did need to stabilize and even modestly reduce the deficit. But the recipe of fiscal balance being the key to economic growth has been grossly exaggerated by its partisans.

For the most part, the 1990s boom had little to do with the Clinton-Rubin fiscal policy. Despite the move from excessive deficits all the way to budget surplus, real (inflation-adjusted) interest rates hardly moved. There was no investment boom. And the spike in productivity after 1995 had nothing to do with deficit reduction.

For one thing, as we keep hearing, the economy is highly internationalized. Money from all over the world pours into the United States. At some point, that dependency becomes unsustainable, especially when coupled with a chronic and escalating trade deficit. But in the early 1990s, both the trade imbalance and the accumulated foreign debt were far smaller than they are today. There was little "crowding out" of business and consumer borrowing by federal deficits in a globalized money market.

The association of deficit reduction with lower interest rates and higher growth was highly misleading for a second reason: the decade of the 1990s was a period of gradual disinflation and of rising productivity. As a legacy of Paul Volcker's "cold bath" cure of very tight money and temporary recession in the late 1970s and early 1980s, much structural inflation had been wrung out of the economy. Regular cost-of-living adjustments vanished from labor contracts. Labor was institutionally a good deal weaker. Foreign competition and outsourcing meant that old concepts such as tight production capacity during a boom lost some of their power to generate pressure for price hikes. As inflation came down, nominal interest rates came down with them. Two-year Treasury bonds declined from a yield of 14.5 percent in December 1981 to 5.1 percent in December 1998. The price of a stock, other things being equal, reflects its expected yield, adjusted for inflation. The lower the inflation rate and prevailing interest rates, the higher the stock price.

Once the Federal Reserve loosened the screws, inflation and interest rates steadily declined, quite independently of any reduction in the federal deficit. In fact, the real interest rate (the nominal interest rate adjusted for inflation) on long Treasury bonds actually *increased* for two years after Clinton's famous 1993 budget deal, because inflation was coming down faster than nominal interest rates. As the economist Dean Baker has pointed out, even at the peak of the Clinton boom—the years 1997 to 2000—real interest rates were higher than in two of the three preceding booms.

Moreover, technological changes made it possible for the Federal Reserve to run a looser money policy and tolerate fuller employment and tighter labor markets without setting off inflation. After three decades of annual productivity growth averaging around 3 percent, productivity growth fell to around 1 percent in the 1970s. Economists are still debating why. Was it the shift from manufacturing to services? Or the entry into the labor market of tens of millions of young (and still unskilled) baby boomers? Perhaps the spike in the price of oil? Or a lag between the introduction of new and costly computer technologies and the economy's ability to use them? Nobel Laureate Robert Solow famously quipped in 1987 that computers were showing up everywhere but in the productivity statistics.

Economic historians have long documented a lag between the invention of new technologies and the capacity of the economy to use them productively. Whatever the cause of the temporary decline, productivity growth came roaring back in the 1990s. The turnaround started in late 1995, when productivity started rising at annual rates in excess of 3 percent. But that increase was in no way the result of higher rates of private investment stimulated by reduced public deficits and lower interest rates—because in the mid-1990s, investment hardly budged. Mainly, it was the investment in computer technology belatedly bearing fruit.

In the Clinton presidency as a whole, investment rates relative to GDP were slightly better than in the recovery of the late 1980s, slightly worse than in that of the late 1970s. And in Clinton's final three years, when investment rates did rise somewhat, much of that investment—in purely speculative sectors such as excess fiber-optic cable—was the wasteful consequence of the stock market bubble, not an efficient contribution to economic well-being.

The overheated boom of the late 1990s also reflected consumer demand. The economists Dean Baker and Robert Pollin, as well as the Fed's own researchers, have demonstrated that the hot economy of Clinton's second term was produced mainly by the wealth effects of the stock bubble (people felt richer and hence spent more) and increased consumer debt. Baker writes, "[A]t the peak of the stock bubble in 2000, households held approximately $5.0 trillion of bubble wealth in stocks." This paper wealth was soon wiped out, but while it lasted, Baker calculates that it led to $150 billion to $200 billion in additional consumption. Because of the concentration of stock ownership, nearly all of this increased spending was by the wealthiest, though it did stimulate the economy generally. In 2000, according to calculations by Robert Pollin, the top 20 percent spent 104.4 percent of their income (for the extra 4.4 percent, they borrowed or drew down savings), compared to 95.1 percent in 1992, before the great stock run-up.

A 2001 study by two Federal Reserve economists, Dean Maki and Michael Palumbo, calculates that the wealth effect of the stock market bubble increased spending by three to five cents for every additional dollar of on-paper financial wealth. Pollin translates those data into $275 billion to $450 billion of economic stimulus. Baker concludes that these wealth effects "explain most of the upturn in consumption seen in this period, as the savings rate fell to what were at the time record lows." While savings relative to disposable household income averaged 9.6 percent in the 1970s and 9.0 percent in the 1980s, it fell to just 3.3 percent in Clinton's final four years in office, as people increased their borrowing. In short, this was a pure consumption boom, supercharged by a stock market bubble. It had almost nothing to do with the virtues of budget balance.

In the mid-1990s, economists had debated whether the rebound in productivity gains truly allowed for faster noninflationary growth. A widely held belief among economists contended that there was a fixed, "natural" rate of unemployment, somewhere around 6 percent, below which tight labor markets and overly tight plant capacity would trigger inflation. That translated to a limit in economic growth rates of 2 to 2.5 percent. *The American Prospect* magazine, in 1997, sponsored a debate, with James Galbraith, Barry Bluestone, and Bennett Harrison arguing that a new, more productive economy permitted fuller employment and higher growth rates, and Alan Blinder, later vice chairman of the Fed, taking the orthodox view that real growth rates of under 2.5 percent were about the best the economy could prudently do. The magazine cover depicted Alan Greenspan as a traffic cop with a radar gun, glumly enforcing a 2.3 percent "growth limit."

But then, much to the delight of the growth advocates, Greenspan soon became something of an inflation dove. His own research convinced him that something new was indeed happening to productivity. Computers were replacing humans in entire areas of the economy, everything from industrial and design processes to automated gas stations and the back-office data processing by insurance companies and banks. Growth in productivity had gone back to the levels of the postwar boom, seemingly for keeps. This persuaded Greenspan that GDP growth rates of 3 and even 4 percent were tolerable without risking inflation. (Productivity growth plus population growth, a rough proxy for labor force growth, about equals the sustainable rate of noninflationary GDP growth.)

Like the gradual disinflation, this productivity gain was happening quite independently of whatever Clinton and Rubin were doing with the budget deficit. Noninflationary economic growth allowed investors to lend money without having to charge an inflation premium. The Fed's policy of keeping short-term interest rates moderate accommodated that growth; the money markets, which determine long-term rates, showed no sign of worrying about inflation. But none of this had much to do with federal budget surpluses.

It would have been ample to get the deficit down to about 2 percent of GDP, a percentage point less than the rate of real economic growth. That would have permitted the all-important ratio of debt to GDP, which had increased during the Reagan and Bush I years, to head back downward. The task was not to bring the public deficit to zero but to get it stable or declining relative to GDP again.

In the late 1990s, 2 percent of GDP equaled about $200 billion a year, which might have been spent on restoring both public investments and the more egalitarian economy that candidate Clinton had advocated in 1993. Even if Republicans in Congress had balked, with budget discipline well in hand Clinton might have gone back to the theme of "Putting people first" and made a fight of it. Money spent directly on research and development probably would have had a much more tonic effect on productivity than money used for deficit reduction.

Joseph Stiglitz, while serving as chair of Clinton's Council of Economic Advisers, loyally promoted the deficit reduction theory. But in his 2003 book, *The Roaring Nineties*, the Nobel laureate wrote:

> [F]rom today's vantage point, I believe we pushed deficit reduction too far. . . . Deficit reduction accelerated the decline in interest rates, which helped recapitalize the banks. But interest rates would have fallen anyway. They were falling before Clinton took office. The technological innovations—the computer revolution—and the process of globalization, changes in the economy that were proceeding before Clinton took office, and that would be little affected by deficit reduction, were making it more attractive to invest in America.

Stiglitz goes on to wish, with hindsight, that instead of devoting tax revenues to deficit reduction, "Clinton had used the additional funds to finance more investments in R&D, technology, infrastructure and education. Given the high returns for those investments, GDP in the year 2000 would have been higher, and the economy's growth potential would have been stronger."

But Clinton and Rubin had themselves a good story about their hard-won fiscal prudence being the key to the long boom, and they were not about to abandon it. A budget surplus had been projected for 2002, but it arrived early. By 1998, the deficit was slain and the budget was in the black. The debt clock on Forty-second Street in New York City was actually shut down. Economists predicted that the economy would be in endless surplus and that the national debt would be paid off by 2012. The Federal Reserve began to worry about what it would buy and sell in its open market operations when no more Treasury securities were in circulation.

The Democrats, wedded as they were to the gospel of budget balance, could not bring themselves to increase public investment much or to rebuild political support for social outlay. Measures such as the earned income tax credit, a wage subsidy disguised as a tax break for the poor, were popular because they rode the tide of tax reduction. Fearful that

Republicans would raid the surplus to cut taxes for the rich, Democrats came up with a budgetary gimmick. Taking advantage of fears that Social Security would run out of money in the middle of the twenty-first century, they created an imaginary device, the so-called lockbox for Social Security, invoked ad nauseam by Al Gore in the 2000 presidential campaign. All of the budget surplus would supposedly be put into that lockbox. Polls showed that one issue more popular than tax cutting was defense of Social Security. By associating resistance to tax cuts with safeguarding Social Security, Democrats hoped they could force the Republicans to keep their mitts off the surplus. George W. Bush, of course, demonstrated otherwise.

If you bothered to read the fine print (and hardly anyone did), there never was a lockbox, in the sense of money from the surplus being permanently transferred into the Social Security trust fund. Rather, Gore simply meant that as the surplus accumulated, the government would eventually draw it down to meet increasing Social Security payout demands. If Social Security had actually been literally segregated from general government finances, it would well have been better defended from Bush's Treasury raids. But this idea had no sympathizers among Clinton's Wall Street advisers such as Rubin, who did not want government controlling huge pools of capital. Once the government began running big deficits again, however, the positive cash flow into Social Security accounts was indeed vulnerable to a raid, and it made the consolidated deficit seem smaller than it really was.

Today there is a deficit problem once again, because of the huge holes blown in the tax code by several rounds of tax cuts. Vice President Dick Cheney said out loud in 2002 what a lot of Republican politicians privately believed: "Deficits don't matter." The public outcry of 1992 had come and gone. Republicans and the business elite seemed to care about deficits when they could be blamed on Democratic "tax and spend" but not when they resulted from Republican tax cuts. Grover Norquist, the Republican tax-cut strategist, articulated the real game: "Starve the beast." The real point of the tax cuts was to create an endless cycle of deficit crises whose cure would be more cuts in spending.

Precious few Republicans put fiscal balance ahead of tax cutting. That left the Democrats as the paladins of deficit reduction. In July 2006, the Democratic House leader and later Speaker, Nancy Pelosi, solemnly pledged that every penny of money gleaned from any reduction in the Bush tax cuts would go for deficit reduction, not new social outlay. This deficit-hawk role is not only thankless but self-defeating.

As a matter of politics, Cheney is right. After seeing the deficit wolf banished in the 1990s, most voters don't care much about deficits in the 2000s. But by sticking Democrats with the green-eyeshade role, Republicans astutely deprive Democrats of pocketbook themes that might actually rally voters. And as a matter of economics, Stiglitz is right: too much deficit reduction is as bad for the economy as too little.

Until recently, the costs of the once again escalating national debt have been concealed by the Social Security surplus and the temporary climate of unusually low interest rates. The budget not offset by Social Security surpluses increased from a small surplus of $2 billion in 1999 to a deficit of $568 billion in 2004. That year, the "consolidated deficit," including money raided from the Social Security funds, was "only" $413 billion, thanks to an infusion of $151 billion in Social Security receipts, making Bush seem less profligate than he actually was. During that five-year period the national debt rose by almost exactly a trillion dollars, yet the interest on the debt actually fell from $229 billion in 1999 to $160 billion in 2004, thanks to Alan Greenspan's temporarily very low interest rates. As interest rates rise, those payments will become more of a burden. The deficit is not yet a crisis, but it is a problem. The most straightforward way to solve it would be to restore the tax code to the way it was before George W. Bush took office. This remedy seems to be far off the radar screen.

Entitlement Hysteria

If anxiety about deficits is somewhat damped down, elite apprehension about "entitlements" remains at a rolling boil. Social Security, the biggest entitlement, is simultaneously America's most popular, expensive, and redistributive social program. Two thirds of people over age sixty-five depend on Social Security for more than half their income; without Social Security, more than a third of America's elderly would be poor. Polls show that upward of 90 percent of Americans have a positive opinion of Social Security. That immense popular support suggests a latent constituency for government programs of economic justice that is activated only in infrequent moments when the usual elite lock on politics is broken. It takes extraordinary political circumstances to enact programs such as socialized retirement security (1935) or socialized health insurance for the elderly (1965), but once enacted such programs become so widely valued as to be politically untouchable.

The Right, therefore, goes after these programs indirectly. In the case of Social Security, critics have been warning for more than two decades of Social Security's incipient insolvency and its supposed wider costs to the U.S. economy. For many of these critics, the not-so-hidden agenda is Social Security privatization. If the hundreds of billions of dollars that now flow into Social Security trust funds annually from payroll tax receipts were ever to flow to Wall Street money managers instead, it would be a stunning bonanza that would dwarf the current insider rake-off of mutual fund fees.

Peter G. Peterson, a former CEO of Lehman Brothers, chairman of the Blackstone Group and the Council on Foreign Relations, cofounder of the Concord Coalition, and commerce secretary under Nixon, has written essentially the same book four times, warning of the coming catastrophe of debt and ruinous entitlement. This project began in 1982, when Peterson wrote a series of articles for the usually liberal *New York Review of Books* at the invitation of his friend the editor Jason Epstein. His 1993 version, *Facing Up*, warned of $14 trillion in "unfunded liabilities" facing future generations, mainly from Social Security and Medicare. The culprit, according to Peterson, is the greed of the middle class and the influence of lobbies such as the AARP.

The Clinton deficit reduction budget, Peterson warned, would still produce deficits well in excess of $300 billion by 2000. In fact, that year the budget was in surplus by $236.4 billion, a surplus equal to 2.4 percent of GDP. Such are the perils of forecasting. But at least Peterson, unlike nearly all other Republican critics of entitlements, was willing to balance his proposed benefit cuts with some tax increases, including higher top marginal tax rates. By the 2004 version of his book, titled *Running on Empty*, Peterson was still calling for rollbacks in Social Security and Medicare benefits—but not rollbacks in the Republican tax cuts.

This is the same Pete Peterson who, as chairman of the Blackstone Group, walked away with $1.88 billion as Blackstone went partly public and sells some of itself to the Chinese government. Peterson's personal gains, many of them derived from buying and selling sound enterprises and stripping their assets, are defended as a contribution to economic efficiency. But social programs that better the lives of hundreds of millions of non-wealthy Americans are deemed by Peterson to be profligate. The contrast between the way Peterson makes his own fortune and the man's homilies on thrift and virtue are so extreme that it is astonishing that he is taken seriously as a social critic.

It would be one thing if the attack on entitlements were merely the work of self-serving Wall Streeters and their ideological allies. But a great many high-minded political centrists have bought the story. David Broder, the widely admired dean of Washington political columnists, writes a column several times a year criticizing the selfish interest groups that defend Social Security and Medicare and the brave politicians who try to gut these programs in the name of fiscal stability. In one emblematic column in May 2006 (among dozens), titled "Bailing the Future Out of Debt," Broder wrote of Bush's valiant efforts to trim entitlements "with a proposal to create private accounts, but it ran into a buzz saw of opposition led by AARP and congressional Democrats and never came to a vote."

The assault on social insurance also has an extensive technical-sounding economics literature. In the late 1980s, the economist Laurence Kotlikoff and two colleagues invented a concept called "generational accounting." According to Kotlikoff, because of the increased life spans of the elderly and the declining ratio of working-age Americans to retired ones, future generations will have to pay tax rates upward of 80 percent if entitlement commitments are to be met. Kotlikoff calculated in a 2004 book that the unfunded liabilities from Social Security, Medicare, and Medicaid were not the alarming $14 trillion predicted by Peterson but $72 trillion! Citing a "menu of pain" prepared by two other economists, Kotlikoff writes that the gap could be closed by roughly doubling payroll taxes, by increasing income taxes by about two thirds, or by cutting Social Security and Medicare benefits by almost 50 percent. Kotlikoff's solution is simple: privatize most of Social Security and replace Medicare with a voucher, and good luck to the senior citizen who can't afford to supplement the voucher with decent insurance.

These are precisely the remedies being promoted by the Bush administration and much of Wall Street. But the dire economic forecasts are only as good as their technical assumptions. When you think about it, the idea of unfunded liabilities is an odd way to comprehend the future obligations of government. As the economist Dean Baker observes, nobody doubts that the Pentagon will continue spending hundreds of billions of dollars a year to defend (and occasionally jeopardize) America's security. Project this assumption forward seventy-five years, and you have an "unfunded liability" in the tens of trillions of dollars. But as long as the U.S. government is in business, there is little doubt that taxes will be collected and the Pentagon will be paid. Likewise for the mandated payouts under Social Security and Medicare.

But isn't there something here to worry about? It's true that a large cohort of baby boomers is entering retirement age and that retired people are living longer. Yet the overall ratio of working people to dependent ones (children as well as pensioners) has been largely unchanged for fifty years. Moreover, the increased number of women in the workforce has increased the fraction of Americans paying into Social Security, as has the faster-than-anticipated increase in immigrants, both legal and illegal, who pay into Social Security and may never take benefits out. Moreover, the pessimistic projections of Social Security's future do not take into account the higher growth rates of recent years. In 1997, the official Social Security Trustees Report projected that the system would run out of funds by 2029. Seven years later, in 2004, the trustees put the date of doom back to 2042. Any system that can gain thirteen years of life in seven years is not collapsing. The bipartisan Congressional Budget Office, using slightly more realistic economic assumptions, put the deficit year at 2052.

What happened to brighten the picture? Faster-than-projected economic growth and population growth meant more workers contributing more money into the Social Security trust fund. The official Trustees Reports, which project growth forward seventy-five years, have been using an exceptionally bleak set of assumptions, rooted in the slower productivity growth of the 1970s. The trustees had been criticized when their assumptions of three decades earlier had proven too optimistic and a Social Security crisis loomed in the early 1980s. So, like the proverbial cat that once landed on a hot stove and never sits on a cold one, they are now being overly jumpy, assuming a highly implausible long-term GDP growth rate of just 1.6 percent. Adjust that upward to something more realistic, and the crisis evaporates. Moreover, the lower-than-expected payroll taxes of the 1980s reflected lower-than-expected workers' pay packets. In other words, the same income shift that enriched the wealthy and flattened the earnings of the working and middle classes shortchanged the funding of Social Security.

Most of the fearmongering about Social Security and Medicare is ideology masquerading as public-mindedness. If we do nothing at all, according to the rather dour 2006 Social Security Trustees Report, the current structure of payroll taxes will be sufficient to pay about 75 percent of future projected benefits after 2040. Another way of looking at this shortfall is that it equals about 2 percent of annual taxable payroll or about 1 percent of GDP. The Congressional Budget Office, with more realistic growth assumptions, estimates the shortfall as less than half of 1 percent of GDP.

How to make up the gap? Robert Ball, the former Social Security commissioner under three presidents and a principal architect of the system's bipartisan restructuring in 1982–83, has proposed a plan that would keep the system solvent indefinitely. Ball would change just three things. First, he would raise the cap on earnings so that 90 percent of all earnings would be subject to Social Security tax, the percentage mandated by Congress in 1981. Right now, payroll taxes (unlike income taxes) are paid at a flat rate on the first dollar of income, and no Social Security taxes are owed on incomes exceeding $90,000, which makes Social Security an exceptionally regressive tax. The highest 25 percent of income escapes Social Security taxation entirely. Second, Ball would supplement payroll taxes with revenues from other sources. President Roosevelt, in 1935, had in fact proposed that once an entire generation had gone through the system and everyone was covered, by the 1980s, general revenues would need to be added to the financing mix. Ball specifically proposes earmarking estate tax proceeds, which hit only the very wealthiest. Finally, he would raise the rate of return earned by the trust fund by allowing a portion of it to be invested by the trustees in a prudent mix of stocks for the long term. This would allow Social Security to get the higher yield typical of equities markets but without fragmenting the system into individual accounts. This last idea would also steal some of the privatizers' thunder.

There are several variations on this approach, some of which slightly reduce the payout rate, either by raising the retirement age or by moderating the annual adjustment for inflation. However, the ratio of Social Security benefits to lifetime earnings is already headed downward, because of the changes legislated by Congress in 1983. Ball, to his credit, manages to maintain solvency without further reductions in benefits. Other defenders of the system, such as the Brookings economist Henry Aaron, would include modest benefit cuts. The larger point is that any shortfall equal to perhaps half of 1 percent of GDP is not a fiscal catastrophe; it is an ideological argument. According to calculations by the Center on Budget and Policy Priorities, the long-term shortfall is almost exactly equal to the Bush tax cuts on the wealthiest 1 percent of Americans. If there is a political will to save the system, this is not a heavy fiscal lift, though in the current climate it is a challenging politics.

Social Security remains well defended in the esteem of the populace. Partial privatization of Social Security was one of the Bush administration's top domestic priorities, but despite a huge amount of self-interested lobbying from the financial industry, the idea fell flat. The basic concept was that younger adults could elect to have part of their payroll taxes diverted into a new system of private accounts, rather like IRAs or 401(k)s. That money would be theirs to invest and use as part of their retirement income. The idea was promoted both as a solution to Social Security's alleged solvency problems and as a politically attractive option to younger voters who had been persuaded by the scaremongering that Social Security might not be there for them, so better to grab some cash money now.

The problem, however, is that the government can't spend the same money twice. The proceeds of the payroll tax are already spoken for. They are the source of payouts to retirees for the next several decades. Divert that money to a new system of private accounts, and the projected shortfall in Social Security will only worsen. Far from solving the perceived crisis, privatization would aggravate it. Some allies of the administration proposed to finesse that conundrum by having the government go deeper into debt. Others wanted to cut the guaranteed portion of Social Security. Many wanted to do both. The details were obscure, but the general public got the drift: a program of partial privatization would not fix whatever might be broken, but it would cut guaranteed benefits. Polls showed the idea costing more support among seniors than it gained among younger voters. Whenever the administration came close to introducing legislation and putting the president's prestige on the line for privatization, Republican legislators and pollsters kept warning that the White House would be handing Democrats a loaded gun.

In fact, partial privatization had substantial appeal in the more conservative wing of the Democratic Party. Bipartisan commissions keep recommending variations of it. The much-maligned liberal advocacy groups did yeoman's work saving many Democrats from themselves, holding wavering legislators accountable to defend what is still the Democrats' best-loved program and the best single commercial for efficient and beneficial government. In 1998 and 1999, according to wellplaced Clinton administration sources, President Clinton himself came very close to advocating a version of privatization. At the time, he also found himself embroiled in a humiliating sex scandal. His uneasy defenders among liberals on Capitol Hill made it very clear, considering the huge political risks they were taking to stand by their frisky president, that this was no time for him to hand Republicans a gift in the form of endorsing privatized Social Security. In some respects, if Social Security survived this assault, we can thank Monica Lewinsky.

Medi-scare

If you don't like social insurance, Medicare presents an even more tempting target than Social Security. Medicare costs, like other health insurance costs, are increasing at more than double the rate of inflation. Medicare faces additional cost pressures because it insures the aged, who have the effrontery to live ever longer (thanks in part to Medicare!). In fact, because of its universality and superior efficiencies Medicare operates more efficiently than comparable private plans.

Whereas the Social Security trust fund, if not supplemented by additional revenue, is projected to run out of money sometime in the 2040s or 2050s, the trustees predict that Medicare's hospital insurance trust funds are likely to be depleted by 2018. Medicare cost the government about $300 billion in 2004, and this sum was only increased by the Bush administration's remarkably inefficient privatized Medicare drug benefit, which took effect in 2006.

Fiscal conservatives, including many Democrats and the Bush administration, advocate replacing public Medicare with a voucher. The elderly could take the voucher and buy coverage offered by private insurers on the open market. The voucher would cap government's costs by providing only the most basic insurance. Because of budget pressures, its value would very likely be eroded over time, shifting more costs onto individuals. Its worth would be further reduced by the much larger middleman expenses of private insurance, leaving affluent elderly able to supplement the basic voucher but most elderly stuck with inferior coverage.

As in the case of privatized Social Security, Medicare vouchers were a near miss for Democrats. In 2000, Democrats on a bipartisan commission came very close to accepting a version of the idea but could not agree on the details. Like Social Security, Medicare is exceptionally popular among the elderly. Polls reported by the Commonwealth Fund showed that 62 percent of Medicare beneficiaries reported that they were satisfied with their quality of care, compared to 51 percent with private insurance. Bush, in the 2004 election year, decided to sidestep Medicare vouchers and propose a liberal-sounding expansion of the program to include drug coverage. This stole a Democratic theme in a way that promoted privatization by stealth.

The cure for the financial pressures on Medicare is paradoxical. The remedy is to enlarge it. If we leave Medicare as a program just for the elderly, budget pressures are likely to nibble it to death. The same 2004 legislation that created the privatized drug benefits mandates a set of budget triggers that will require Congress to make deep cuts in benefits. Ideologically, a socialized program that is superior to its private counterparts is a real menace to conservatives. It is hard to imagine Medicare surviving as an island of universalism in a sea of privatization.

The best, and quite possibly the only, way to redeem Medicare for the long term is to build on its successes and gradually expand it into universal national health insurance. Medicare already covers more than 40 million people. When you add those covered by Medicaid, State Children's Health Insurance Program (SCHIP), the military services, the Veterans Administration, and other ultimately public sources, more than 40 percent of all medical costs are borne by government. The private part of the system, with its fragmentation, marketing costs, profiteering, and efforts to insure the well and avoid the sick, is far less efficient than the public part. The most efficient form of insurance is a universal pool.

In the private parts of the health system, business "solves" the budget crisis by steadily off-loading more out-of-pocket costs to consumers. Society bears a huge hidden cost in the form of needed medical care that people do without because they can't afford it. Medicare's budget problems are more transparent. When benefits are cut, there is a public outcry.

By making Medicare universal, we could afford good insurance for the entire population. There would continue to be cost pressures, because of long-term trends entirely unrelated to the form of health insurance. The population keeps living longer, and science keeps inventing costly ways of keeping people alive and healthy. Difficult choices have to be made, or medical care is literally capable of absorbing half of our GDP. Nations with universal systems spend their limited moneys far more efficiently than we do. They don't have duplicative specialty facilities such as for-profit outpatient surgeries competing to skim off the most profitable cream at the expense of the rest of the system. Their national health systems pay wholesale rather than retail prices for drugs. They treat mammograms like the public health screening measures that they are, rather than as billable profit centers. As a consequence, universal systems do better at the whole range of preventive medicine for adults and children, and they keep their populations healthier. Despite the reputation of the public sector for bureaucratic red tape, the universal systems burden their physicians with far less paperwork and second-guessing of medical decisions than our private insurance bureaucracies do. Because of its superior efficiencies, Medicare has actually had a lower rate of inflation than private insurance, despite the generally younger and healthier population insured by private carriers and their clumsy efforts to "manage" care.

A bogeyman in this debate is "rationing." Some universal systems, such as those of Britain and Canada, do have queues for elective procedures. But America already has rationing—cruel rationing on the basis of social class. Denying insurance to 45 million mostly lower-income Americans is rationing. Inventing the concept of a "preexisting condition" and making insurance prohibitively expensive for cancer survivors is a form of rationing. When stripped-down HMOs that fail to cover many services are imposed on employees and their families by cost-cutting employers, that is also a form of rationing. There is no such thing as a preexisting condition under Medicare or any other universal system, which tends to have far less rationing than a system based on private insurance. Moreover, under any health insurance system, the very wealthy still have the ability to purchase privately whatever services they want. But in most other advanced countries, the universal health systems are highly valued by the vast majority of the population and private alternatives are mainly supplemental.

The universal systems also reinforce an ethic of service rather than profiteering on the part of doctors, the kind of ethic that draws most aspiring practitioners into the healing arts in the first place. In the United States, many doctors whose incomes are whipsawed by managed care companies find themselves looking for profitable sidelines. Physicians in universal systems tend to be far less commercial in their outlook. When my son had a serious accident in London and needed emergency surgery, I asked the best-informed doctor I knew whether to use the National Health Service or seek out a private specialist. "Don't go near the private surgeons," my friend said. "The NHS has the best people." And my son received superb care.

As a political strategy, I have advocated a gradual transition that would extend Medicare to more and more of the population, by age group. Start by giving all young people under age twenty-five a Medicare card. On average, the young tend to be healthy. Expanding Medicare to the young would be relatively cheap. Adding the healthy and inexpensive young to the same pool as the sicker and costlier old would make actuarial sense. Politically, it would create a rolling constituency for universal Medicare, because upon turning twenty-six people would be appalled to realize that they were losing coverage.

Then, from the other end of the age spectrum, Medicare could be made available to people aged fifty-five and over. This is the age group for which private insurance becomes astronomically expensive to purchase if they lose their employer coverage. By joining a universal pool, they could get good insurance at the best available rates, with subsidies on a sliding scale. By this point, Medicare would be covering well over half the population, and there would be growing popular support for extending it to everyone.

Jacob Hacker proposes the same outcome via a different route. He would have government require that all employers either provide their workers with decent health insurance or pay the costs of their employees joining what Hacker calls Medicare-Plus. The noninsured could join by paying premiums on a sliding scale based on income. Hacker's approach astutely brings into the reform coalition those employees or corporations or trade unions who are happy with their current insurance—groups that are otherwise unfriendly to national health insurance. These groups and individuals could continue to insure privately, and would not resist the reform out of fear that the public program might cover less than their current insurance. Eventually, the vast majority of Americans would be in Medicare. Hacker offers the political insight that emphasizing the uninsured, though compassionate, is a losing strategy. Most Democrats, thinking small, find that their proposals never get much traction. The political future of health reform is to link the uninsured with the worried insured and the underinsured—the vast majority.

Other nations with universal health care systems, incidentally, cover current costs mainly with current revenues. The picture of a fiscal crisis based on the Medicare trust fund's "running out of money" in 2018 is not an insoluble crisis. The perceived fiscal meltdown is purely a consequence of the fact that the most efficient strategy for covering everyone and containing costs is outside national debate.

The Return of Rubinomics

Shortly after the Democrats' surprising gains in the 2006 midterm election, Robert Rubin delivered a high-profile speech to the Economic Club of Washington, making a brave call for a tax increase and reform of entitlement programs. The main purpose of both was to rein in the budget deficit. These goals remain Rubin's top priorities and his counsel to Democrats.

The British have an expression that fits Rubin's budget politics:

horse-and-rabbit stew—a seemingly equal blend of one horse and one rabbit. In Rubin's policy stew, budget balance is the horse and new social investment is the rabbit. The big identified problem is deficits and entitlements. The small problem is insufficient social outlay.

Rubin's latest initiative is called the Hamilton Project. Named after America's first Treasury secretary and housed at the centrist Brookings Institution, the Project was launched in early 2006. It professes to be an effort to combine restored fiscal responsibility with a new generation of opportunity and security programs for working Americans. Rubin personally raised the money for the project, mostly from Wall Street, and has donated several hundred thousand dollars himself.

The program's rhetoric is unimpeachable. According to its basic document, "An Economic Strategy to Advance Opportunity, Prosperity, and Growth":

> The Project's economic strategy reflects a judgment that long-term prosperity is best achieved by making economic growth broad based, by enhancing individual economic security, and by embracing a role for effective government in making needed public investments. Our strategy—strikingly different from the theories driving current economic policy—calls for fiscal discipline and increased public investment in key growth-enhancing areas.

The authors caution that along with underinvestment in public goods, the most serious problem facing the American economy is the projected public deficit and debt, which will only be exacerbated as the baby-boom generation retires. Yet, while promising to increase public investment and reduce the projected deficits, the Project promises to be "budget neutral." The Project also employs a rhetoric linking economic growth to economic security: "The more confidence that people can achieve in their personal finances—through both savings and social insurance—the more confidence they can place in the future, making them more likely to seize opportunities and bounce back from risks." This implies more than token levels of spending.

How to square that circle? There are only two ways: either increase taxes dramatically or offset new program outlays with even steeper program cuts elsewhere.

Take a look under the hood of this gleaming vehicle, and the answer emerges. The top priority of the Project's sponsors is fiscal discipline. Rubin is willing to roll back the Bush tax cuts on the wealthiest, but primarily for budget balance. When I pressed him in an interview about whether America needed *net* increases in social outlay, he declined to say that it did.

Most of the Hamilton Project's policy papers propose small-scale changes in existing programs aimed at making them more marketlike and efficient. For example, one proposal would modify the unemployment compensation program by making it more like welfare. Instead of an entitlement to a set number of weeks of benefits, laid-off workers would be required to take lower-wage jobs as a condition of receiving even time-limited aid. Compensation funds would make up for less than half of the income loss. There would be no net increase in social outlay. This approach would accelerate the movement of the former blue-collar middle class into low-wage service jobs. The change is not complemented by a serious plan to increase the supply of good jobs. This proposal might make a small number of laid-off workers slightly better off in the short run, but it would be a path of downward mobility for most participants, and would fire nobody's imagination.

Another Republican-sounding program would create tax incentives for workers to fund rainy-day accounts, which they could tap if they were laid off or incapacitated. In other words, instead of using the power of government to collect taxes on a progressive basis and using the proceeds to improve the living standards of American workers, this approach requires downwardly mobile workers to prepay the cost of their own dislocation.

Rubin is also a devoutly orthodox free trader. Ostensibly, the Hamilton Project is promoting a grand bargain: to increase social investment so that those displaced by trade can find new opportunities, and then everyone can support the standard trade recipe. But there has been serious resistance to this proposal from the trade unions, because adequate social investment to create good jobs never seems to be forthcoming. At one awkward public session of the Hamilton Project, its sponsors were challenged to produce the increased social outlay as a precondition for the next round of trade liberalization rather than at some subsequent point in the vague future. They demurred. Covering the event for *The Washington Post*, the business reporter Steven Pearlstein wrote:

> The problem is that, when you scratch the surface, the free-trade members of the Democratic establishment turn out to be more committed to Part A of the formula, more globalization, than they are to

Part B, making sure the benefits from globalization are widely shared. For them, it's really not a package deal. And if push comes to shove, which it always does in trade politics, they'd welcome more globalization even without the compensatory social policies. How do I know this? Because they said so. At the [Hamilton Project] conference's closing session, I asked former Treasury secretaries Robert Rubin and Larry Summers and former deputy Treasury secretary Roger Altman if any of them would be willing to support the idea of a "time out" on new free-trade initiatives until there was some tangible progress toward greater economic security for U.S. workers. To a man, they recoiled at the idea.

Rubin has also spent great effort trying to promote a grand bargain of budget balancing, using his extensive Republican contacts at the Treasury, of which his former partner, Henry Paulson, became secretary in mid-2006. Well-placed sources tell me Rubin even spoke to President Bush personally. Rubin was selling a deal in which Democrats would put entitlement caps on the table—deep reductions in Social Security and Medicare—in exchange for Republicans' willingness to roll back some of Bush's tax cuts. He unveiled his plan in *The Wall Street Journal*, rather generously (and spuriously) allocating the blame for the lack of fiscal discipline to both parties. But while the Republicans were eager to create a bipartisan entitlement commission, to reduce the value to voters of the Democrats' crown jewels, they were not budging on taxes. Rubin is circumspect about whom he spoke with and what exactly he proposed, but he confirms that no senior Republican would put taxes on the table. In this respect, the Republicans saved Rubin from a deal that would have crippled two Democratic crown-jewel programs, Social Security and Medicare, which are the Democrats' prime claim to supporting an equitable society.

There have been influential Wall Street Democrats before. In the late 1920s, John J. Raskob, the party treasurer and executive of General Motors and DuPont, was a powerfully conservatizing influence on the pre-Roosevelt Democratic Party. The treasury secretaries under Democratic presidents Roosevelt, Truman, Johnson, Kennedy, and Carter all were fiscal and regulatory conservatives, as were such Democratic Party leader-cum-lobbyist types as Bob Strauss and Tony Coelho in the 1970s and 1980s. But none of these Democrats combined Rubin's power in financial markets, his admiring press, and his broad sway over the party's economic posture. Other men have stood at the pinnacle of Wall Street. No one else has simultaneously been at the pinnacle of the Democratic Party.

In April 2004, AFL-CIO President John Sweeney grew concerned that John Kerry was getting too much of his economic advice from the Wall Street wing of the party. Kerry had just completed his primary sweep. In the general election, he would need the unions. Sweeney proposed a private meeting to discuss living standards as a campaign issue, and the candidate invited the labor leader to his Beacon Hill home. Sweeney arrived at the Kerry manse, bringing his policy director, Chris Owens, and Jeff Faux of the Economic Policy Institute. There, seated in the elegant living room, were Robert Rubin and two longtime lieutenants: investment banker and former Rubin deputy Roger Altman, and fellow Clinton alum Gene Sperling—Kerry's key economic advisers.

In a three-hour conversation, the group discussed the deficit, taxes, trade, health care, unions, and living standards. Eventually, Kerry announced that the meeting needed to wrap up, because "Bob has to get back to Washington." Rubin responded that, no, he could stay as long as Kerry wanted. Sweeney and his colleagues were ushered out the door; Rubin, Altman, and Sperling remained. "Wall Street was in the room before we arrived," Faux recalled to me, "and they were there after we left." In the current presidential election, Rubin is playing a similar role with front-runner Hillary Clinton, and he is very influential with the Democratic House and Senate leadership as well.

A blind spot in the usual media criticism of the Democratic Party's capture by "interest groups" is the failure to even conceive of Wall Street as an interest group. In the familiar account, the obstacles to the party's modernization and political renewal are such groups as abortion-rights advocates, blacks, gays, and unions. Candidates can score points with pundits for showing independence by taking on, say, the unions on school vouchers; or showing distance from the African-American leadership by backing away from affirmative action; or rejecting civil libertarian opposition to the death penalty; or seeking some kind of middle ground on gay marriage and abortion rights.

Such actions are said to show political courage by resisting "politically correct" politics and entrenched interest groups. But taking on the most powerful Democratic Party interest group of them all—Wall Street—is viewed as a sign of recklessness, unsoundness, demagoguery, and political suicide. A mark of Wall Street's ubiquitous power in defining the limits of the politically thinkable is that its power is hardly noticed.

The personification of this power is Robert Rubin. His rise is not just personal, but structural. He epitomizes Wall Street's bipartisan lock on financial policy.

Rubin is widely admired as a public-minded leader and the man who engineered the Clinton recovery. As I have suggested, that premise is contradicted by the economic evidence. The conflicts between his role as a very senior Wall Street executive and his status as leading economic adviser to the Democratic Party go largely unremarked. Today, Rubin's outsized influence narrows, if not strangles, the ability of Democrats to offer fundamental economic reforms that might rally the support of middle and working class America. I asked Rubin how he thought a program based on budget austerity, capped entitlements, and mostly small-scale improvements in social programs could possibly be a winning program for Democrats during a time when most voters feel squeezed economically. "The politics is the hardest part," Rubin admitted.

The supposed fiscal risks all have relatively easy solutions. America can easily afford decent social insurance that benefits the vast majority of people who are not independently wealthy. We just need to decide to pay for it. We can easily bring the deficit down to a sustainable 1 or 2 percent of GDP by restoring the tax code that we had in 2000 and still finance Social Security, Medicare, and new social investments to compensate for the shift of risks onto individuals, as well as financing other national needs such as adequate public infrastructure.

The systemic risks caused by increased speculation, however, are much more problematic, and they will remain that way until we adjust our politics. Globalization of finance and commerce makes it all the easier to deregulate and all the more difficult to maintain a system of equitable and secure capitalism at home. Not surprisingly, Wall Street Democrats are as passionate as Republicans about liberating commerce and capital to operate globally, free from the hard-won constraints of managed capitalism.

CHAPTER SEVEN

EQUALITY, EFFICIENCY, AND GLOBALISM

GLOBAL COMMERCE UNDERCUTS the model of managed capitalism and the equalizing mechanisms of the nation-state. It presents challenges of governance far more difficult, both politically and institutionally, than the governance of capitalism inside a sovereign country. By undermining national countervailing institutions, global commerce has made it easier politically for the owners of capital to move the market system back more than a century, to an era when property rights were paramount and offsetting social rights nonexistent; when there was little taxation of capital and even less regulation of labor or of the environment.

Global commerce enables transnational corporations to play off one country against another—but it doesn't always allow them to escape the consequences of their own self-interested folly. Indeed, the history of modern capitalism is a chronicle of national governments enacting rules not just to make society more equitable but to save the market system from itself. Far from obviating that need, globalism makes the project much harder to achieve.

One ray of hope, however, lies in the fact that, despite globalization and the pressure to dismantle managed capitalism, business still requires some things from government, among other things the enforcement of its property rights. And even if business prefers weak regulation, it needs common regulatory standards so that the commercial environment is not a crazy quilt of varying national laws. Although business tries to have standards decided by industry self-regulation, it cannot get rid of government entirely. Everything from accounting standards to the treatment of transnational banks, food safety, and antitrust rules requires some system for regulation, and ideally regulatory convergence in different countries.

It is not efficient, for example, for agribusiness to have to deal with one set of food safety standards in the United States and a different one in the European Union, or different antitrust regimes in different markets. Though globalization tends to produce a "race to the bottom" by disadvantaging nations with costly systems of social overhead and worker protection, it doesn't dispense with the rules of commerce altogether. In a few cases, such as the European Union's antitrust standards, which are tougher than those in the United States, or the Kyoto Accord, globalization may even produce the beginning of a race to the top. But the relatively undemocratic and unaccountable way in which trade rules are negotiated still generally tilts the field against citizens and in favor of organized capital.

Property Rights, Labor Rights

An emblematic case of this double standard is the way in which the trading system has gone about dealing with intellectual property rights and labor rights. Strictly speaking, neither has anything to do with the rules of trade as traditionally understood, which were mainly about tariffs. Until the Uruguay Round of trade negotiations, consummated in 1994, intellectual property was not part of the trade agenda. There was, and still is, a very weak international body called the World Intellectual Property Organization (WIPO) and an equally weak labor counterpart, the International Labour Organization (ILO). Though major nations had signed various conventions on intellectual property and on respect for such "core labor rights" as a ban on child labor, in both cases the standards were largely unenforceable.

In the discussions leading up to the Uruguay Round, aggressive lobbying by several U.S.-based industries, most notably the pharmaceutical and motion picture industries, persuaded the Reagan administration to put intellectual property on the trade agenda. They came up with a negotiating category called TRIPS, for Trade-Related Aspects of Intellectual Property Rights. Their argument was that nations that expected to benefit from exports to the U.S. market should respect intellectual property rights—patents, trademarks, and copyrights—and not just any version of property rights, but something close to the U.S. system.

In principle, this goal was perfectly legitimate. American industry was suffering from wholesale piracy of everything from proprietary formulas for drugs that had cost billions in research dollars to knockoffs of movies and software disks. If the United States was going to open its markets to imports, it was only fair that trading nations not steal products that would otherwise have been exported to them by the United States.

However, the devil is in the details. Regulation of intellectual property is a balancing act between rewarding innovators and diffusing the fruits of that innovation to society as a whole. When the framers of the U.S. Constitution gave Congress the authority to legislate protection of patents, trademarks, and copyrights, Congress initially provided relatively short terms of protection, and that in an era when the pace of innovation was far slower than it is today. In recent years, industry has successfully lobbied Congress for ever-longer protection, and the patent laws have been changed in ways that give excessive protection to supposed innovators. This exaggerated protection is economically inefficient, since it comes at the expense both of future innovation and of present diffusion of knowledge. It results in excess profits—what economists call "monopoly rents"—that harm both potential competitors and innovators, as well as consumers in the United States and overseas.

For example, despite the fact that the Human Genome Project is mostly taxpayer-funded, with research properly in the public domain, private industry has filed tens of thousands of patent claims on more than a hundred thousand human gene sequences. Drug companies have patented traditional remedies made of materials in the public domain long used by native peoples. The more that this science is balkanized, the more researchers are deterred from advances, because of the fear of infringing on someone else's patent. Investments in intellectual property litigation become more important than investments in the research itself.

The process of research depends on having a large information commons, in which broad knowledge is in the public domain. In the past, scientists have been forceful defenders of free, rather than proprietary, information. When Jonas Salk was asked why he hadn't patented his newly invented polio vaccine, he replied, "Could you patent the sun?"

Lately, American industry has sought to patent, if not the sun, nearly everything under it. In the trade context, the cost falls disproportionately on poor people in poor nations, who cannot afford to pay commercial prices for AIDS treatment and many other lifesaving drugs that could be produced generically as social goods. During both the Clinton and Bush administrations, U.S. trade negotiators aggressively sided with U.S. drug companies. Only concerted resistance by developing nations and nongovernmental advocacy groups resulted in a partial retreat by the drug makers. After he left office, Clinton helped broker some of these deals.

The excessive protection of the intellectual property of some—but not all—of U.S. industry is instructive for our larger story about trade, in three respects. First, it is an example of the fact that there is no such thing as free trade. If trade were purely free, there would be no intellectual property rights. (Several successful industrial countries, including Switzerland and the Netherlands, had no patents at all until the early twentieth century. The United States, in the nineteenth century, did not recognize foreign patents.) With true free trade, India's pharmaceutical makers would be at liberty to manufacture generic versions of drugs invented by American manufacturers, and China's software companies could make knockoffs of Microsoft Windows.

The solution is not to ignore intellectual property protection in trade. That denies innovators the legitimate fruits of their creation. But there is no intuitively correct answer about what kind of regime for intellectual property to establish or precisely what degree of protection to offer.

Some American industries, such as pharmaceutical manufacturers, are, by any reasonable standard, overprotected. Others are underprotected because of the failure of many East Asian nations to live up to the terms of the intellectual property accords they signed in 1994. Intellectual property protection is only as good as its enforcement, and enforcement by China, South Korea, and Japan, among others, is notoriously biased against foreigners. East Asian nations also use their market power to coerce licensing or transfer of proprietary technology, another violation of the spirit of respect for intellectual property.

As the reader will have observed, a word that keeps recurring in this discussion of intellectual property rights is that slippery word "protection." The jeremiads against "protectionism" miss the mark because commerce itself depends on some protections that can only be enforced by states, or by common-law litigation in courts created and operated by states, or by international bodies authorized by states. These include protections of property, of foreign assets against seizure, of debt repayment, and of sanitary standards in food commerce, among many other protections. Within very broad limits, what to protect and what not to protect in a market economy is indeterminate for economic efficiency. We could imagine stronger or weaker bankruptcy, antitrust, patent, and worker safety laws. Depending on the particulars, the result could be a more—or less—efficient economy. We could likewise imagine a trade regime with weaker or stronger protection for intellectual property or for labor. And we could envision a trade system that did not allow exporting nations to reap an artificial cost advantage by despoiling the environment.

The actual protections that we get are not the result of seminar room deliberations about economic efficiency or of optimizing the blend of efficiency and equality. They are the fruits of political power. The drug industry is more highly organized than the labor movement or the small business sector, so the tax-subsidized pharmaceutical companies get too much protection, while many smaller entrepreneurs seeking market access to Asia find their patented products and technologies pirated.

But the "free-market" solution of just getting rid of all "protections" is nonsensical. In a democracy, there is no way to avoid the fact that decisions are made via the political process. Deciding *not* to protect intellectual property—or labor or the environment—is just as political an affair as deciding to protect it.

In recent negotiations, business lobbyists have been powerful enough to get intellectual property rights onto the trade agenda. For the most part, labor lobbyists have been too weak to have labor rights included.

Why labor rights? When workers in two different countries with very different living standards and wages are thrown into direct competition, their wages tend to converge. It would be nice if that convergence were upward—Mexican and Chinese wages rapidly rising toward American standards. But that is not what is occurring. With hundreds of millions of workers competing for jobs and no minimal standards of decency, that convergence is more likely to be downward. As the Harvard economist Dani Rodrik has pointed out, even American economists who favor free trade would oppose allowing employers in the United States to resort to child labor or slave labor. But as long as the workers are overseas, we give those practices a free pass.

Western financial and business elites are very adroit at using workers in Third World countries as the poster children for their own brand of free-market economics. Supposedly, more laissez-faire trade would give these poor nations the capital they need to grow, as well as access to markets in rich countries. In this narrative, workers in the advanced countries who want to maintain a regulated form of capitalism are pursuing their selfish goal at the expense of their poorer Third World brethren (it's always charming to hear these arguments advanced by multimillionaires).

But this framing powerfully confuses the debate. At a conference in October 2006 on the impact of low-wage foreign labor on U.S. living standards, I heard a well-meaning commentator indignantly declare, "When I see Chinese peasants, I don't see 'low-wage labor'; I see poor people." The premise is that American workers should feel guilty for defending a fraying social compact that gives them a decent share of the American economic product. In the same spirit, former *New York Times* columnist John Tierney chided critics of low-wage domestic employers such as Wal-Mart, "Shouldn't you be more worried about villagers overseas subsisting on a dollar a day?"

Consider what this glib formulation conceals. The premise is that economic growth is both necessary and sufficient to increase living standards and that laissez-faire trade optimizes both the rate of growth and the diffusion of prosperity. But the whole history of industrial society demonstrates that a socially tolerable income distribution, and the efficient operation of capitalism itself, depend on extra-market mechanisms. Moreover, American workers can use the democratic process to promote a managed form of capitalism, because they are citizens of a democratically governed nation-state with the authority to regulate the market economy. There is no global polity, hence no democratic mechanism to regulate global capitalism, except at one remove. To a far greater degree than domestic social policies, trade policies have been effectively captured by an elite. So even if we could imagine win-win global labor policies, which could help both Wal-Mart's retail sales force in America and workers in China producing for Wal-Mart to gain a larger share of the fruits of their labor, such policies are not on the trade agenda.

Supposedly, by initially working for starvation wages, Third World workers embark on a path to higher growth and better living standards. Eventually, their increased demand generates a virtuous circle of higher consumption and further investment. But as Jonathan Hiatt and Deborah Greenfield of the AFL-CIO observe, "The implicit assumption that poor country workers will benefit from the comparative wage advantage of their national economies applies only if workers are able to capture the economic benefits of their labor. . . . Employers rarely pay workers more than they are obliged to, [so] workers can only capture this share if they are able to exert some bargaining power in the labor market."

A wage is a price—the price of labor. If workers in Michigan and Michoacán are working with the identical production technology, and the going rate for semiskilled labor is $20 an hour in the former and $2 an hour in the latter, this disparity will not last for long. Even if the American worker is personally twice as productive as the Mexican counterpart, most of the "productivity" is a function of the technology, not the human effort. If capital is mobile and comparable production technologies are available, workers' productivity levels will soon converge.

In principle, wages will rise with productivity. But whether wages actually rise with productivity in practice depends on the relative bargaining power of workers and their employers. As Wal-Mart introduces ever more sophisticated systems for inventory control, its workers become more productive. But their wages don't rise. And Wal-Mart uses its immense purchasing power to make sure that Chinese workers' wages don't rise with increased productivity either.

In postwar America, wages did rise with productivity. Government policies permitting organization and recognition of trade unions, and regulating labor in other ways such as wages-and-hours laws, facilitated that process. However, in a world with hundreds of millions of desperately poor people and many repressive governments that do not respect labor rights, wages will not follow productivity upward; or they will do so at such a slow pace that they will powerfully drag other wages downward.

The domestic social compact of the postwar era was built on a tripod: one part aggregate demand at high levels; one part state regulation, to give labor more equal bargaining power with business; and one part social insurance. The international institutions created in the mid-1940s by moderate leftists were intended to counteract the deflationary tendency of global private finance. This was a society that most Americans valued. But globalization clearly undercuts workers' bargaining power because it frees industry to seek cheaper and less empowered labor. When we import Chinese products, we hope not to import China's norms of political democracy and civil liberty. Why should we import China's norms about how workers should be treated?

As a challenge for trade policy, the problem divides into several parts. To the extent that foreign wages are being held down repressively, cutting into living standards in the United States and other advanced nations, this repression can be understood as an illicit subsidy. The artificially depressed labor costs, well below what the workers' productivity warrants, reduce the final price of the product, just as a government subsidy would. So the system needs basic labor standards as a trade issue as well as a human rights issue. When low wages go hand in hand with other mercantilist trade practices aimed at capturing strategic advantage, separate remedies are needed to temper the illicit mercantilism. If we solve those two problems, there still may remain a residual problem: labor-intensive countries with lower living costs paying workers more modest wages for comparably productive work or legitimately making superior products at more attractive prices and thus cutting into U.S.

market share. But if public policy addresses the first two issues—labor repression and other forms of mercantilism—the residual problem will be far smaller.

There was a period in the history of the trade debate when most economists simply denied that this was a problem. As production moved offshore, they argued, living standards in the Third World would rise. Even if wages were highly unequal, that demand had to go somewhere, and some of it would buy goods and services from the United States. If America retained its prowess in research, technology, and a highly educated workforce, we would create new jobs, at even better wages than the jobs we had lost. And in any case, losses to U.S. workers would translate into gains for U.S. consumers as lower foreign wages translated into cheaper imported products. But this account excluded several key factors.

In a world of asymmetric trade and industrial policies, it doesn't logically follow that foreign nations will buy as much as they sell. Yes, America has a knack for inventing new things, such as computer software. But the structural trade deficit makes clear that new technology and new production are occurring disproportionately offshore. And at the level of the global economy, there is something akin to a "reserve army" phenomenon. Once trade barriers fall, the sheer number of worldwide workers seeking employment depresses prevailing wages. Absent government policies to support workers' bargaining power, wages simply lag rising worker productivity. And far from acting to increase workers' bargaining power, many regimes actively suppress it.

Sagging wages create an old problem: depressed worldwide demand. Once economists insisted that total supply had to equal total demand. Since Keynes, most economists have recognized that it's not in fact the case that "the demand has to go somewhere." Depressions occur because demand is insufficient to purchase the available supply. The high savings rates in many Third World countries are the flip side of depressed wages and consumer demand. The theory of comparative advantage, among its other unreal assumptions, presumes equilibrium at full employment. But the actual global economy, with so many desperate people being forced off the land and either taking jobs at desperation wages or swelling the ranks of the urban unemployed, is a far cry from full employment.

At the level of the global economy, norms of what makes for a decent society, and their enforcement, are at best embryonic. The basic standards of the International Labour Organization do not permit child labor, slave labor, and prison labor to qualify as legitimate forms of comparative advantage. These prohibitions are recognized both in the World Trade Organization charter and in U.S. trade law. But in practice, U.S. diplomacy seldom treats even the most extreme labor abuses as unfair trade practices.

Social Rights and Trade

This all suggests the need for an explicit linkage between trade access and labor standards. If we in the democratic West value high living standards and rights of citizens and workers as well as property rights, it is just as legitimate to condition trade on basic social minimums as it is to condition trade on respect for intellectual property. After all, in order to "trade" domestically, employers are required by law to pay minimum wages, to maintain safe workplaces, to refrain from hiring children, to respect collective bargaining rights, and to pay into worker retirement trust funds. If we think these ideas promote a decent economy domestically, they do not cease to make sense when commerce is global. As the world becomes one big marketplace, it is reasonable to apply labor standards worldwide, though not identical standards in every country.

The ideal of broadly diffused living standards rising in tandem with workers' productivity is at worst neutral for economic efficiency and often positive. This is a value choice, not an economic imperative, for there are many paths to growth. China in the 1980s and 1990s shows that a country can have a stunningly high growth rate while it brutally represses labor and holds down wages. Japan, at a similar stage of development in the 1950s and 1960s, had a more equal income distribution than the United States—and does to this day. The Japanese model combined a more egalitarian society with a prodigious growth record comparable to China's. The fact that Japan and China both grew by using "beggar-my-neighbor" strategic trade practices at the expense of other nations is a separate problem.

Not surprisingly, the idea of linking trade access to labor rights is fiercely resisted by business. When the Beijing government, partly in response to Western criticism of working conditions, put out a draft law for comment in the spring of 2006, proposing greater rights for trade unions, it was attacked by the American Chamber of Commerce in China. U.S. businesses warned that proposed protections against arbitrary layoffs could slow Western investment in China. Some companies even compared the proposed union rights to the old days of a more socialistic China (even though every democratic country in the world allows free trade unions). Such nerve—the People's Republic of China, which had been conveniently providing cheap and docile labor for global capital, was behaving like . . . a bunch of Communists! But American multinationals needn't worry. Beijing has no intention of allowing truly independent trade unions. The gesture about stronger labor rights was mostly a feint.

If acceptance of ILO standards, including the right to organize free trade unions, were linked to the privileges of membership in the World Trade Organization in an enforceable manner, wages in Third World countries would be more likely to rise in tandem with rising worker productivity. Some American jobs would still be lost because of the lower prevailing living costs in poor countries, but the artificial advantage of repressed labor would be sharply reduced.

In March 2004 and again in June 2006, the AFL-CIO petitioned the U.S. trade representative (USTR), contending that the repressive Chinese labor system was in effect an unfair subsidy and not a form of natural comparative advantage reflecting China's relative poverty and lower productivity. Both petitions were summarily rejected by the Bush administration. Both petitions requested trade sanctions under Section 301 of the 1974 Trade Act, which permits retaliation against unfair trade practices. Describing China's system as "government-engineered labor exploitation," the 2006 petition described the strictly enforced migration from rural villages to urban factories:

> When migrants enter the factory system they often step into a nightmare of twelve-hour to eighteen-hour work days with no day of rest, earning meager wages that may be withheld or unpaid altogether. The factories are often sweltering, dusty, and damp. Workers are widely exposed to chemical toxins and hazardous machines, and suffer sickness, disfiguration, and death at the highest rates in world history. They live in cramped cement-block dormitories, up to twenty to a room, with each worker's space limited to a bed in a two-tiered bunk—comparable in space, discomfort, and privacy to prison cells in the United States. They typically face militaristic regimentation, surveillance, and physical abuse by supervisors during their long day of work and by private police forces during their short night of recuperation in the dormitories. Ten to twenty million workers in China are children. No one knows the precise number, because statistics of that kind are state secrets, and anyone disseminating such data is sub-

ject to criminal punishment. Another one to six million are detained without fair trial and forced to labor in China's prison system, under threat of violence and torture. . . . Global corporations from Wal-Mart to Procter & Gamble to Delphi to Dell relentlessly squeeze labor costs in their Chinese affiliates and suppliers and use the threat of low-wage competition to roll back decades of hard-won gains in wages, benefits, and dignified treatment for workers in the United States. The severe exploitation of China's factory workers and the contraction of the American middle class are two sides of a coin.

In rejecting the petitions, the Bush administration did not deny the deplorable conditions in China or even their effect on American jobs and wages. Rather, U.S. officials cited ongoing (and largely cosmetic) discussions with the Chinese government. The Beijing regime initially exchanged letters of understanding with the U.S. Department of Labor, promising to improve working conditions, but no such improvement occurred. And in 2005, the annual report of the U.S. Congressional-Executive Commission on China declared that the Beijing government had simply "avoided discussions with the international labor community on Chinese workers' rights."

Although it is rarely appreciated and even more rarely used by the executive branch, Section 301 of the Trade Act explicitly provides that denial of basic workers' rights is an unfair trade practice subject to remediation or retaliation. The listed basic rights are freedom of association, freedom to bargain collectively, and freedom from forced labor and child labor, as well as state-enforced minimum wages and occupational safety and health standards. Congress added these provisions in 1974, when competition from exploited foreign workers was first becoming a problem, specifically to discourage trade advantage based on labor repression. But the U.S. government has refused to apply this criterion to China despite overwhelming evidence. In fact, in its recent reports on enforcement efforts on Section 301, USTR describes its extensive efforts to protect intellectual property—and says nothing on the subject of labor conditions, despite the mandate in U.S. law.

Modest progress in two bilateral trade deals negotiated by the Clinton administration, however, suggests that linkage between trade and labor rights is administratively and diplomatically possible. In negotiating a trade agreement with Jordan, the Clinton administration, heavily prodded by its trade union allies, included a clause providing that both signatories affirmed their commitment to ILO core labor standards.

However, in the case of a dispute, the agreement's enforcement language is so weak as to be almost meaningless. Moreover, Jordan is both a monarchy and a key U.S. ally in a region where Washington can count on few friendly Arab governments. The idea of the United States getting tough with the Jordanians over Jordan's labor standards is just about inconceivable.

A somewhat stronger agreement was negotiated with Cambodia. In a little-noticed and unprecedented bilateral trade deal, the United States in 1999 explicitly tied an increase in Cambodia's quotas for garment exports to the United States to the country's progress in allowing labor unions to operate freely and upholding other core labor rights. This unique deal grew out of a complaint by the Union of Needletrades, Industrial and Textile Employees (UNITE), the U.S. garment and textile workers' union, that repressive labor conditions in Cambodia were leading to unfair low-wage competition, as Cambodian exports to the United States increased.

As signed in 1999, the trade deal gave the Cambodians a bonus of up to 14 percent in its annual quota, to the extent that the ILO certified that its garment factories were in compliance with core ILO standards, including enforcement of minimum wages and the freedom of unions to organize. Thanks to this linkage, the Cambodian labor movement has been able to unionize a major garment factory in Phnom Penh, winning gains in wages and working conditions. The government has issued regulations making it more difficult for employers to retaliate against workers seeking to organize unions and it has cracked down directly on several abusive employer practices. In 2003, a newly formed union federation representing hotel and other service workers won another major victory when the government's new system of labor arbitration upheld the unions' complaint that hotel operators were pocketing the "service charge" levied on guests in lieu of tips instead of paying it to workers. The Raffles hotel chain was compelled to give workers back pay and to rehire hundreds of workers who had been fired for complaining. None of this likely would have occurred without the trade-labor linkage. It's proof positive that wages do not spontaneously rise with increased productivity and increased global commerce. Whether they do or not is a function of rules and of bargaining power.

With this kind of linkage, consumer and labor pressure can also be applied to U.S. multilateral companies such as the Gap and Nike that produce in, or purchase from, Cambodia to do business only with enterprises that honor core labor standards. And the U.S. labor movement can work closely with its Cambodian counterpart to use these pressure points to make sure the nominal guarantees result in reforms. With a stronger labor movement, political candidates who support workers' rights have increased their seats in the Cambodian national legislature.

Not only did this accord help the fledgling free labor movement in Cambodia gain a foothold, it rewarded Cambodia's progress with a quota increase that translated into an estimated ten thousand additional jobs. The fact that these jobs paid higher wages than they otherwise would have serves to reduce the pressure on U.S. workers to accede to the lowering of their own wages.

It's a heartening story. However, the entire quota system for textiles and apparel expired in 2004, and with it the labor provisions of the U.S.-Cambodia deal. In other recent trade negotiations, labor goals have been even weaker.

One could imagine using the Cambodia model as the germ of a very different strategy of linkage between trade and labor, in which a nation's ability to enjoy exports free of tariffs or quotas would depend on its embrace of core labor rights. This is not nearly as far-fetched as it sounds. There was a time when Europe and the United States had very limited trade with the then-Communist countries. The essence of the Communist economy was that prices were not set by markets, so there was no pretense that trade with Communist Bulgaria, for example, was in any sense "free trade." It was administered trade, and it was entirely appropriate that the trade be regulated by tariffs, quotas, and government licenses. By analogy, it is entirely appropriate to insist that nations that want barrier-free commerce with the West need to respect basic norms that have long been part of the West's social compact: labor rights as well as property rights.

In May 2007, some Democratic leaders in Congress offered President Bush new trade negotiating authority in exchange for a provision that pending bilateral agreements would include labor and environmental provisions. Most observers concluded that these would be mere window dressing. A serious version of a labor-trade linkage would require the ILO to certify that the nation in question was in compliance with the ILO's core labor standards, most important the right to organize free trade unions and to bargain collectively. Any fair review would hold that the United States is not currently in compliance because of the government's indulgence of gross violations of the Wagner Act. Just as the side agreements on labor and the environment under NAFTA (negotiated by President Clinton) turned out to be meaningless sops to Democrats in

Congress, it is even more improbable that the Bush administration would concede serious enforcement rights.

Battering Down Taxes

An economy that includes social investment aimed at expanding opportunity and security incurs public costs. Education, socially provided health care, worker retraining, environmental protection, services for the elderly, all require government outlays. The nations that value these social protections pay for them with a mix of out-of-pocket charges and taxes.

Organized business is increasingly mobilized against taxes, as a matter of both profit maximization and free-market ideology. The more that global capital becomes portable, the easier it is for business to avoid jurisdictions with high or progressive tax structures. And conservative administrations in the major countries increasingly help business allies to win lower tax rates, weaken enforcement, or avoid taxation with off-shoring schemes that often barely skirt the law and sometimes cross the line into illegality.

Tax competition—the playing off of one nation against another to lower tax rates and enforcement practices—has succeeded in drastically reducing the level of corporate taxation in all of the advanced nations that are members of the Organization for Economic Cooperation and Development (OECD). In 1997, for example, the British chancellor of the Exchequer, Gordon Brown, declared in his annual budget speech, "I want the U.K. to be the obvious first choice for new investment. So I have decided to cut the main rate of corporation tax by two percent, from 33% to 31%, the lowest rate ever in the U.K. This means we will have the lowest corporation tax rate of any of our major competitors." In 2000, the Canadian government went the British one better, promising to gradually reduce the tax rate on corporate profits from 28 percent to 21 percent over five years.

In March 2007, Gordon Brown, preparing to take over as prime minister, led a successful campaign to cut the British corporate tax rate yet again, to 28 percent. The Germans followed suit, announcing plans to cut the German rate from 39 to 30 percent. Meanwhile, the Germans have raised taxes on workers and consumers to make up the revenue loss. Many Germans rightly complain that part of their tax payments go to the European Union, which sends regional development subsidies to new E.U. member nations such as Slovakia—which turn around and offer extremely low tax rates with which to lure corporations and jobs away from Germany. In the ten years between 1995 and 2005, the average corporate tax rate in member nations of the European Union was cut by 8.1 percentage points in older members of the European Union and even more, 10.8 points, in newer members from eastern and central Europe competing for foreign investment.

For ideological conservatives opposed to taxation and social outlay, this race to the bottom in tax policy produces a secondary gain. As taxes on capital are reduced, either social outlays must be reduced or the taxes lost must be shifted onto workers and consumers. That shift, in turn, leaves ordinary people bearing a relatively higher tax burden in exchange for relatively fewer services and makes a welfare state harder to defend politically. In all of the advanced democracies, taxes paid by business have steadily been reduced. This reduction has been achieved both by lower nominal rates that are applied to corporate profits and to investment income, and through deliberately weakened enforcement practices.

In the United States, median-income workers in 2006 paid a much higher combined rate in payroll taxes, income taxes, and sales taxes than they did in 1966, even though total public outlay relative to GDP was almost identical. In the 1960s, corporate tax receipts produced 16.1 percent of all federal revenue. Though corporate profits are a higher fraction of GDP than ever, corporate tax revenues fell to 9.4 percent in the 1990s and around 7 percent of federal tax receipts today. The same pattern has occurred in nearly every OECD member country.

A related effect of globalization is a huge increase in the opportunities for semilegal tax avoidance as well as criminal tax evasion, both abetted by conservative governments that are happy to see corporations escape taxation one way or another. Arguably legal tax avoidance schemes have become so complex in recent years that national tax authorities mostly throw up their hands. Even mainstream corporate tax planning, using global accounting maneuvers, costs national treasuries several hundreds of billions of dollars each year. Meanwhile, the auditing resources of the IRS have been shifted from corporations and the complex tax avoidance partnerships used by the wealthy to investigations of the modest earned income tax credit available to the working poor.

A multinational corporation with operations in several countries can arrange its internal bookkeeping to minimize taxes owed. Within limits, this tactic, known as transfer pricing, is legal. It is the reason that the tax counsels of large corporations can earn seven-figure salaries for saving their companies nine- and ten-figure tax bills.

Take the case of Intel. With operations in more than thirty countries, it tries to locate new facilities in nations that grant it extensive tax holidays. Intel does not pay U.S. corporate tax on its income from foreign operations, because U.S. law provides that foreign-source income is taxed only when repatriated as dividends. As long as Intel keeps investing in new offshore facilities, it can keep most of its profits from being taxed. The process of tax competition produces a kind of downward leapfrog game. At any given time, the nation with the highest rate of taxation on income from capital is warned by its business interests that it is putting them at a competitive disadvantage. Today, despite enforcement practices that have left the United States with one of the lowest effective tax rates on capital, the nominal rates are above average and business groups continue to demand relief in the name of competitiveness.

This game of global tax competition is played by wealthy individual investors as well as corporations. In 1984, the Reagan administration succeeded in abolishing the withholding tax on interest paid to foreigners. Since then, according to the international tax scholar Reuven Avi-Yonah, "No major nation has been able to impose such a tax for fear of driving mobile capital elsewhere." And a great many investors are able to arbitrage tax enforcement across international borders by putting money into foreign banks, letting the interest compound, and never reporting it as taxable income. Tax scholars have estimated the otherwise taxable capital kept beyond the reach of national tax authorities to be about $9 trillion. Needless to say, this is a game mostly for the rich that shifts the tax burden onto the middle class and the poor.

Beyond tax competition aimed at nations with well-established tax law systems, the existence of offshore tax havens facilitates the process of tax evasion. Avi-Yonah gives the example of a wealthy Mexican who wishes to invest in the bonds of an American corporation and illegally avoid taxation on the interest income by either the Mexican or the U.S. government:

> All he needs to do is set up, for a nominal fee, a Cayman Islands corporation to hold the bonds. The interest payments are then made to the Caymans corporation without any U.S. tax withheld. . . . The individual does not report the income to the Mexican tax authorities, and they have no way of knowing that the Caymans corporation is effectively an "incorporated pocketbook" of the Mexican resident. Nor are the exchange-of-information provisions of the U.S.-Mexico tax treaty of any help, because the IRS has no way of knowing that

the recipient of the interest payments is controlled by a Mexican resident.

Tax haven countries not only benefit from trading with the OECD countries but serve as enablers of illicit and costly tax evasion. Scholars who study tax evasion put the combined annual cost to the treasuries of the United States and western Europe at around half a trillion dollars. In the U.S. case, we lose an estimated $150 billion a year from transnational tax evasion—enough money to finance universal prekindergarten and public child care services three times over or to pay for the expansion of Medicare into universal health insurance.

A tax haven is a nation with a very low or no income tax on corporations or investors and no tax treaty with nations such as those of Europe and North America that have normal systems of tax reporting and collection. Typically, Western countries have treaties with one another mandating information sharing, so that they can detect evasion schemes using foreign bank accounts. Switzerland has long been a haven of a more moderate sort, offering bank secrecy to attract money of dubious provenance. In recent years, especially since September 11, 2001, the Swiss, under pressure from other Western countries, have begun bringing their banking and tax laws into closer conformity with the rest of the OECD.

Because tax haven countries do not have reporting agreements with other countries—and have extreme bank secrecy laws, it is difficult or impossible for the tax authorities of Western nations to track illegal transactions using havens, except when a tax avoider gets careless or an accomplice or a whistle-blower turns state's evidence. Tax evasion schemes take a variety of forms. In addition to the kind of individual tax evasion described above, a corporation based in the United States or western Europe may move its domicile of record to, say, Grand Cayman. Supposedly, commerce that occurs in the United States or Europe requires taxes to be paid in the appropriate jurisdiction, based on complex formulas. With creative accounting, however, a corporation can book its transactions as if they occurred in the tax haven. There are thousands of corporations whose "home office" is a plaque on the door of a law firm located in the Caribbean. A more flagrantly illegal use of a tax haven is simply to hide assets or earnings entirely.

In principle, it would not be difficult for the advanced countries to put tax havens out of business. The major trading nations would simply enact reciprocal national laws, requiring any bank, corporation, partnership, or individual doing business both in the treaty country and with a bank or corporation located in a tax haven to report to domestic tax authorities all financial transactions using the tax haven. Alternatively, the major nations could flatly prohibit commerce with countries that refused to sign tax enforcement treaties. What prevents governments from doing this is of course the political power of organized business.

An epic case of the power of business to frustrate international tax enforcement is the fate of a rather modest initiative proposed by the governments of the United States and western Europe. In 1998, major Western governments launched the Project on Harmful Tax Practices, under the auspices of the OECD. What the initiative did *not* attempt to do is as significant as what it did. It made no effort to curb tax competition based on tax rates or to discourage transnational corporations from playing off one country against another to win tax breaks; that brand of tax competition had become accepted as normal. The OECD initiative was aimed at sheer illegality.

Small offshore countries like Aruba and the Cayman Islands are pure tax havens—nations whose economies are built around a blend of tourism and money laundering. The Cayman Islands, for example, derive about 30 percent of their gross national product from their banking industry, almost all illicit commerce, tax evasion, or as the nominal domicile of enterprises such as hedge funds seeking to avoid national regulations (why else bank in the Cayman Islands?). The initial proposal targeted the forty-one most egregious tax havens. The basic idea was to request these countries to modify their bank secrecy laws to share information on transactions involving foreign nationals—or face economic sanctions from the OECD countries.

What happened next speaks volumes. Conservative think tanks, backed by organized business interests, began a campaign against the proposed enforcement agreements. Note that the proposed agreement was not aimed at what has become normal tax avoidance accounting, much less the effort to play off countries against one another to reduce tax rates—only at outright illegality. But conservative tax policy advocates, such as Daniel Mitchell at the Heritage Foundation, have repeatedly declared that if taxation is a form of theft or a drag on the economy, then tax evasion is economically efficient and even a form of virtuous civil disobedience.

Mitchell, in a brief widely circulated by the Heritage Foundation, argued that "tax competition should be celebrated, not persecuted." He described the proposed enforcement program as "an affront to free trade" and "an attack on sovereignty" of small nations. Of course, when U.S. muscle is brought to bear to defend corporate intellectual property rights or to collect debts incurred by banks to often corrupt Third World dictators, American free-market enthusiasts never criticize these moves as attacks on sovereignty.

Corporate lobbyists and the corporate tax counsel bar quickly got to the Republicans. When the Bush administration took office in January 2001, one of the first acts by incoming Treasury Secretary Paul O'Neill was to kill U.S. support for the OECD enforcement initiative. The attacks of September 11, 2001, using money transferred from various off-shore accounts, occurred just months later. Since 9/11, the Bush administration has increased its pressure on banks to supply information aimed at combating money laundering with national security implications but has continued to resist the use of similar information-sharing measures intended to reduce tax evasion. IRS resources continue to be directed away from audits of international corporations and the tax avoidance partnership schemes of wealthy individuals—and onto small taxpayers.

The dramatic increase in global commerce would create a tax enforcement challenge under any circumstances, because it is difficult to monitor economic activity by U.S.-based persons and corporations that occurs beyond national borders. Major nations would need to sign enforcement and information exchange treaties with one another and with every smaller country that offers an opportunity for tax evasion. Alternatively, they might pool tax collection and enforcement by creating a new transnational organization. But neither has occurred—because conservative governments backed by business interests serve as enablers of tax evasion.

The Global Market as Underdeveloped Law

Looked at in a longer perspective, the broad problem of global regulation of the market needs to be understood in the context of several hundred years of development of national civil, criminal, commercial, and social law. This evolution occurred within sovereign states and grew into highly refined systems of due process, with rules of evidence, precedents, appeals, and the like.

Only in the twentieth century did advanced nations begin to add social and environmental rights to the well-established body of property rights. But as we have seen in the case of labor standards, international tax enforcement and intellectual property protection, transnational systems for the enforcement of rights and duties are far cruder and more rudimentary administratively, as well as biased against the idea that property rights should be balanced against social rights.

For example, the way the WTO works, complaints may be lodged by companies or unions, but it is up to national governments to prosecute them. WTO panels are far less subject to the rules of judicial fairness and due process than are national courts of law. Dispute panels operate in secret, there is no public participation, no independent test of expertise or impartiality, and no appeals process. "*Ex parte* contacts" (communications with the judge outside of the formal proceeding) and conflicts of interest are not prohibited, and a member of a WTO panel serving in the role of judge may also be a business consultant.

When a nation is found in violation of a WTO commitment—let's say it improperly subsidizes an export product and injures the exports of a competing nation or its labor standards violate U.S. trade law—the grieving party has to decide whether it is worth the candle to impose the remedies authorized by the WTO, for example, countervailing tariffs equal to the amount of the improper subsidy. For enforcement purposes, the grieving party is the government of the country where the actual complainant is domiciled. When that nation is the United States, the leader of the entire commercial and military system, Washington often concludes that it doesn't want to set off a trade war and that it has higher diplomatic priorities. The actual injured party is often out of luck—or concludes that it had better come to terms with the perpetrator of the injury.

Several good, highly technical books have been written on the governance of the multiple dimensions of globalized commerce as a legal, administrative, and political challenge from A to Z—everything from antitrust enforcement to rules for transporting animals to zoos. According to one encyclopedic compendium, *Global Business Regulation*, by John Braithwaite and Peter Drahos, globalization has begun to produce some ratcheting up of standards, most notably in some areas of environmental policy and in intellectual property rights. While globalization has engendered some hopeful processes such as the Kyoto Accord, it has also accelerated the exploitation of once-pristine rain forests and traditional fishing grounds. But after an exhaustive survey of various substantive areas of commerce and law, the authors conclude that in the key area of financial regulation, "[r]atcheting down has been the dominant dynamic—globalizing deregulation."

Globalization is relevant because it intensifies the opportunities for corporate dominance. As it turns out, for the most part globalization biases the regulatory process against strong counterweights to private markets. Much regulation of cross-border commerce is accomplished privately by contract and by industry-dominated trade organizations. A great deal of this works well enough to sort out competing commercial interests but not to balance them against the public interest. Energy companies have carved up the world's oil fields, and if they poach on one another's claims, lawyers are at the ready. But countervailing global environmental standards are far from adequate. Commercial interests try to sort out who has the rights to which fishing grounds, but the world's fish stocks are rapidly dwindling, and a recent report projects the near extinction of the most widely consumed species within a few decades. Private agreements among individual fleets do not solve the larger collective action problem. A massive struggle is similarly under way between private companies seeking to commodify the world's drinking water supplies, inevitably raising prices, and public-minded forces working to maintain water as a public good.

Almost by definition, conflicts of this sort are more balanced and more transparent when played out within a national polity where there are well-established traditions of deliberation, democracy, and law. Private contract law is good enough to allow banks to extend credit across borders and collect debts in normal circumstances. But, as we have seen, in times of crisis, banks go running to governments, even as they lobby governments not to limit their ability to make risky loans.

Can Islands of Social Justice Survive?

As globalization adds to the political forces that undercut managed capitalism, an intriguing question is whether nations or groups of nations that opt for a more equitable and stable form of social market economy can survive politically, economically, or institutionally. To put a finer point on the question, can they survive by using regulations, social investments, taxes, and income transfers to counteract the effects of the global market on a more secure and egalitarian brand of capitalism? Or must they also challenge the rules of globalization and liberation of market forces that undermine their domestic managed economy?

The most instructive case in point is, of course, the European Union. European capitalism gets an undeservedly scornful press in the United States for its alleged "sclerosis." To read the usual commentaries, one would think that Europe's mixed economy was about to collapse into a morass of high unemployment, lagging entrepreneurship, and taxpayer backlash.

The facts diametrically contradict the stereotypes. For starters, European rates of per capita productivity growth are comparable to those of the United States. It is productivity growth that ultimately drives economic growth. Some of Europe, with its more regulated labor markets, ostensibly has higher rates of unemployment than the United States. But if you compare apples with apples—the percentage of working-age adults who are employed—social Europe actually manages to provide more jobs, as well as better jobs, for its population than the United States does.

According to the OECD, the employment rate of American men in 2003, for example, was 76.9 percent—almost identical to that of men in the nations with the most advanced welfare states, Norway, Sweden, Denmark, and Finland, where it was 75.8 percent. But in the Nordic countries, which have much more generous social policies to allow parents to reconcile work and family responsibilities, the rate of female employment was 70.5 percent, compared to 65.7 percent in the United States. So social Europe beat free-market America by about 2 percentage points in providing jobs for the entire population. And of course the working conditions, wages, vacation days, and social protections are far superior in Europe. Even France, with its lower population growth (and bad reputation), has had a higher rate of job growth in recent years than the United States—an average of 1.5 percent per year between 1995 and 2003, compared to 1.3 percent in the United States.

By most of the other indicators that economists use to assess the health of economies, social Europe is doing at least as well as free-market America. It has higher savings rates, far better balanced trade accounts, and better fiscal discipline. To the extent that financial markets are an accurate barometer of economic confidence, the markets are voting overwhelmingly to trust the euro over the dollar. The euro, widely ridiculed as a monetary impossibility when it was launched, in quarters such as *The Wall Street Journal*, was trading below parity with the dollar when it became legal tender in 2002. At this writing, it costs about U.S. $1.38 to buy one euro, and the dollar is continuing to sink.

Despite its stronger unions, higher wages, better living standards, and social protections for ordinary citizens (or maybe *because* of them), the trends in unit-labor costs in manufacturing in recent years have actually been better in most of Europe than in the United States. Unit-labor costs measure what industry has to pay workers relative to their output. When unit-labor costs are declining, it signifies that the economy is becoming more productive. When they are rising, it means employers are overpaying workers relative to productivity and must sacrifice either jobs or profits or pass along the costs to the public in the form of inflation. In the period between 1990 and 1999, according to the OECD, improvements in unit-labor costs in Austria, Belgium, Finland, France, Germany, Italy, the Netherlands, and Sweden exceeded the performance in the United States.

How could this be? For one thing, Europe tends to invest far more in its workers than the United States does. Europe views employees more as productive assets rather than as expendable cogs. The flip side of greater worker protections is greater corporate and social investment in workers' skills. Germany has the world's highest labor costs, but also very high worker productivity, and it continues to lead the United States in numerous categories of manufacturing. To some extent, its relatively high unemployment reflects the fact that German workers are so productive that it needs fewer workers per unit of output. For another thing, social bargaining institutions, far from corresponding to the press caricature of runaway union bosses pressing for exorbitant settlements, actually serve to keep wage increases closely in line with productivity growth. According to a study by Jonas Pontusson, one of the most careful students of comparative forms of capitalism, there is a positive correlation between nations with strong trade unions and social protections and falling unit-labor costs.

Nations such as Sweden, Norway, Denmark, and Finland have long relied on unions as social partners that share a broad concern for the well-being of the economy as a whole. As long ago as the 1950s, three Swedish economists, representing the unions, the Social Democratic Party, and the employers' federation, devised a social model based on what they called an active labor market policy combined with a "solidarity wage policy." In this model, unions and employer federations would work collaboratively to narrow differentials in wages. This would reward companies that used innovations rather than wage cuts to increase their profits. It would also more nearly equalize incomes across industries and occupations. The active labor market policy, in turn, would serve to invest money in the skills of workers, rather than simply paying unemployment compensation to workers who were temporarily idle. Some of those training and reemployment outlays have also been used by the Swedes as part of their industrial and regional development policy. For example, if a town in the north of Sweden with a highly skilled pool of workers has lost, say, shipbuilding jobs, the national pool of worker-training funds can be used to subsidize the labor costs of a new employer.

The Swedish version of active labor market policy seemed to stall in the 1980s but subsequently recovered. The model has undergone several refinements since it was introduced half a century ago. Today, northern Europe spends about ten times what the United States does per capita on different brands of active labor market policy. The Danes and the Dutch, both with high rates of unemployment and expensive programs of unemployment insurance in the 1990s, have transformed their economies by using their labor market outlays more dynamically, with a strategy known as flexicurity, which makes the workforce more productive and increases the supply of private-sector jobs. Dutch unemployment levels today are below U.S. levels, but the Dutch have not sacrificed their broad-based programs of opportunity, security, and equality.

Moreover, when unions are party to a social compact that ensures that wage increases will grow only with productivity, it has a salutary effect on macroeconomic policy. Central banks can tolerate fuller employment without worrying that tight labor markets will produce excess worker bargaining power and set off inflation. This path, however, does not always realize its full promise. The former German central bank, the Bundesbank, had an aversion to inflation, perhaps the result of the hyperinflation of the 1920s. German central bankers were also traumatized after 1989, when the integration of the former East Germany, lubricated by the exchange of largely worthless East German ostmarks for deutsche marks on a 1-to-1 basis, required the printing of a lot of money and a brief bout of most un-German inflation. Other European nations have long complained that the overly cautious monetary influence of the Bundesbank needlessly slowed Europe's growth rates. The creation of the new European Central Bank in Frankfurt in 1998 was an attempt to inject greater balance onto European monetary policy. With the euro still a relatively new currency, the ECB has inherited some of the biases of the Bundesbank. Many critics contend that with friendlier central bankers, Europe could allow lower interest rates and higher growth without kindling inflation.

The broad point here, despite a lot of misleading information, is that Europe's economy does about as well as that of the United States—*on average*. What is radically different is who gets the benefits. Thanks to Europe's social model, the benefits are much more broadly diffused.

Where Europe does overwhelmingly better than the United States is in the way it delivers for the vast majority of people. Not only are wages far more equal, Europeans receive universal health coverage, and public opinion polls show that Europeans are more satisfied with their medical care than Americans. Child care and prekindergarten are financed socially in most of Europe. Public policy requires benefits and protections unheard of in the United States. The European Union mandates, for all member countries, paid sick leave and at least twenty days of paid vacation. Some countries mandate twenty-five days of annual vacation, and many collective bargaining agreements provide even more. The Nordic countries provide generous paid maternity benefits. On average, typical Europeans spend about two hundred fewer hours a year in paid employment than their American counterparts. Virtually all of the higher average U.S. gross domestic product is accounted for by longer working time.

Economic opportunity and living standards are distributed far more broadly—not because the middle class is heavily taxed to pay for the nonproductive poor but because the elites' incomes are not as exorbitant and there are far fewer dependent poor. Defining poverty as an income below 50 percent of the median, the United States has a poverty rate of 17 percent, according to the Luxembourg Income Study. The major nations of continental Europe all have rates of under 9 percent. Only Britain, Italy, and Ireland have rates in the double digits, and all are lower than ours.

To read the conservative press, you would think that Europe's citizens were in a state of advanced revolt against their brand of socially mediated capitalism. But something much more interesting is occurring. In the slow-growth 1980s, neoliberal center-right parties were gaining supporters by attacking the welfare state. Not today. In the current decade, Europe's neoliberal parties are working to make the welfare state more dynamic, innovative, and efficient. Hardly any voters support politicians who want to scrap social protections. The Dutch and Danish versions of flexicurity are the work of both center-right parties and Social Democrats. Centrist parties in France, Germany, and Sweden are all seeking ways to make their welfare state serve economic dynamism, not giving it up.

All of this suggests two big lessons. First, a more social brand of capitalism can be at least as efficient as the American model, and a lot more equitable. And second, once that model reaches critical mass—when it benefits the broad working population and not just the elderly or the poor—it is too popular for politicians of any stripe to tamper with. Newt

Gingrich well understood that lesson in 1993 when he made sure to block any form of government-organized universal health insurance, lest working-age voters harbor a friendly view of social investment and of liberal Democrats.

Europe's model of capitalism, however, still faces a big threat—not from its own citizenry but from the market pressures of globalism. A crucial question is whether social investment and labor market regulation can continue taming market forces to benefit the citizenry, or whether the market pressures imported by globalization will fatally undermine the European model—unless the terms of globalization are revised.

Managed Capitalism Meets Globalism

To some extent, the European Union offers a measure of shelter from the wider forces of globalization. The continent of Europe is a larger fortress for a social model of capitalism than any single country. The European Union has managed to expand to include poorer counties such as Portugal, Spain, Greece, and Ireland, and later several eastern European nations, without wrecking the social model of its wealthier countries. It has done so using a mix of regional development funds and Union-wide standards.

The history is instructive. When the antecedents of the European Union were launched in the 1950s, they were an effort to bring more liberal trade to countries suddenly too small to make it on their own and to strengthen the economy of the entire region. In those years, the six-nation European Coal and Steel Community (launched in 1951) and the six-member European Economic Community (begun in 1957) were understood as extensions of a freer market. To compete with the United States, Europe needed to transcend the constrictions of small, national states and organize its economy on a continental scale. In those years, it was the center-right parties and the European business community that embraced what was then known as the Common Market, strongly seconded by the United States, which wanted a bulwark against the spread of communism.

But by the 1980s, the ideological meaning of European integration had undergone a reversal. This was the era of Ronald Reagan and Margaret Thatcher in the United States and the United Kingdom, respectively, and of the first durable postwar social democratic governments in France and Germany. The center-left European parties realized that if their social model were to stand up against the pressures from the

Anglo-Saxon nations and resurgent global market forces, social Europe, not just market Europe, needed stronger, continent-wide institutions. What began as merely a customs union in 1957 was expanded, via deliberate statecraft, into a single market by 1993, with a single currency by 1999, and an emergent continental polity.

As market institutions were integrated, so, increasingly, were social and political ones. More political power was delegated by member nations to the E.U. executive, now partly accountable to a popularly elected European Parliament. A whole theory and vocabulary of constitutional law informed the emerging European confederation, with such principles as harmonization (convergence of national policies), subsidiarity (the idea that nothing should be done by the European Union that could be better done by its member states), and concerns about a democratic deficit (bureaucrats in Brussels should be popularly accountable). Increasingly, the European Commission, the executive branch of the European Union, issued binding directives on social policy, so that protections would be Europe-wide and industry would be less able to stimulate a regulatory race to the bottom.

However, globalization, at least on its current terms, is making the European project more precarious. We have seen how corporations are able to use tax competition to undercut the fiscal base of social investment. In terms of income distribution, a pure market tends to produce outlandish rewards for big winners. American-style corporate pay structures are infecting egalitarian Europe. The Continent has shifted to a more neoliberal mood. Deregulation is undermining the strategy of using a regulated labor market to maintain more equitable compensation systems. Laissez-faire is at odds with industrywide or national bargaining over wages and benefits. And as European-based firms face competition from low-wage areas of rising productivity, such as China, it becomes harder to exist as an island of decent labor compensation.

Nations once well defended by superb traditions of craft production and uniquely high quality products abruptly find themselves assaulted by low-wage Asian competition. In Italy, networks of artisan firms producing everything from high-end shoes and fashion items to precision machinery and cutlery are losing market share. The Italians have intensified their effort to brand "Made in Italy" as standing for quality and workmanship, even as they find themselves compelled to contract subassembly to the Chinese.

And even as the nations of the European Union have redoubled efforts to build a more dynamic and less bureaucratic welfare state, the increased financial engineering of deregulated global capital markets puts the whole project at risk. European politicians of both the center-right and center-left point to the success of Denmark, where a series of reforms in the 1990s under the label flexicurity combined reduced labor regulation with increased outlays on training for displaced individuals. Thanks to these reforms, Denmark enjoys new economic dynamism and a lower unemployment rate than the United States, and has not sacrificed broad social benefits or income equality. Yet the man who, as prime minister, brokered these reforms, Poul Nyrup Rasmussen, warned in a 2007 report that the whole European social and economic model was at risk because hedge funds and private-equity firms are able to swoop in and to eviscerate Europe's productive corporations and its collaborative labor relations. The Rasmussen report concluded, "In a number of fields in our social market economy, we see subordination to the logic of financial markets: the declining rate of real investment as a percentage of cash flow; the steady increase of dividends and extreme executive salaries, stock options and management fees—and even less income retained internally in companies as LBOs extract more value; the decline of capital stock relative to the gross profit; investment in R&D stagnating or declining as a percentage of expenditures; and deteriorating working conditions."

For example, Denmark's former national telephone company, TDC, was fully privatized in 1998. In December 2005, it was taken over by a consortium of five private-equity companies, including Blackstone and KKR, for just under 12 billion euros, a price 40 percent above its current market price. At the time, this was the largest European LBO on record. Financing was mostly by debt, which radically worsened TDC's balance sheet. The company's debt-to-assets ratio has gone from 18 percent to about 90 percent, and its new debt is at a higher interest rate. Despite the higher debt service costs, the new owners promptly paid themselves a cash dividend of 5.9 billion euros, a windfall equal to four times the company's annual earnings. This was on top of 524 million euros in management, legal, and transaction fees. It is hard to imagine a sector less well suited to the short-term profit mentality of private-equity firms than telecommunications, where operating companies need funds for continuous investment in R&D, infrastructure, and employee training. The private-equity owners of TDC followed the formula of extracting assets and then trying to cut costs mainly by squeezing labor. Multiply the TDC story times a thousand, and you have a bullet aimed at the heart of Europe's strategy of long-term investment built on a high quality workforce and labor-management harmony.

If Europe is to defend its social model, it will need to combine reforms of its outmoded bureaucratic aspects with vigorous regulation of its capital markets so that it is not swamped by imported laissez-faire. Globalization makes that task much harder. Politically, Europe's centrist and center-right politicians and their corporate allies would like to see Europe become more like the United States, not less. They have not distinguished between the aspects of globalization that put salutary competitive pressure on Europe's managers and workers from the influences that are predatory and destructive. Germany is another nation whose social model is placed at risk by the incursions of private equity. But when the German government led by Chancellor Angela Merkel proposed tighter regulation of hedge funds and private equity in early 2007, they found themselves politically isolated. The Commission of the European Union has proposed only the mildest forms of industry self-regulation.

How have these crosscurrents affected the European model? The most careful students of European income distribution have pointed to a modest increase in inequality in the past decades, though it is the details that are most instructive. According to data from the OECD and the Luxembourg Income Study, the United States has at least twice the degree of inequality of most of Europe, as well as far greater economic insecurity, and the gap is widening.

Both the United States and Europe have been growing more unequal in the past two decades, Europe at a somewhat slower rate. Using standard statistical measures, only the Netherlands, Switzerland, Ireland, and France became (slightly) more equal in the 1980s and 1990s. Denmark's income distribution was roughly unchanged. In the Netherlands, Switzerland, and Ireland, a combination of low unemployment and increased social protections produced increased equality. France relied almost entirely on social outlays. The rest of Europe became slightly more unequal. For the most part, it was countries with advanced systems of social investment that did the most effective job of resisting market-driven inequality and countries such as the United States and the United Kingdom since Reagan and Thatcher that had the biggest increases in inequality.

Digging deeper below the surface, Jonas Pontusson points to increases in labor market inequality—wage differentials and deregulation—as the biggest single source of Europe's widening inequality. He concludes:

The discrepancy between changes in gross earnings inequality and disposable income inequality suggests that the Nordic welfare states, most particularly the Danish welfare state, have largely offset inegalitarian labor market trends or, in other words, compensated low income households for their relative losses through more progressive income taxation or through redistributive transfer programs.

In other words, the most advanced nations in the European social model of capitalism—thus far—have been able to contain the effects of global marketization on equality and security by working their welfare states harder and more flexibly. Other nations with less heroic equalizing institutions have suffered modest increases in inequality. Despite premature accounts of its demise, however, the European model has not yet hit a political tipping point, with affluent voters bailing out of the bargain—because the model provides opportunity and security benefits to the vast majority of voters. But as the global market economy continues to make incursions, social Europe will have to face an ever more difficult challenge of maintaining this balancing act without altering the rules of trade.

What does Europe's experience suggest for our broader story about the squandering of America? Economically, it indicates that a different brand of capitalism is possible—an equally efficient one that provides both a broader diffusion of economic benefits and opportunities and a reduction in economic risks to citizens, workers, families, and the economic system as a whole without sacrificing economic dynamism. Politically, Europe suggests that a better-managed and more equitable form of market economy requires a radically different brand of politics—one with mobilized citizens, governments with a clear sense of social purpose, and trade unions and other countervailing institutions that promote a broad public awareness of the need for social balance in a market economy—and that this brand of citizen politics can fight the increased political power of organized capital to at least a draw. However, unless constraints are placed on global regulation of capital—a project that is almost impossible to achieve in a single country or even a continent—Europe's social market economy will find itself increasingly in jeopardy despite its broad popularity among its citizens.

It bears repeating that European parties of both the center left and the center right champion programs of economic security and broadly diffused economic prosperity. Their differences are mainly of tactics and degree. European politics include strong Social Democratic parties and allied unions, who have a clear ideology of what kind of society they want and a set of strategies to achieve it. Center-right parties, often Christian Democratic, have an equally cogent view of a just society, anchored in Catholic social teaching (and very different from the antigovernment, laissez-faire views of most American Christian fundamentalists). A third group that supports antidotes to the destabilizing forces of global capitalism are center-right nationalist parties, typified by the French neo-Gaullists, who see social rights as guaranteed by a strong state. European neoliberals, who would leave everything to markets, run a distant fourth.

All the groups are serious about fiscal stewardship. And the forces that support a social model of capitalism are serious and systematic about building durable social counterweights to markets. This common social model, etched into the DNA of the European Union and offsetting the power of global organized business, is anchored in democratic politics.

America can't simply emulate Europe. But we once had this brand of politics in the United States, and it undergirded a much more attractive, efficient, and equitable economy. It was not as far-reaching as Europe's version, but its achievements included a broader diffusion of prosperity and the establishment of programs such as Social Security and Medicare that benefit the vast majority of people—programs that would not be enacted or even proposed by a majority of today's politicians.

Harnessing capitalism for broad prosperity and security, both domestically and globally, requires a very different politics. Can we regain it?

CHAPTER EIGHT

TRADE AND THE NATIONAL INTEREST

CHAPTER SEVEN EXAMINED how globalization can undercut labor standards and social rights, unless the protections of the nation-state are extended to the global arena, or are made far more robust at home. More generally, trade policy poses two broad questions for American policy: By what principles and rules should money and goods flow across national borders? And within the system of global trade rules, what policies are good for the United States as a nation?

Recent U.S. administrations have bungled both challenges. They have promoted an architecture for the system that is at odds with everything we have learned over more than a century about the benefits of a managed brand of capitalism. And the obsession to bring "free trade" to the world has often entailed the sacrifice of America's own domestic economy.

Trading Away Prosperity

Trade policy is the most striking area where America's true interests are obscured—and defeated—by a complex tangle of geopolitical objectives, ideology, and the concentrated power of industry and finance. For more than three decades, the United States has promoted a series of trade policies whose end result has been a chronic structural deficit that has left us financially dependent on foreign central banks, the near collapse of America's manufacturing sector, and the destruction of a high-wage social contract.

There are three parts to this story. The first has to do with America's military and geopolitical role. Since the early postwar period, America's aims as leader of the Cold War alliance against communism crowded out geoeconomic goals affecting our ability to compete in the world. In the immediate postwar years, this potential conflict in national objectives had little consequence, because of America's towering economic dominance. Later, as the United States found itself competing against its own military allies—and even against potential adversaries such as China—that practiced highly nationalistic forms of strategic trade, this warping of America's diplomatic priorities had immense consequences. Even after the Cold War ended, America's self-conception as sole superpower led it to subordinate economic goals to military ones.

The second part of the story reflects the power of an ideal: free trade. This concept is ground into the lenses of the economic profession. You literally cannot be a mainstream economist in good standing without accepting the broad premise of the theory of comparative advantage, first proposed by David Ricardo in 1817. Supposedly, free trade benefits both trading parties, just as other forms of specialization increase economic efficiency at home. I pay my barber to cut my hair. In turn, he buys the newspaper that carries my column. Even if I were pretty good at cutting my own hair, it makes more economic sense for me to pay him to do what he does best, so that I can spend my time doing what I do best. Adam Smith was the first to point out the efficiencies of specialization.

As with domestic economics, according to Ricardo, so with international trade. If England is better at producing cloth, Ricardo wrote, and Portugal at making wine, both benefit from trade. Over two centuries, this basic idea has been refined and restated in abstruse algebra, and it remains as central to standard economics as the Holy Trinity is to Christianity (and just as rooted in faith).

The third part of the story reflects the increasing influence of America's financial elites. With the completion of the Uruguay Round of trade negotiations, the implementation of NAFTA, and the launching of the World Trade Organization (all during the 1990s), America's "free trade" goals have been less about reducing tariffs, quotas, or other obstacles to commerce as traditionally defined, and more about giving financial interests access to other economies, unfettered by the traditional instruments of managed capitalism.

Ideas have moved nations throughout history—the idea of monotheism, the idea that European nations would prosper by acquiring colonies, the idea that it was manifest destiny for the United States of America to extend from coast to coast, and the ideas of communism, Nazism, and constitutional democracy. Political ideas have their greatest reach when they can serve a practical political interest. It is hard to think of a more perfect marriage of idea and self-interest than the way the free-trade ideal was captured and redefined by American financial elites in the middle and late twentieth century.

This liaison was relatively new. Right up until the eve of World War I, American industry thrived by embracing protection. In the nineteenth century, the United States was a catch-up nation industrially. If it had followed the prescription of David Ricardo and just imported the finished products that Britain produced more efficiently, America would have continued to exploit its natural comparative advantage in cheap land, farm products, and raw materials, leaving Britain to maintain its industrial lead indefinitely.

Instead, American leaders beginning with Alexander Hamilton thought it was smarter for the nation to pursue advantage in industry as well as agriculture. So the United States industrialized behind high tariff walls. Not only did we have tariffs, but we used what today would be called an industrial policy. The railroads were given land grants equal to 8 percent of the surface area of the United States—land that they could rent or sell to finance construction. It was a pure government subsidy of an emerging industry. Beginning in 1862, the government invested in public universities to promote the mechanical arts and in agricultural extension to foster technical advances in farming. World War II and the Cold War functioned as immense, if tacit, technology policies.

Every other emergent nation reached similar conclusions. Each practiced its own variations on economic nationalism, many with far more direct government involvement in the industrial economy than in the United States and far more nakedly protectionist policies. France and Germany, and later Japan, Korea, Brazil, India, and China, all developed their industries pursuing diverse forms of what economists today call strategic trade, or neomercantilism.

The appeal of acquiring industry is not hard to discern. Even if a nation has plenty of raw materials, extractive industries tend to be economically static. Many economists have commented on the paradox of mineral-rich nations being mired in poverty. In practice, mineral wealth is often exploited by foreign corporations, and of course the materials eventually run out. Even agriculture, though more technically dynamic, is less so than industry and is dependent on fluctuations of world commodity prices.

Manufacturing allows nations to begin with fairly simple production and move quickly up the ladder. There are multiple linkages among manufacturing, technology, education, workers' skills, high-productivity jobs, and national wealth. Though the theory of comparative advantage counsels that nations should maximize their well-being simply by importing such products from the most efficient current exporter, the leaders of most developing nations are more astute than the standard economic model. It makes sense to use government policies to capture leadership in dynamic sectors of the economy.

As the economist Laura D'Andrea Tyson, later Bill Clinton's chief economic adviser, observed in a 1992 book titled *Who's Bashing Whom?*

> Technology intensive industries violate the assumptions of free trade theory and the static economic concepts that are the basis for U.S. trade policy . . . During the last decade, new developments in trade theory have demonstrated that, under conditions of increasing returns, technological externalities, and imperfect competition, free trade is not necessarily and automatically the best policy. Promotional and protectionist policies by foreign governments can harm domestic [U.S.] economic welfare by shifting industries with high returns and beneficial externalities away from domestic producers and domestic production locations. Conversely, comparable policies at home can improve economic welfare, sometimes at the expense of other nations.

Tyson peppered the book with disclaimers, calling herself a "cautious activist." But though Clinton named Tyson chair of his Council of Economic Advisers shortly after her book appeared, he did not take her advice on trade and industrial policy. Doing so would have put him squarely at odds with the elite consensus of American industry and finance.

Practice at Odds with Theory

For two decades, several other mainstream economists have assembled a potent case against free trade as an accurate description of how the world actually works, what optimizes economic growth, or as the preferred policy for the United States. But in the world of diplomacy, business, and elite opinion, nothing changes. Anyone who challenges free trade is deemed by business elites and editorial writers to be a toady for special interests and an economic idiot. Economists who say otherwise speak with extreme care.

As early as the mid-1980s, a group of mainstream economists challenged the core premises of the theory of comparative advantage. Students of Asian mercantilism, such as Alice Amsden, an economist at

MIT, demonstrated that the most successful Asian nations violated just about every premise of the Ricardian model. Other critics included Tyson and her colleagues at the Berkeley Roundtable on the International Economy, as well as James Brander of the University of British Columbia and Barbara Spencer of Boston College. The most prominent was a young prodigy named Paul Krugman, then at MIT.

Long before Krugman became famous as a newspaper columnist, he was an acclaimed technical economist and an astute critic of the standard view of trade. Krugman trod carefully, since the theory of comparative advantage is among the most universally espoused tenets of standard economics. In technical papers written between 1983 and 1986, Krugman observed that the received wisdom about free trade was substantially wrong.

In standard theory, countries trade to exploit natural differences of climate, skills, culture, resources, and so on. Trade allows nations to benefit from one another's natural strengths. Though such natural endowments are still relevant and trade is generally beneficial, Krugman wrote, since World War II "a large and generally growing part of world trade has come to consist of exchanges that cannot be attributed so easily to underlying advantages of the countries that export particular goods. Instead, trade seems to reflect arbitrary or temporary advantages resulting from economies of scale or shifting leads in close technological races." In some cases, he added, comparative advantage can be created. By strategically intervening to capture the advantage in industries with technological dynamism, nations can produce spillover benefits for their economies.

This revisionism, especially when articulated by prestigious and mainstream economists, was explosive. It came to be known in the profession as the "New View" of trade. It was, of course, not new to economic historians, to students of industrial policy, or to Japanese, Korean, French, and German mercantilist planners. But it was a highly heretical concept within mainstream American economics. Krugman had to be taken seriously, not just because he was a respected card-carrying neoclassical economist but because he could demonstrate the proposition more with reference to elegant algebraic models than with industrial and diplomatic history.

Having cautiously embraced this view, Krugman almost immediately (and prudently) distanced himself from its implications. His early writings warned that even though gains from industrial targeting and strategic trade policy were possible, it was not at all clear that governments would act wisely in their pursuit of strategic advantage. And there was the usual risk that each nation's strategic efforts would degenerate into "beggar-my-neighbor" trade policies and even trade war.

In the more than two decades since Krugman edited a volume of papers by several trade economists associated with the New View of trade, the success of Asian mercantilism has only demonstrated ever more clearly that the theory of comparative advantage is substantially a myth. Even Paul Samuelson, the Nobel laureate, dean of American economists, and author of the modern, technical version of Ricardo's hypothesis, the Hecksher-Ohlin-Samuelson theorem, wrote in a 2003 paper in the *Journal of Economic Perspectives* that trade is not necessarily a win-win proposition for both partners. One nation can sometimes gain at the expense of another.

Yet the romance between the economics profession and the ideal of free trade seems destined to be a permanent marriage, no matter how much cheating goes on by the real economy. The tendency of main-stream economists to keep reverting to their support of free trade is reinforced by the preferences of the business elite. If you wish to be taken seriously in the corridors of power, you had better be a free trader. Economists who are somewhat heterodox on other issues bend over backward to reassure their colleagues, their publics, and themselves that yes, they still believe in free trade.

In the Clinton administration, Laura Tyson became a close ally of Robert Rubin and ceased being an advocate for managed trade. She went on to serve as dean of the business school at the University of California at Berkeley, then as dean of the London Business School, remaining a "cautious activist." Her colleague on the Council of Economic Advisers, Alan Blinder, later vice chairman of the Federal Reserve, has recently written articles in *Foreign Affairs* and *The American Prospect* warning that outsourcing and the loss of good American jobs in services as well as manufacturing to other countries are a much bigger threat than most economists think. "[T]he greatest problem for the next generation of American workers may not be lack of education," Blinder wrote, "but rather offshoring—the movement of jobs overseas, especially to countries with much lower wages, like India and China."

But Blinder took great care to include a disclaimer: "Ever since Adam Smith and David Ricardo, economists have explained and extolled the gains in living standards that derive from international trade. Those arguments are just as valid for trade in services as for trade in goods. There really *are* net gains to the United States from expanding service-sector trade with India, China, and the rest. The offshoring problem is not about the adverse nature of what economists call the economy's eventual equilibrium. Rather, it is about the so-called transition—the ride from here to there." The peer pressure among economists not to disavow the precepts of free trade produces a seemingly scientific basis for the political preference of financial elites.

Promoting America's Disadvantage

Just as there is a potent economic and political logic in catch-up nations' deciding to practice economic nationalism, there is a reciprocal logic in why dominant nations promote their version of free commerce. If you are more efficient than any other producer, you naturally commend free trade as a universal virtue, in the same way that the biggest kid on the block calls for a fair fight. Britain was the first nation to proclaim the benefits of universal free trade in the early nineteenth century, just as America began doing so in the mid–twentieth century, and for exactly the same reasons. Some critics have termed this "the imperialism of free trade"—the leader tries to lock in the first-mover advantage for all time and prevent others from catching up.

The leading promoter of free trade, however, is often hypocritical. Britain's embrace of free trade was complicated by its colonial empire and its policy of giving "imperial preference" to its colonies. America's sponsorship of free trade was contradicted by its immense military machine, which had a variety of unacknowledged economic benefits in terms of subsidy of emergent technologies. Hegemonic powers tend to give themselves a free pass on such contradictions.

America's promotion of free trade, as a universal ideal and practice, also comported beautifully with the global ideological struggle between capitalism and communism. Free trade was the international face of free-market capitalism. The United States was so economically dominant that the fact that most of our capitalist allies did not actually practice free trade was seen as a minor footnote. Besides, it was thought, if America served as a model of free trade in its own behavior and rewarded other nations for moving in the direction of free trade, there would gradually be convergence.

This diplomatic stance, which gradually hardened into one of the core pillars of American foreign economic policy, also served American industry. Some companies could thrive by producing mainly for the domestic market, others by exporting, still others by locating branch plants overseas. However, as noted, there were also some loopholes on the American side. Not only did the huge Cold War military machine, successor to the World War II total-mobilization economy, function as government subsidy to industry and science by producing a steady flow of contracts as well as research dollars, which for a time helped maintain American industrial leadership, but American agriculture, heavily subsidized and protected by tariffs, quotas, and subsidies, was somehow exempt from the theory and practice of free trade.

But in the 1940s and 1950s, free trade was what America was selling to the world, along with a cornucopia of products. At the time, it all made perfect sense. The policy became a rock-solid article of faith, shared by the powerful business community and by presidents of both parties and certified as scientifically sound by the economics profession.

Then the ground shifted, and the benefits of the bargain were not so clear. American producers got their first rude awakening from the Japanese. Almost overnight, it seemed, Japan was not just exporting cheap toys and textiles but also making steel, semiconductors, automobiles, and advanced electronic products, often superior to and cheaper than their American competitors'. And Japan's closed system was largely impenetrable to the wide range of products in which U.S. producers still maintained superiority.

But America's geopolitical and commercial culture remained wedded to the promotion of free trade. Washington had expended significant diplomatic capital on several trade "rounds" aimed at making the world more open to free movement of goods and capital. The early postwar multilateral trade negotiations, culminating in the Tokyo Round in 1977, were aimed mainly at reciprocal reductions in tariffs. Then, beginning with the Uruguay Round, which began in 1986 and concluded in 1994, the United States promoted the dismantling of so-called non-tariff barriers, such as quotas, subsidies, and covert forms of mercantilism such as domestic cartels. The problem, however, is that while the United States became progressively more open, foreign mercantilism simply took new, aggressive forms, most notably in East Asia, and America's trade imbalance began its inexorable rise.

Japan turned out to be the leading edge of a rival Asian model of capitalism that was fundamentally different from the model America was promoting. Far from producing convergence, America's sponsorship of a free-trade system and effort to model good behavior by disdaining economic nationalism only served to enable wider divergence and to harm domestic industry—good jobs and technologies located in

America. These suffered. But American-based corporations and banks adapted to foreign mercantilism and thrived. They did so by shipping jobs and funds overseas. Their political support for one-sided free trade only intensified. The distinction between American production and U.S.-based corporations was often lost.

The power of the neomercantilist model, especially its East Asian variant, totally contradicted the reigning U.S. ideology. The U.S. response was mainly studied denial. If America was losing its industrial leadership, it must be because American workers and managers were less productive than their more nimble competitors. The cure was lower wages, greater rewards for CEOs, and more companies being put at the mercy of speculative financial markets. If America had a structural trade imbalance, classical economics said that the cause had to be the country's low rates of domestic savings and investment. It could not be the consequence of other nations' trade and industrial policies, because the theory said that those policies couldn't work.

Confounded by East Asian Capitalism

As the United States keeps promoting and trying to model laissez-faire, East Asia continues, with great success, to operate its economy more on the model of Japan. Though the particulars vary, in the East Asian variant of capitalism, the main instruments include

- Government subsidies and allocation of cheap capital to help domestic producers develop technologies, gain a foothold, and increase domestic and global market share
- The pricing of exports below the cost of production in order to gain a foothold
- Market-closing measures or favoritism for domestic enterprises to keep U.S.-based producers from competing in the East Asian nation's home market, except as purchasers or partners
- The use of cartels to carve up markets and set prices
- The coercive capture or outright theft of U.S. intellectual property
- Domestic content requirements, sometimes coupled with subsidies, to coerce or entice U.S. producers to locate their advanced production in the local country, often including the compulsory licensing or transfer of proprietary technologies in partnership with local companies
- In the Chinese case, working conditions that are often akin to slave labor

The Asian economic model, with its several variations, commits countless sins against the idealized conception of free markets that American administrations attempt to export to the world. Indeed, our government spends far more diplomatic effort on exporting ideology than on exporting American products.

Some of the instruments of East Asian capitalism simply reflect a different concept of the appropriate roles of the state and private entrepreneurs in economic development. Others are outright cases of theft and extortion, such as the piracy of intellectual property and coercive demands for technology transfer and location of production as a condition of selling to local markets. Still other mercantilist tactics occupy a gray area, such as the use of immense government subsidies to lure U.S. plants to relocate offshore. This practice is not explicitly illegal under WTO rules, but it gives asymmetric advantages to nations that offer such measures. In addition, the leading Asian nations keep their currencies artificially undervalued, to provide a further advantage to their exports and discourage imports.

These practices pose a challenge to the U.S. economy, to the ideal of laissez-faire, and to the project of reconciling very different systems of law and conduct so that trade can flow without unduly favoring one nation over the other. They systematically draw technologies, production opportunities, and jobs out of the United States, without returning the benefits that would flow from more symmetrical trade. The chronic U.S. trade deficit and the loss of key industries are the proof. With the exception of intermittent policy offensives, such as a belated skirmish over intellectual property rights and occasional forays to reduce currency imbalances, most American policy makers and economic theorists remain in denial of the fact that these instruments of strategic trade *work*. To concede that they do would be to reject the entire laissez-faire model.

Using this model, the Japanese were able to overtake the United States in much of consumer electronics and then to make huge inroads in the whole range of advanced technologies. Japan's entire industrial system was an affront to Western ideas of laissez-faire, and it worked all too well. When Japan desired to capture a technology where the United States was the leader and most efficient producer, its Ministry of International Trade and Industry (MITI) worked with Japanese cartels to allocate capital to Japanese producers and to close home markets to U.S. products. In the meantime, Japanese patent laws made it hard for U.S. competitors to safeguard their technology.

The American response was ideologically confused. Some of President Reagan's advisers concluded that if Japan was making superior products, this had to be the market speaking (even if the market was being violated). The need to reward Japan as a loyal Cold War ally reinforced the impulse to take a very soft line on trade. Others felt there were national security reasons for the United States to maintain leadership in key technologies with military implications. Because of the general aversion to anything smacking of industrial policy or other government interventions in the market's allocation of capital, there was little support for the idea that the United States should seek to remain competitive in the whole range of advanced industries and technologies as an end in itself. The market would decide that.

There was a willful refusal by American leaders to acknowledge that the shift of industrial leadership from the United States to Asia was not a free-market verdict. And much to the consternation of our trading partners, U.S. trade negotiators also refused to admit that a great deal of our prior trade leadership itself reflected extramarket forces. America led the world in the manufacture of aircraft, for example, because of the extensive spillover from military outlays to commercial applications. Our leadership in pharmaceuticals was the result of a tacit industrial policy system: the government appropriated extensive funds for basic research, extended generous patent protection, and provided reliable testing and a seal of approval from the Food and Drug Administration. While other nations were making substantial inroads in computer technology, the United States managed to hold on to its leadership in software and microprocessor design via a duopoly that came to be known as "Wintel"—the Microsoft Windows operating system and the Intel chip.

Intel, prodded by the Pentagon, limited the foreign licensing and production of its most advanced technologies. Many students of free markets faulted Microsoft for using improper market power to crush innovators, helped by lax antitrust enforcement. But the Wintel fortress, precisely because it violated some of the ideals of the free market, did allow the United States, in one key area of the new economy, to fend off other nations' habitual violations of market economics and trade rules.

Though some East Asian nations became more marketlike in some respects, such as having somewhat open consumer economies, in their production systems they continued to use various forms of state assistance and state-guided development strategies combined with high domestic savings rates, and they became export powerhouses. With the United States as the only major nation whose government did not care where production was located, the American economy became the residual recipient for the exports of these rapidly growing economies. Our manufacturing economy suffered, and our trade deficit became permanent and structural. India's fast-growing economy, for example, sends about 65 percent of its exports to the United States and only 3 percent to Japan. With Japan having roughly half the GDP of the United States, its share of India's exports should be about ten times as large as it currently is.

Although China and India have received more of the recent attention, Japan's chronic mercantilism continues. Given its continuing state-led industrial policy, Japan remains relatively inhospitable to imports. Meanwhile, all of East Asia has embraced variants of the Japanese model. And with the emergence of China, the threat has taken on a whole new magnitude.

America's disdain for industrial policies makes it harder for us to get back into the game. For example, a broad coalition of groups has proposed a "New Apollo" project, which would have the government invest in energy independence for the United States. The U.S. government spends only about $3 billion on energy R&D, compared to $28 billion in the biomedical sector. Increased public investment on energy independence based on renewables would have multiple benefits. It would reduce our dependence on imported fuels, improve our trade imbalance, put the United States at the forefront of new and dynamic energy technologies, and create millions of jobs.

By analogy, in the 1980s a government-business partnership called SEMATECH, on a more modest scale, helped the U.S. semiconductor industry retain its world leadership in the face of foreign industrial policies. SEMATECH combined research subsidies with a tough trade policy that compelled Japan to cease trying to use illegitimate means (subsidies, quotas, cartels) to squeeze out superior U.S. semiconductor products. The only reason the government went along with this rare deliberate industrial policy was concern about the need for U.S.-produced semiconductors for America's national security. But today, in an even more politically conservative environment, a new Apollo Project aimed at U.S. leadership in new energy technology would violate both the prevailing ideology and the World Trade Organization's rules (promoted by the United States) against industrial subsidies. Japan, China, and the European Union, by contrast, have no scruples about using public outlays to capture advantage. The United States, however, is so intent on trying to convince them of the error of their ways that the last thing it wants is a high-profile technology policy of its own.

Because the United States' trade policy lacks a strategic focus, its response to foreign challenges has been episodic and inconsistent. The consequence is that vital industries and technologies developed in the United States are losing market share, leaving it with a structural trade imbalance. It is this reality of other nations' practicing strategic trade—not the low U.S. domestic savings rate or the federal budget deficit—that explains most of the wide and growing trade gap, which will soon top one trillion dollars. Even more significant than the size of the trade deficit is the percentage of imbalance. Our imports are fully 57 percent higher than our exports, and that ratio is growing. The U.S. trade imbalance increased by 17.5 percent in 2005 alone. In 2005, our negative trade balance with China was $201 billion. That imbalance was the result of $243 billion in imports and just $42 billion in exports. For Japan, the figures were $138 billion in imports and $55 billion in exports. As other nations capture advantage in technology-intensive products, we are increasingly importing the most advanced products and exporting raw materials, or we are exporting materials for assembly and reimport. Given the truculence with which the U.S. government advances its perceived national interest in military and geostrategic areas, it seems almost bizarre that we should be so weak when it comes to advancing our trade interests.

Gulliver in Uniform

For three decades, trade officials have periodically proposed taking a harder line against Japanese, Chinese, or Korean predatory trade tactics, but more often than not the interests of the American economy have taken a backseat to the high politics of war and peace. During the Cold War era and even today, we needed Japan and Korea as key Far East allies. After the opening to China, we needed the Chinese as a counterweight to the Soviets and then as an intermediary with the North Koreans—and of course as a creditor.

U.S. military leadership also undercuts American commercial success directly, in a paradoxical and little-appreciated fashion. Beginning in the earliest days of the Cold War era, the Pentagon pressed its NATO allies to purchase American military products. The idea was both to promote American control over sensitive technologies and to ensure that the alliance's forces would be using compatible equipment. Because the European nations were economically weak, often with balance-of-payments problems, the Pentagon and U.S. defense contractors brokered deals that included what are known as "offsets": if a NATO country purchased a certain amount of U.S. military hardware, the United States would off-set those purchases, either by allowing a lot of the parts to be made in-country or by arranging to purchase a like amount of miscellaneous products made in the client nation. In those years, the United States had a huge balance-of-trade surplus and dominance in manufacturing indus-try, so the commercial effect was of little consequence.

But offsets became built in to the way military trade operated and served as a perk for America's allies. Today, unlike in the early Cold War era, the United States has the world's largest trade deficit and a dwindling manufacturing base. Military products are one of the few industrial goods where American manufacturers still dominate (not be-cause of comparative advantage, but because of government outlays). But whenever a foreign customer/ally negotiates an arms purchase, the offsets demanded are bigger than ever.

According to an authoritative review by Owen Herrnstadt of the cost of offsets, between 1993 and 2005, U.S. companies reported 8,007 offset transactions in 45 countries. The monetary value of these transactions totaled $37.3 billion. Nearly all of this represented manufacturing pro-duction that could have been done in the United States, improving our trade balance, providing good jobs for U.S. workers, and keeping Amer-ican industry at the forefront of production technology. Instead, because Washington places military goals ahead of economic ones, this eco-nomic activity went overseas. Boeing, for example, has a $4.4 billion contract to provide forty F-15 fighters to South Korea. The South Koreans (who enjoy a lopsided trade surplus with the United States) negotiated a deal to have most of the parts made locally, creating high-wage jobs that otherwise would have stayed in the United States, improving our manufacturing base and balance of trade. The Koreans are also allowed to supply parts for F-15s that Boeing sells elsewhere. Sometimes the negotiated offsets are far removed from the immediate sale. After Poland joined NATO, Lockheed won a contract to supply $3.8 billion worth of F-16s. According to *The New York Times*, the offsets from Lockheed and its industrial partners, which Lockheed pays, include subcontracts for Poles to make commercial jet trainers as well as parts for business aircraft like the Gulfstream and Piper for export to the United States and to make the Pratt & Whitney engine for the F-16. There is also a venture with Accenture for a new technology company in Łódź and a partnership with the University of Texas to start a technol-ogy accelerator at the University of Łódź.

The desire to bind foreign governments to American military leadership undermines U.S. commercial goals. American military contracts become instruments of foreign industrial policies. Commerce in weapons systems is trade in which governments are intimately involved: as purchasers of products on the foreign side; as contractors whose long-term relationship with the military supplier allows the products to be developed on the American side; and as setters of rules regarding which technologies are too sensitive to transfer. All this is about as far from laissez-faire commerce as it gets, and its current effect is to displace U.S. manufacturing. Yet time and again, our government puts military objectives ahead of commercial ones.

A Separate Peace

The apparent muddle in U.S. trade goals is no muddle at all when it is understood as the self-interest of Wall Street. Both the financial industry and multinational corporations benefit immensely from the current brand of globalization. They set the terms of debate and the goals for the United States. For investment bankers, having the whole world open to American capital offers much broader opportunities for speculation, long-term investment, and fee income.

But what about other businesses? You would think that the manufacturing industry, which is not without political influence, would be shouting from the housetops about coerced technology transfer, unfair state-led competition, and theft of intellectual property. Business is still waging a good fight to stop outright piracy of intellectual property, but a real transformation has occurred in the past quarter century. Once, the affected industries—steelmakers, automakers, machine tool manufacturers, textile producers, developers of semiconductors—did add up to a powerful lobby for more symmetrical rules of trade. But today, despite the intensification of foreign mercantilist practices and their spread to more nations, most U.S. multinational corporations have adjusted to the warped rules of the trading system because they gain more than they lose. As long as Boeing makes the sale, why should its executives care where the jobs are? Korean workers are a lot cheaper than American ones.

Powerful American companies such as General Electric, IBM, Boeing, Intel, and Motorola contribute mightily to America's dwindling export share of advanced technology. Once, these companies were crusaders for fairer terms of trade. In the 1980s, several of these U.S. multinationals set up a think tank, the Economic Strategy Institute, to research and expose foreign mercantilist practices and promote a tougher U.S. government stance. But Washington has been such an unreliable ally that, except in the one area of intellectual property protection, most U.S. multinationals have essentially fashioned a separate peace with East Asian mercantilism. They can make more money by going to the other side of the wage divide, the currency divide, and the subsidy divide, producing in places where labor costs are far lower, currencies artificially depressed for export purposes, and government benefits much higher. The carrots and sticks offered by China and other Asian nations, combined with the U.S. government's passivity, are just too powerful to resist.

Today, demands for offsets, domestic content, and technology transfer pervade commercial deals as well as military ones. When GE, for example, wishes to do business in China, the Chinese government demands that advanced production be located in China and that sensitive technologies be shared with local partners. In March 2003, according to *The Wall Street Journal*, GE won a $900 million contract to sell high-tech electricity generation turbines to China. The potential market is huge. China plans to purchase more than $10 billion in power generation equipment in the next decade. To win the contract, GE had to agree to allow a lot of the manufacture to take place in China, and to transfer manufacturing guidelines for its state-of-the-art 9F turbine, in which GE had invested more than half a billion dollars. Chinese officials were quite candid that China itself hoped to eventually manufacture similar turbines, aided by the technology transfer.

When China joined the WTO in December 2001, it agreed to gradually phase out what amount to extortionate technology-sharing demands. But although GE bargained hard, it did not file any official complaints. Doing so would have been a serious affront to its prospective business partners. The U.S. government did not complain either. Washington prohibits only the transfer of technology with the most sensitive military applications. For American industry to lose export opportunities, jobs, and commercial technology because of foreign coercive trade practices is evidently no big deal for our government.

U.S. companies may bargain hard over these demands, but the sticks are often more than offset by carrots—subsidies that can run into the billions of dollars to build state-of-the-art factories, twenty-year tax holidays, government-financed training for workers, and of course access to China's cheap workforce. So GE as a multinational corporation, on balance, concludes that it reaps a net benefit from the bargain. But what is a net benefit for GE is not a net benefit for the United States. The trade imbalance worsens, and the drain of advanced technology and good jobs continues. So does the intellectual and political muddle. America still has the world's finest research universities, but critics of American education mistakenly conclude that U.S. industry is moving its research facilities to Asia because of the appeal of Asian scientists rather than Asian mercantilism. And because of the very low purchasing power of Chinese workers and the relatively low Chinese purchases of U.S.-made capital goods (which are increasingly produced overseas as part of the deal), there is no offsetting gain to U.S. exports. The consequence is political as well as economic. U.S. multinational industry, which might be a lobby for fairer trade, is co-opted by foreign mercantilists.

Just as striking is the asymmetry in the role of governments. China and Korea, as well as smaller nations such as Taiwan, Singapore, and Malaysia, are constantly trying to lure advanced American companies to locate offshore. Their government agencies are literally better informed about the state of key American companies and industries than our own government is. Their emissaries target strategic companies and technologies and arrive armed with attractive subsidy packages. The U.S. government has no such policies—indeed, the Department of Commerce has run conferences with foreign governments and corporations to help U.S. companies explore offshoring opportunities. Because we officially promote a laissez-faire ideology, little government effort is expended to encourage foreign production to locate here.

The disparity of subsidy policies is also instructive. East Asian subsidies tend to be strategic. Ours are the random products of regional economic development policies and national military needs. Some state and local governments offer modest subsidies, mostly in the form of tax breaks. But there is nothing comparable on the American side to the strategic targeting by foreign national governments, and the scale of Asian government subsidy money dwarfs anything on offer in the United States.

For example, Intel, one of America's high-tech jewels, is gradually moving much of its production to China. Intel was offered subsidy packages from states such as New Mexico adding up to tens of millions of dollars—compared to subsidies from the government of China well into the billions. The only thing that prevents the most advanced Intel technology from moving to China is national security controls by the Pentagon. The Commerce Department, myopically genuflecting to free trade, could not care less.

Driving Our Entrepreneurs Offshore

Consider the iconic experience of a high-tech pioneer named Igor Khandros, a man who epitomizes both the appeal of America as a haven for foreign-born entrepreneurs and the myopia of U.S. government policy. Khandros, a metallurgical engineer, managed to get permission to emigrate from Kiev in the then-Soviet Ukraine in 1978. He found his way to Rome, was turned down for visas by Israel and New Zealand, and eventually made it to New York. Going to school at night, he earned a doctorate in materials sciences and went to work for IBM's Yorktown research center in the Hudson Valley. In 1993, moving to Livermore, California, Khandros launched his own company, FormFactor, using a new technology of his own invention for the testing of wafers used in computer chips. He attracted venture capital and the collaboration of Intel, took the company public, and quickly built a $400 million enterprise with more than 1,000 U.S. employees and 80 percent of its sales in exports. In 2006, the national semiconductor trade association, Semiconductor Equipment and Materials International (SEMI), honored Khandros with its annual award "for his innovations in parallel testing, microspring contactors and wafer probe cards."

Here was the American dream personified. America's cultural openness, its superb universities, its broad venture capital markets, all worked as advertised to generate yet another brilliant start-up. With this engine of innovation, what's to fear from trade?

The problem is the lethal combination of foreign piracy, foreign subsidy, and mistaken U.S. government priorities. Khandros's testing technology was so good that it was soon pirated by a Korean company called Phicom, even though Khandros had taken out worldwide patents on his innovations. Phicom's copies were so exact that customers sometimes mistakenly shipped Phicom products to FormFactor for repair, believing them to be FormFactor products.

Khandros sued in Korea. The Korean trial court, which almost never sides with foreigners in patent piracy cases, actually found for Khandros. But the holding was overturned on appeal. The court held that Khandros's intricate inventions were "obvious manufacturing art" and thus not subject to patent protections.

It is possible to sue foreign exporters for patent infringement in U.S.

courts, which are more impartial. But with so much semiconductor manufacturing now taking place offshore, Korea's Phicom can thrive without selling in the U.S. market and thus does not need U.S. patent authorization. But it is illicitly eating into FormFactor's market share nearly everywhere else. In principle, Korea is a party to WTO commitments to respect intellectual property, but in practice, Korea controls how that commitment is enforced.

Very frustrated, Khandros learned that the United States was negotiating a free-trade agreement with Korea. Since piracy is a violation of the rules of trade, here was some leverage. Clyde Prestowitz, a former high-ranking trade official who has emerged as the dean of critics of U.S. trade policy, offered to take Khandros to senior Washington officials to tell his story and request his government to seek redress. They went to the U.S. trade representative, the State Department, the National Security Council. Nobody was particularly interested; America had bigger fish to fry with the South Koreans.

By coincidence, that very week the government of Singapore, having learned of FormFactor's battle with the Koreans, approached Khandros with a lucrative offer: If he would relocate his operations to Singapore, the government would offer him new R&D funding, a reduced tax load, and lower labor costs. FormFactor would still have the same patent fight with the Koreans, but it would at least have lower operating costs and more money to invent new technologies. Khandros had one last Washington meeting, with a high Commerce Department official who could not have known of the confidential approach by Singapore. The official said he was sorry, there was nothing the U.S. government could do. He helpfully concluded by asking Khandros, "Have you thought of moving to Singapore?"

The apparent shortsightedness embodied in this all-too-typical episode is not random or accidental. This Commerce Department official, not surprisingly, comes out of U.S. multinational industry. In the private sector, this is simply how the game is played: onshore or offshore, just get the best deal you can. The result is often good for private business but bad for America. The more this business perspective dominates government policy, the more the national interest is overlooked. The occasional fighting entrepreneur like Khandros is no match for the system.

The Hidden Dragon in the Theory

The disconnect between America's diplomatic objectives for the trading system and America's national economic interest plays out in both the

World Trade Organization and in our bilateral trade deals. Once again, the emblematic case is China.

China, with its combination of a still-Leninist one-party regime, a quasi-capitalist but state-led export economy, and close to a billion increasingly productive workers laboring at a fraction of Western wages, particularly confounds the official U.S. assumptions about how trade is supposed to work. From the perspective of orthodox economics, China fits no known intellectual category of economy. It is like the proverbial bumblebee, which, as a matter of aeronautical engineering, is incapable of flight.

China violates most of the rules of market economics, yet it is being rewarded with a 10 percent annual growth rate. It practices multiple forms of mercantilism yet is treated very gingerly (and wishfully) by the United States in hopes that it will mature into a normal democratic and capitalist economy. The sheer scale of the Chinese workforce, and the disparity between its productivity and wages, present unprecedented challenges to the theory and practice of U.S. trade policy. However, our policy toward China remains largely unchanged. In the meantime, American corporations have flocked to China as a low-wage export platform.

In the 1990s, the United States and the rest of the trading system had one powerful piece of leverage over China: the Beijing regime dearly wanted to be admitted to the WTO, in order to reduce tariffs on Chinese exports and to confer international legitimacy on what was (and is) still a despotic regime. The United States, without bargaining very hard over the details, acquiesced to Beijing's wishes, partly because it saw China as a counterweight to Russia. But both the Clinton and Bush administrations also hoped that by letting China into the WTO, they would create more opportunities for commerce and investment and accelerate the maturation of China into something more closely resembling a market economy. They are still waiting. China today remains a Leninist state with no democratic or labor rights, a highly mercantilist brand of capitalism orchestrated by the one-party government, and immense leverage over the United States as the leading holder of our outsized foreign debt.

Beyond geopolitics, the biggest reason for a China WTO deal and the continued soft treatment of Beijing was the appetite of American business. Even if China were not a prime customer for consumer products, its growing economy offered a superb low-wage platform from which American companies ranging from Wal-Mart to Intel could bring in imports. According to official statistics from China's General Administration of Customs, by 2005 fully 58 percent of China's total exports and 64 percent of its exports to the United States are generated by foreign companies or Chinese joint ventures with foreign companies.

So there was a huge business and financial constituency for closer commercial relations with China, never mind the impact on the trade imbalance. The U.S. government, which has gone to the mat on countless other global negotiations, has been reluctant to push the Chinese very hard on trade reciprocity, much less human or labor rights. But in the WTO discussions, the Treasury Department, representing financial elites, did make a serious push in one area: access to China's financial markets. Wall Street saw China as a vast market for financial services—and a new source of deals.

In April 1999, over the objection of the U.S. trade representative and the State Department, Treasury Secretary Rubin made faster financial liberalization the make-or-break condition of a WTO membership deal. This was in the immediate aftermath of the Asian currency crisis, which China had been spared because it had *not* liberalized. The Chinese could not accept that condition. That April, Premier Zhu Rongji, a relative reformer, was in Washington to finalize a WTO agreement. But he went home empty-handed and was soon displaced. It was not until the Bush administration that China's accession to the WTO was consummated in 2001.

James Mann, a former Beijing correspondent for the *Los Angeles Times* and one of the most astute observers of U.S.-China diplomacy, writes in his book *The China Fantasy* that in the late 1980s, just after the Tiananmen Square massacre, the West had substantial leverage over terms of a WTO deal because at the time China was far more vulnerable economically:

> The Japanese government had suspended a package of $5.6 billion in loans to China after the massacre, and the World Bank froze more than $2 billion in interest-free loans. Economic growth dropped to such low levels that, for a time, there was fear of a recession. If ever there was a time when the United States held considerable economic leverage over China, this was it. The [George H. W.] Bush administration didn't seek to use this leverage. Under his policy of engagement, Bush opened the way for a resumption of World Bank and Japanese loans to China and gradually restored normal contacts. Within a couple of years, Deng Xiaoping succeeded spectacularly in

reviving China's economic growth, and by the time Bush gave way to a new administration in Washington, the moment of American economic leverage had passed.

Bush's successor, Bill Clinton, accepted the Democratic nomination for president in 1992, promising "an America that will not coddle dictators, from Baghdad to Beijing." But in the case of China, Clinton's emphasis on human rights quickly gave way to the pressure of business interests that wanted to do deals with the Chinese.

Not only is there general support for this model of U.S.-China trade by business as a class. Individual policy makers profit handsomely when they move to the private sector. "The proclivity of American elites to refrain from public criticism of China's repressive system is reinforced all the more by the influence of money," Mann writes. "In Washington, U.S. political leaders and cabinet members know if they become involved in dealing with China and don't become identified as critics of the regime in Beijing, when they leave office they can move on to lucrative careers as advisers, consultants, or hand-holders for corporate executives eager to do business in China." This describes a bipartisan cast of former secretaries of state Henry Kissinger and Madeleine Albright, former defense secretary William Cohen, former national security adviser Sandy Berger, former U.S. trade representatives Mickey Kantor and Charlene Barshefsky, and hundreds of lower-ranking former officials.

American political and commercial elites have convinced themselves that "engagement" with China and encouragement of China's participation in the global economy will inexorably lead the Chinese to become more like us. A darker possibility is that we will become more like them—a nation with an authoritarian government in league with financial and commercial elites that dominate a vast pool of low-wage labor. American business serves as Beijing's enabler. Wal-Mart presses China for even lower wages, and companies like Google, Yahoo!, and Microsoft, whose slogans promote the Internet as a source of personal liberation, have readily come to terms with Chinese censorship.

Mann quotes Bill Clinton as defending an unreformed China's entry into the WTO as "the best way to integrate China further into the family of nations and to secure our interests and our ideals." Mann then adds:

The fundamental problem with this strategy of integration is that it raises the obvious question: "Who's integrating whom?" Is the United States now integrating China into a new international economic order based on free-market principles? Or, on the other hand, is China now integrating the United States into a new international order where democracy is no longer favored and where a government's continuing eradication of all organized political opposition is accepted or ignored?

Mann was speaking of Beijing and other regimes that manage to amalgamate an aggressive capitalism with an authoritarian system of government. He might have been describing the brand of single-party state promoted by Karl Rove. Mann concludes, "We need politicians who will call attention to the fact that America has been carrying out a policy that benefits business interests in China far more than it helps ordinary working people in either country."

All the T-Bills in China

China has continued to behave like anything but a normal capitalist nation. But today the United States has far less leverage over China's trade policy (or any other China policy), because China is America's leading creditor. Although China's deliberate pegging and undervaluation of the yuan to promote its exports is a relatively discrete and easy-to-remedy problem, as well as a violation of the norms of trade, the Bush administration repeatedly rejected a hard line even on that issue. In May 2006, then Treasury secretary John Snow, nominally complying with a 1988 law requiring a twice-yearly review of exchange rate issues, declined to identify China as a currency manipulator, an explicitly unfair trade practice under both the WTO and domestic law. Snow pronounced the administration to be "extremely dissatisfied" with China's refusal to let the yuan's value be set by trading markets but complimented the Chinese for letting the yuan appreciate—by 2 percent.

Asian mercantilism puts the American economy deeper into hock. Asia keeps accumulating dollars, whose value it props up, and keeps lending the money back to us. Today, the balance of economic leverage between Washington and Beijing is the opposite of what it was less than two decades ago, in the aftermath of the Tiananmen Square massacre. Only a fool would call this the fruits of free trade.

China, with one fourth of America's foreign-held Treasury debt, purchased $87 billion of U.S. Treasury debt in 2006, or 47 percent of the total. The United States and China have a pathological codependency. We borrow the money with which to buy their low-wage products. The money piles up in China's banks, which turn around and lend it back to the United States so that we can keep buying. Even though a rational free-market investor would not accumulate so much dollar-denominated debt because of the risk of devaluation, Chinese banks are not ordinary profit-maximizing investors. It is in China's interest that the game continue, because the United States is the prime market for its industrial expansion. The loans are only so much paper. The technologies China acquires and the jobs it creates are real. The symbiosis has reached a point where American officials are afraid to push for adjustment too hard. Robert Rubin, while Treasury secretary, favored a strong dollar, even as most international economists were arguing that the dollar needed to depreciate, especially against the East Asian currencies. In an interview with me, Rubin explained that East Asian central banks, by propping up the dollar, were actually "doing us a favor."

Although the United States periodically makes diplomatic noises about the importance of China letting its currency float normally in currency markets, Washington doesn't mean it. The tough talk, coupled with very token measures by the Chinese, is intended mainly to head off action by critics in Congress. Rubin's former partner at Goldman Sachs, Treasury Secretary Henry Paulson, has modestly turned up the rhetoric on China, but Paulson doesn't really want a significantly cheaper dollar any more than Rubin did. Paulson, like Rubin, wants just enough Chinese "progress" to keep Congress from enacting retaliatory measures. And so the game continues.

The optimists hope that as long as central banks in general keep buying Treasury securities, private foreign investors will be reassured that the dollar will not crash. Some observers draw an analogy between the China-U.S. codependency and the original Bretton Woods system, which lasted nearly thirty years. In that era, the dollar was king and it was the United States that chronically ran a trade surplus. We lent the money we kept accumulating to our debtor nations so that they could buy American products, rather as China does to us today.

But the analogy is far from comforting. In the postwar era, the United States was economically and militarily hegemonic. It played that role more or less benignly. Would we be happy with China playing the hegemonic role? Moreover, the United States explicitly swore off mercantilist trade and economic policies so that Europe and Japan could rebuild their war-torn economies. China, by contrast, is the world's premier mercantilist nation.

The Debate We Should Be Having

If you accept the broad premise of this book (and the evidence of twentieth-century history), a managed form of capitalism is far better for most people, better for broadly diffused prosperity, better for economic efficiency, and better for the stability of the system as a whole. The nation-state is necessarily the venue of that economic management, because it is the locus of government and of political democracy. There is no global government, only very partial and largely unaccountable institutions of international regulation. The only entity close to a transnational democratic polity is the European Union. But the European Union solves the problem of reconciling private commerce with managed capitalism on only one continent and Europe's model is coming under increasing threat by the current brand of globalization.

"Free trade" is a synonym for laissez-faire capitalism operating across borders. But if laissez-faire is not the optimal form of capitalism domestically, it is not the best brand of capitalism internationally. The free-trade story is at odds with the way capitalism actually works, the way capitalism has been domesticated within the advanced countries to provide broadly diffused benefits, the way most trading nations pursue advantage, and the way trade diplomacy operates. In practice, the pursuit of "free trade" causes the U.S. government to sacrifice the national interest for the self-interest of economic elites.

In American politics today, there is almost no serious discussion of how to reconcile the goals of expanded cross-border commerce and Third World development with that of maintaining high and egalitarian living standards in the United States and the other countries with decent social compacts. The official United States agenda for trade evades the real issues that our economy needs to confront if we are not to lose what remains of social protections, decent wages, and the broader ability of the United States to compete as an advanced economy. If we had a different balance of political power, we would be having an entirely different national conversation. The real issues raised by globalization are these:

- How can we preserve the instruments of a mixed economy when commerce increasingly crosses borders? Which necessary regulatory functions can best be performed by national governments? Which ones can be accomplished by reciprocal conventions and treaties that set common goals? Which require global institutions of governance, with substantial delegation of sovereignty? Which necessitate conditional, as opposed to open, trade. What other constraints on capital flows are necessary?

- What is the national interest of the United States in maintaining a society of broad prosperity and technological dynamism? How is that national interest complicated by international trade? How can we prevent globalized corporations from playing off governments against one another, so that nations that value social investment, taxation of capital, regulation, and high wages are not punished by capital flight to nations that have none of these?

- How can the advanced democracies protect their social models from the pressure to reduce wages and social benefits without disadvantaging the development needs of poor countries that need to export in order to grow? How can workers in the Third World and in the advanced nations get back on the same side?

- How can we prevent nations that pay lip service to free trade but practice strategic trade from breaking the rules and capturing leadership in advanced products at our expense? How can we prevent domestic industry from being seduced by a combination of illegal subsidies, illicit strong-arming, and dirt-cheap labor that leads transnational corporations to locate their advanced production as well as routine production abroad?

- What rules of engagement are necessary to allow nations with very different economic development models to pursue their own preferred strategies, but with an equitable distribution of burdens and benefits? When trade puts downward pressure on wages and on the state's ability to tax, can we somehow maintain a good society by the heroic use of social investments? Or do we also need to revise the rules of trade?

Different people will offer different answers to these questions, of course. The point is that we should be debating them, not evading them. As this book suggests, my own answer is that our democratically elected national government needs to demand much more reciprocal rules of trade, and to find ways to bring the instruments of managed capitalism to the global economy. We need to align the interests of corporations once again with the interests of citizens. Some of this endeavor will require transnational forms of regulation, such as the Kyoto protocols and the core labor standards of the ILO, and conventions among governments to prevent offshore tax evasion and end runs around national regulation of finance. Some of it will require much more robust domestic social investments, so that individuals and families are sheltered against economic dislocations beyond their personal control and are given the tools to compete. The point is that the history of the past century has proven that managed capitalism is superior to laissez-faire capitalism, more efficient as well as more equitable, and it should not be sacrificed on the altar of utopian free markets, global or otherwise.

Seen this way, the increase in global commerce presents an entirely different challenge from the conventional goal of promoting universal "free trade." Universal laissez-faire would indeed be one way of organizing a global economy—but it would fly in the face of the lessons of twentieth-century history and produce a system far more unstable and far more unequal than the economies built by the advanced democracies. Regulating transnational capitalism may be administratively and diplomatically challenging, but the deeper challenge is political. Until domestic politics change, the U.S. agenda for the global system will persist on its destructive path.

CHAPTER NINE

THE RETURN OF SPECULATIVE GLOBAL FINANCE

THERE WAS A TIME in recent history when global commerce was understood as the servant of a just domestic society, not the master. In 1944, as World War II was ending, the United States and its wartime allies devised a new international financial and trade order. With the Great Depression fresh in everyone's memory, the goal was to create a postwar monetary and trading system that would allow national governments to manage their domestic economies to promote high employment, balanced growth, economic stability, and a socially defensible income distribution.

A worldwide depression had discredited laissez-faire, both domestically and globally. Among the factors that had deepened the Great Depression were bouts of competitive currency devaluation, defaults on international loans, and the collapse of trade. Laissez-faire, as a transnational principle, made it more difficult to operate a managed form of capitalism at home, in several respects. A monetary system based on gold was deflationary, because discoveries of gold did not necessarily occur at the pace needed by economic growth. Globally, there was no counterpart to the "elastic currency" provided at the national level by central banks like the Federal Reserve. So countries with high rates of growth pulled in imports and ended up with balance-of-payments deficits; they were punished for their success or forced to defend their currencies with austerity policies. This logic had created a deflationary bias for the whole system. By the same token, the trading system needed to ensure that nations played by roughly reciprocal rules, so they did not try to prosper by a beggar-thy-neighbor strategy. For the statesmen of the 1940s, with their vivid memories of Depression-era breadlines and Depression-bred dictators, trade had to be reconciled with the overarching domestic goal of full employment.

In the Bretton Woods system of the immediate postwar era, the architects of the new rules for international commerce and finance got the balance about right. The ingeniously designed International Monetary Fund was intended to create structural incentives for economic growth rather than deflation. Exchange rates were pegged and managed by governments, so that national economies were not at the mercy of private speculative capital movements. Indeed, with fixed exchange rates there literally were no speculative markets in international currencies, because no money could be made. The IMF was available to help nations that fell into temporary balance-of-payments problems, so that they didn't have to deflate their way into balance and create a drag on the entire system. Pressure was to be put on surplus nations to expand, rather than on deficit countries to contract.

The new World Bank, meanwhile, underwrote reconstruction loans, so that redevelopment did not depend on the caprices of short-term private financing. National economies were freed to pursue their own strategies of development, whether state-led or private.

A few years later, in 1948, the United States and its allies negotiated an International Trade Organization, to reconcile liberalized trade and full employment. In the United States, the conservative Eightieth Congress refused to ratify it, and the weaker General Agreement on Tariffs and Trade, by default, became a skeletal set of basic trade principles. The GATT system allowed liberalization of trade at a socially bearable pace and did not attempt to interfere with member nations' economic development strategies. All the major Western governments, center left or center right, were committed to domestic policies anchored in a regulated brand of capitalism, to balance market goals with social goals.

The United States found itself in the happy position of being both beneficent and fat. One is reminded of Mark Twain's definition of confidence: a Christian holding four aces.

Uniquely, the United States had come out of the war suffering no economic damage. On the contrary, war spending had retooled our entire industrial machine, after more than a decade of depression. But America's allies, the conquerors as well as the conquered, were in dire economic condition. Whether because farsighted statesmen were in power or because of the looming competitive appeal of communism to destitute peoples, or because the Depression, the New Deal, and the war had left a political legacy of an interventionist state, the U.S. government of that era practiced an exemplary form of enlightened self-interest.

Though it is little appreciated today, global finance built on principles of managed capitalism did not occur without a political fight. As the Roosevelt and Truman administrations promoted public institutions such as the IMF, World Bank, and Marshall Plan, the financial conservatives of that era argued that private financial flows would be ample to restart normal international commerce and to rebuild war-torn Europe and Japan. Conservatives had made the same argument after World War I, with catastrophic results. They had added war reparations to the burden of Germany's economic recovery and created no transnational public institutions to temper the speculative, destabilizing, and ultimately deflationary influence of private capital flows. Their legacy was the Great Depression.

The difference between the 1920s, the 1940s, and our own era has nothing to do with economic fundamentals, which are unchanging. The main difference is in who had the political power to make these decisions. Of these three economic periods, only in the 1940s did sponsors of managed capitalism prevail.

The post–World War II system, however, did not work exactly as its architects had imagined. In the early postwar years, the United States, rather than the new multilateral institutions, became the economic and financial flywheel. The dollar, rather than the intended new system of IMF credits, became the key reserve and trading currency. The Marshall Plan, and later dollar exports based on what was then a chronic U.S. trade surplus, loomed larger than the World Bank in Europe's postwar reconstruction. The United States was the overwhelmingly superior economic power, and Congress was not about to cede sovereignty to these new multinational economic institutions, except as American surrogates. Even so, the new system facilitated a mixed form of capitalism, both in the United States and elsewhere. Social goals and market goals were balanced. All of that would soon change.

Back to Austerity

For the first quarter century after World War II, the U.S. dollar was the de facto global currency. As other nations recovered, this system could not continue without either creating inflation in the United States or depriving the world economy of the reserves it needed in order to expand. These contradictory pulls intensified in the 1960s, as global growth increased and the United States struggled to finance the Vietnam War. When the Bretton Woods system of fixed exchange rates anchored by the U.S. dollar finally collapsed in the early 1970s and currencies were allowed to float, one side effect was the growth of currency speculation. Another was increased short-term, often speculative lending to sovereign nations by private banks, surpassing the lending by such public institutions as the IMF and the World Bank. The OPEC hike in the price of oil, followed by the bout of "stagflation" in the United States and the resultant rise in dollar interest rates, left many developing countries at the mercy of international creditors.

A political side effect was an ideological windfall for the Right. A decade of slow growth and inflation discredited the model of managed capitalism, put its political supporters on the defensive, and added to the prestige of laissez-faire economists. Beginning in the late 1970s, the ideological mood, spurred by Margaret Thatcher in the United Kingdom and later Ronald Reagan in the United States, shifted to one of extreme laissez-faire. The plight of debtor nations was used by private banks and their allies in Whitehall and the U.S. Treasury as an opportunity for forcibly converting them to an economic recipe of Thatcherism.

The IMF mutated from an institution intended to anchor high growth and mixed market systems into one that served mainly private creditors' interests. The IMF began promoting a model based on financial speculation, seeking to impose a single brand of capitalism on all nations. The approved IMF model included low taxes, especially on capital; low social outlay; conservative fiscal policies; and a strategy of financial market opening that placed the interests of private finance far above the interests of small nations that did not wish to become prisoners of speculative herd instincts.

The new formula was known as the Washington Consensus, named for the three institutions that devised it and that act as its enforcers, all located in downtown Washington, D.C.: the IMF, the World Bank, and the U.S. Treasury. Any nation that got into balance-of-payments difficulties in the 1980s or 1990s had to agree to a program of market opening, especially of financial markets, as well as budgetary austerity, to qualify for an IMF bailout. The IMF seal, in turn, certified the debtor nation as worthy of taking on additional private debt.

These measures supposedly would reassure foreign private lenders of the "soundness" of the local economy. But typically, the austerity only pushed the economy deeper into recession; the new debt either financed short-term consumption or bailed out old creditors; and the debtor country was typically saddled with even higher interest payments. The IMF recipe did nothing for long-term development. To appreciate the perversity of the formula, imagine the United States in the Roosevelt era embarking on an austerity program designed to satisfy foreign lenders as a cure for the Great Depression. The developing nations that thrived in the 1980s and 1990s were precisely those of East Asia, with regulated financial markets, that had rejected the Washington Consensus.

The United States also displayed many forms of hypocrisy. Though America continues to run a trade deficit so large that it would cause any other nation to be hauled before the IMF and made to launch an austerity program, America continues to use what Charles de Gaulle once called the "exorbitant privilege" of paying foreign debts in its own currency, creating dangerous imbalances for its own economy and for the world.

The era of global financial speculation produced a double risk. It not only increased the hazard of greater losses to American financial institutions and their investors but put entire economies at risk of deep depression caused by events entirely beyond their control, with "contagion" effects to other countries.

In terms of our trilogy of equality, efficiency, and risk, global financial speculation flunks all three criteria: Economies become more unequal, both within and between nations. Huge sums of money are wasted. And the entire system is put at greater risk. However, a small number of traders get very rich.

Please note that I am using the word "speculation" not as a pejorative for private financial flows in general but in a more precise way. Developing countries need nothing so much as capital. The damage is done not by long-term investment in actual enterprises but by short-term loans and financial bets on currency movements, because that sort of money can fly out just as quickly as it rushes in—which is, of course, what has actually occurred in country after country.

Liberated market forces are conventionally said to increase economic efficiency. But speculative financial forces are subject to fads and herd instincts. Rather than producing the equilibrium described in economic textbooks, they tend to increase volatility, exaggerate cycles, and undercut long-term investment. When this dynamic operates globally, where there is no sovereign, it is more difficult for central bankers, national governments, regulators, and transnational institutions, even operating in concert, to contain the negative effects.

Bank Holiday

With the liberalization of global commerce, a new challenge is the global regulation of finance. While some advocates of free markets think that currency traders should be free to speculate to their hearts' content, even the most euphoric of the laissez-faire crowd takes a far more sober view of banks. Though banks are private institutions, they are part of a nation's monetary system, and a banking collapse can take down the entire economy.

Three decades ago, cross-national governance of banking was a trivial concern, because national regulation strictly limited the role of foreign banks in a domestic economy. While a few U.S. financial institutions did have a major presence in some Third World economies, the ability of U.S. banks to perform normal commercial services in Europe, or of European banks to operate in the United States, was narrowly circumscribed. Japan was totally closed to foreign banking (and this policy did not stop Japan from growing at 10 percent a year for two decades).

Responding to the domestic banking industry's desire to operate worldwide, the Reagan administration in the 1980s, as part of the Uruguay Round of trade talks, came up with another nontraditional area for trade: financial services. The idea was that banks should be given free rein globally and that foreign-owned banks operating outside their home countries should enjoy exactly the same rights and privileges as domestic ones. This was part of the broader agenda of liberating financial flows of all kinds from national regulation.

However, banks based in different countries are subject to entirely different regulatory structures. This disparity creates subtle competitive advantages and disadvantages, as well as concern that the entire system's safety could get away from nation-bound regulators.

For example, diverse nations have different regulatory philosophies about a bank's "capital adequacy"—the ratio of the bank's equity capital to the volume of loans it is permitted to make. Banks take in deposits and invest the money in a variety of assets, from ordinary loans to complex derivative deals. They make their money on the spreads. Lately, thanks to other forms of deregulation that allow proliferation of complex financial instruments, banks' investments have become far more speculative.

The smaller the amount of the bank's own capital to cover the occasional bad bet, the greater is the risk that an unanticipated trend will cause the whole bank to go under, requiring government bailouts and destabilizing the whole system. The intensification of the Great Depression was in part the result of the contraction of credit that occurred as borrowers defaulted on loans and the entire banking sector shrank. In recent times, a more modest version of the same credit contraction syndrome occurred in the 1980s, as bank and thrift institutions had to absorb large speculative losses. Regulators today worry about the huge risks of speculative bank activity that is hard to monitor, such as deals with hedge funds and exposure to derivatives bets.

With a single worldwide banking market, it doesn't work to have divergent national regulatory standards. For example, in Japan, with its more planned form of capitalism, banks are typically permitted to be more highly leveraged (less capital, more loans), on the theory that the Ministry of Finance is keeping close watch on the whole affair. German banks are permitted to perform both commercial and investment banking services—no Glass-Steagall Act for the Germans. In fact, the German system allows the breach of the even more fundamental barrier (in Anglo-Saxon law) between banking and ordinary commerce. Financial powerhouses such as Deutsche Bank own substantial shares of German industry. Even though a foreign bank doing business in the United States becomes subject to some aspects of U.S. financial regulation, the fact that its parent institution is rooted in a fundamentally different system of law and supervision creates possible competitive advantages as well as greater systemic risks, as banks book any given banking activity in the jurisdiction with the weakest regulation of that activity.

With the Uruguay Round, globalization of financial services supercharged the politics of bank deregulation in the United States. American bankers were quick to complain that they were subject to tougher constraints on mergers than their foreign competitors, who were now free to set up shop in America's domestic market. Global competition also became the trump in the campaign to repeal what was left of Glass-Steagall. Bankers and their political allies warned that if German and British and Japanese banks were free to offer the full range of services but their American counterparts were not, a lot of financial activity might move offshore. Likewise for the listing and trading of securities. It was another way that globalization produced a regulatory race to the bottom.

Not surprisingly, this process troubled the regulators. There was no easy way of harmonizing every aspect of national regulation, but a great deal might be accomplished by at least harmonizing standards for capital adequacy. The 1980s, as noted, was not a great decade for commercial bankers. The industry lost hundreds of billions of dollars in nonperforming Third World loans and other speculative endeavors. If regulators had applied strict accounting standards, several New York banks would have been judged insolvent. Several major foreign banks also took a huge hit. This was the background to the several rounds of government bailouts. As banking became internationalized, regulators from the major nations generally shared the views that bank capital needed to be rebuilt and that capital adequacy standards in different nations needed to be brought into greater harmony. Otherwise, the race to the bottom would take the form of the bank or banking system with the greatest taste for risk leading others down the road to speculative perdition.

There were, however, two major institutional obstacles. First, there is no international bank regulatory agency. Second, by the 1980s the speculative business of banking had become so complex that measuring capital-to-asset ratios was no easy matter. Bank assets are no longer simple affairs like loans, where it is easy for regulators to assess the value of the collateral and whether the loan is performing. Increasingly, banks are "counterparties" (suppliers of money) in complex derivatives transactions, which can blow up all at once, as well as being investors in other kinds of securities. Different categories of bank assets carry different degrees of risk.

The closest thing to an international banking agency (and it isn't very close) is an obscure institution called the Bank for International Settlements, based in Basel, Switzerland. The BIS is less a regulatory agency than an industry-dominated clearing collaborative and venue for occasional policy discussion. Just as the Federal Reserve handles the clearance of interbank transactions in the United States, the BIS is responsible for coordinating and monitoring the daily settling up of international bank transactions. With the encouragement of domestic regulators such as former Fed chairman Paul Volcker, New York Fed president William McDonough, and later Alan Greenspan, the Bank for International Settlements took on the task of helping to broker a common standard for bank capital.

In the Basel Capital Accord of 1988, signatories agreed to a common capital adequacy standard and set of criteria aimed at harmonizing standards that require banks to rebuild capital when their lending ratios became dangerously thin. So far, so good. But the proverbial ink was scarcely dry when innovations in speculative financial transactions rendered the Basel Accord substantially moot. In the 1990s, regulators began pursuing a second Basel Accord, to track what banks actually did and set capital standards accordingly. This became known as Basel II.

Meanwhile, regulators in the United States had been working with banks to rebuild their depleted capital and improve their ratios of capital to assets. Despite the general mood of deregulation, a systemic banking meltdown was such a dire prospect that the George H. W. Bush administration and the Democratic Congress agreed on legislation in 1991 toughening the FDIC Act. The 1991 law, for the first time, created statutory requirements for the ratio of bank capital to bank investments, as well as a system for prompt "corrective action," monitored by regulatory agencies, when ratios dwindled below prudent levels. Interestingly, in the years since that law was passed, banks have both rebuilt their capital and reached new levels of profit. Note the implication for our larger story: good regulation and healthy banking are complements, not opposites. However, the internationalization of banking presented both political and administrative complications, frustrating the efforts to negotiate a second, far more sophisticated Basel Accord.

The international politics added a second layer to a complex domestic politics in which the banking industry holds the whip hand. It would not be an exaggeration to say that banks have something close to a veto over the regulatory system. Though this is ostensibly a government system of regulation, in practice it is consensual industry self-regulation— blessed, certified, and enforced by national government. Globalization only increases the banks' leverage because of the concern that effective regulation will drive capital offshore. In the United States, the Treasury and the bank-dominated Federal Reserve tend to be advocates for the banks, while the more independent regulatory agencies are likely to have more of a public interest perspective. Treasury secretaries are often recruited from Wall Street, to reassure capital markets, and they bring the Wall Street view to government deliberations. By contrast, the FDIC, whose trust funds are at risk of having to bail out failing banks, often acts as the tougher regulator.

In the run-up to Basel II, it was the Federal Reserve, in the person of William McDonough, that took the lead. McDonough, then president of the Federal Reserve Bank of New York, needed the political support of the big New York banks for any international capital adequacy formula, because they had the political power to persuade Congress to overturn anything they found objectionable. So in the negotiations over Basel II, the banks themselves have been major players.

In the development of Basel II, the regulators were persuaded that the banks knew more than the regulators did. The banks, presumably, had a huge stake in managing risks. They had spent a small fortune on elaborate models intended to hedge and balance the risks in their portfolios. In the Basel II formulas, the regulators agreed to take the banking industry's own risk criteria and then apply different capital standards to different categories of investments and risks, known as "buckets." This agreement was close to being approved in 2005 and 2006, when some of the regulators and their technical experts took a closer look. What they found was alarming. It turned out that the proposed new standards, rather than shoring up the ratio of bank capital to bank loans and other investments, would actually permit many institutions to degrade the status quo and lessen their capital ratios.

In 2005, a "Quantitative Impact Study" by the regulatory agencies reviewed the expected effect of the proposed standards on the banks expected to participate in Basel II. Regulators were horrified that the study showed an anticipated *decline* in required bank equity capital, with a median decline of 26 percent. Half of the participating banks reported projected declines of more than 31 percent. One bank would be allowed a decline of nearly 50 percent.

Despite the Bush administration's close ties to industry and its ultra-laissez-faire philosophy, several congressional leaders in both parties did not like what they saw. Fortuitously, the chairman of the FDIC happened to be a highly knowledgeable and pro-regulation Democrat, Martin Gruenberg, former staff director of the Senate Banking Committee under Senator Paul Sarbanes. The law requires representation of the minority party on the FDIC's board. By long-standing convention, senior congressional members of the minority party generally get to select the minority members of regulatory commissions to be appointed by the president. In the atmosphere of the Bush administration's general laxity in keeping current with regulatory appointments, the White House had not bothered to fill the vacancy in the FDIC chair, leaving Gruenberg, the Democratic deputy chairman, serving as acting chairman for thirteen months in 2005–06. When Bush, in June 2006, finally did get around to appointing a Republican chair, Sheila Bair, she shared most of Gruenberg's misgivings about Basel II.

The episode, not yet resolved in mid-2007, was a big embarrassment both for McDonough and for Susan Schmidt Bies, the member of the Federal Reserve Board of Governors designated to deal with issues of international bank regulation. McDonough essentially tried to broker a deal with the big money center banks, assuring them that the new Basel standards would treat them gently. When the backlash ensued against what turned out to be overly lenient standards and regulators tried to toughen them, the big banks withdrew their support.

Capital standards for transnational banking are clearly a problem that "the market" cannot solve. As industry lobbyists, their political allies, and more public-minded regulators from various countries grapple with this vexing political and institutional challenge, a status quo persists that is a virtual invitation for banks to speculate with other people's money, exposing the entire system to ever-increasing risks. With domestic banking moving ever farther down the path of deregulation, adequate transnational regulation of banks will be a very heavy lift, technically, institutionally, and politically.

The Costs of Hot Money

When the U.S. stock market was sluggish during 2005, a lot of "smart money" poured into what Wall Street likes to call emerging markets and what ordinary people call their countries. Asian, North African, and South American stock markets briefly boomed. But then the smart money decided these stock markets had risen about as high as they were going to go for now, and the money poured out. The markets tumbled. This exaggerated swing had nothing whatever to do with economic fundamentals. Mainly, it reflected increasingly powerful hedge funds copying one another's behavior.

Likewise, in the summer of 2006, oil prices soared. Hedge funds had become nervous about the Middle East, summer gasoline demand slightly exceeded projections, and supply was tight. These speculative forces bid up the price of crude oil to unsustainable levels. As autumn came, and with it a supply glut, prices at the pump tumbled by more than a dollar. Political cynics imagined the Bush family calling their Saudi friends to increase supply or Dick Cheney getting on the phone to oil executives, asking them to lower retail prices in anticipation of the election. That may even have happened, but it didn't need to. The extreme swings in retail gas prices reflect how speculative hedge funds needlessly exaggerated economic, seasonal, and geopolitical factors.

These two examples did not have catastrophic economic effects, merely inconvenient and unsettling ones. But other such speculative movements did play havoc with real economies and will again. Two vivid illustrations are the second Mexican credit collapse of 1995 and the Asian currency crises of 1997–98.

The Mexican crisis was the direct consequence of another entirely gratuitous "free-market" initiative, the North American Free Trade Agreement of 1993. The NAFTA area was not a true free-trade area or common market. The agreement, spanning thousands of pages that few people read, was written by and for business interests that wanted easier access to cheap Mexican labor and that hoped to use NAFTA to get rid of regulations. The Clinton administration so oversold NAFTA that American banks and other investors poured far more money into Mexico than the Mexicans could invest prudently. The rapid inflow bid up the value of the peso and financed a brief and unsustainable consumption boom. To attract the money, Mexico offered high-yield bonds effectively denominated in dollars, called Tesobonos, so that U.S. investors would not face any risk of peso devaluation. But as the boom peaked and investors began to cash out, the peso started losing its value and bonds began trading at a discount. Mexico found itself unable to attract enough new money to pay off its bondholders, quickly ran short of reserves, and again faced the risk of default.

Treasury Secretary Robert Rubin and Fed Chairman Alan Greenspan personally lobbied Congress for a most unmarketlike $40 billion bailout. When Congress refused to go along, the Treasury, with Greenspan's blessing, somewhat dubiously dipped into its emergency currency stabilization fund to lend Mexico the necessary money to make whole foreign (mostly American) investors in Mexico's bonds. The U.S. government, bailing out market excesses created by its own bad trade policy, came to the rescue, protecting U.S. investors but leaving Mexico, for the second time in little more than a decade, hobbled with even more debt.

Rubin, in his memoirs, reflects on the difficult decision to rescue Mexico as it played out in the Clinton cabinet, where he had just been named Treasury secretary. "[I]ntervention would almost surely be criticized as 'bailing out' wealthy American and European investors who had speculated on developing markets. Putting public funds on the line was likely to be massively unpopular and politically risky," he wrote. Rubin added the further concern that "[i]nvestors, after being insulated from the consequences of risk in Mexico, might pay insufficient attention to risks next time, or operate on the expectation of official intervention." In the end, Rubin reported, "We concluded—I think rightly—that Mexico couldn't be helped *without the side effect of helping some investors*" (emphasis added).

It is instructive how blind even the most intelligent people can be when it comes to associating their self-interest with the public interest. Goldman Sachs, where Rubin had been cochairman, was the largest underwriter of Mexican bonds. Bailing out investors was described as being just an unfortunate side effect; in fact, it was the whole point. The U.S. Treasury is not in the habit of rescuing Third World nations when no private U.S. interests are at stake.

Rubin also notes in passing that in an earlier era, this sort of highly volatile Third World sovereign lending simply didn't exist. Loans to sovereign governments "had been illiquid, changing hands only in privately negotiated transactions with large point spreads." But by the 1990s, "highly liquid capital moved at the speed of light through fiber-optic cables. . . . Orders could be executed at any hour. The result was that developments in markets in one place could have instantaneous effects in any other place, and crises could spread much more rapidly."

Rubin doesn't reflect on whether the new volatility that creates the spread of panicky contagion is either efficient or necessary, or why it is now the norm. This shift is the result of deliberate policy changes that promote international speculation. As a Wall Street man, whose colleagues profit from such transactions, he takes it for granted that trading markets in foreign currencies are desirable and inevitable. He's also wrong on the history and role of technology. Seventy-five years ago, panic also spread from one currency to another at the same speed of light, using copper wire rather than optical fiber. The reason, then as now, was the lack of controls on speculation in currencies. In the intervening years, when such speculation was prohibited, there was no such volatility.

But prior to the 1980s, developing nations had plenty of access to capital, either internally generated in the case of powerhouses like Japan and Korea, or foreign private capital investment, but not on such volatile terms. The earlier era of greater prudence in lending did not seem to hurt the Third World. Latin America, for example, grew at an annual rate of more than 5 percent in the 1950s, '60s, and early '70s, far better than in the speculative 1980s and '90s. Asian nations grew at prodigious rates precisely to the extent that they kept their domestic capital markets insulated from the pressures of global speculation. And nearly all of East Asia's capital was generated domestically.

Like the twin Mexican crises, the Asian currency panic of the late 1990s was also the sequel to too much deregulation. In this case, the IMF and U.S. trade negotiators, carrying out the ideology of global laissez-faire as promoted by major U.S. and European banks, had put pressure on newly emergent Asian countries to fully open their financial markets. Investors in the rich countries wanted direct access to these markets, which had higher growth rates than those of mature economies. Financial middlemen stood to make fortunes. They wanted to be able to make loans, trade currencies, invest in companies, broker joint ventures, buy local banks—in short, to treat these high-growth economies as appendages of Wall Street. This formula was congenial to some of the locals, who either were true believers in laissez-faire or stood to gain personally as the agents of American business interests. These nations also exported products to the United States and wanted Washington's goodwill.

Global money traders are notoriously subject to fads. In the 1990s, East Asia was the next new thing. As noted, the East Asian countries had managed very high growth rates precisely by violating the precepts of the Washington Consensus. Their brand of capitalism was managed. It relied on close ties between local business and government, very low interest rates, high domestic savings, and a degree of consensual planning. It was explicitly closed to foreign financial speculation.

Once these relatively small countries succumbed to U.S. and IMF pressure to liberalize, their currencies became objects of speculation. In the late 1990s, traders and investors poured money into the newly opened economies of East Asia, creating a brief artificial boom. When the returns failed to meet inflated expectations, they pulled out just as fast. This caused a run against these countries' currencies. In the summer of 1997, Thailand's currency, the baht, came under speculative attack. When Thailand's central bank could no longer defend it, the baht abruptly fell by some 25 percent.

There was nothing fundamentally wrong with the Thai economy, which had been growing at an annual rate of about 9 percent for more than a decade. But the hot money had concluded that the so-called East Asian miracle had peaked. The speculative shorting of Asian currencies spread rapidly to Malaysia, Indonesia, the Philippines, and even the prodigious economy of South Korea. Then, as always, the International Monetary Fund came in, as it were, to shoot the wounded.

In order to "restore investor confidence," the IMF, seconded by Washington and Wall Street, demanded austerity programs as the response to a recession created substantially by foreign speculators. The recipe included higher taxes and lower public spending, so that "sound" budget policies would raise the trading value of currencies under speculative attack by foreign investors. The Nobel laureate economist Joseph Stiglitz subsequently wrote, "IMF policies not only exacerbated the downturns but were partially responsible for the onset: excessively rapid financial and capital-market liberalization was probably the single most important cause of the crisis."

People who make economic policy are not supposed to hold such views, since international liberalization of capital and product markets is the reigning bipartisan policy. Stiglitz, after chairing Clinton's Council of Economic Advisers, went on to become chief economist and senior vice president of the World Bank, often clashing openly with the more orthodox economists of the Clinton administration and the IMF. I personally heard a surprisingly candid confrontation about the wisdom of the IMF formula between Stiglitz and Lawrence Summers, then deputy Treasury secretary, at one of the public sessions of the annual meetings of government and business leaders in Davos, Switzerland. High public officials simply did not get into this kind of public spat. Stiglitz was soon fired. Reportedly, it was Summers who forced Stiglitz out of his World Bank post in 2000. Not long afterward, Stiglitz won the Nobel Prize for his lifetime work on the imperfections of markets.

Stiglitz was amused by the fervor with which the IMF and the Treasury denounced the East Asian economies once their currencies came under attack. "According to the IMF," he wrote, "the Asian nations' institutions were rotten, their governments corrupt, and wholesale reform was needed. These outspoken critics were hardly experts on the region." How, Stiglitz wondered, "if these countries' institutions were so rotten, had they done so well for so long?" Then he had an epiphany.

The IMF and the World Bank had deliberately avoided studying the region, though presumably its success should have made it a model for others. It was only under heavy pressure from the Japanese that the World Bank finally undertook a study of economic growth in East Asia (the final report was titled "The East Asian Miracle") and then only after the Japanese had offered to pay for it. The reason for the World Bank's reluctance, Stiglitz concluded, was obvious: the countries had been successful not only in spite of the fact that they had not followed most of the dictates of the Washington Consensus, but *because* they had not.

As traders shorted Asian currencies, driving them down further, the crisis deepened. Domestic demand in all these countries took a hit, creating a regional recession. American markets became very nervous. On October 27, 1997, the Dow Jones Industrial Average lost 554 points in a day. Western banks were reluctant to roll over loans even to solid economies like South Korea's. The South Korean economy was hemorrhaging reserves at the rate of a billion dollars a day. The Asian financial crisis threatened to spread to Russia and Latin America.

In December 1997, Greenspan and Rubin decided they had to come to South Korea's rescue. They were far from happy with this intervention, because South Korea was not following the IMF recipe. Its development formula included very close business-government collaboration and even directed lending of the sort frowned upon in Washington and New York (except after the fact in the context of bailouts). Help for South Korea was delayed, according to Rubin's memoirs, while Washington pressured the South Koreans to alter their whole economic model.

But the stakes—the prospects of a broader systemic collapse—were too high to play a bluffing game. Eventually, in late December, Rubin called the heads of several New York banks and told them their government wanted a "standstill agreement" to roll over existing loans as they came due. William McDonough brought several foreign banks into the bargain. That gave the South Koreans breathing room to stave off a collapse, and by spring their economy had begun to recover. Greenspan sweetened the deal by keeping domestic interest rates low, despite his concern that cheap money was fueling a stock market boom that he had already branded dangerously unsustainable in his "irrational exuberance" speech more than a year before. In other words, an entirely gratuitous global opening to speculative forces caused the U.S. central bank to pursue a monetary policy that it considered unwise for domestic purposes and that set in motion a further speculative spiral.

In recent years, the IMF has pulled back from its recipe of enforced austerity and mandatory financial market opening. Nothing fails like failure. After the East Asian collapse, many governments vowed never again to work with the IMF. The correlation between the developing nations that have followed the IMF recipe and those that have prospered is nearly a perfect refutation of the IMF's view of how economies work. In this decade, there has been a quiet financial revolution in South America, as Argentina and Brazil have paid off the last of their debts to the IMF, and most Latin American countries have just stopped doing business with the Fund, whose outstanding loans are now just a fraction of their peak.

Debt and Delusion

Perhaps the most stunning irony is that the nations of East Asia that most violated America's preferred recipe about flinging open their financial markets, and that were most insulated from the speculative pressures commended by U.S. elites, have now become America's prime creditors. China, Japan, and South Korea did not want or need American financial capital (though they cajoled or coerced the transfer of American research and technology). With their managed economies, huge export earnings, and high domestic savings rates, they had more than enough capital for their own development needs and some to spare. As their strategic trade policies produced chronic U.S. trade deficits, they more than willingly financed the debt.

As part of their mercantilist strategy, the central banks of East Asia intervened in currency markets, to keep their currencies undervalued in order to make their products artificially cheap in world markets. The high value of the U.S. dollar compared to Asian currencies in trading markets today is substantially the product of Asian mercantilism. The Asian nations happily go on lending dollars like so much play money, despite the risk that the dollar might lose some of its value. It's small risk to bear in exchange for continuing to build their technologies and export economies at America's expense.

Normally, as national economies strengthen, national currencies appreciate. This is particularly true of countries that run trade surpluses. But as these surpluses accumulate, the central banks of East Asia buy dollars and then invest them in U.S. securities. The dollar, despite America's chronic trade deficits, has mostly held its value against Asian currencies thanks to these interventions. If trade were working the way it is described in economic textbooks, currency realignments would lower the value of the dollar, thus raising the cost of imported products, making American exports a better deal in global markets and bringing the trade accounts into closer balance. But because foreign central banks have their thumbs on the currency scales, this process of equilibrium doesn't occur.

The net debt owed by the United States to foreigners rose to about $2.7 trillion in 2005, an increase of $333 billion over the previous year. In fact, the current account (mostly trade) deficit is much higher than that increase in the debt—in 2005 it was $792 billion. The reason our total debt to foreigners did not increase by that full amount is that Americans also make investments overseas. Even with such investments, however, our net foreign indebtedness has been rising at a very rapid rate. Foreigners now hold almost 60 percent of all outstanding Treasury securities, up from 20 percent in the mid-1990s.

The excessive dependence of the U.S. economy on foreign borrowing increases the risk of a domestic depression and even a global one. The problem is not the national debt but the reliance on foreign creditors. The foreign debt, in turn, reflects the structural trade deficit. We have been borrowing our prosperity for better than two decades, and the ratio of foreign borrowing to GDP is growing. The longer an adjustment is deferred, the more serious will be the collapse.

When I studied economics in college, we were taught that the national debt was no big deal, because "we owe it to ourselves." In the 1960s, when the debt was a larger fraction of GDP than it is today, that was literally true. Foreigners held less than 4 percent of the U.S. national debt. In 2004, fully 98 percent of the net increase in Treasury debt was bought by foreigners, and 95 percent in 2005. The proportion of outstanding debt held by foreign creditors rises every year. In 2005, foreigners put a net $391.7 billion into U.S. corporate bonds and $79.1 billion into corporate stocks, plus buying most of our government debt—more than a trillion dollars of net investment inflow into the United States. The rate of this increased dependency is staggering. As recently as 1990, U.S. capital markets supplied all of our long-term capital needs, and our foreign capital accounts were roughly in balance. Our annual rate of foreign borrowing has doubled just since 2002.

A real decline in American living standards has already been baked into the national cake. It has simply been disguised, for now, by the borrowing from abroad, which must eventually be paid—in ever-higher interest payments, the sell-off of U.S. assets that generate income, or an eventual dollar crash. About half of our foreign debt is held by foreign governments. However, the central banks of allied nations cannot keep this game going indefinitely, much as they might wish to help, because the other half of America's international creditors are still private.

So the game depends on the market's belief that the dollar will hold its value. Given the volatility of speculative markets, this is no basis for confidence. Live by the market, perish by the market. Indeed, any other currency with this record of deepening imbalance would have long since crashed. This risk, at least, gets some public attention. But the remedies commended by the usual suspects—budget balance and higher savings rates—mostly miss the point. America's trade imbalance is now structural; it reflects the fact that other nations practice a kind of mercantilism that we disdain, and the fact that our manufacturing base has shriveled. Balancing the budget would increase the domestic rate of savings and reduce our need to attract foreign capital, but that would not make up for the imbalance between exports and imports.

Eventually, a country that runs a chronic trade deficit must suffer a decline in the value of its currency. Most economists calculate that it would take a devaluation in the range of 30 percent to put America's trade deficit on a downward path. Some contend that a decline of 30 percent of the value of the dollar would not be bad. Imports would become more expensive, but that would be good for both domestic production and exports. Since virtually all of our foreign debt is denominated in dollars, a cheaper dollar would mean a write-off of that much debt. Paul Volcker points out that the dollar went through a period of overvaluation in the 1980s and declined by about 25 percent against major foreign currencies, and nothing terrible happened. However, that occurred during a period when the dollar was artificially high because of Volcker's own policies of very high interest rates and there was no overhang of foreign debt. As the Fed relented and allowed interest rates to come down, it was natural that the dollar should depreciate. Today, by contrast, dollar interest rates are low. The only reason the dollar is holding its value is that foreign central banks want it that way and manipulate their own currencies accordingly.

Moreover, the U.S. trade balance was much healthier two decades ago and our capital balance with the rest of the world was still positive. We owned more foreign assets than foreigners owned U.S. assets. Today, our negative balance keeps escalating. Even though a steep dollar decline would produce a kind of windfall by cheapening the debt we owe other nations, it is very unlikely that the United States, with a plummeting dollar, would be able to enjoy the low interest rates of recent years. Markets are famous for overshooting. If the dollar lost the confidence of global money markets, the Federal Reserve would almost certainly raise interest rates. And higher interest rates would be a serious drag on both households and corporations heavily dependent on cheap money.

The United States may have a huge trade deficit, but it is an engine of innovation and a great place to invest, as well as a safe one. So foreigners will keep investing in dollar securities.

There are several flaws in this view. The claim of a global savings glut strains credulity, especially given that China and India, with well over 2 billion inhabitants, are growing at unprecedented rates. Growth requires prodigious investments of capital. The illusion of ample capital and low interest rates has been largely the result of loose money policies by central banks. But this era is ending because of concerns about inflation. And when central banks tighten interest rates, capital is suddenly scarce.

The United States retains some power to receive special treatment for several reasons: most of the world's official reserves are held in dollars; so many trade transactions are still denominated in dollars; the United States still has the world's deepest capital markets; and America's huge trade deficit is the flip side of a lot of people's valued exports. A dollar crash is in nobody's interest, so the game goes on. On the other hand,

World War I was also in nobody's interest. History is littered with mis-calculations and calamities that nobody really wanted.

A Doomed Dollar?

When imbalances are extreme, events have a way of getting out of hand. At some point, the dollar must cease defying the law of gravity. A trade deficit of 7 percent and an accumulated foreign debt of 25 percent of GDP may not be enough to trigger a flight from the dollar and self-fulfilling prophecies of a dollar collapse. But what about a deficit of 10 percent? Or 15 percent? A dollar decline may be triggered by some random event. Once the dollar starts falling, investors will stampede to dump dollar securities, and the aftermath will be nasty.

As we must know by now, markets are not entirely rational. In February 2005, one line in a routine report by the Bank of South Korea referred in passing to diversification of currency holdings. The report caromed around the Internet. The markets took it as a deliberate signal that the South Koreans would sell some dollars. The dollar immediately plummeted. China has begun to diversify its foreign assets, buying stocks as well as T-bills. Imagine if the United States and China got into a conflict over Taiwan's repeated threats to declare independence, the uneasy China-India relationship, China's new nuclear ambitions, or any of several other geopolitical issues where Beijing and Washington do not exactly see eye to eye. And suppose China decided to send the United States a signal of its muscle by selling off just a few dollar assets. Or suppose that Sino-U.S. tensions increased and currency traders merely worried that China might begin dumping dollars.

Most economists believe that the dollar is seriously overvalued against Asian currencies because of these trade and debt imbalances; that the overvaluation contributes to the trade deficits by overpricing U.S. exports; and that the longer we defer an adjustment, the further the dollar has to fall. Even though the Federal Reserve has been tightening interest rates since June 2004 and the interest rate spread between dollar and euro rates has widened in the dollar's favor, the dollar continues to sink against the euro. That has to reflect a long-term erosion of confidence in the dollar.

No less an expert than Volcker contends that the codependency of escalating trade imbalance and central bank purchases of dollars is unsustainable, and that a dollar crash followed by a recession is only a matter of time. If the U.S. currency were to tumble in world financial markets, the Federal Reserve would not be able to orchestrate the kind of rescue it has pulled off so many times on other fronts, because even the Fed does not have limitless reserves and limitless power to sweet-talk markets. The roughly half of Treasury securities held abroad not by foreign central banks are heavily held by offshore hedge funds, famous for herd instincts and instant reversals. In a dollar crash, the Fed would be torn between a policy of tight money to stem the dollar's fall and loose money to keep the economy out of severe recession. It could not do both.

A popular topic of debate among economists is whether the debt crisis will end with a "hard landing" or a "soft landing." A hard landing means a dollar crash, followed by high interest rates and a severe recession. A soft landing means gradual devaluation of the dollar, at a slow enough pace that foreign investors will not dump dollar securities. Another route to a soft landing is a slowdown of growth in the United States. Consumers with less money to spend will cut back on purchases of imported products as well as domestic ones.

But while a dollar crash would be more destabilizing, the end result of the soft landing is not fundamentally different from that of the hard landing. Either way, the consequence would be a decline in U.S. living standards. Given our heavy dependence on imports, a 30 percent decline in the value of the dollar translates to a sharp spike in import prices—everything from the price of energy to imported food—and an equivalent decline in living standards. Every year, we borrow 7 percent of our prosperity from abroad, and that debt accumulates. If we have to give up that debt habit and pay it back with interest, we will be that much poorer, even without an abrupt dollar crash.

In understanding what is causing the rising foreign debt, we need to remember that there are two distinct elements: our low savings rate and our large trade imbalance. America's domestic rate of savings is close to zero. Household savings rates have been falling for two decades, and in 2005 and 2006 households were net borrowers. Business savings (profits) have been rising, but government "dis-savings"—the public deficit—offset the increase in corporate profits, leaving the overall national savings rate very low. To meet our economy's normal need for private capital and to finance the public debt, the money has to come from somewhere. Increasingly it has come from abroad.

Even with a low savings rate, if the United States had equal trade accounts with the rest of the world, far less net foreign debt would be incurred. Our purchases from abroad would be reciprocated with purchases by our trading partners. We would be borrowing only the investment capital that exceeded our supply of domestic savings. That would still be a problem but a far more manageable one. But if every year we buy nearly $800 billion more than we sell, we have to borrow the difference to finance those purchases, as well as the money we need to pay for domestic investments.

When it comes to trade deficits, there is a debate among economists about the dynamics of cause and effect, and remedy. There is certainly a connection between savings rates and trade imbalances. A country with a very high savings rate consumes relatively less, from both domestic and foreign producers. Other things being equal, lower consumption means a lower propensity to import. The orthodox school contends that the imbalances in America's capital and trade accounts are nothing more than the logical consequence of the low domestic savings rate, perhaps compounded by an overvalued dollar. If we have a low savings rate and consume 97 percent of what we produce, that leaves just 3 percent to invest. And if we require 12 percent of our economic output for investment and to finance the public debt, we are 9 percent short. The only place to get that money is from overseas.

That explains the equivalence between the savings shortage and the imported capital, but what about imported products? Standard theory also holds that the net inflow of imported money has to equal the net inflow of imported goods, because the goods must be paid for—if not by barter, then by borrowed cash.

But that syllogism begs the question of cause and effect. In the orthodox view, what's required to reduce the trade imbalance and the ensuing foreign borrowing is to increase our national savings rate. But our savings rate rose in the late 1990s and the trade imbalance kept widening. In the 1950s, we had relatively low domestic savings compared with the rest of the world and a huge trade surplus. The different strategic economic policies of other trading nations add up to a separate and powerful source of U.S. trade imbalances, very likely the prime cause.

At bottom, the global financial system presents two huge challenges for U.S. policy. First, how can we contain global speculative forces so that they don't continue to create purely financial crises that undermine the potential of the real economy? On that front, there is moderately good news. The world's nations have rebelled against the formula of the Washington Consensus and have reclaimed a measure of sovereignty over their fiscal and monetary systems. The IMF no longer imposes a one-size-fits-all model (and if it did, the United States would be the prime candidate for austerity and rehabilitation). There is also the beginning of an effort to develop common global regulatory standards, which itself is a recognition that laissez-faire needs some help.

The second challenge is probably more difficult—digging our way out of a mountain of foreign debt without triggering a steep recession in the process. In both cases, it would lead to better policy if U.S. leaders disentangled goals for the architecture and management of a globalized economy from goals for the United States as one actor within that economy—and from ideological goals that remain in the realm of economic fantasy. In both cases, the premise that laissez-faire is the optimal form of capitalism takes us further away from good policy, either for the United States or for the system.

CHAPTER TEN

THE SQUANDERING OF DEMOCRACY

THIS BOOK has addressed the squandering of America in its several economic dimensions and identified a common source: the elite capture of politics and the destruction of countervailing popular institutions. Once, these institutions animated democracy and broadened prosperity in a virtuous circle that strengthened civic life and elected stewards of a managed form of capitalism.

We have examined the squandering of managed capitalism and its dual consequences: greater economic risk to the system, greater disparity in the allocation of risks and rewards for individuals. We have also looked at the squandering of American solvency by the same elites that regularly proclaim their alarm about the (far more manageable) financial costs of social insurance. And we have explored the squandering of American industrial leadership. To go into detail about two other grave defaults—the wreckage of constructive U.S. influence in the world and the pillaging of the natural environment—would require at least another book (and there are already several good books on these subjects). But these two additional squanderings are worth keeping in mind, because they reflect the same malign influence of heedless and unrestrained elites.

This chapter is about the squandering of our democracy—the weakening of both our democratic institutions and our Democratic Party and the absence of a real alternative to the elite domination of economic agendas. In a market economy, where concentrated wealth has disproportionate political power, the only thing that keeps elites from wreaking self-interested havoc is robust democracy; but democracy is also in disrepair, and the multiple pathologies described in this book are the result.

Democracy Degraded

Political democracy has been undermined in several mutually reinforcing respects. The resurgence of money as prime political currency is one huge factor. Not only does money crowd out political participation, the influence of money has blunted the populism of the Democratic Party as the voice of the common American, thus further discouraging popular involvement in politics.

Mass media, focus groups, TV advertising, and the treatment of politics as just another form of marketing and mass entertainment have served to further distance citizens from their democracy. Politics has always had its entertainment aspect. The live debates of nineteenth-century America, such as the Lincoln-Douglas debates, were not just principled arguments that helped educate the citizenry about the great issue of the day, slavery. They were also popular entertainment, watched by millions. But in that era politics did not have to compete with professional sports, movies, radio, TV, iPods, or the Internet.

The Internet has been a double-edged sword for political community. It can create instruments of popular mobilization such as MoveOn and Meetup, and can give small political donors increased influence relative to large ones. It can create virtual communities, some of them political. But the Internet is also part of the onward march of solipsism, in which citizens never have to leave their rooms. A decade ago, *The American Prospect* published a piece by Robert Putnam entitled "The Strange Disappearance of Civic America," which became the germ of Putnam's celebrated book *Bowling Alone*. Putnam described an America in which all forms of face-to-face social association were dwindling. This trend, of course, has political implications.

Theda Skocpol has written of the shrinkage of genuine forms of association that once engaged citizens in democratically controlled mass-membership organizations, into letterhead organizations run by paid professionals. A century ago, according to Skocpol's research, there were more than twenty-five mass-membership organizations with active memberships of more than 1 percent of the adult U.S. population each. These were members who went to meetings of local chapters, deliberated public questions, and elected delegates to state and then to national conventions. These organizations were sometimes political, sometimes merely civic, often progressive, sometimes oriented to local small business. But they contributed to the enrichment of political life because they were classrooms for democracy. They were organizations for regular people, not just elites.

Today, there are a few remnants of this shrunken world: the labor movement on the progressive side and a few groups, such as the National Rifle Association and organized Christian fundamentalists, on the conservative side. A handful of other democratically controlled mass-membership groups exist, smaller than their predecessors, such as the League of Women Voters, the National Farmers Union, and ACORN.

The emblematic example of today's ersatz membership organization is the American Association of Retired Persons (AARP). It plays the role of advocate for the elderly but is primarily a front organization for the sale of insurance products. Its "members" need only pay five dollars to get a discount card and receive pitches for a lot of co-branded AARP products. It has no real chapters or true members, and its leadership is not democratically elected. As a consequence, its political influence is entirely unreliable. AARP does defend Social Security (it could hardly do otherwise and have any legitimacy). However, in 2003, a well-connected Republican operative and adman, Bill Novelli, took over as AARP's chief executive officer. As a marketing vehicle for insurance products, the organization is very close to the commercial insurance industry. Novelli was instrumental in using AARP to provide political cover for President Bush's version of a prescription drug program, written by and for the insurance and pharmaceutical industries, that ill served the AARP membership.

Moreover, the same economic stress that causes the typical two-parent family to work nearly five hundred more hours a year than comparable families of a generation ago leaves people with less time to participate in politics. Once, when most women were homemakers and there was less of a family time squeeze, both women and men had more time for politics. Parents feel lucky if they can make it to PTA meetings, much less show up at zoning hearings, go door to door for the March of Dimes, or participate personally in political campaigns. Even many local "volunteers" for ideologically liberal groups such as campaigns against toxic drinking water turn out to be paid canvassers working on commission. For all the benefit to authentic local civic deliberation, they might as well be selling Fuller brushes.

The declining turnout is far from symmetrical with regard to class. In affluent communities, voting participation has scarcely declined in a generation. It is the turnout among the lower middle class and the poor that has drastically decreased. Political scientists report that as institutions of working-class political recruitment and mobilization decline, participation in all its forms diminishes with them—attending meetings, having informed opinions, registering, and voting. In the nation's lowest-income congressional districts, fewer than 10 percent of eligible voters actually vote. Poor people have not been well treated by the system, and it has been decades since they had a credible champion. The poor are more skeptical to begin with about politics changing their lives for the better. The more politics seems rigged, the less they bother.

In the run-up to the November 2006 midterm elections, *The New York Times* reported that Democrats were very concerned that black voters, despite their antipathy to the Bush administration, were not likely to vote in high numbers, precisely because they were so disgusted with politics itself. This worry was backed up by a Pew Research Center poll that found blacks twice as likely in 2006 as in 2004 to express little or no confidence in the voting system, with the numbers rising from 15 to 29 percent.

All this leaves real local politics the province of insiders, creating further distance between the citizenry and its democracy. Nationally, elites have never been more effective at dominating political agendas. At the local level, if ordinary people do not have time for local politics, you can be sure that local real estate developers do.

Paradoxically, when George W. Bush puts cronies into key government positions, leaving a wake of corruption and wreckage of agencies like the Federal Emergency Management Agency (FEMA), the damage isn't limited to the Republican Party. The cynical, inept Republican stewardship reinforces the Republican message that government is no good and intensifies the popular turning away from politics.

The consequence of all of the above is declining interest in politics, declining voter turnout, and declining faith that politics matters, especially among voters who would vote for progressive candidates if Democrats gave them more of a reason to vote. Ironically, it is precisely these voters who most need effective politics and government because they are most at the mercy of the market.

Democracy Assaulted

Democracy is a complex, multifaceted affair. As the country's founders well understood, democracy is not simply majority rule. America's deliberately nonparliamentary brand of democracy is built on careful checks and balances. The essence of *procedural* American democracy has been about the rights of political minorities, the liberties of citizens generally, and constraints on arbitrary executive power. Since the Roosevelt era, the essence of *substantive* American democracy has been the enlargement of social and economic rights to increase security and opportunity, as well as the expansion of political participation.

Both aspects of democracy have come under further assault in the Bush era. Under Bush, for the first time since the end of Reconstruction in 1877, the federal government sought to narrow the franchise rather than broaden it, colluding with corrupt state Republican parties to deny qualified citizens the right to vote, as well as manipulating vote counts. The most basic civil liberties were sacrificed on the altar of combating terrorism. The executive branch claimed new, extraconstitutional powers to ignore laws enacted by Congress and duly signed by the president. The Republican majority in Congress consigned the Democratic opposition to a purely token role. Key laws were passed under suspensions of the rules, in which texts of bills were not even available to be read. New legislation that passed neither house was written in conference committees in which lobbyists were present but not Democrats. Gerrymandering and voter suppression made it more difficult for the opposition party to oust incumbents. Bush succeeded in putting enough allies on the federal bench that the courts have largely ceased to serve as a check on his excesses. In these several respects, our democracy itself neared a tipping point. Only the extreme hubris and policy failure of Bush's Iraq war, coupled with economic distress and some dumb luck (George Allen Jr.'s *macaca* moment) allowed Democrats to narrowly take back Congress in November 2006.

If Democrats expect to regain a public mandate, repair democracy, and broaden prosperity, they need to be credible as champions of ordinary people. In the mid-twentieth century, American progressive leaders were politically strategic in their institution building. They not only used popular politics to support social institutions; they used the logic of social policies to reinforce the politics. When Franklin Roosevelt devised the Social Security system (with the support of progressive Republicans), he deliberately financed it with payroll charges, planning to add supplements from general revenues only later, so that voters would experience it as something they had paid for in advance and *earned*, not as a giveaway program. Programs such as the G.I. Bill of Rights drew upon a reservoir of wartime social solidarity and served to reinforce it. They created a sense that we were all in this together.

By contrast, in American politics today, markets are rampant, radical individualism is strategically promoted by the economic elite, and two groups are largely AWOL: effective, ideologically coherent Democrats and conscientious, public-minded Republicans. We'll come back to the Republicans in a moment. The more puzzling story is the default of the Democrats.

What's the Matter with Democrats?

The recent weakness of the Democratic Party is both institutional and ideological. Republicans are better funded and more effective at the mechanics of politics. At both the national and state levels, the Republican Party machinery is more reliable and sophisticated at important mechanics, such as demographic targeting and get-out-the-vote efforts. Republican state parties have an institutional existence between elections as well as in campaign seasons. Democratic politics are more of a candidate-centered pick-up team that must be rebuilt almost from scratch for every campaign. In many states, organized labor is the surrogate Democratic Party, and in half of America neither the unions nor the state party has much institutional presence. The "Section 527" organizations permitted under the campaign finance laws to make independent expenditures to support or oppose candidates became a major presence in 2004, funding voter registration and get-out-the-vote work. These were bankrolled largely by liberal billionaires. When John Kerry lost the presidential election, the billionaires, in investment banker fashion, decided to cut their losses on a bad bet and pulled the plug on more than two years' work of institution building. The enterprise had to be rebuilt almost from scratch in 2006.

As the 2006 election showed, institutional superiority isn't always decisive. But the Democrats were positioned to make gains in 2006 less because they offered a cogent alternative than because Republicans made every blunder imaginable, and then some.

The more instructive Democratic weakness is ideological. Although some Democrats clearly embrace populism, Republicans seem to know what they stand for and Democrats as a party don't. You can put the entire Republican economic ideology on a bumper sticker: Markets Work, Governments Don't. This easy-to-grasp economic philosophy is complemented by a simple social philosophy: Poor People Reflect Poor Values. If everyone would just stay in school, work hard, get married, and respect traditional values and religious faith, poverty would vanish.

This dual credo may have elements of truth when it comes to a small minority of dissolute poor, but it offers nothing to a broad, well-behaved working and middle class that finds itself working harder for less, in an era when markets often reduce security and living standards. The Republican ideology plainly contradicts the lived experience of most American voters. Yet Democrats have only begun to turn that economic reality into political pay dirt with a few high-profile populist victories, and it remains to be seen what Democrats as a party can deliver.

The progressive economic philosophy that Democrats of the last century effectively shared with their European cousins during the era from roughly 1932 to 1968 couldn't quite fit on a bumper sticker, but it could be summed up in about a paragraph:

Markets are useful engines of economic growth, but they are not reliable at providing employment security, much less decent wages, retirement, education, or health care. Nor can we trust markets to police the honesty of financial institutions, the cleanliness of air and water, the safety of workplaces, or the stability of the economy as a whole. So alongside markets, we need social investments financed with progressive taxation, as well as public regulation of the market's self-cannibalizing tendencies. A well-managed economy operated according to these principles can be at least as efficient as a laissez-faire one (which underinvests in people)—and a lot fairer.

Of course, politicians didn't talk like this; policy wonks did. But the same public philosophy could be simplified as a slogan that was once widely accepted as real: *Democrats are the party of working people.* In this case, working people were defined as at least 80 percent of the population—the large majority of voters who were a few paychecks away from poverty if they lost their jobs, plus every retired person who depended on pensions and Social Security.

We explored in chapter two how the several equalizing institutions of the post–World War II boom were gradually dismantled by administrations friendly to politically resurgent business. By the early 1990s—fully fifteen years ago—the stagnation of living standards and the rising insecurity of working- and middle-class people were already a vivid public issue. It was the economy, stupid—and still is. That reality animated the 1992 manifesto of candidate Bill Clinton, who memorably declared that people who work hard and play by the rules should not be poor. His successful campaign was the last time that Clinton put pocketbook populism at the center of his credo.

Numerous commentators have argued in different ways that the

Democratic Party's socially avant-garde stances, coming on the heels of the Vietnam War and its cultural schisms, have damaged the Democrats with white working-class voters. The classic exposition of this view is Thomas Frank's *What's the Matter with Kansas?* A more pessimistic version of the same analysis is offered by Thomas Edsall, in his book *Building Red America.* In this view, by embracing such positions as support for affirmative action, gay rights, abortion rights, and secularism, while offering little to help the shrinking pocketbook, Democrats have fatally alienated socially conservative, white working-class voters, especially white men, most emphatically in the Deep South, where the combination of racial liberalism and social liberalism has proven particularly toxic.

Frank contends that working-class voters manipulated by the religious Right are suffering from a case of false consciousness; if they knew what was in their self-interest, they'd vote for the Democrats. Edsall counters that the Democrats have become such a party of economically elite social liberals that they aren't offering much to the white working class. Both authors have pieces of the truth, and one common theme is painfully clear: if socially liberal Democrats ever expect white working-class voters to look beyond avant-garde Democratic views on issues such as tolerance, Democrats had better start delivering tangible pocketbook benefits.

But today's Democrats have scant credibility as pocketbook progressives. The reasons are many and self-reinforcing. In the 1970s, just as organized business was recovering its latent political and ideological influence, centrist Democrats began turning away from the postwar model of managed capitalism. It was Jimmy Carter who first declared that government is not the solution but the problem. Carter had only the weakest alliance with trade unionism. As industry intensified its campaign to break unions, Carter had the support in Congress in 1978 to pass legislation to strengthen enforcement of the Wagner Act, but he spent no political capital on the issue, and the bill ultimately failed by two votes in the Senate. It was also Carter, and the centrist economists who advised him, who began the project of large-scale economic deregulation, making the conventional wisdom about the superiority of markets effectively bipartisan. So as early as the late 1970s—fully three decades ago—the role of the Democratic Party and trade unionism as counterweights to the power of business and the ideology of markets was already declining, and some of that weakness was self-inflicted.

This was also the period when the conservative think tanks began what would be a massive expansion. Conservatism became a movement. By the time Ronald Reagan took office, offering a more full-throated version of market fundamentalism, business had an open field in which to carry out its agenda.

As big money became more important in politics, Democrats found themselves on the weak side of a potent asymmetry. Not only did Republicans have more money. Republicans seeking financial support from wealthy donors enjoyed a nice congruence of ideology and self-interest: Business was paying Republicans to behave like Republicans—to carry out a laissez-faire agenda in which both donor and recipient believed. But when Democrats raised money from big business, there was an ideological disconnect. Economic populism was what had made Democrats the majority party. Yet wealthy donors, with a handful of exceptions, were paying Democrats to be *less* populist. They were rewarding the Democrats for deserting their natural constituency and ideology of managed capitalism.

Many self-described "business Democrats" hoped they could wean their party from progressive taxation and economic regulation and gain support for freer trade. Clinton's support for NAFTA and China's entry into the WTO was mainly about winning "credibility" with business. But this stance cost the Democrats dearly with their economic base voters.

By the 1990s, scores of Democrats in the House and Senate reliably voted with organized business on issues that tangibly harmed ordinary people—bills making it easier for stock promoters to cheat small investors, undercutting the right of little people to sue if they were maimed by corporate negligence, making it easier for corporations to loot workers' pensions, helping credit card companies to impoverish people if they declared bankruptcy because of huge medical expenses; bills tilting tax relief to the very top, such as deep cuts in the estate tax paid by the top 1 percent rather than relief for working people. As many as eighty House Democrats, including several African-American representatives from some of America's poorest communities, often helped Republicans win enactment of bills plainly harmful to the Democratic base. Business interests, led by the tobacco industry, used a loophole in the campaign finance laws to pour money into the Congressional Black Caucus's affiliated foundation, creating a multimillion-dollar slush fund and weaning many black legislators from their usual support for consumer legislation.

At the same time as many Democratic legislators vote against the pocketbook interests of their constituents, individual wealthy Democratic donors tend to be fervent supporters of liberal social issues—abortion rights, gay rights, and affirmative action, as well as idealistic causes such as global climate change and opposition to genocide in Darfur. These positions are either anathema to cultural conservatives or far removed from the lives and struggles of working people. But these issues are the ones that dominate fund-raising events on Park Avenue and Rodeo Drive.

As a result, the typical Democratic candidate driven by the logic of campaign finance ran as a social liberal, a foreign policy idealist, and an economic moderate. This was said to be a sensible position to attract suburban swing voters. But the result was often ideological mush on pocketbook issues, combined with great clarity on liberal social issues that functioned as lightning rods in much of the white South.

The Democrats' feeble stance on popular economics was compounded by a perceived weakness on defense, one not really deserved. The 1972 George McGovern campaign, at the height of the backlash against the Vietnam War, may have had a neoisolationist tinge. But the Clinton era surely had a more coherent, competent, and effective national security record than Bush's. However, as Drew Westen observes in his book *The Political Brain*, the Democrats' equivocation on *nondefense* issues communicates irresolute leadership in general. And especially during a perceived threat to national security, voters want a leader who is resolute. The majority of voters who disagreed with George W. Bush on issue after issue nonetheless respected the fact that he was clear about what he stood for. That suggested a president who would defend the country. "The Republican Party," Westen concludes, "could not have captured the imagination of either working-class or middle-class voters if the Democratic Party had learned to speak their language and to speak to their concerns."

Split as they were between progressive and probusiness factions, Democrats could not muster the votes to address the multiple sources of distress for working families, even during an administration when they briefly had the White House and both houses of Congress. When Democrats enacted the Family and Medical Leave Act of 1993, the best they could achieve was a law that requires large corporations to provide just twelve weeks a year of *unpaid* leave. Only about 54 percent of Americans were covered at all. And this was the high-water mark of Clinton-era social legislation. It did signal that Democrats are on the side of working families, but in such a feeble way that it gained little traction with economically stressed voters.

Nor did Democrats send a clear signal on pocketbook issues during their years of opposition. Given the fact that they had control of neither the White House nor Congress, it was not in the cards for them to pass serious legislation. They might have looked at that reality and decided to be bold. Instead, they went for small-bore, largely token programs, such as modest increases in the minimum wage or piecemeal expansions of health coverage. Even if enacted, such programs would not transform the economic situation of most working people.

Uncertain Trumpets

The fecklessness of recent Democratic presidential nominees is often mistakenly understood as merely personal, epitomized by the 2000 model Al Gore, a robotic candidate who seemed a captive of his handlers, and John Kerry, who all too often lived up to his Republican caricature as a flip-flopper. But the fact that men like them rise to the top of Democratic politics and then fumble winnable elections is no accident. Weak candidacies and uncertain trumpets are the logical product of muddled ideology. And the faint ideology is, in turn, the product of the immense power of organized business in today's American politics.

If a Democratic presidential candidate is whipsawed between a base that craves a pocketbook champion and economic elites offering the self-interested counsel that "class warfare" is to be avoided at all costs, that candidate will sound like mush. You could see this tension play out in the campaigns of Gore and Kerry, who both had the added unfortunate habit of listening to far too many tactical advisers (representing the two wings of the party) and then trying to split the difference.

One day, Gore would take the advice of his New Democrat consultants and offer bland moderation. The next day, his pollsters would point to the electorate's hunger for economic remedies, and he would sound a bit populist. His enraged New Democrat allies would then leak to the press that Gore was off message, and the following day the candidate would tack back toward moderation. About the only thing that both the progressives and the New Democrats agreed on was that the middle class was hurting, though they quite disagreed on the program and the rhetoric. So Gore was left to blurt out the words "Middle Class!" as if this were a politics. And later, Kerry's equivocation made even Gore look good.

On the issue of trade, most working Americans grasp that the current rules of trade are not good for them. Commentators such as Lou Dobbs tap a vein of pocketbook frustration that could be the grist for either inward-looking nativism or a new progressive politics based on internationalizing the principles of managed capitalism. But with the exception of Dick Gephardt, who took a pummeling as a "protectionist" in the 1988 primaries and again in 2004, no major Democratic presidential nominee has made a serious call for revising the rules of trade. Clinton took a moderately hard line on abuses by China in the 1992 campaign, only to become the most complete enabler of China's trade policies.

Kerry, in 2004, wanted to show the Democratic base that he was on their side economically. But he also wished not to offend the economic elites. So the best he could manage was to call for arcane changes in the tax code, so that the tax system would not reward "Benedict Arnold CEOs" for moving jobs offshore. This poll-tested slogan sounded good, but few knew exactly what Kerry meant. The slogan did not bespeak any serious understanding of the trade problem or any commitment to fundamental change, nor did Kerry. Tax favoritism for offshoring jobs is perhaps a third-tier cause of job loss, if that. Nor did the slogan, in the end, resonate with voters. It was more weak tea.

A reinforcing source of the diminished Democratic Party is the immense success of Republicans, over nearly three decades, in systematically disparaging government and emasculating public institutions that voters actually value—and the failure of too many Democrats to fight back. The social compact of a bygone era is scorned by the Right as "tax-and-spend." Progressive taxation was once used by government to underwrite outlays that helped ordinary people. In its heyday, tax-and-spend worked, both economically and politically. People concluded that it was a good deal. Regulation was also part of the package, and it too protected citizens from the vicissitudes of rampant markets.

To wreck a politics of progressive taxation and social investment, the Right changed the terms of who was taxed and what the taxation bought. The tax load was shifted off business and onto workers and citizens. The Right deliberately used tax cuts for rich allies to create permanent deficits, as a "starve the beast" strategy denying government resources and forcing cuts in programs that people value, such as Pell Grants. What could be clearer class warfare from the top? But pocketbook issues are so depoliticized that most ordinary people don't grasp the connection, and too few Democrats help them connect the dots. The result is that people know that their own economic life has become a little harder on yet another front, but they feel their frustrations are largely beyond politics.

The political scientist Jane Mansbridge reports an experience while she was conducting in-depth interviews with working-class women. She visited a single mother living in a ramshackle house at the end of a dirt road littered with the frames of rusted-out cars. The woman, a beautician, was highly articulate about her daily economic frustrations. After listening sympathetically to the woman's account of her daily life, Mansbridge asked what she thought government might do to help. The woman replied, "Cut taxes some." Social investments that might offer some tangible benefit were largely beyond her experience and imagination. Given the recent increases in payroll and sales taxes on the working poor, she was not wrong about taxes.

Research by the Princeton political scientist Larry Bartels on the odd support of working-class voters for tax cuts aimed at the very wealthy underscores just how much yardage Democrats must gain back to reclaim a program of activist government. Bartels, in a paper titled "Homer Gets a Tax Cut," looked at public opinion data from the 2002 National Election Survey on support for estate tax repeal. He found that voters of every social class, even strong critics of the increasing gap between rich and poor, supported repeal.

> Even among people with family incomes of less than $50,000 (about half the sample), 66 percent favored repeal. Among those who wanted to spend more money on a variety of federal government programs, 68 percent preferred repeal. Among people who said that the difference in incomes between rich and poor has increased in the past 20 years and that it is a bad thing, 66 percent favored repeal. Among those who said that government policy is a "very important" or "somewhat important" cause of economic inequality (almost two-thirds of the sample), 67 percent preferred repeal. Among people who said that the rich are asked to pay too little in federal income taxes (more than half the sample), 68 percent favored repeal. And, most remarkably, among those respondents sharing all of these characteristics—the 11 percent of the sample with the strongest conceivable set of reasons to support the estate tax—66 percent favored repeal.

Polls show that most Americans mistakenly believe themselves to be wealthy enough that their children will have to pay taxes on their estates, and they resent being taxed on their imagined riches. Yet that's not the whole story. Five years later, most American voters once again support estate taxes, as well as a progressive income tax. Today's contradictory set of attitudes on taxing the wealthy reflects the Republicans' success in recent years in disparaging and disabling government to the point where ordinary people have a hard time imagining that a politics of tax-and-spend could produce concrete pocketbook benefits, and the Democrats' too-feeble response.

Hard-pressed voters do not get to vote themselves a wage increase or a cut in the price of gas. The one chance they do have to cast a ballot that directly influences their wallet is when they vote for a ballot initiative on taxes or for a politician who promises to cut taxes (or accuses his opponent of raising them).

The politics of permanent deficits and the shift of taxes onto ordinary working people at a time of pocketbook distress has done just what Republicans hoped. It has largely depoliticized economic hardship. It has made voters resistant to any kind of taxation—and Democrats averse to proposing even progressive tax reforms that would raise taxes only at the top and cut net taxes for most people. In the Bush era, Republicans who sponsored politics and programs opposed by substantial majorities of Americans invariably fell back on two trumps: "Democrats Won't Keep You Safe" and "Democrats Will Raise Your Taxes." Strip government of resources, put cronies in charge who are incompetent at running it, and people will stop seeing government as their ally. Even Democrats will think twice about defending government.

In mid-2006, I was at a conference chairing a panel discussion on public investment, featuring Pennsylvania's effective and pragmatic Democratic governor Ed Rendell. The governor devoted his talk to several small-scale examples of how he was working to make government more efficient. For example, he had ordered the sale of the gas-guzzler cars in the state fleet, and replaced them with smaller, more fuel-efficient vehicles. He had figured out how to do more with less. The unmistakable subtext was that ordinarily, government is wasteful, and he, Rendell, was a good guy for making it less inefficient. Like much of the rhetoric of presidents Carter and Clinton, the Democratic message, reflecting (and unfortunately reinforcing) the presumed mood of the times, was "Hey, we Democrats don't much like government either."

When question time came, I asked Governor Rendell if he had ever had occasion to make a speech reminding voters of all the necessary and constructive things they get from their government. After all, a key difference between Democrats and Republicans is that Democrats believe that government is a necessary instrument of the good society and

Republicans don't. So shouldn't Democrats like Rendell spend some of their political capital, as leaders and teachers, to remind voters what's good about government?

I might as well have been speaking Bulgarian. Rendell looked at me quizzically—and responded by rattling off several more things he had done to make government slightly less awful.

Rendell is hardly alone. The unfortunate fact is that much of the time, Democrats do the Republicans' work for them by reinforcing the attacks on government and its instruments of social investment, progressive taxation, and economic regulation, instead of reminding voters that most people depend on these institutions.

In 1992, one of the themes of the Clinton-Gore campaign was Reinventing Government. We needed to make government more modern and more efficient. After Clinton took office, this idea was formalized into a program under the vice president, with a name that suggested Gore at his most bureaucratic: the National Performance Review. Much as Governor Rendell managed to subtly disparage government even as he claimed credit for running it more efficiently, the Gore National Performance Review became less an exercise in defending public purposes or reminding voters of the need for affirmative government than an effort to show that Democrats could be just as ruthless as Republicans in shrinking government. At best, government was depicted as a necessary evil rather than a public good.

In releasing his first report on the work of the Reinventing Government task force, Gore boasted:

> We also expect that the reinventions we propose will allow us to reduce the size of the civilian, non-postal workforce by 12 percent over the next 5 years. This will bring the federal workforce below two million employees for the first time since 1967. This reduction in the workforce will total 252,000 positions—152,000 over and above the 100,000 already promised by President Clinton.

These habits of doing the Republicans' ideological dirty work are hard to break. But a little leadership can go a long way. In the 2006 Massachusetts gubernatorial campaign, Republicans and conservative Democrats had been pressing for a cut in the state's income tax rate. Two of the three candidates in the Democratic gubernatorial primary, as well as the Republican candidate in the general election, Kerry Healey, "took the pledge" to cut the tax. The slogan of the tax-cutting forces was "It's your money." The one holdout was Deval Patrick, then a long shot, and pollsters warned that he was taking a big risk. But here's what Patrick said: "It's your money. But it's also your road that needs fixing. It's your overcrowded school. It's your broken neighborhood and it's your broken neighbor. It's time for us to start taking responsibility for that." The sky didn't fall. On election day, Patrick won handily.

Elite Captivity

Democrats offer feeble political leadership on pocketbook issues because too many are in the pockets of the same wealthy elites as the Republicans. Exhibit A is the Democratic Leadership Council. The DLC was founded after Walter Mondale's forty-nine-state loss in 1984. It was a coalition of southern Democrats who wanted a more centrist Democratic stance on social and racial issues; defense Democrats who wanted to purge the party's McGovernite tendencies on war and peace; and corporate Democrats who wanted a party less easy to depict as antibusiness. This recipe would supposedly help Democrats regain lost territory in the South and among so-called Reagan Democrats, cultural conservatives, and swing voters.

To some extent, the early DLC was engaging in a principled debate, and it was not entirely wrong. The 1980s were the heyday of identity politics. Often, the Democratic Party platform seemed a medley of the cultural Left. Some Democrats did sound like naive pacifists who could not be trusted with the national defense. These stances were anathema in localities where Democrats had once won the affection of cultural conservatives by delivering pocketbook benefits.

But getting rid of cultural radicalism or military softness the better to pump up economic populism was emphatically *not* the DLC formula. The DLC wanted the Democrats to be moderates not just on cultural and defense issues but on economic questions, too. The DLC got most of its funding from K Street—the home of the same business lobbies that successfully pressed for getting rid of the model of managed capitalism. DLC Democrats were usually the first to defect to Republicans on pocketbook issues. One of the early leaders of the DLC, an Arkansas governor named Bill Clinton, followed some of the New Democrat cultural formula, taking a poke at a rapper named Sister Souljah to indicate that he would not pander to racial radicalism and deliberately permitting the execution of a seriously retarded convict named Ricky Ray Rector to signal his toughness on crime. At the same time, he alarmed his DLC supporters by adding a note of economic populism—which lasted just long enough to propel him to the White House.

What started out as an arguably principled debate by the DLC soon degenerated into the corporate capture of one major wing of the party. Today the DLC and its think tank arm, the Progressive Policy Institute, serve as a lobby against economic populism. The DLC, unlike the labor movement, has no grassroots component and no expertise in running campaigns. But during the Clinton administration, several of its key people served in senior policy positions. It could enlist the president of the United States to speak at its fund-raising dinners. And joining the DLC certified a Democratic candidate as a sound investment for business dollars.

The DLC serves as a propaganda machine against any kind of Democratic politics that smacks of class or that requires serious public outlay to remedy economic distress. In the post-Clinton era, this has worked to fragment the Democratic coalition and muddle its economic message. One of the most politically destructive lines of DLC argument is that activist government is politically and socially passé because in a postindustrial economy, most people are doing just fine. This claim can be advanced only by cherry-picking data and misdefining the nature of Democratic social programs.

The urtext for this viewpoint is a long piece published by the DLC in April 2006 by the economist Stephen Rose, titled "The Trouble with Class-Interest Populism." The article begins by arguing that "the core argument in the liberal case for class-interest populism is deeply flawed." Rose cites two basic reasons. First, he contends, "people no longer choose candidates primarily on the basis of 'pocketbook' issues as they did when the New Deal coalition dominated national politics." And second, he adds, "Even if people did vote primarily on pocketbook issues, the group that could reasonably be categorized as having a clear, class-based interest in voting for Democratic policies would comprise less than a quarter of the population." Rose goes on to contend that just 23 percent of the population "can be categorized as having a direct personal interest in supporting the social safety net programs that the public associates with the Democratic Party—programs that help living in poverty or just a few rungs above it."

Note the sleight of hand and the straw man. Democrats' social programs have never been only for the poor. The greatest Democratic achievements are institutions like Social Security, Medicare, the G.I. Bill of Rights, federal aid to education, and kindred programs that benefit the working middle class—well over 80 percent of the population. Only by misdefining "Democratic" social programs as merely for the poor, near poor, and nonelderly does Rose get the target population down as low as 23 percent. His statistic is derived from looking at beneficiaries aged twenty-six to fifty-nine, which slyly leaves out most beneficiaries of Social Security, Medicare, and college aid.

Rose claims that Social Security and Medicare are no longer strongly identified with one party. But when Bush tried to privatize Social Security, Democrats found it to be good politics to come to its defense. And when Bush added a costly, inefficient, and inadequate privatized prescription drug program drafted by and for the drug and insurance industries and grafted it on to Medicare, one of the first things progressive Democrats did was to sponsor legislation giving government the power to negotiate drug prices and requiring the government to offer a public Medicare drug program.

To the extent that Democrats have lost credibility as champions of the working middle class, it is precisely because they have been listening to the counsel of the DLC. Rose cites polls showing that the majority of Americans consider themselves middle class. From this, he concludes, "So it is obviously unreasonable to argue that the entire self-described middle class should perceive a clear class interest in voting Democratic." But this inference has it exactly backward. The middle class today has many of the same economic vulnerabilities as the working poor: the risks of losing jobs, pensions, incomes, and health insurance; rising costs of college tuition and home ownership relative to income. With the middle class increasingly subject to economic vulnerabilities that used to be limited to the working poor, a class politics championing the bottom 80 or 90 percent is just what's needed.

Serving as a perfect bookend to the DLC advice to avoid any kind of pocketbook populism is the counsel of Wall Street Democrats who put fiscal discipline ahead of other goals. The leading exemplar of this brand of Democrat is Robert Rubin and his Hamilton Project. Rubin's name keeps coming up in this book, and for good reason. He epitomizes the Democrats' paralysis on pocketbook issues for ordinary people and the party's disabling capture by financial elites. A Democratic Party that takes its strategic advice and economic program from the DLC and Robert Rubin reassures the bond market and the well-heeled donors. But it does little to improve the economic condition of working Americans, or to regain their political affection.

What's the Matter with Republicans?

On the Republican side, our nation desperately needs leaders with a sense of stewardship. Some patrician Republicans still fit that description, but they are a dying breed. There were once large numbers of Republicans who put the well-being of the republic ahead of personal wealth. This was, after all, the party of Abraham Lincoln, who not only emancipated the slaves but gave us the land-grant college system and the Homestead Act in the name of broadening opportunity; the party of Theodore Roosevelt, a crusader for the environment, limits on economic concentration, and the progressive income tax; and the party of George Norris, a champion of public investment. Even Richard Nixon supported a guaranteed annual income and universal, government-mandated health insurance. When inflation got out of control, Nixon used wage and price controls rather than the blunter instrument of deliberately creating a general recession.

Republican-oriented business leaders once presided over a corporate welfare state, in which generous wages and benefits and partnerships with unions were seen as decent ways to reward workers' loyalty. Large corporations were also proud benefactors of local communities. Most of that is gone, and corporate executives are more interested in grabbing the biggest possible pay packet and in showing Wall Street quarterly earnings, accurate or otherwise, that boost stock prices (tied to options benefits for themselves).

Yet, another brand of Republican conservatism is possible. George W. Bush has articulated an "ownership society," in which government helps people realize the American dream of ownership—of homes, health insurance policies, and retirement security. Bush's own version was empty rhetoric, but there is actually a principled debate to be had here. In the 1990s it went under the name "Conservative Opportunity Society." It would include, for example, vouchers to pay for health insurance, for affordable housing, and for public or private education, and it would subsidize individual nest eggs to build opportunity and secure retirement. All of this is said to maximize choice and efficiency by dint of being more marketlike, but it does require public outlays.

Republicans like Jack Kemp, the former congressman who served as secretary of housing and urban development under Reagan and was Bob Dole's running mate in 1996, have long championed this approach. One can argue about whether social goods are truly provided more efficiently by market forces, but that is a separate debate. The trouble is that a serious version of this opportunity model costs public money. And in the Bush era, tax cutting has invariably crowded out social initiatives. The result is that Republican-sounding approaches, such as housing vouchers and training vouchers, are funded at minuscule levels. Proposed private versions of Social Security would strip the guaranteed portion of the system of assets and leave people at greater risk.

Take, for example, one signature program, known as "asset development." In a pioneering book published in 1991 titled *Assets and the Poor: A New American Welfare Policy*, Michael Sherraden of Washington University argued that income transfers did little for the poor over the long run other than to prevent outright destitution. What distinguished the middle class from the poor, Sherraden contended, was not so much income as *assets*—financial assets such as owner-occupied homes and savings accounts, as well as human-capital assets such as skills. If we want a durable solution to poverty, therefore, we need to help the poor equip themselves with assets.

Sherraden proposed what he called Individual Development Accounts. The poor would deposit small amounts of money into these accounts. The government would match the deposit, on a sliding scale. This strategy would both inculcate the very middle-class habit of saving and accelerate the process of enabling poor families to accumulate assets. The accounts could be drawn upon for a variety of approved purposes, such as education, training, and acquisition of a home, thus increasing human-capital assets as well.

Here was a wonderfully marketlike brand of conservative social engineering, music to the ears of both Republicans and New Democrats. It was nicely differentiated from the conventional welfare state. It used social transfers not to promote dependence but to enable self-reliance.

Sherraden's idea caught on in foundation and policy circles. One think tank, the Corporation for Enterprise Development, transformed itself into a tireless booster of the idea. A vice president of the Ford Foundation, Melvin Oliver, became a major supporter. By the late 1990s, the field of asset development could boast a whole academic-industrial complex, with studies, expert evaluations, and conferences.

Sherraden's 1991 blueprint put the first-year cost of his IDA program at about $28 billion, or about $45 billion in today's dollars. In 1998, then senator Rick Santorum of Pennsylvania, a conservative of the Jack Kemp school, introduced legislation to underwrite Individual Development Accounts. His bill passed with wide bipartisan support. The program was funded at about $80 million a year, one quarter of 1 percent of what Sherraden had proposed—enough to help just a few thousand poor families acquire assets. The appropriations were further cut under Bush.

Sherraden's most recent research finds that the typical target household has such scant disposable income that it could manage to save only about $20 a month, even with the incentive of generous government matches. But even if this approach had real promise, we'll never find out what it might achieve, because Republicans, despite the rhetoric of markets and opportunity, have given priority to tax cuts for the already rich.

Here is a metaphor for the larger policy debate that America isn't quite having. Whether we use "marketlike" mechanisms or direct public outlays, it takes tax dollars to broaden opportunity and prosperity. Unfortunately, what exists is tokenism on the Democratic side—proposals funded at so puny a level that they will not transform anybody's life, imagination, or political allegiance; and on the Republican side, a happy-sounding politics of bait and switch.

Fiscal Fraud

The most serious Republican default is on the fiscal front. Before Ronald Reagan, Republicans were the party of fiscal responsibility. In the 1992 election, spurred by the independent candidacy of H. Ross Perot, the unsustainably large federal deficits created by the tax cuts of Republican presidents Reagan and Bush the elder briefly became a symbol of political irresponsibility. A few Wall Street Republicans, joined by some fiscally conservative Democrats, created the Concord Coalition, which increased the public pressure to restore balance. Clinton's 1993 budget, including tax increases on the wealthiest 2 percent as well as cuts in program outlays, cut the deficit roughly in half over four years. Clinton went on to achieve a budget surplus by 1999.

The George W. Bush administration then gratefully used the hard-won surplus for tax cuts tilted to the wealthy. Curiously, the fiscally conservative Republicans who had made such an issue of deficits in 1992–93 were nowhere to be seen. The Concord Coalition was a shadow of its former self. An emblematic case of the failure of Republicans to put fiscal responsibility ahead of tax cutting is illustrated by the work of Maya MacGuineas, once a senior aide to former Senate Finance Committee chairman Pete Domenici of New Mexico. MacGuineas, working out of the scrupulously nonpartisan New America Foundation, is a sincere fiscally conservative Republican. She leads a letterhead group of deficit hawks called the Committee for a Responsible Federal Budget.

When MacGuineas published a blueprint in September 2005 for reducing the deficit by $200 billion, it included ingenious savings both large and small. She proposed $36.1 billion in military spending cuts; $30 billion in cuts in "corporate welfare," such as reductions in farm subsidies; a downward adjustment in the consumer price index as a disguised cut in Social Security; and more than $13 billion in Medicare reductions via income testing. She proposed a onetime $25 billion surtax to help pay the costs of recovery from Hurricane Katrina. Conspicuous by its absence, however, was the 800-pound gorilla of budget imbalance: the three rounds of Bush tax cuts, which together will cost the Treasury around $4 trillion over a decade.

Shortly afterward, I was invited to debate MacGuineas before an audience of foundation executives. Why, I asked her, were the major Bush tax cuts not on the table? She responded that she wanted a deficit reduction plan that was politically realistic. Republicans would not take seriously a plan that included even a partial reversal of Bush's tax cuts, no matter how dire the deficit projections.

Much of the squandering of our prosperity and economic security has occurred on the Republicans' watch. American politics sorely needs a Republican Party that reverts to the role of fiscal steward or principled libertarian. As the Bush administration went into free fall in late 2006, Republican factions began quarreling among themselves. Perhaps out of the infighting will come a reborn Republican Party that once again cares about the fate of the republic. But for now, the best thing about Bush's collapse is that it opens the door to a resurgent Democratic Party, a revival of American democracy itself—and perhaps even serious engagement with grave national challenges.

The Fantasy of Bipartisanship

One of the most politically disabling conceits of this era has been the premise that America suffers mainly from a symmetrical excess of partisan zeal. To read much of the political science literature and the writings of many commentators, you would think that American politics today were deadlocked between ideologically extreme, government-hating conservatives and equally rigid, statist liberals—with the dismayed electorate turned off by the polarization, partisan bickering, and failure to address real problems. A Google search of "partisan bickering," incidentally, turns up 391,000 hits. It has become one of the great media clichés.

The Washington Post's David Broder is personally responsible for dozens of the "partisan bickering" citations. Broder writes a variation of this same misleading column several times a year. "The public is tired of the partisan bickering, tired of the gridlock and eager to elect people who will focus on the real problems and work together to find solutions," Broder wrote just before the 2006 midterm election. "If that lesson is reinforced by the election results, Washington will change. Congress will be run by people who talk with each other, across party lines."

Joe Klein, in *Time* magazine, tells the same story. His postelection cover piece was headlined "Why the Center Is the New Place to Be," a story that he has written dozens of times. The heroes of this conception of politics are bipartisan types, like John McCain, Joe Lieberman, and the so-called Gang of Fourteen, whose compromise ostensibly saved the Senate in 2005 from the "nuclear option" of banning filibusters on Supreme Court appointments. In fact, the Gang provided bipartisan cover for Bush to force a winning, filibuster-free Senate vote for the archconservative judge Samuel Alito.

A June 25, 2007, *Time* magazine cover piece lauding California Governor Arnold Schwarzenegger and New York Mayor Michael Bloomberg mentioned generic "partisan blockage" and failures of "Washington" to solve public problems no fewer than nine times. The fact that the Bush administration is responsible for the cuts in aid to cities and states, and refuses normal give-and-take with Democrats to address national ills, barely rated mention.

Even liberals in good standing sometimes fall into this trap: *The New York Times*' Bob Herbert, about as reliable a liberal op-ed voice as we have, returned from a speaking engagement at a national issues conference at DePaul University on the eve of the 2006 election. "Voters hungry for a serious discussion of complex issues are fed a steady diet of ideological talking heads," he wrote. "I was struck by the extent to which the people who attended the forums were interested in seeking out practical, nonpartisan, non-ideological solutions to the wide range of problems discussed."

This kind of writing reinforces the premise that politics is failing to solve problems because of symmetrical ideological zeal. The reality, of course, is that most of the zeal, discipline, extremism, and destructive policies are on one side.

Recent history is hardly a case of partisan deadlock failing to address national problems. It is rather a story of Republicans using fierce party discipline to ram through a program not sought by a majority of American voters and taking no prisoners politically. If national problems, such as the escalating deficit and dwindling health insurance coverage are not being solved, it is because the Republicans were determined to push a program that made the problems worse. They were in no mood to split the difference with moderate Democrats, so there was no centrist grand compromise waiting in the wings, sandbagged by partisan bickering.

Yet this myth has very potent appeal. Robert Frost once described a liberal as "a man too broadminded to take his own side in a quarrel." This seems a near-perfect description of the calls for a new centrism from today's moderate Democrats as the cure for the bickering that they implausibly blame on both sides.

The DLC's Will Marshall and Al From, in one of their periodic manifestos, declared, "America needs a third choice that replaces the left's reflexive defense of the bureaucratic status quo and counters the right's destructive bid to simply dismantle government." (When did you ever see Republicans belittling the Right as equally outmoded as the Left and calling for a "third choice"?)

Ted Halstead and Michael Lind of the New America Foundation, both self-identified Democrats, wrote in their 2001 book, *The Radical Center,* "We chose this name [Radical Center] to differentiate our principles and policies from those of the Democratic Left and the Republican Right. To us, it seems obvious that the familiar varieties of liberalism and conservatism . . . are largely irrelevant in the . . . first half of the twenty-first century." (Again, can you imagine such rhetoric coming from Republicans?)

Matthew Miller, a former Clinton budget official, wrote in his 2003 book, *The Two Percent Solution,* "What American politics urgently needs, therefore, is not a new left, but a new center. Domestic debate needs to be re-centered around a handful of fundamental goals on which all of us can agree, whether we call ourselves Republicans, Democrats, or Independents."

Miller, in researching his book, traveled around the country and interviewed both conservatives and liberals. He concluded that, but for partisan bickering, there was potential common ground. He calculated that for an additional 2 percent of GDP in public outlay (currently about $250 billion), we could give everyone a living wage, good health insurance, and decent schools, plus get big money out of politics. But you have to wonder what political planet Miller is living on. Where are the

Republicans willing to increase public spending by $250 billion a year if only Democrats would just compromise?

Among the conservative think tanks and Republican strategy groups, you will find no moderate Matthew Millers commending a grand bargain with liberals. You will find right-wing ideologues who are dead serious about winning. William Kristol, Karl Rove, and Grover Norquist did not prevail by disdaining a new Right and commending a new center. Rather, the conservative strategy is simply to destroy liberalism.

Miller can't quite seem to comprehend what the Right is up to. He reports that his interviews "with conservative thinkers and activists left me stumped. Most of them insisted they were as concerned with equal opportunity and the problems of disadvantaged Americans as were Democrats, and resented the way their party was caricatured as heartless or indifferent." He offers several hypotheses to explain this apparent puzzle of seeming Republican indifference to social justice. In the end, he concludes that the Right is suffering from, of all things, "cognitive dissonance." Evidently they really do care about the poor; they just don't grasp that their program is harming the poor. Miller should forget cognitive dissonance and remember Occam's razor. There is a much simpler and more plausible explanation: They really *don't* care about the poor.

It would be wonderful if politics could rise above party and ideology, just as it would be wonderful if the heavens rained money. Ever since the Progressive Era, an American ideal has been the quest for "nonpolitical," technical solutions to problems that are, unfortunately, inherently political. Most serious public issues, like it or not, are ideologically colored, even if the ideology is tacit. Should we raise taxes or cut spending to balance the budget? Whose taxes should we raise? Which spending should we cut? Should we as a society provide health coverage to all? Or should we leave the poor to charity? There are no politically neutral answers to these questions. These decisions, alas, are guided by an underlying public philosophy, a set of ideas about what makes for a good society—an ideology. It's true that good public policy should also be guided by evidence and practical experience that sometimes challenges ideological preconceptions. And during some periods of public life there has been far more willingness to reach across party lines. But the excessive partisanship in America today is almost entirely Republican.

This idea of party polarization and resultant blockage has also become something of a trope in the political science profession. It is easy to demonstrate statistically an increase over the past two decades in party cohesion in congressional roll-call voting. The main causes are the eclipse of the old, racist, Dixiecrat wing of the Democratic Party (replaced by the nearly complete dominance of Republicans in the white South) and the displacement of liberal and moderate Republicans. With the demise of these two outlying factions, Democrats are more likely to vote with Democrats and Republicans with Republicans, especially the latter. But greater party loyalty on roll-call votes is hardly the same thing as a symmetrical shift of both parties to the ideological extremes.

As anyone who has followed recent American politics knows, the real story is an ideological shift of the entire spectrum to the right. The ideological difference between the two parties has widened because Democrats generally have moved moderately toward the center on most issues, while Republicans have moved more extremely rightward. Before 1975, the typical Democratic senator or representative supported a more explicitly managed form of capitalism. Few Democrats in Congress were willing to vote for deregulation, and most wanted to expand social spending. The most influential group in the House Democratic Caucus was the resolutely progressive Democratic Study Group, whose membership included nearly all non-Dixiecrat Democrats. There was no DLC. And there were far more moderate and liberal Republicans willing to support progressive taxation, social investment, and economic regulation.

Democrats have become more liberal since then only in their support for previously nonexistent tolerance issues, such as gay rights and reproductive choice. The Republican leadership, meanwhile, has mounted a vicious attack on moderates in their ranks known by the dismissive acronym RINO, standing for Republicans In Name Only. Suspected RINOs have been stripped of committee chairmanships, have had to fight primary opponents sponsored by allies of the leadership, and have been hounded from Congress.

For most of American history, presidents relied on bipartisan coalitions to pass legislation, as LBJ did with civil rights bills. Bill Clinton frequently resorted to "triangulation," even while the Democrats still controlled both houses of Congress. NAFTA, for example, passed the House with about two thirds of Democrats voting against it and most Republicans supporting it. Likewise for welfare reform. But between 2001 and 2006, as Republican Speaker Dennis Hastert famously vowed, no legislation would be brought to the floor unless it had the backing of "a majority of the Majority." That is, a bill could have the support of nearly three quarters of the House—all the Democrats and 49 percent of Republicans—and it would never see the light of day. This happened with several pieces of legislation, such as an increase in the minimum wage. Democrats voted more cohesively in the Bush era, in part because the agenda was so thoroughly rigged by the Republican leadership. The political scientists Jacob Hacker and Paul Pierson, in their 2005 book, *Off Center*, carefully examined the data and demolished the thesis of symmetrical partisan polarization.

Go further back in twentieth-century American history, and you will find strong partisanship and leadership on the Democratic side, often facilitated by progressive Republicans. When Franklin Roosevelt sponsored such New Deal initiatives as public power, the Wagner Act, much tighter regulation of Wall Street, and Social Security, he could count not only on the strong majority of (non-southern) Democrats but on (mostly western) progressive Republicans. The precursor of the Wagner Act, the 1932 Norris-LaGuardia Act prohibiting "yellow-dog" employment contracts (forbidding workers from belonging to a union), bears the name of its two Republican sponsors.

Lyndon Johnson, like Roosevelt, depended on the strong party unity of northern and western Democrats, coupled with the crossover support of key moderate Republicans such as Senate Minority Leader Everett McKinley Dirksen. Most Republicans opposed Johnson on many pieces of major social legislation such as Medicare, but none of the landmark civil rights bills would have been enacted without Republican support to offset the die-hard Dixiecrat opposition.

The lesson for our own era is that partisan deadlock is a myth. Solutions to national problems occur when the majority party has a vision and enjoys support within its own ranks; if it can win the support of some enablers in the opposition party, so much the better. (The Dixiecrats were an anomaly, tantamount to a third party.) What's interesting about the Bush era is that Bush has played the same leadership role as Roosevelt and Johnson did, but, unlike FDR and LBJ, he did not take office with a popular mandate for radical change. He did not even win the popular vote, and he campaigned as a moderate. What Bush did manage to do was move a radically conservative agenda by relying on fierce party discipline.

In this context, most of the self-described congressional centrists on the Democratic side were not champions of a successful compromise agenda. Mainly, they provided bipartisan cover for the Bush agenda. A classic case in point is the ranking Democrat on the Senate Finance Committee, Max Baucus of Montana. Time after time, Baucus serves as Bush's enabler, supporting Republican tax cuts and Republican assaults on regulation and social insurance. Baucus was regularly invited to House-Senate conference committees as a reward for supporting Republican legislation, even as House Democratic conferees were excluded. Former Democratic senator John Breaux used to play a similar role. He cochaired the "bipartisan" Breaux-Thomas Commission, which pushed for privatized forms of Social Security and Medicare. All this blurs the Democrats' identity and message.

Base Affections

It was once a staple of political science that politicians naturally tried to win the affections of the "median voter." Almost by definition, that fabled citizen was found in the political center. George W. Bush, in one of history's great cases of bait and switch, positioned himself in the 2000 campaign to appeal to the centrist voter. He did so knowing that relatively few voters actually supported the far-right agenda that he later would enact. From the vantage point of 2007, it is hard to believe the way Bush campaigned just seven years ago.

In a stirring passage in his convention acceptance speech, Bush invoked

> single moms struggling to feed their kids and pay the rent. Immigrants starting a hard life in a new world. Children without fathers in neighborhoods where gangs seem like friendship. . . . We are their country, too. . . . When these problems aren't confronted, it builds a wall within our nation. On one side are wealth and technology, education and ambition. On the other side of the wall are poverty and prison, addiction and despair. And, my fellow Americans, we must tear down that wall.

One could imagine Bobby Kennedy or Lyndon Johnson—or even Al Gore on a good day—uttering just those words.

"To seniors in this country," Bush earnestly declared, "you earned your benefits, you made your plans, and President George W. Bush will keep the promise of Social Security—no changes, no reductions, no way."

"Medicare," he added, "does more than meet the needs of our elderly; it reflects the values of our society. We will set it on firm financial ground, and make prescription drugs available and affordable for every senior who needs them."

In the third presidential debate, Bush told Gore, "You know I support a national patients' bill of rights, Mr. Vice President. And I want all people covered." He called for grants to the states "so that seniors—poor seniors—don't have to choose between food and medicine."

Bush pledged to change the tone in Washington, to govern as a bipartisan the way he had done as governor of Texas. "I know it's going to require a different kind of leader to go to Washington and say to both Republicans and Democrats, 'Let's come together,'" he said.

Bush repeatedly promised to balance the budget and insisted that the nation could afford a tax cut without slipping into deficit. He even criticized a House Republican plan to achieve budget savings by cutting the Earned Income Tax Credit. "I don't think they ought to balance their budget on the backs of the poor," he said.

All these declarations were, of course, lies. While all recent presidents have periodically gone back on promises and some have told explicit untruths, what's interesting is that the multiple untruths told by this president are something very rare in politics: *ideological lies.*

Hypocrisy, as La Rochefoucauld observed, is the homage that vice pays to virtue. In the case of Bush, campaign lies were the homage that Republican sloganeering paid to the popularity of progressive Democratic ideology.

Imagine instead that Bush had hit the campaign trail promoting a Social Security shift that would increase the system's deficits, requiring cuts in benefits and an increase in the retirement age; that he promised a tax cut that cost more than twice Social Security's long-term shortfall. Imagine that his patients' rights bill was advertised as authored by the HMO industry—and as prohibiting patients denied care from suing their insurer; that he touted a Medicare drug plan written by the drug and insurance industries that left a $2,250 "doughnut hole" in annual coverage; that his environmental policy would scrap one protection after another and let industry rewrite the rules; that he pledged to demonize Democrats who resisted his policies; that his No Child Left Behind program pledged to freeze funding for Head Start and money for child care—and to go back on a bipartisan deal to increase federal funds for poor public schools in exchange for high-stakes testing.

Campaigning on that set of views, Bush would have been the minority candidate of a minority party. There would have been no cliff-hanger in Florida and no narrow Supreme Court resolution of *Bush v. Gore.* Yet that set of views has been his actual program. And his need to prevaricate suggests the popularity of progressive economic themes.

More interesting still, Bush got away with it, at least long enough to be narrowly reelected in 2004. How did he do it? The attacks of September 11, 2001, certainly helped, as did Senator Kerry's lackluster campaign. But Bush also did something that completely defies the "median voter" thesis: he played almost entirely to his base, soothing moderate voters, where he could, with empty rhetoric. The viability of this strategy was spelled out in a detailed memo by his senior pollster, Matthew Dowd, who argued that if Bush really fired up religious fundamentalists and other social conservatives, he could gain a bare majority by moving to the right rather than to the center. This might not have worked but for the climate of permanent warfare, which, for a time, attracted some swing voters.

What saved the republic from a prolonged period of one-party rule on behalf of a program supported by only a minority of Americans, and perhaps the destruction of our democracy itself, was not flaws in the Republican political strategy but something much more old-fashioned: hubris. Bush's Iraq policy failed because his top officials ignored the warnings of intelligence professionals. His contempt for the enterprise of government manifested itself in blunders too grotesque to ignore, such as FEMA's bungling of Hurricane Katrina. In the end, the coup de grâce was old-fashioned corruption, some of it bordering on farce: Tom DeLay, the hammer who pounded a very slim House majority into a disciplined force, having to resign under indictment; House Appropriations Committee chairman Bob Ney being convicted of accepting bribes and refusing for a time to resign; Representative Randy Cunningham being sentenced to a long prison term; and, most weird of all, the page scandal involving a gay Republican congressman, Mark Foley. It turned out that a party that had gained traction with antigay ballot initiatives had closeted gays in its top leadership positions.

With the notable exceptions of the insurgent Democratic Senate and House challengers who captured Republican seats by running as economic populists, the 2006 elections seemed more a case of Republicans losing than of Democrats winning. Lots of Democrats followed the advice of the old tactical cliché: when your opponent is doing himself in, just get out of the way. Like many clichés, this one is mostly wrong. There is a latent base of disaffected voters, making up a large majority of Americans, waiting for leadership. If Republicans were able to get so far using leadership and party discipline on behalf of a program *not supported by a majority of Americans*, just imagine what a little Democratic courage might do on behalf of a program that actually served the broad majority.

REDEEMING AMERICA

I BEGAN *The Squandering of America* by noting the odd depoliticizing of issues that ought to be at the center of American public debate, notably the stagnant living standards for most Americans during a period of economic boom. Writing just after the 2006 midterm election, one can sense the ending of a political era and a new political opening. What remains to be seen is whether insurgent ideas and opposition politics will seize the moment.

As the Bush administration entered its final two years, more and more Americans were heard to say that it would take at least a generation to repair the damage—the mess in the Middle East, the lost stature of the United States in the world, the failure to address global climate change. This book has addressed a parallel set of problems: narrowed prosperity, escalating foreign debt, increased economic risk, diminished democracy.

All of these problems have solutions, and America has surely endured worse. The republic faced far more dire times when its new capital was burned by the British in 1814, when the union was nearly sundered in 1861, and when a nation still mired in depression faced the gathering force of Hitler, Stalin, and Tojo in 1941 and dictatorship seemed mightier than democracy. We are fully capable of surmounting our present economic challenges.

A rebuilding of equalizing institutions could broaden American prosperity. A very different set of regulatory policies could once again harness capitalism for the broad public good. A new approach to trade, industry, and technology could bring America's foreign accounts back into balance and reduce the threat to the dollar and to our living standards. A restoration of progressive taxation could restore fiscal order and substantially increase investment in people. And a period of effective Democratic—with a capital D—governance could revive America's two-party system and repair our democracy. But all this will take uncommon political leadership, as well as liberation from widespread myths.

There is a circularity to our current political blockage. If citizens had more faith in political remedy, political leaders might be bolder. If more progressives could get elected, they might enact policies that broadened prosperity and offset the inequality and instability of private markets. If the polity once again helped middle-class and working people, citizens might regain confidence in public institutions, progressive leaders, and politics itself. As my grandfather used to say, if we had ham, we could have ham and eggs—if we had eggs.

With the weakness of the labor movement and other institutions of popular politics, the most likely way to turn this vicious circle into a virtuous one is with leadership that speaks to the lives of regular people and offers hope. Occasionally, there is a glimmer of that kind of leadership. Barack Obama, speaking a language of hope, is the rock star in the Democratic firmament. Al Gore, once he opted not to run for president, felt liberated enough to give the kind of speeches that voters had hungered for in 2000, ones that could have propelled him to the White House.

Consider some of the Democratic progressives who get elected in very unlikely places by speaking a language of pocketbook populism. The aforementioned Sherrod Brown, running against a popular and relatively moderate incumbent, carried Ohio counties that Democrats just don't win. He won fifty-one counties, compared to the seventeen that Kerry won in 2004. Brown, facing the usual charge of "tax-and-spend," even turned the tricky issue of tax relief to his advantage. When his opponent, Senator Mike DeWine, ran ads boasting about the Bush tax cuts he had supported, Brown's ads asked voters, "Did you get any of those tax cuts, or did they all go to Mike DeWine's wealthy friends?" Voters didn't have to think very hard to know the answer.

Paul Wellstone, who died in a plane crash while campaigning during the final weeks before the 2002 election, was probably the most left-wing member of the Senate. But Wellstone managed to get elected twice, and would have been elected again, in one of America's most closely divided states, by speaking for ordinary Minnesotans and being clear about what he stood for. Even voters who disagreed with Wellstone on many specifics admired his gumption and voted for him as a rare honest politician.

There is another recipe, of course. Democrats like Montana's Max Baucus are also elected from swing states, as centrist enablers of Republican policies. But why bother?

Learning What We Know

The columnist Ellen Goodman once wrote that political and social change occurs "when people learn what they already know." Goodman was specifically referring to what housewives knew from their daily lives in the 1950s, tacit knowledge that women had to relearn as a *political* fact.

Women were socialized to be homemakers and only homemakers; the role was so taken for granted that it seemed as natural as breathing. Subconsciously, many women knew that something was amiss. They were generally denied entry into the skilled professions; they were steered to help wanted ads headed "Male" and "Female," where "female" meant primarily support positions; and most didn't think twice about it. This was just the way things were. Women were denied resources for intercollegiate sports. Women's incomes were not counted in a couple's mortgage applications. And bosses could make sexual passes at female employees with impunity—not because all this was the natural order of things but because a specific social order dictated these terms and was very convenient for the men who benefited from it.

The division of gender roles seemed so immutable that it took radicals to step outside the political assumptions of the day. They were widely ridiculed as bra burners. Remarkably enough, in less than a single generation, radical feminism percolated outward because it spoke to women's lived experience. Soon the law prohibited discrimination in employment based on sex. Leading colleges and professions opened their doors to women. Sexual harassment, a concept that did not even exist in the 1950s, was defined as a crime. And "male chauvinist," a phrase invented by the Communist Party in the 1930s, became part of the common language. Men, too slowly, became better domestic citizens. All this occurred because women learned, politically, what they already tacitly knew.

Something similar occurred in the populist revolt of the 1880s and the 1890s, when farmers and workingmen grasped that their economic plight was the result of a particular financial system biased in favor of creditors, one whose terms could be changed politically, and began their project of serious organizing. And it occurred in the 1930s, when factory workers grasped that they had the power to confront industry and organize trade unions. In the face of today's passivity on the part of both leaders and voters, it seems hard to believe that change can occur as quickly as it often has in American political history. But in 1959, who would have imagined that civil rights would be the top national issue just five years later in 1964 and that the president of the United States would pledge in a nationally televised address, "We shall overcome."

By the same token, most working- and middle-class Americans know that something is seriously amiss in today's economy. They are working too hard and not getting enough of the rewards. Their economic situation has become far more precarious. But people need to relearn that their situation is not a natural disaster. It is the result of ground rules that have been set by political forces. And helping people to learn what they already know requires nothing so much as political leadership.

There have been several efforts to improve Democratic "messaging" and "framing," as if getting more clever at rhetoric were a substitute for being clear about one's beliefs. The fact is that economic progressives have managed to get elected in the most improbable places by standing for the well-being of regular Americans.

Going forward, leaders would do well to articulate a few bold, clear ideas that identify them with the economic frustrations and aspirations of citizens—and along the way rehabilitate the idea of public remedy. Instead of programs of byzantine complexity to fill in the gaps in private health insurance without frightening the health insurance industry or the Business Roundtable, why not support a proven idea that can be summed up in three easy words—"Medicare for all"—and dare private industry and the Republicans to oppose it?

Bill Clinton would have done far better had he offered a straightforward health plan that did not try to split the difference with big business and the insurance industry. His 1993 plan was designed so that private insurers would get the business of providing the coverage and large corporations' costs would be capped. Hardly anyone outside the Capital Beltway understood the plan.

Despite the profit potential, the business elite and the Republicans quickly turned against the plan, correctly seeing an expansion of government-sponsored social insurance. William Kristol famously declared that Republicans should oppose Clinton's plan "sight unseen," and Newt Gingrich followed the advice. By the time the 1994 elections came, the widely supported goal was forgotten, and Clinton seemed a weak president unable to enact his program. Had Clinton proposed something far simpler and bolder, "Medicare for all," and pinpointed the insurance industry and the Republicans as the obstacles to it, the 1994 midterm elections could have been a referendum on a popular reform that he and the Democrats might well have won.

Why not take back some of the tax cuts on the wealthiest and broaden the "family welfare state" described in chapter one, so that every child can begin life as something of a trust-fund baby? The only demographic group to vote solidly Democratic in the 2004 presidential election was voters thirty and under. This is the generation facing impossibly high costs of first-time home ownership, burdened with college tuition debt and steep barriers to being able to afford to have children. An economic bill of rights for the young could win the affections of an entire generation.

My purpose here is not to write a platform, only to suggest the immense political value of bold policies that would offer practical help to regular Americans, even if enactment is not on the near horizon. Congressman Maurice Hinchey, a populist Democrat who was elected by a Hudson Valley district including depressed cities such as Kingston, a seat that had been safely Republican since 1910, argues that Democrats need policies that break the prevailing paradigm. Hinchey suggests, among other policies like universal health care, an immediate increase in the minimum wage to $10 rather than the $7.25 that Democrats got Congress to approve for 2009. "If I went out in the streets of Kingston," Hinchey told me, "and said to people that the minimum wage is not going up to $7.25 until 2009, they would say to me, 'That is all you Democrats are going to do? Why did I vote for you?'"

The Politics of Transformation

Once, national policies such as Social Security, the G.I. Bill of Rights, and Medicare made a huge positive difference in the lives of millions of working Americans, on a scale that was economically and politically transformational. Today such policies are literally unthinkable. They are precluded by the assumptions of political debate, reflecting the power of the elite consensus and the passivity of popular institutions.

Restoring something like the distribution of income, wealth, security, and possibility that prevailed during the postwar social compact would require a popular resurgence to serve as a counterweight to the political and economic power of organized business. It would entail a restoration of progressive taxation and a rehabilitation of public outlay on a scale sufficient not just to restore fiscal balance but to underwrite new social investments running into hundreds of billions of dollars a year. Europe manages an income distribution of prosperity even more equal than the one that obtained in America's postwar boom, despite the corrosive effects of laissez-faire trade. But to achieve this goal, Europe spends nearly 15 more percentage points of GDP socially rather than privately, compared to our practices in the United States.

This scale of transformation seems inconceivable. But at a time of increasing individual risk, there is a tacit hunger for policies such as health coverage "that can never be taken away," as Clinton put it; for universal pension coverage that cannot be looted by financial engineers or lost to the vagaries of corporate takeovers and bankruptcies. Families stretched thin by the need for two incomes would welcome universal, high-quality preschool, child care, and after-school programs. All of these approaches would serve the middle class as well as the poor and build cross-class political coalitions.

Progressive Democrats lack the votes to achieve any of these policies in the current Congress. But as Maurice Hinchey's comment about a higher minimum wage suggests, they should launch them into public discourse. If polls and the success of Democrats who won Republican seats running as populists in 2006 are any guide, Democrats would be pleasantly surprised by the public response.

In the same way, restoring a financial economy that would serve the goal of connecting investors to entrepreneurs, rather than inviting insiders to reap windfall gains by manipulating paper, would require a degree of reregulation of the sort not seen since the New Deal. Here, too, progressives lack the votes to change policies in the near term, but they should have the courage to start a debate and begin changing conventional assumptions of what is possible.

In these days of partisan blockage, there is a fatal temptation to go for half a loaf and end up with political crumbs. Progressives need to be alert to the issue of which kinds of incremental reform open new possibilities and which ones merely reinforce programmatic fragmentation and popular cynicism.

Policy proposals ought to be measured against their transformative, versus merely palliative, potential. And there are plenty of opportunities for politically intelligent strategies of incremental reform. A good current example is the Medicare drug program.

By demanding that President Bush allow the government to offer citizens the option of a prescription drug program under the public Medicare system, Democrats in early 2007 grasped the potential of legislative politics as a teaching tool, win or lose. The debate reminds the public that the plan enacted by Bush is mainly a subsidy to the insurance and pharmaceutical industries; that a fragmented, for-profit approach to drug coverage is far less efficient than public Medicare, which can provide better insurance at the same cost without the infamous "doughnut hole" of vanishing coverage. It offers a "heads I win, tails you lose" politics for Democrats. Either Bush defers to Democratic leadership and ideology on a popular issue or he blocks it, putting himself visibly in bed with two unpopular industries and making both the industries and the Republicans even more unpopular.

One more case in point is the logic of minimum-wage and living-wage ballot initiatives. The 2004 Florida initiative to raise the minimum wage by a dollar tangibly helped only about 5 percent of the Florida population. But it carried every Florida county and got over 70 percent of the vote. It teased out a latent coalition and surfaced the issue of economic vulnerability. It was a terrific organizing tool. The grass roots led; politicians followed. The Florida initiative received about a million votes more than Bush did and over 2 million more than Democratic presidental candidate John Kerry. Had Kerry strongly identified himself with it, he could have been president.

The good news is that American voters are in many respects ahead of most politicians. In the past few years, there have been significant changes in public opinion, creating a real opening for progressive leadership. According to the pollster Ethel Klein, who has prepared an authoritative summary of shifting public perceptions on economic issues, by spring 2007 every major public opinion poll was reporting that increasing majorities of Americans felt that ordinary people were at serious economic risk, that government should do more rather than less, and that the gap between "the rich and everyone else" was unacceptably wide. For example, in January 2007, the Gallup organization found that 86 percent of Americans polled said that our performance in addressing the gap between rich and poor was inadequate. And in April 2007, Gallup reported that a larger percentage of citizens favored heavier taxes on the rich than they did in the Depression year 1939! The Gallup report concluded: "In summary, the data show that:

- A significant majority of Americans feel that money and wealth should be distributed more equally across a larger percentage of the population.
- A significant majority of Americans feel that the rich pay too little in taxes."

The Wall Street Journal/NBC poll reports a dramatic increase in those looking for a greater government role in helping people meet economic needs. In 1992, only 32 percent wanted government to do more. By early 2007, that share had grown to 52 percent, while the percentage preferring to leave economic challenges to individuals and business fell from 62 percent to 40 percent.

	GOVERNMENT SHOULD DO MORE TO SOLVE PROBLEMS AND HELP MEET THE NEEDS OF PEOPLE	GOVERNMENT IS DOING TOO MANY THINGS BETTER LEFT TO BUSINESS AND INDIVIDUALS	MIXED/DK
2007	52%	40%	8%
2002	45%	43%	12%
1997	41%	51%	8%
1992	32%	62%	6%

Source: The Wall Street Journal/ NBC, Ethel Klein.

As shown in the March 2007 report of the nonpartisan Pew Research Center for the People and the Press, "Trends in Political Values and Core Attitudes: 1987–2007," there is an unmistakable swing back toward broad public support for a managed form of capitalism. Even in 1994, the year the Republicans took control of Congress, 57 percent of Americans agreed that "Government should care for those who can't care for themselves." By 2007 that percentage soared to 69 percent. In partisan terms, Pew found a Democratic Party advantage of 50 to 35, up from equal party preference as recently as 2002. The voters are hungry for policies that restore security and opportunity. The question is whether Democrats will lead.

Averting Economic Calamity

By temperament, I am an optimist (one has to be, as a liberal Democrat in the present era). I did not set out to write an alarmist book. But the deeper I got into the details of the U.S. economy, the more alarmed I became.

The risks of writing a book predicting economic trouble are multiple. One can be dismissed as a dour purveyor of doom and gloom, particularly if the forecasted trouble continues to be deferred. Or the trouble can arrive ahead of schedule and one can be overtaken by events. Nobody can predict precisely when an economic calamity might occur, only note that too many preconditions are in place. Timing aside, however, these risks are all too real and need to be taken very seriously.

It's possible to project forward a decade and consider the consequences if reform in each of the worrisome financial areas continues to be blocked. And the likely consequences are actually quite different in different realms.

In the area of individual economic privation, the sad reality is that people are capable of suffering even greater pocketbook distress without producing a political explosion, especially if the pace is gradual and there is scant political leadership. After World War I in Great Britain, high unemployment and declining living standards persisted for more than two full decades. In Brazil, the extremes of inequality are greater than in the United States. The affluent live behind gates with security systems and guards in close proximity to favela slums and simply don't go to major parts of big cities. The voters intermittently elect leftist governments, and not much changes.

In our country, one could imagine a further widening of income inequality, more Americans going without needed health care, more elderly people having to work into their seventies and even eighties as pensions dwindle, more children denied life chances, and more of a squeeze on working parents. This would be a deeply unattractive society, but it would not necessarily collapse.

In the area of financial risk, however, the predictable consequences are more dire. A likely scenario is a loss of confidence in the dollar. That, in turn, could lead to a deep recession and a set of very unhappy choices for American policy makers. Should the Federal Reserve raise interest rates in the hope of restoring a dollar inflow, even at the cost of exacerbating the recession? Or should it cut rates and invite further international capital flight? The gradual erosion in living standards would turn into a much steeper decline, for the elite as well as for ordinary people.

Can this future be prevented? Perhaps, but the time to start was yesterday. It would require drastically different trade policies that demand more reciprocity by mercantilist trading partners, as well as different fiscal policies. The necessary remedies will also require a very different politics—Democrats who rise to the occasion and rebuild a modern brand of managed capitalism; Republicans who look beyond their own narrow financial self-interest.

Another big risk is that an external shock such as a rise in energy and food prices will increase inflationary expectations, leading to a rise in long-term interest rates. Higher interest costs, in turn, could cause the excessively leveraged speculative investments of hedge funds and private equity to crash, with cascading effects on the real enterprises that they own, and on the rest of the real economy. In some respects, this scenario would resemble the dot-com crash of 2000–01, driven by a new wave of financial engineering. But this time a rebound may not be so easy. When higher interest rates burst the bubble, the engineers of recovery will encounter an economy hobbled by foreign debt, one that has already squandered its fiscal resources on high domestic deficits.

If the economy were to suffer a serious crash, politics could well turn very ugly. As Roosevelt proved, it is possible to recover from a depression and financial collapse by using government to regulate financial markets, rebuild demand, increase social investment, and put people back to work. That recipe, however, is totally antithetical to the prevailing wisdom about efficient economics and out of fashion politically. Even with a hidden depression rather than a crash, the failure to seriously engage with the downside of globalism has its own set of alarming political dynamics. As living standards fall for ordinary people, especially for socially conservative white male, blue-collar workers, the know-nothings gain more influence. We've already seen this in an anti-immigrant backlash. In the absence of a managed economy that offers balanced opportunity and security, vulnerable workers scapegoat foreigners and minorities. The elite, globalist Right is playing with social dynamite by not paying attention.

What about political democracy itself? Historians will record that America, in 2006, narrowly averted losing its democracy. The Rove-Cheney-Bush machine had a cynical formula for building a permanent majority and reducing the opposition to window dressing. Their strategy failed only because of the Republicans' staggering foreign policy hubris and cascading domestic scandals. If the Republicans remain in executive power beyond 2008 and take back Congress by substituting hot-button social issues for ones that demand economic resolution and by manipulating the machinery of free elections, there is a real risk that the United States will be a democracy in name only. This has happened elsewhere. For six decades, Mexico had all the trappings of nominal democracy; the opposition party just never got to govern. The same has been true of postwar Japan.

It was Bismarck who said that divine providence protects idiots, drunkards, children, and the United States of America. The republic has faced worse challenges, and one must be optimistic that it will survive this one. But if our society is to reclaim broadly shared prosperity, we had better revive our democracy.

ACKNOWLEDGMENTS

I appreciate my colleagues at *The American Prospect*, collaborators in the project of reviving the politics of a just and dynamic economy. Preliminary versions of some of these ideas appeared in the *Prospect*'s pages. Thanks especially to Paul Starr, Harold Meyerson, Diane Straus Tucker, Ben Taylor, Robin Hutson, Ezra Klein, Bob Reich, and to the *Prospect* board. I also thank the several other editors whose work has enriched my own: Ash Green at Knopf, Renee Loth, Marjorie Pritchard and Dante Ramos at *The Boston Globe*, Steve Shepard at *BusinessWeek*, and most recently Mike Hoyt at the *Columbia Journalism Review*.

I continue to learn from the heterodox members of the economics profession, especially Joseph Stiglitz, Barry Bluestone, Dani Rodrik, Edward Wolff, Paul Krugman, Alicia Munnell, Robert Blecker, David Howell, Andy Sum, Bill Spriggs, Richard Freeman, and Jamie Galbraith. I have also benefited from the work of other social scientists, including Reuven Avi-Yonah, Dan Tarullo, Richard Parker, Theda Skocpol, Jacob Hacker, Richard Valelly, Drew Westen, Suzanne Berger, Peter Gourevitch, Jonas Pontusson, Janet Gornick, Tom Shapiro, Larry Brown, David Smith, Katherine Newman, Kathleen Gerson, and John Mollenkopf.

Thanks also to the leaders of the loose network of collaborators in think tanks and advocacy groups who are working to rebuild a progressive politics that emphasizes pocketbook issues, especially to Miles Rapoport, Tamara Draut, David Callahan, Nomi Prins, and Michael Lipsky at Demos; to Jeff Faux, Larry Mishel, and Jared Bernstein at the Economic Policy Institute; to Alan Houseman and colleagues at the Center for Law and Social Policy; to Bob McIntyre at Citizens for Tax Justice; to Dean Baker, Mark Weisbrot, and John Schmitt at the Center for Economic and Policy Research; to Bob Borosage and Roger Hickey at Campaign for American's Future; to Sid Wolfe and Lori Wallach of

Public Citizen; to several people in the labor movement too numerous to mention but special thanks to Ron Blackwell, Damon Silvers, Thea Lee, Richard Trumka, Owen Herrnstadt, and Ron Bloom.

I appreciate several current and former government officials whom I interviewed on background.

Thank you to Joan Fitzgerald, Barry Bluestone, Dean Baker, Jared Bernstein, and Ethel Klein, for reading portions of the manuscript, and to my agent, John Brockman.

I also appreciate several foundation leaders for encouraging or supporting my work, including Craig Kennedy and Randy Soderquist of the German Marshall Fund of the United States, Ralph Gomory of the Alfred P. Sloan Foundation, Steve Heintz of the Rockefeller Brothers Fund, Richard Leone at the Century Foundation, Lance Lindblom of the Nathan Cummings Foundation, Eric Wanner of the Russell Sage Foundation, Rick McGahey at the Ford Foundation, and several others who support the work of the *Prospect*.

Special thanks to Daphne Hunt and David Soll for research assistance; to dear friends and fellow writers Ross Gelbspan, Richard Rothstein, Marcia Angell; and to my family—Polly Levy, Gabriel and Jessica Kuttner, Owen and Jack Stewart, Shelly Fitzgerald and Vincent Lorenzo, and to my beloved Joan.

NOTES

INTRODUCTION: FAILURES OF POLITICS

9   *Everything for Sale:* Robert Kuttner, *Everything for Sale: The Virtues and Limits of Markets* (New York: Alfred A. Knopf, 1997).

13   two serious economists: James Glassman and Kevin Hassett, *Dow 36,000: The New Strategy for Profiting from the Coming Rise in the Stock Market* (New York: Random House, 1999).

14   countervailing power: John Kenneth Galbraith, *American Capitalism: The Concept of Countervailing Power* (Boston: Houghton Mifflin, 1952).

14   my first book: Robert Kuttner, *Revolt of the Haves: Tax Rebellions and Hard Times* (New York: Simon and Schuster, 1980).

CHAPTER ONE: A HIDDEN DEPRESSION

16   Pension coverage: See Jacob Hacker, *The Great Risk Shift: The Assault on American Jobs, Families, Health Care and Retirement* (New York: Oxford University Press, 2006).

16   median income: Jared Bernstein and Elise Gould, "Income Picture: Working Families Fall Behind," Economic Policy Institute, Washington, D.C., August 29, 2006, citing U.S. Census Bureau data.

16   "the Great Compression": Claudia Goldin and Robert A. Margo, *The Great Compression: The Wage Structure in the United States at Mid-Century* (Cambridge, Mass.: National Bureau of Economic Research, 1991).

16   economy steadily became more unequal: Lawrence Mishel et al., *The State of Working America, 2006–2007* (Ithaca, N.Y.: Cornell University Press, 2006), 55, citing U.S. Census Bureau data.

17   "politics of excluded alternatives": Walter Dean Burnham, *Critical Elections and the Mainsprings of American Politics* (New York: W. W. Norton, 1970).

19 A May 2006 poll: "From Underperforming to Overperforming," Greenberg Associates, Washington, D.C., May 2006.

19 a June 2006 poll: Jeffrey M. Stonecash, "Inequality and the American Public," Third Annual Maxwell Poll, Campbell Public Affairs Institute, Syracuse University, Syracuse, New York, October 2006.

19 A July 2006 survey: Steven Greenhouse, "Three Polls Find Workers Sensing Deep Pessimism," *The New York Times*, August 31, 2006.

20 In September 2005: Ian Dew-Becker and Robert J. Gordon, "Where Did the Productivity Growth Go?," Brookings Institution, Washington, D.C., September 2005.

20 Piketty and Saez: See "Income Inequality in the United States, 1913–1998," Working Paper no. 8467, National Bureau of Economic Research. Regular updates of Piketty and Saez's research are available from Emmanuel Saez at emlab.berkeley.edu/users/saez.

20 top 1 percent: Mishel et al., *The State of Working America*, 65.

21 Between 1947 and 1973: Ibid., 45, citing Census Bureau and Bureau of Labor Statistics data.

21 Increase in wages and in Wall Street bonuses: Andy Sum et al., "Who Stole Christmas from U.S. Frontline Workers?" Northeastern University Center for Labor Market Studies, Boston, Mass., December 24, 2006, 5.

21 concentration of wealth: Edward N. Wolff, "Recent Trends in Wealth Ownership," Jerome Levy Economics Institute Working Paper no. 300.

22 401(k)s: Alicia H. Munnell and Annika Sundén, "Coming Up Short: The Challenge of 401(k) Plans," Brookings Institution, Washington, D.C., 2004.

23 Average college tuition charges: College Board, "Trends in College Pricing 2004," available at www.collegeboard.com/prod_downloads/press/cost04/041264TrendsPricing2004_Final.pdf.

23 prices of various goods and services: Jared Bernstein and Sylvia Allegretto, "Assessing the Middle Class Squeeze," Economic Policy Institute, Washington, D.C., February 2006.

23 health insurance premiums: Henry J. Kaiser Family Foundation, "Employer Health Benefits: 2005 Annual Survey," available at kff.org/about/marketplace.cfm.

24 actual average housing prices: Floyd Norris, "What Happens If Inflation Is Overstated?" *The New York Times*, June 9, 2006.

25 "Affluenza": John de Graaf et al., *Affluenza: The All-Consuming Epidemic* (San Francisco: Berrett-Koehler Publishers, 2001).

25 commending self-denial: Damon Darlin, "Advice to All You Graduates; Let's Start with That Daily Latte," *The New York Times*, June 10, 2006.

26 Home ownership rates: Dowell Myers, "Advances in Homeownership Across the States and Generations: Continued Gains for the Elderly and Stagnation Among the Young," Census Note 8, Fannie Mae Foundation, Washington, D.C., October 2001.

26 help with the down payment: Thomas M. Shapiro, *The Hidden Cost of Being African American: How Wealth Perpetuates Inequality* (New York: Oxford University Press, 2004), xx.

26 declining economic fortunes: Tamara Draut, *Strapped: Why America's 20- and 30-Somethings Can't Get Ahead* (New York: Doubleday, 2005), 8.

27 At the 80th percentile: Current Population Survey, "FINC-06. Percent Distribution of Families, by Selected Characteristics Within Income Quintile and Top 5 Percent in 2005," available at http://pubdb3.census.gov/macro/032006/faminc/new06_000.htm.

27 intergenerational and inequality: Gary Solon, "Cross Country Differences in Intergenerational Earnings Mobility," *Journal of Economic Perspectives* 16, no. 3 (2002): 59–66; Michael Hout, "How Inequality May Affect Intergenerational Mobility," in *Social Inequality*, ed. Kathryn M. Neckerman (New York: Russell Sage Foundation, 2004), 969–987.

27 Home ownership rates: U.S. Census Bureau, "Historical Census of Housing Tables," available at www.census.gov/hhes/www/housing/census/historic/owner.html.

28 number of hours worked by married couples: See discussion in Mishel et al., *The State of Working America*, 86–90.

28 feminist road not taken: Kathleen Gerson, "What Do Women and Men Want," *The American Prospect*, March 2007, A8–A11.

28 more than 80 percent of mothers: Ibid.

29 *The Two-Income Trap:* Elizabeth Warren and Amelia Warren Tyagi, *The Two-Income Trap: Why Middle-Class Mothers and Fathers Are Going Broke* (New York: Basic Books, 2003), discussion at 50–54.

29 a combined income: Ibid.

30 effects of women's mass entry: Arlie Hochschild with Anne Machung, *The Second Shift: Working Parents and the Revolution at Home* (New York: Viking Penguin, 1989).

30 Quebec program: Michael Baker, Jonathan Gruber, and Kevin Milligan, "Universal Childcare, Maternal Labor Supply, and Family Well-Being," Working Paper no. 11832, National Bureau of Economic Research, Cambridge, Mass., December 2005.

31 20 percent or greater drop: Hacker, *The Great Risk Shift*, 2.

31 an Ownership Society: Speech by George W. Bush, September 2, 2004, available at www.whitehouse.gov/news/releases/2004/09/20040902-2.html.

34 the money in these plans: Munnell and Sundén, "Coming Up Short."

35 Kasriel study: Gretchen Morgenson, "After the Debt Feast Comes the Heartburn," *The New York Times*, November 27, 2005.

35 A 2006 study: Alicia Munnell and Annika Sundén. "401(k) Plans Are Still Coming Up Short," Center for Retirement Research, Boston College, 2006.

37 decline in the personal savings rate: U.S. Department of Commerce, www.bea.gov/briefrm/saving.htm.

37 Only 36 percent of Americans: Patrick Purcell, "Retirement Savings and Household Wealth," Congressional Research Service, Washington, D.C., May 2006.

37 increase in consumer debt: Mishel et al., *The State of Working America*, 269.

38 A recent report: Jason C. Booza, Jackie Cutsinger, and George Galster, "Where Did They Go? The Decline of Middle Income Neighborhoods in Metropolitan America," *Living Cities Census*, Brookings Institution, Washington, D.C., June 2006.

38 Home equity withdrawals: Damon Darlin, "Mortgage Lesson No. 1: A Home Is Not a Piggy Bank," *The New York Times*, November 4, 2006.

39 U.S. household savings rates: John C. Carrington and George T. Edwards, *Financing Industrial Investment* (London: Macmillan, 1979).

39 home ownership rates: U.S. Census Bureau, "Historical Census of Housing Tables," available at www.census.gov/hhes/www/housing/census/historic/owner.html.

40 The Warrens point out: Warren and Tyagi, *The Two-Income Trap*, 71–95.

40 A 2005 Harvard Medical School study: David U. Himmelstein, Elizabeth Warren, Deborah Thorne, and Steffie Woolhandler, "Illness and Injury as Contributors to Bankruptcy," *Health Affairs* 24 (2005): 63–73.

41 share of insurance premiums: Lawrence Mishel, "Employers Shift Health Insurance Costs onto Workers," Economic Policy Institute, August 16, 2006, available at www.epinet.org/content.cfm?id=2461.

41 85 million Americans: Families USA, "Health Care: Are You Better Off Today than Four Years Ago?," September 2004, available at www.familiesusa.org/assets/pdfs/Are_You_Better_Off_rev20053139.pdf; Pamela Farley Short, Deborah R. Graefe, and Cathy Schoen, "Churn, Churn, Churn: How Instability of Health Insurance Shapes America's Uninsured Problem," Commonwealth Fund, November 2003, available at www.cmwf.org/usr_doc/Short_churn_688.pdf.

42 cost savings: Dean Baker, "The Savings from an Efficient Medicare Prescription Drug Plan," Center for Economic and Policy Research, January 2006, available at www.cepr.net/publications/efficient_medicare_2006_01.pdf.

42 15.3 percent of GDP: *OECD Health Data 2006* (Paris: OECD, June 26, 2006), available at www.oecd.org.

CHAPTER TWO: THE ASSAULT ON THE GOOD SOCIETY

45 open-ended focus group: Damon Silvers, communication to the author.

45 Annmarie: Theda Skocpol, *The Missing Middle: Working Families and the Future of American Social Policy* (New York: W. W. Norton/Century Foundation, 2000), 141; and comment to the author, 2006.

46 classic scholarly exposition: Simon Kuznets, "Economic Growth and Income

Inequality," *American Economic Review* 45 (March 1955): 1–28. See also Amartya Sen, *Development as Freedom* (New York: Anchor, 1999).

51 Social Security payroll tax: Social Security Administration, "OASDI: Coverage, Financing and Insured Status," available at www.ssa.gov/history/pdf/t2a4.pdf.

52 History of the Social Security tax shift: See David Cay Johnson, *Perfectly Legal: The Covert Campaign to Rig Our Tax System to Benefit the Super Rich—and Cheat Everyone Else* (New York: Portfolio Press, 2003).

52 the very wealthiest are paying a net tax rate of about 17.5 percent: Ibid., 17.

53 $300 billion a year: IRS, "The Tax Gap," available at www.irs.gov/pub/irs-utl/tax_gap_facts_figures.pdf. See also Max Sawicki, ed., *Bridging the Tax Gap* (Washington, D.C.: Economic Policy Institute, 2005), estimate at 2.

53 Domestic spending relative to GDP: Council of Economic Advisers, *Economic Report of the President, 2006* (Washington, D.C.: Government Printing Office, 2006), Tables B-78 and B-79, 376, 377.

54 Declining coverage of unemployment compensation: "The Administration's Fiscal 2007 Budget Request for Unemployment Compensation," testimony by Howard Rosen before the House Ways and Means Committee Subcommittee on Human Resources, May 4, 2006.

54 union membership tends to offset: Peter Hart Associates and PowerPoint presentation by Karen Ackerman, AFL-CIO, October 2006.

55 53 percent: Ruy Teixeira, "Public Opinion Watch," Center for American Progress, August 31, 2005, available online at www.americanprogress.org/issues/2005/08/b1013709.html.

55 Union benefits: Mishel et al., *The State of Working America*, 179–188.

55–56 Hourly Wage table: Ann C. Foster, "Differences in Union and Non-Union Earnings in Blue Collar and Service Occupations," available at www.bls.gov/opub/cwc/cm20030623ar01p1.htm#10.

59 less than half the aid: College Board, "Trends in Student Aid 2006," available at www.collegeboard.com/prod_downloads/press/cost06/trends_aid_06.pdf.

59 A 2006 research study: Kati Haycock, "Promise Abandoned: How Policy Choices and Institutional Practices Restrict College Opportunities," a Report by the Education Trust, August 2006, available at www2.edtrust.org/NR/rdonlyres/B6772F1A-116D-4827-A326-F8CFAD33975A/o/PromiseAbandonedHigherEd.pdf.

61 Sam Zell: Katharine Q. Seelye and Richard Siklos, "Chicagoan Puts Up $315 Million to Win $8.2 Billion Tribune Co.," *New York Times*, April 3, 2007.

63 His most recent research: George J. Borjas, "The Labor Market Impact of High-Skill Immigration," Working Paper no. 11217, National Bureau of Economic Research, Cambridge, Mass., March 2005.

64 In a 1983 article: Robert Kuttner, "The Declining Middle," *The Atlantic Monthly*, July 1983, 60–72.

66 shift in demand for skills: Alan Blinder, "Outsourcing: Bigger Than You Thought," *The American Prospect*, November 2006, 44–46.

66 "the increasing inequality": Benjamin Friedman, *The Moral Consequences of Economic Growth* (New York: Alfred A. Knopf, 2005), 351.

66 "a dirty little secret": Thomas L. Friedman, *The World Is Flat* (New York: Farrar, Straus and Giroux, 2005), 265.

67 "Girls: finish your homework" quote: Ibid., 237.

67 just not plausible: Ian Dew-Becker and Robert Gordon, "Where Did the Productivity Growth Go?," Brookings Institution, Washington, D.C., September 2005, 75.

67 "Any skills mismatch": Michael J. Handel, "Skills Mismatch in the Labor Market," *Annual Review of Sociology* 29 (2003): 135–65, quote at 138.

67 "One of the more unexpected findings": Ibid., 158.

CHAPTER THREE: WALL STREET RULES

73 "irrational exuberance": Francis Boyer Lecture, American Enterprise Institute, December 5, 1996, available at www.federalreserve.gov/BoardDocs/speeches/1996/19961205.htm.

75 CEOs' pay: Graef Crystal, *In Search of Excess: The Overcompensation of American Executives* (New York: W. W. Norton, 1991).

76 Executive pay increased another 14 percent: Lucian Bebchuk and Yaniv Grinstein, "The Growth in Executive Pay," available at http://papers.ssrn.com/sol3/papers.cfm?abstract_id=648682.

78 Global Crossing . . . WorldCom: See discussion in Nomi Prins, *Other People's Money* (New York: New Press, 2004), 250–253.

79 Congressional pressure on Arthur Levitt: Arthur Levitt, *Take on the Street: What Wall Street and Corporate America Don't Want You to Know; How You Can Fight Back* (New York: Random House, 2002).

80 Prins quote: Prins, *Other People's Money*, 101.

82 "That's the trouble": Michael Lewis, "Jonathan Lebed: Stock Manipulator, S.E.C. Nemesis—and 15," *The New York Times Magazine* online, February 25, 2001.

84 The Insull family: M. L. Ramsey, *Pyramids of Power: The Story of Roosevelt, Insull, and the Utility Wars* (New York: Bobbs Merrill, 1937).

84 "It is said": Ferdinand Pecora, *Wall Street Under Oath: The Story of Our Modern Money-Changers* (New York: Simon and Schuster, 1939), 224–225.

85 Albert Wiggin . . . Charles E. Mitchell: Ron Chernow, *The House of Morgan: An American Banking Dynasty and the Rise of Modern Finance* (New York: Atlantic Monthly Press, 1990), 356; Pecora, *Wall Street Under Oath*, 21–25.

85–86 "We assume that": Fred Schwed, Jr., *Where Are the Customers' Yachts? Or*

A Good Hard Look at Wall Street (New York: John Wiley & Sons, 1940, 1955), 69–70.

86 Schwed on controlling margin: Ibid.

87 Just over 1 percent: John Kenneth Galbraith, *The Great Crash* (Boston: Houghton Mifflin, 1955), 78.

88 the powers the Securities Act did not grant: Joel Seligman, *The Transformation of Wall Street: A History of the Securities and Exchange Commission and Modern Corporate Finance* (New York: Aspen Publishers, 2003), 70.

88 William O. Douglas quote: In Seligman, *The Transformation of Wall Street*, 71–72.

88 Frankfurter, "bankers' strike": In Seligman, *The Transformation of Wall Street*, 79.

88–89 draft of 1934 Act: In Seligman, 85–86. See also Pecora, *Wall Street Under Oath*, 269.

89 Pecora, 75 percent of the trades: Pecora, *Wall Street Under Oath*, 270.

90 Richard Whitney: See Chernow, *The House of Morgan*, 423–499.

91 Federal Reserve and Eccles: Marriner S. Eccles, *Beckoning Frontiers: Public and Personal Recollections*, ed. Sidney Hyman (New York: Alfred A. Knopf, 1951). See also William Greider, *Secrets of the Temple: How the Federal Reserve Runs the Country* (New York: Simon and Schuster, 1987), 308–314.

91–92 open market operations: Greider, *Secrets of the Temple*, 312.

92 Judge Healy quote: Pecora, *Wall Street Under Oath*, 162.

93 studies showed consumer savings: Cited in Seligman, *The Transformation of Wall Street*, 262–263.

93 electricity rates: Richard Rosen, Marjorie Kelly, and John Stutz, "A Failed Experiment: Why Electricity Deregulation Did Not Work and Could Now Work," Tellus Institute, Boston, Mass., March 2007.

95 history of movement for federal chartering of corporations: See Seligman, *The Transformation of Wall Street*, 230; and Ralph Nader, Mark Green, and Joel Seligman, *Taming the Giant Corporation* (New York: W. W. Norton, 1967).

95 cost of bad bank loans: Lowell L. Bryan, *Breaking Up the Bank* (Homewood, Ill.: Dow Jones-Irwin, 1988), 42–44.

95 cost of savings and loan failures: Michael A. Robinson, *Overdrawn: The Bailout of American Savings* (New York: Dutton, 1990), 290.

96–97 growth of money market mutual funds: Joe Nocera, *A Piece of the Action* (New York: Simon and Schuster, 1994), 197.

97 growth of commercial paper: Robert Litan, *What Should Banks Do?* (Washington, D.C.: Brookings Institution, 1987), 42–43.

97 John Brooks, *The Go-Go Years* (New York: Weybright and Talley, 1973), 158.

99 "the market for corporate control": Henry G. Manne, "Mergers and the Market for Corporate Control," *Journal of Political Economy* 73 (1965): 110–112.

100 "efficient market hypothesis": The classic statement is Eugene F. Fama, "Random Walks in Stock Market Prices," *Financial Analysts Journal* 21, no. 5 (September–October 1965): 55–59.

100 Berle and Means 1932 book: A. A. Berle and Gardiner Means, *The Modern Corporation and Private Property*, rev. ed. (New York: Harcourt, Brace and World, 1967).

103 Volcker quote: Jacob M. Schlesinger, "The Deregulators," *The Wall Street Journal*, October 17, 2002.

104 Butcher quote: John J. Curran and Darienne L. Dennis, "Does Deregulation Make Sense?," *Fortune*, June 5, 1989, available at http://money.cnn.com/magazines/fortune/fortune_archive/1989/06/05/72063/index.htm.

CHAPTER FOUR: FINANCIAL ENGINEERING AND SYSTEMIC RISKS

107–08 Keynes quote: John Maynard Keynes, *The General Theory of Employment, Interest and Money* (New York: Harcourt, Brace, 1936).

109 LTCM's trillion-dollar exposure: Roger Lowenstein, *When Genius Failed: The Rise and Fall of Long-Term Capital Management* (New York: Random House, 2000).

109 "secretive, close knit mathematicians": Ibid.

110 Greenspan's view on derivatives: Alan Greenspan, "Risk Transfer and Financial Stability," speech, Chicago, May 5, 2005, available at www.federalreserve.gov/Boarddocs/speeches/2005/20050505/default.htm.

110 Rubin denunciation of Born: Robert E. Rubin, Alan Greenspan, and Arthur Levitt, Joint Statement, May 7, 1998, available at www.treasury.gov/press/releases/rr2426.htm. Also, Brooksley Born, Testimony on the Over-the-Counter Derivatives Market Before the U.S. Senate Committee on Agriculture, July 30, 1998.

111 expert panel: Bank for International Settlements, "OTC Derivatives: Settlement Procedures and Counterparty Risk Management," 1998, available at www.bis.org/pub/ecsc08.pdf.

111 Hennessee Group: Hennessee Hedge Fund Review, September 2006, www.hennesseegroup.com/Hedge_Fund_Review_index.html.

112 *Fortune* estimates: Andy Serwer, "Let's Make a Deal," *Fortune*, July 13, 2005.

114 Marshall Wace: Henny Sender and Anita Raghavan, "Worry amid Hedge Fund Boom: Privileged Access to Information," *The Wall Street Journal*, July 27, 2006.

115–16 Rhodes op-ed: "A Market Correction Is Coming, This Time for Real," *Financial Times*, March 29, 2007.

116–17 Role of *The Wall Street Journal*: See, e.g., "Fannie's Friends on the Hill," editorial, *The Wall Street Journal*, May 9, 2005.

117 "illusions deliberately and systematically": Office of Federal Housing Enterprise Oversight, "Report of the Special Examination of Fannie Mae,"

May 2006, available at www.ofheo.gov/media/pdf/FNMSPECIALEXAM
.PDF.

118 In the first ten months of 2006: Ray Unger, "Sometimes 'Can't Miss' Deals
Can Miss by a Lot," *The Capital Times*, December 8, 2006, available at
http://www.madison.com/tct/business/stories/index.php?ntid=110382.

119 One study of management buyouts: James Surowiecki, "Private Lies," *The
New Yorker*, August 28, 2006.

119–20 Katz calculation: Sharon P. Katz, "Earnings Management and Conservatism in the Transition Between Private and Public Ownership: The Role
of Private Equity Sponsors," Working Paper, January 2006.

121 Burger King: "Burger King: Where's the Beef?" *BusinessWeek*, April 10,
2006.

121 Blackstone Group: "Gluttons at the Gate," *BusinessWeek online*, October
30, 2006, available at www.businessweek.com/magazine/content/06_44/
b4007001.htm.

121–22 loans to pay out dividends: *The Wall Street Journal*, January 4, 2007,
quoted at http://money.cnn.com./2006/01/05/news/companies/private_
equity_dividends.

122 Intelsat: Greg Ip and Henny Sender, "In Today's Buyouts, Payday for Firms
Is Never Far Away," *The Wall Street Journal*, July 25, 2006.

122 Grohe: Rasmussen Report, 184–185.

123 price of HCA swaps: Serena Ng, Dennis K. Berman, and Kara Scannell,
"Are Deal Makers on Wall Street Leaking Secrets?" *The Wall Street Journal*,
July 28, 2006.

123 Cerberus: "What's Bigger than Cisco, Coke, or McDonald's?" *BusinessWeek*,
October 3, 2005.

124 "Don't fall for": Steven Pearlstein, "Making a Play for the Dumb Money,"
The Washington Post, March 21, 2007.

124 "Frankly, there is so much": Ibid.

125 *Chronicle of Philanthropy*: Maria Di Mento, Ben Gose, and Peter Panepento,
"Strong Endowment Growth," *Chronicle of Philanthropy*, June 4, 2007.

129 Tobin Tax: Mahbub ul Haq et al., *The Tobin Tax: Coping with Financial Volatility* (Oxford, England: Oxford University Press, 1996).

CHAPTER FIVE: THE CASINO CONTINUES

130 Privately funded task force: Committee on Capital Markets Regulation,
Interim Report, December 5, 2006, available at www.capmktsreg.org/index
.html.

131 Material weakness, stock performance, and comment: Glass, Lewis & Co.,
"The Materially Weak," Denver, Colo., February 2007.

132 Macey quote: Jonathan Macey, "What Sarbox Wrought," *The Wall Street
Journal*, April 7, 2007.

132 Goldman Sachs: Herb Greenberg, "Goldman Disagrees with Paulson," March 14, 2007, available at www.marketwatch.com.

132 U.S. share of IPOs: Charles D. Niemeier, "American Competitiveness in International Capital Markets," September 30, 2006, Public Accountability Accounting Oversight Board, Washington, D.C., 7.

133 maligned Sarbanes-Oxley Act: See David Henry, "Broadcom's Options Bombshell," *BusinessWeek*, September 8, 2006.

133 restatements of past financial reports: "The Error of Their Ways," Glass, Lewis & Co., Denver, Colo., February 27, 2007.

133 Thomson Financial survey: Adam Lashinsky, "IPOs Still Love U.S. Markets," *Fortune*, February 1, 2007.

133–34 subprime loans increased: "At a Mortgage Lender, Rapid Rise, Faster Fall," *The Wall Street Journal*, March 11, 2007.

134 One industry study projects that about 32 percent: Damon Darlin, "Lenders May Prove Adjustable," *The New York Times*, March 31, 2007, citing First American CoreLogic study.

135 founders of New Century: available at www.thestreet.com/funds/follow-money/10344120.html.

135 23 percent of subprime loans: Greg Ip and Damian Paletta, "Regulators Scrutinized in Mortgage Meltdown," *The Wall Street Journal*, March 22, 2007.

136 John M. Robbins warned: "MBA Questions Freddie Mac's New Underwriting Standards for Subprime Lending," February 29, 2007, available at www.mortgagebankers.org/NewsandMedia/PressCenter/48715.htm.

137 Mutual fund assets increased: John C. Bogle, *The Battle for the Soul of Capitalism* (New Haven, Conn.: Yale University Press, 2005), 177.

138 "Equity fund investors paid": Ibid., 158.

138 Comparable return: Ibid., 159.

138 "[T]he investor put up 100 percent of the capital": Ibid., 163.

139 mutual fund directors' compensation: Roy C. Smith and Ingo Walter, *Governing the Modern Corporation* (Oxford, England: Oxford University Press, 2006), 139.

139 Buffett quote: Berkshire Hathaway, Inc., 2000 Annual Letter to Shareholders, quoted in Smith and Walter, *Governing the Modern Corporation*.

141 A study by the finance professors: Randall A. Heron and Erik Lie, "What Fraction of Stock Option Grants to Top Executives Have Been Backdated or Manipulated?" working paper, July 14, 2006, available at www.biz.uiowa.edu/faculty/elie/Grants%207-14-2006.pdf.

141 200 million to one: James Bandler and Charles Forelle, "UnitedHealth Cites 'Deficiency' in Options Grants," *The Wall Street Journal*, May 12, 2006.

141 Hemsley: Eric Dash and Milt Freudenheim, "Chief Executive at U.S. Health Insurer Forced Out," *The New York Times*, October 15, 2006.

143 Hirschman's famous formulation: Albert Hirschman, *Exit, Voice and Loyalty* (Cambridge, Mass.: Harvard University Press, 1970).

143 Ellerman's history: David Ellerman, *Property and Contract in Economics: The Case for Economic Democracy* (Oxford, England: Blackwell, 1993).

143 economic visionary: Louis O. Kelso and Mortimer J. Adler, *The Capitalist Manifesto* (New York: Random House, 1958).

144 For a discussion of "blockholding," see Peter Gourevitch and James A. Shinn, *Political Power and Corporate Control* (Princeton, N.J.: Princeton University Press, 2005).

145 "shelter from the storms": William Greider, *The Soul of Capitalism* (New York: Simon and Schuster, 2003), 228.

146 "Owners of the World, Unite": Bogle, *The Battle*, 47.

146 Congressional Budget Office: Cited in Mishel et al., *The State of Working America*, 249.

147 Okun: Arthur Okun, *Equality and Efficiency: The Big Tradeoff* (Washington, D.C.: Brookings Institution, 1974), 119.

147–48 Smith and Warner, *Governing the Modern Corporation*, 91.

152 unlikely fan of interventionist government: Milton Friedman, "A Natural Experiment in Monetary Policy Covering Three Episodes of Growth and Decline in the Economy of the Stock Market," *Journal of Economic Perspectives* 19 (Fall 2005): 145–150.

155 Corrigan: See account in Greider, *Secrets of the Temple*, 447–448.

155 Corrigan mission to Saudi Arabia: See Bob Woodward, *Maestro: Greenspan's Fed and the American Boom* (New York: Simon and Schuster, 2000), 73.

156 S&L costs: Martin Mayer, *The Greatest Bank Robbery Ever* (New York: Charles Scribner's Sons, 1990), 35.

159 Greenspan and Long-Term Capital Management: Woodward, *Maestro*, 193–208; Rivlin comment at 206.

159 Greenspan and the stock bubble: John Cassidy, *Dot.con: How America Lost Its Mind and Money in the Internet Era* (New York: HarperCollins, 202), 268.

160 Greenspan, assets should rise no more than income: Alan Greenspan, "Technology and the Economy," remarks before the Economic Club of New York, January 13, 2000, available at www.federalreserve.gov/boarddocs/speeches/2000/200001132.htm.

CHAPTER SIX: BUDGET ANXIETY AND RUBINOMICS

165 "bond traders": Bob Woodward, *The Agenda* (New York: Simon and Schuster, 1994), 126.

165 "We're all Eisenhower Republicans": Woodward, *The Agenda*, 95.

166 Dean Baker on interest rates: Dean Baker, "Short-Term Gain for Long-

Term Pain—The Real Story of Rubinomics," Center for Economic and Policy Research, Washington, D.C., February 2006.

166 Solow's famous quip: Robert M. Solow, "We'd Better Watch Out," *The New York Times Book Review* online, July 12, 1987.

167 "[A]t the peak": Baker, "Short-Term Gain."

167 Robert Pollin: See Robert Pollin, *Contours of Descent* (London: Verso Books, 2005).

167 two Federal Reserve economists: Dean M. Maki and Michael G. Palumbo, "Disentangling the Wealth Effect: A Cohort Analysis of Household Savings in the 1990s," April 2001, available at www.federalreserve.gov/pubs/feds/ 2001/200121/200121pap.pdf.

167 Baker concludes: Baker, "Short-Term Gain."

168 Blinder: Alan S. Blinder, "The Speed Limit: Fact and Fancy in the Growth Debate," and "Can't We Grow Faster?" (debate among Alan Blinder, Barry Bluestone, and Bennett Harrison), *The American Prospect*, November–December 1997.

169 Stiglitz quote: Joseph Stiglitz, *The Roaring Nineties* (New York: W. W. Norton, 2003), 52.

169 Stiglitz on R & D and infrastructure: Ibid.

171 deficit of $568 billion: Congressional Budget Office, "Historical Budget Data," Table 1, p. 2, January 26, 2006, available at www.cbo.gov/budget/ historical.pdf.

171 falling interest costs: Ibid.

172 Peterson books: Peter G. Peterson, *Running on Empty: How the Democratic and Republican Parties Are Bankrupting Our Future and What Americans Can Do About It* (New York: Farrar, Straus and Giroux, 2004); Peter G. Peterson, *Gray Dawn: How the Coming Age Wave Will Transform America—and the World* (New York: Times Books, 1999); Peter G. Peterson, *Will America Grow Up Before It Grows Old?: How the Coming Social Security Crisis Threatens You, Your Family, and Your Country* (New York: Random House, 1996); Peter G. Peterson, *Facing Up: How to Rescue the Economy from Crushing Debt and Restore the American Dream* (New York: Simon and Schuster, 1993).

173 Broder column: David Broder, "Bailing the Future Out of Debt," *The Washington Post*, May 21, 2006.

173 "generational accounting": Laurence J. Kotlikoff and Scott Burns, *The Coming Generational Storm* (Cambridge, Mass.: MIT Press, 2004).

173 Dean Baker observation: Dean Baker and Mark Weisbrot, *Social Security: The Phony Crisis* (Chicago: University of Chicago Press, 2002).

174 Trustees Report: Social Security Trustees Report, available at www.ssa .gov/OACT/TRSUM/trsummary.html.

174 Congressional Budget Office Projection: Congressional Budget Office, "The Outlook for Social Security," June 2004, available at www.cbo .gov/showdoc.cfm?index=5530&sequence=0.

174–75 Ball plan: Robert M. Ball, "Meeting Social Security's Long-Range Shortfall," Century Foundation, September 2006, available at www.tcf.org/list.asp?type=PB&pubid=531.

175 Henry Aaron: Henry Aaron, "Perspective on the Draft Interim Report of the President's Commission to Strengthen Social Security," Brookings Institution, Washington, D.C., 2001.

177 Commonwealth Fund: "Medicare vs. Private Insurance: Rhetoric and Reality," The Commonwealth Fund, New York, October 1, 2002.

180 Hacker on Medicare-Plus: Jacob Hacker, "Health care for America," Economic Policy Institute, Washington, D.C., January 11, 2007.

180 Robert Rubin, speech to Economic Club of Washington, November 9, 2006, available at www.economicclub.org.

181 Hamilton Project: Economic Strategy: Roger C. Altman et al., "An Economic Strategy to Advance Opportunity, Prosperity, and Growth," April 2006, available at www1.hamiltonproject.org/views/papers/thp_strategy .htm.

181 "The more confidence that people can achieve": Ibid.

182 Hamilton unemployment proposal: Lori G. Kletzer and Howard Rosen, "Reforming Unemployment Insurance for the Twenty-first Century Workforce," October 2006, available at www1.hamiltonproject.org/views/papers/200609kletzer-rosen_wp.htm.

182 proposal for workers to prepay: Jeffrey R. Kling, "Fundamental Restructuring of Unemployment Insurance: Wage-Loss Insurance and Temporary Earnings Replacement Accounts," September 2006, available at www1 .hamiltonproject.org/views/papers/200609kling_wp.htm.

182–83 Pearlstein article: "A Winning Strategy for the Democrats: Barter for Free Trade," *The Washington Post*, July 26, 2006.

185 Rubin on the politics: Interview with the author.

CHAPTER SEVEN: EQUALITY, EFFICIENCY, AND GLOBALISM

188 Jonas Salk: Interview with Edward R. Murrow on *See It Now*, April 12, 1955.

189 Asian enforcement of intellectual property: See Pat Choate, *Hot Property: The Stealing of Ideas in an Age of Globalization* (New York: Alfred A. Knopf, 2005). See also Office of the U.S. Trade Representative, "2006 Report to Congress on China's WTO Compliance," December 2006, especially 76–82. See also Hearing Before the U.S.-China Economic and Security Review Commission, June 7–8, 2006, available at www.uscc.gov.

190 Rodrik: Dani Rodrik, *Has Globalization Gone Too Far?* (Washington, D.C.: Institute for International Economics, 1997), discussion at 30–35.

191 Tierney: John Tierney, "Shopping for a Nobel," *The New York Times*, October 17, 2006.

191 Hiatt and Greenfield: Jonathan P. Hiatt and Deborah Greenfield, "The

Importance of Core Labor Rights in World Development," *Michigan Journal of International Law*, 26 (2004): 39–62.

195 AFL-CIO petition: Sec. 301 Petition of the AFL-CIO before the Office of the U.S. Trade Representative, June 8, 2006.

196 Congressional-Executive Commission on China, "Annual Report 2005," October 11, 2005, available at www.cecc.gov/pages/annualRpt/annualRpt05/CECCannRpt2005.pdf?PHPSESSID=fea16cecebacc6b5195c3520139a0f5d.

196–97 Office of the United States Trade Representative, "2006 Special 301 Report," April 28, 2006, available at www.ustr.gov/Document_Library/Reports_Publications/2006/2006_Special_301_Review/Section_Index.html.

197 U.S.-Cambodia trade deal: See discussion in Hiatt and Greenfield, "The Importance of Core Labor Rights," 55–59.

199 British chancellor: Gordon Brown quoted in *Having Their Cake and Eating It, Too: The Big Corporate Tax Break* (Brussels: International Confederation of Free Trade Unions, 2006), 7, available at www.taxjustice.net/cms/upload/pdf/tax_break_EN.pdf.

199 Canada: Ibid.

199–200 tax rates in European Union: Ibid.

200 shift of IRS auditing resources. See discussion in David Cay Johnston, *Perfectly Legal: The Covert Campaign to Rig Our Tax System to Benefit the Super Rich and Cheat Everyone Else* (New York: Portfolio, 2003), 129–156.

201 Avi-Yonah: Reuven S. Avi-Yonah, "Globalization, Tax Competition and the Fiscal Crisis of the Welfare State," *Harvard Law Review* 113 (May 2000): 1573.

201 Avi-Yonah on tax havens: Ibid.

202 loss of revenue: Joseph Guttentag and Reuven S. Avi-Yonah, "Closing the International Tax Gap," in *Bridging the Tax Gap*, ed. Max Sawicki (Washington, D.C.: Economic Policy Institute, 2005), 101.

203 OECD project: Organization for Economic Cooperation and Development, "Harmful Tax Competition: An Emerging Global Issue," Paris, 1998.

203 Mitchell: Daniel Mitchell, "An OECD Proposal to Eliminate Tax Competition Would Mean Higher Taxes and Less Privacy," Heritage Foundation Backgrounder no. 1395, Washington, D.C., September 18, 2000.

205 John Braithwaite and Peter Drahos, *Global Business Regulation* (Cambridge, England: Cambridge University Press, 2000), quote at 5.

207 Europe's employment rate: From OECD, "Economic Outlook," cited in Jonas Pontusson, *Inequality and Prosperity: Social Europe vs. Liberal America* (Ithaca, N.Y.: Cornell University Press/Century Foundation, 2005), 87.

207 French job creation: Ibid.

207 launch of the euro: See David Malpass, "The Euro's Broken Promises," *The Wall Street Journal*, October 21, 2002.

207–08 unit-labor costs: Pontusson, *Inequality and Prosperity*, 106.

208 positive correlation with trade unionism: Ibid.

210 Hours worked in Europe: Mishel et al., *The State of Working America*, 318.

210 Poverty rates: Luxembourg Income Study, www.lisproject.org/keyfigures/povertytable.htm.

213 Rasmussen Report: Poul Nyrup Rasmussen and Ieke van den Burg, "Hedge Funds and Private Equity: a Critical Analysis," Socialist Group in the European Parliament, Brussels, March 2007, 81.

213 TDC experience: Rasmussen report, 204–205.

214 U.S. inequality: Mishel et al., *The State of Working America*, 329.

214–15 Pontusson quote: Pontusson, *Inequality and Prosperity*, 40.

CHAPTER EIGHT: TRADE AND THE NATIONAL INTEREST

220 Laura D'Andrea Tyson, *Who's Bashing Whom?* (Washington, D.C.: Institute for International Economics, 1993), 3.

221 Paul R. Krugman, ed., *Strategic Trade Policy and the New International Economics* (Cambridge, Mass.: MIT Press, 1986).

222 Paul A. Samuelson, "Where Ricardo and Mill Rebut and Confirm Arguments of Mainstream Economists Supporting Globalization," *Journal of Economic Perspectives* 18, no. 3 (Fall 2004): 135–146.

222 Alan Blinder, "Outsourcing: Bigger Than You Thought," *The American Prospect*, November 2006, 26.

223 imperialism of free trade: See John Gallagher and Ronald Robinson, "The Imperialism of Free Trade," *The Economic History Review*, 2nd ser., vol. 6, no. 1 (1953).

227–28 history of U.S.-Japan relationship: See Clyde R. Prestowitz, *Trading Places* (New York: Basic Books, 1986).

229 trade statistics: Department of Commerce, Bureau of the Census, Office of the U.S. Trade Representative, "U.S. International Trade in Goods and Services: Exhibit 13. Exports, Imports, and Trade Balance by Country and Area: 2005 Annual Totals," June 13, 2006, available at www.census.gov/foreign-trade/Press-Release/2005pr/final_revisions/.

230 Authoritative review of offsets: Owen E. Herrnstadt, "Outsourcing and the Lack of a Comprehensive U.S. Policy: What Do Other Countries Know That We Don't?" Unpublished paper, April 2007, citing *Offsets in Defense Trade, Eleventh Report to Congress*, conducted under Section 309 of the Defense Production Act of 1950, as Amended, U.S. Department of Commerce Bureau of Industry and Security, Washington, D.C., January 2007.

230–31 military content deals: Leslie Wayne, "Polish Pride, American Profits," *The New York Times*, January 12, 2003.

232 GE won a $900 million contract: Kathryn Kranhold, "China's Price for Market Entry: Give Us Your Technology, Too," *The Wall Street Journal*, February 26, 2004.

234 Khandros award: See http://wps2a.semi.org/wps/portal/_pagr/115/_pa.115/274?dFormat=application/msword&docName=P039362.

235 Khandros episode: Author's interviews.

237–38 Mann quote: James Mann, *The China Fantasy* (New York: Viking, 2007), 80.

238 Clinton, accepted Democratic nomination: William J. Clinton, acceptance speech to the Democratic National Convention, New York, N.Y., July 16, 1992, available at www.presidency.ucsb.edu/shownomination.php? convid=7.

238 Mann on U.S. political leaders advising the Chinese: Ibid., 59–60.

238–39 "Who's integrating whom?": Ibid., 105.

239–40 China purchased $87 billion: Floyd Norris, "Washington Dares to Challenge the Lender It Depends Upon," *The New York Times*, April 14, 2007.

240 "doing us a favor": Author's interview.

CHAPTER NINE: THE RETURN OF SPECULATIVE GLOBAL FINANCE

245 For a history of Bretton Woods, see Richard N. Gardner, *Sterling-Dollar Diplomacy* (New York: McGraw-Hill, 1969), and Robert Kuttner, *The End of Laissez Faire* (New York: Alfred A. Knopf, 1991).

247 For a good critique of IMF policies, see Joseph E. Stiglitz, *Globalization and Its Discontents* (New York: W. W. Norton, 2002); also Robert A. Blecker, *Taming Global Finance* (Washington, D.C.: Economic Policy Institute, 1999).

251 Basel Capital Accord of 1988: Bank for International Settlements, available at www.bis.org/publ/bcbs04a.htm.

253 "Quantitative impact study": Remarks by Martin J. Gruenberg to the Conference of State Bank Supervisors Annual Conference, Washington, D.C., May 19, 2006.

253 Basel II conflicts: Author's interviews. Also see Daniel K. Tarullo, Testimony on the New Basel Capital Accords, Senate Committee on Banking, Housing and Urban Affairs, November 10, 2005.

255 Mexican bailout: See accounts in Robert E. Rubin and Jacob Weisberg, *In an Uncertain World* (New York: Random House, 2004), 3–38, and in Woodward, *Maestro*.

255 Rubin and Weisberg, *In an Uncertain World*, 5, 8.

256 Rubin on loans to sovereign governments: Ibid., 118.

257 Stiglitz on the IMF: Stiglitz, *Globalization and Its Discontents*, 91.

258 Stiglitz and Washington Consensus: Ibid., 90–91.

259 Rubin and Korea: Rubin and Weisberg, *In an Uncertain World*, 228–241.

260 debt owed by U.S.: Floyd Norris, "More Than Ever, the U.S. Spends and the Foreigners Lend," *The New York Times*, October 1, 2005.

260 foreign holdings of Treasury securities: Ibid.

261 foreign purchases of U.S. debt: Floyd Norris, "In Long-Term American Treasury Securities They Trust," *The New York Times*, February 21, 2006.

261 annual rate of foreign borrowing: Ibid.

262 Volcker: Author's interview.

263 Bank of South Korea: Paul Blustein, "Korea to Limit Its Dollar Holdings," *The Washington Post*, February 23, 2005.

264 costs of dollar adjustment: See discussion in C. Fred Bergsten and John Williamson, eds., "Dollar Adjustment: How Far? Against What?" Institute for International Economics, Washington, D.C., November 2004.

CHAPTER TEN: THE SQUANDERING OF DEMOCRACY

268 Putnam: Robert Putnam, *Bowling Alone* (New York: Simon and Schuster, 2001).

268 Skocpol: Theda Skocpol, "How Americans Became Civic," in *Civic Engagement and American Democracy*, ed. Theda Skocpol and Morris P. Fiorina (Washington, D.C.: Brookings Institution Press, 1999).

270 *The New York Times*, Pew and American Democracy Research Center, "November Turnout May Be High," October 11, 2006, available at http://People_Press.org/reports/display.ph p3?Report ID=291.

274 Frank: Thomas Frank, *What's the Matter with Kansas?* (New York: Metropolitan Books, 2004).

274 Edsall: Thomas Edsall, *Building Red America* (New York: Basic Books, 2006).

275 defecting Democrats: See Robert Kuttner and Asheesh Kapur Saddique, "The Defectors," *The American Prospect*, October 2005.

276 Westen: Drew Westen, *The Political Brain* (New York: Perseus, 2007).

276 Westen quote: Ibid., 8.

279 Mansbridge: Conversation with the author.

279 Larry Bartels, adaptation published as "Unenlightened Self-Interest," *The American Prospect*, June 2004.

280 Rendell: panel discussion at "Take Back America" conference, Washington, D.C., July 2006.

281 Gore quote: "The National Performance Review," September 1993, available at www.ibiblio.org/Nprintro.html.

282 Deval Patrick quote: available at www.progressivedems.org/DevalPatrick Eval.htm.

283 Rose piece: "The Trouble with Class-Interest Populism," Progressive Policy Institute Backgrounder, Washington, D.C., April 2006, available at www.ppionline.org/ppi_ci.cfm?knlgAreaID=114&subsecID=144&contentID=253831.

286 Sherraden's book: Michael Sherraden, *Assets and the Poor: A New American Welfare Policy* (Armonk, N.Y.: M. E. Sharpe, 1991).

287 Sherraden's most recent research: Michael Sherraden, "From Research to Policy: Lessons from Individual Development Accounts," *Journal of Consumer Affairs* 34, no. 2 (2000): 159–181.

288 MacGuineas budget proposal: Maya MacGuineas and Alicia Cheng, "Closing the Hurricane Gap," *The New York Times*, October 7, 2005.

289 Broder on "partisan bickering": David Broder, "Will Voters Pull the Trigger," *The Washington Post*, October 12, 2002.

289 Klein: Joe Klein, "Why the Center Is the New Place to Be." *Time*, November 20, 2006, 38.

289 *Time* magazine cover piece: "The New Action Heroes," *Time*, June 25, 2007, www.time.com/time/magazine/article/0,9171,1633089-1,00.html.

289 Herbert quote: Bob Herbert, "The System's Broken," *The New York Times*, October 30, 2006.

290 Robert Frost: cited at http://en.wikiquote.org/wiki/Robert_Frost.

290 Will Marshall and Al From: "The New Progressive Declaration," July 1996, available at www.dlc.org/ndo/_ci.cfm?kaid=868subid=1948contentid=839.

290 Halstead and Lind: Ted Halstead and Michael Lind, *The Radical Center* (New York: Doubleday, 2001), 15–16.

290 Matthew Miller: Matthew Miller, *The Two Percent Solution* (New York: Public Affairs, 2003), xi.

291 Miller, "cognitive dissonance": Ibid., 32–33.

293 Hacker and Pierson: Jacob Hacker and Paul Pierson, *Off Center* (New Haven, Conn.: Yale University Press, 2005).

294 Bush convention speech: Available at www.2000gop.com/convention/speech/speechbush.html.

295 La Rochefoucauld: Maxim 218, cited at http://en.wikiquote.org/wiki/La_Rochefoucauld.

296 Dowd memo: See Edsall, *Building Red America* (New York: Basic Books, 2006), 50.

EPILOGUE: REDEEMING AMERICA

299 Ellen Goodman quote: Ellen Goodman, "Betty, You Changed Our Lives," *The Washington Post*, February 7, 2006.

301 Hinchey quote: Hinchey to the author.

303 Gallup data: poll of January 25–28, 2007, cited in unpublished memo by Ethel Klein to the author.

303 Gallup report April 2007: www.galluppoll.com/content/default/aspx?ci=27208.

303–04 *Wall Street Journal*/NBC data: Ethel Klein memo to the author.

304 Pew study: The Pew Research Center for the People and the Press, "Trends in Political Values and Core Attitudes: 1987–2007," Washington, D.C., March 22, 2007, available at http://people-press.org/reports/display.php3?ReportID=312.

306 Bismarck: Cited at http://en.wikiquote.org/wiki/Otto_von_Bismarck.

INDEX